HEALING
FOODS

HEALING FOODS

LONDON, NEW YORK, MELBOURNE, MUNICH, AND DELHI

DK LONDON
Editor Susannah Steel

Project Editor Shashwati Tia Sarkar
Senior Art Editor Tessa Bindloss
Editorial Assistant Christopher Mooney
Managing Editor Dawn Henderson
Managing Art Editor Christine Keilty
Senior Jacket Creative Nicola Powling
Jacket Design Assistant Rosie Levine
Producer, Pre-Production Raymond Williams
Senior Producer Jen Scothern
Art Director Peter Luff
Publisher Peggy Vance

DK INDIA
Senior Editor Chitra Subramanyam
Senior Art Editor Balwant Singh
Editor Ligi John
Art Editor Prashant Kumar
Assistant Art Editor Tanya Mehrotra
Managing Art Editor Navidita Thapa
DTP/CTS Manager Sunil Sharma
DTP Designer Anurag Trivedi
Photo Research Aditya Katyal

First published in Great Britain in 2013 by
Dorling Kindersley Limited
80 Strand, London, WC2R 0RL
Penguin Group (UK)

DISCLAIMER See page 352

A CIP catalogue record for this book is available
from the British Library.

ISBN 978-1-4093-2464-5

Colour reproduction by Opus Multimedia Services
Printed and bound in China

Discover more at **www.dk.com**

CONTENTS

RECIPES THAT HEAL 146

KEY TO ICONS

These icons are used throughout to signpost you to dietary benefits for different health areas.

- HEART AND CIRCULATION
- DIGESTION
- URINARY
- RESPIRATORY
- DETOX
- METABOLIC BALANCE
- IMMUNE SUPPORT

- ENERGY BOOST
- MUSCLES AND JOINTS
- SKIN AND HAIR
- MIND AND EMOTIONS
- EYE HEALTH
- MEN'S HEALTH
- WOMEN'S HEALTH

ABOUT THE AUTHORS

Susan Curtis has practiced as a homoeopath and naturopath since the mid-1980s and is the Director for Natural Health for Neal's Yard Remedies. She is the author of several books, including *Essential Oils*, and co-author of *Natural Healing for Women*. Susan has two grown-up children and is passionate about helping people to eat well and live a more natural and healthy lifestyle.

Pat Thomas is a journalist, campaigner, broadcaster, and passionate cook. She is the author of several books on health and environment, and has worked with leading campaign organisations to outline sensible strategies for healthy and sustainable eating. She is a former editor of *The Ecologist* magazine and was the director of Paul McCartney's "Meat Free Monday" campaign in the UK. She currently sits on the Council of Trustees of the Soil Association – the UK's premier organic certification body – and is the editor of Neal's Yard Remedies' natural health website, *NYR Natural News*.

Dragana Vilinac, medical herbalist, comes from a family with a long lineage of traditional herbalists. Her life's purpose is the exploration and education of the healing dynamics between plants, planet and people. She has worked in the field of western, Chinese, and traditional Tibetan (Bhutanese) medicine since the 1980s, and has been a consultant on international development projects related to herbal medicines in Europe and Asia. She has co-authored books with the theme of plants as food and medicine. Dragana is the Chief Herbalist for Neal's Yard Remedies.

INTRODUCTION

"LET FOOD BE THY MEDICINE
AND MEDICINE BE THY FOOD"

HIPPOCRATES

THE FOOD WE EAT HAS AN OVERREACHING EFFECT
ON OUR HEALTH AND **WELL-BEING**, WHETHER
WE ARE CONSCIOUS OF IT OR NOT. BECOMING
MORE AWARE OF YOUR DIET AND THE **HEALING
PROPERTIES** OF FOOD WILL HELP YOU TO MAKE
NECESSARY ADJUSTMENTS TO MEET THE NEEDS
OF **YOUR BODY** – AND IT WILL DO AN ENORMOUS
AMOUNT TO MAINTAIN AND IMPROVE YOUR **HEALTH**.

THE PROTECTIVE POWER OF FOOD

Nutritional science has shed much light on the importance of "whole food": we now understand that nutrients in our food work synergistically to promote health – and that processed food, denuded of many of its intrinsic nutrients, can promote disease. We also know of 50 or so essential vitamins, amino acids, minerals, and essential fatty acids that we need to get on a regular basis from our diet, and over 1,200 phytonutrients in fruits, vegetables, beans, grains, and animal products.

A RAINBOW OF PHYTONUTRIENTS

Phytonutrients are the bio-active compounds in plants ("phyto" means plant) that supply their colour and flavour. Although not essential to life in the way that vitamins and minerals are, they support health in a variety of ways.

Antioxidants, for example, protect the body from free radicals, the unstable molecules that are produced through metabolism and exposure to pollution, and which cause disease by damaging vital tissues and organs.

Antioxidants by colour

COLOUR	PHYTONUTRIENT	BENEFITS	FOUND IN
Green			
	Lutein	Protects eyes; boosts immunity; and supports healthy tissues, skin, and blood	Kale, collard greens, cucumber, courgette, peas, avocado, asparagus, green beans
	Chlorophyll	Detoxifying; helps build red blood cells and collagen; boosts energy and well-being	All leafy green vegetables, sprouted grasses, and microalgae
	Indoles	Has anti-cancer properties; supports healthy hormone balance	Brussels sprouts, broccoli, bok choi, cabbage, and turnips
Orange/yellow			
	Carotenes (incl. alpha-, beta-, and delta-carotene)	Source of vitamin A; has anti-cancer and heart-protective properties; protects mucous membranes	Orange and yellow fruits and vegetables (peppers, winter squash, carrots, apricots, mangoes, oranges, grapefruit)
	Xanthophylls (incl. zeaxanthin and astaxanthin)	Source of vitamin A; has anti-cancer properties; protects eyes and brain; strengthens the immune system	Red fish (e.g. salmon), eggs, most orange and yellow fruits and vegetables
Red			
	Lycopene	Protects against heart disease, cancer (especially prostate), and vision loss	Fresh and cooked tomatoes, watermelon, goji berries, papaya, and rosehips
	Anthocyanins	Can help reduce the risk of heart disease, cancer, and neurodegenerative diseases	Cranberries, strawberries, raspberries, cherries, and red cabbage
Blue/purple			
	Anthocyanins	Fights free radicals; has anti-cancer properties; supports healthy ageing	Blueberries, aubergine, grapes, grape juice, raisins, and red wine
	Resveratrol	Has anti-cancer properties; helps balance hormone levels	Grapes, grape juice, red wine, mulberries, and cocoa
White			
	Allyl sulphides	Boosts immunity; has anti-cancer and anti-inflammatory properties	Onions, garlic, scallions, and chives
	Anthoxanthins	Helps lower cholesterol and blood pressure; helps reduce the risk of certain cancers and heart disease	Bananas, cauliflower, mushrooms, onions, parsnips, potatoes, garlic, ginger, and turnips

DIFFERENT DIETARY PATTERNS

While we would not advocate a rigid approach to a particular diet, there are things that can be learnt and adopted from traditional diets. Humans are very adaptable and it is interesting to see the ways in which different cultures have adapted their diets to remain healthy in widely different environments.

TRADITIONAL DIETS

INUIT

The Inuit people of the Arctic have traditionally had very little access to cereals or fresh fruit and vegetables, but the manner in which they hunt and eat their mostly fish- and meat-based diet meets their nutritional needs. For example, vitamins and minerals that are derived from plant sources in other areas of the world are also present in most Inuit diets: vitamins A and D are present in the oils and livers of cold-water fishes and mammals, for instance, while vitamin C is obtained through sources such as caribou liver, kelp, whale skin, and seal offal. Since these foods are typically eaten raw or frozen, the vitamin C they contain – which would be destroyed by cooking – is instead preserved.

MEDITERRANEAN

Another traditional diet that has received publicity in recent years is the Mediterranean diet. This diet is based on mainly fresh vegetables and fruit with some whole grains, healthier oils like olive oil and those from fresh fish, red wine, and smaller quantities of meat. Studies throughout the world have shown that following a strict Mediterranean diet offers substantial protection against heart disease, cancer, and Parkinson's and Alzheimer's diseases. The biggest study into this diet has shown that it can reduce the number of deaths from these diseases; it also found that people who follow this diet show significant improvements in health, and are nine per cent less likely to die young.

JAPANESE

Traditional Japanese cuisine is rich in fat-soluble vitamins from seafood and organ meats and minerals from fish broth, and contains plenty of beneficial lacto-fermented foods such as tempeh and miso. Although portions tend to be relatively small, they are both filling and very nutrient-dense. In fact, Japanese people who follow this traditional diet tend to be some of the healthiest, least obese, and longest-lived people in the world.

ANCESTRAL/PALEOLITHIC

Also referred to as the caveman or hunter-gatherer diet, this modern nutritional plan is based on an ancient diet of wild plants and meat that early humans were likely to have habitually eaten during the Paleolithic era – a period of about 2.5 million years that ended around 10,000 years ago with the development of agriculture. Early humans were foragers who would have grazed opportunistically on seasonally available plants and not made the, often arbitrary, distinctions we do between weeds and crops and medicinal and culinary herbs. Although the hunter-gatherer diet comprises commonly available modern foods – mainly fish, grass-fed, pasture-raised meats, vegetables, fruit, fungi, roots, and nuts – it largely excludes legumes, dairy products, grains, salt, refined sugar, and processed oils, which define the Western diet (overleaf). Studies of the Paleolithic diet in humans have shown improved health and fewer incidences of diseases such as diabetes, cancer, obesity, dementia, and heart disease.

WHAT MANY OF THESE DIETS have in common is that they are plant-based, with meat reserved for feast days and occasional treats. They include plenty of oily fish so are rich in the omega-3 fatty acid DHA. Their overall balance of essential fatty acids is healthier (i.e. higher in omega 3 than 6, unlike modern diets), and they are high in antioxidants. People who follow these diets rely on seasonal fresh food produced without industrial chemicals, which means they eat a wide variety of nutrient-dense foods necessary for optimal heath throughout the year. They tend to eat sensible portions and rarely "snack" between meals.

THE WESTERN DIET

By contrast, the modern Western diet, also called the Western pattern diet, is characterized by high intakes of red meat, sugar and artificial sweeteners, high-fat foods, salt, and refined grains. It also typically contains hydrogenated and trans-fats, high-sugar drinks, and higher intakes of processed meat. This diet, based on studies of western populations, is associated with an elevated incidence of obesity, death from heart disease, cancer (especially colon cancer), and other western pattern diet-related diseases. The high consumption of grains – as breakfast cereals, breads, cakes, biscuits, pasta, and so on – means that grain has become a significant source of carbohydrate-energy, minerals and, in the case of whole grains, of fibre and B vitamins. However, it is now thought that this reliance on cereals may come at a high cost to our health. Modern strains of high-gluten cereals, combined with an over-reliance on wheat-based products and an industrial approach to the processing of grain-based foods, can place a strain on our digestive systems and nutrient balance. For example, an increasing number of people have developed gluten intolerance, or gluten sensitivity, which can vary from coeliac disease to feeling bloated if they eat too many cereal-based foods in a day.

> "IT IS NOW THOUGHT THAT RELIANCE ON CEREALS MAY COME AT A HIGH COST TO OUR HEALTH."

Cereals contain what have been termed "anti-nutrients" that may prevent the digestive system absorbing several essential nutrients. The most researched anti-nutrients are the phytates found in the bran or outer hull of most grains, and which is part of a seed's system of preservation – it prevents the seed sprouting until conditions are right. The phytate known as phytic acid can block the absorption of essential minerals such as calcium, magnesium, copper, iron, and especially zinc, in the gut. This may be why a diet high in improperly prepared whole grains may lead to serious mineral deficiencies and bone loss, and why consuming large amounts of unprocessed bran often initially improves bowel regularity, but may lead to irritable bowel syndrome and, in the long term, other adverse effects.

So although cereals can be a useful part of a diet, they do require careful preparation because of their anti-nutrient properties. Many cultures throughout the world have developed ways of preparing types of grain for human consumption. Soaking, sprouting, and souring are very common aids for grain preparation, and ensure the neutralization of phytates, enzyme-inhibitors, and other anti-nutrients with which seeds are naturally endowed. Some traditional preparation methods involve complex, comparatively labour-intensive steps that produce what are now considered unusual foods from common grains, but which were once part of common dietary practices. The traditional sourdough method of preparing rye bread, for example, which was widespread throughout eastern Europe, helps to make rye flour far more digestible.

Modern diets in general also tend to include a larger number of beans and legumes, and, more recently, soya derivatives. Although including beans in your diet can be a useful source of fibre and protein, these foods also contain phytates. The phytate in soybeans, for example, means they are low in calcium and one reason why they are less healthy than you might think, though fermenting helps to make soya a more nutritious food. It is interesting to note that the traditional Japanese diet includes a lot of soya, but it is usually fermented in the form of tempeh or miso. In addition, Japanese preparation techniques eliminate most of the anti-nutrients in other legumes and in grains. Soya milk is not fermented and so can be a cause of digestive problems and calcium depletion, as well as being a fairly potent phytoestrogen – potentially useful for reducing hot flushes in menopausal women, but not so suitable for children or everyone else.

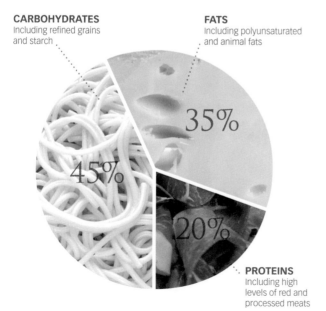

CARBOHYDRATES
Including refined grains and starch

FATS
Including polyunsaturated and animal fats

35%

45%

20%

PROTEINS
Including high levels of red and processed meats

WESTERN DIET FIGURES

In a Western diet, the main nutritional building blocks of fats, carbohydrates, and protein are often processed, nutrient-poor foods high in sugar, refined grains, and saturated fats.

VARIETY IS THE SPICE OF LIFE

The good news is that if you currently eat a modern Western diet, you can easily adapt your eating habits to dramatically improve your health. Including a variety of nutrient-rich, low-energy foods such as vegetables and fruit in your diet both helps with weight control and can have a positive effect on your health: eating a varied diet ensures we get a steady supply of highly bioavailable nutrients that help to reduce the likelihood of conditions such as Alzheimer's disease, dementia, anxiety, depression, arthritis, some types of cancer (including breast and bowel cancer), and heart and circulatory disease.

DIETARY DIVERSITY

No single food or food group can supply all the nutrients we need, which is why a diverse diet is so important. Research consistently shows that dietary diversity protects against the onset of type 2 diabetes, for example, by balancing blood sugar levels and protecting against blood vessel damage. A varied, seasonal diet rich in plant foods can also lower your total risk of cancer and has been shown to protect against some very specific cancers of the digestive tract. To improve the balance and variety of your diet, choose foods like multigrain breads and muesli that have variety "built in", and eat side-dishes and condiments such as fruit and vegetable salads, sprouted

pulses, fresh salsas, pickles, and chutneys. Stir fries, casseroles, and soups with many ingredients are another easy way to increase the diversity of your diet. Or when grocery shopping, regularly buy a fruit or vegetable that is not familiar to you to prepare and eat. Following a varied diet also tends to be more satisfying and so reduces your sugar, salt, and saturated fat consumption – all risk factors for heart disease. Including more spices and herbs in your food can also boost its flavour and nutritional density: adding a handful of chopped fresh herbs to lettuce in a salad, for example, can add up to 75 per cent extra antioxidants to the food.

Vary your diet

TYPICAL DIET	DIVERSE DIET	
BREAKFAST Wheat bran cereal with milk, sugar and banana; orange juice; tea with milk	**BREAKFAST** Oat porridge made with milk, sprinkled with dried fruit, sunflower and pumpkin seeds, and seasoned with cinnamon and maple syrup; rosehip and hibiscus tea	 **Sourdough rye bread** p328
LUNCH Wheat bread, ham, cheese, and lettuce sandwich with mayonnaise for spread; a piece of fruit	**LUNCH** Lentil soup (p212) made with ginger, turmeric, shallots, garlic and chilli; served with slice of rye bread (p328) spread with butter; a piece of fruit	
DINNER Chicken (or other meat) served with a vegetable and rice	**DINNER** Salmon with dill and tamari sauce (p268) served with an adzuki and mung bean salad (p226) with tomatoes and a mixed citrus and herb dressing	 **Hummus with coriander** p196
SNACK Potato crisps	**SNACK** Multiseed crackers (e.g. wheat, pumpkin seed, linseed, poppy seed) spread with Hummus (p196) made with chickpeas, tahini, coriander, paprika	
TOTAL OF 13 FOODS	**TOTAL OF 35 FOODS**	

AS NATURE INTENDED

The success of traditional diets such as the Mediterranean and Inuit diets in sustaining good health and well-being (p11) lies in the fact that they each contain a carefully balanced range of seasonal nutrient-rich foods that are available from local sources. To get the very best from locally grown fresh produce, however, it is worth considering buying organic, as foods that are produced this way contain more of the nutrients that make these seasonal foods so beneficial to our health.

LOCAL AND SEASONAL

Adjusting your diet with the seasons can mean that, as well as being beneficial for your body's "energies", you will eat more fresh foods that can be locally sourced. Choosing local and seasonal should also encourage you to make healthier choices, and can increase a general feeling of well-being as you become more in tune with the cycles of nature. This doesn't mean that you need to become rigid or obsessive about what you eat and when; some foods, such as avocados or bananas, may simply not grow where you live. It is the principles you base your dietary habits on that are key. The 80:20 rule – eating 80 per cent of local, seasonal, unprocessed foods and 20 per cent of more exotic foods, or "treats" – is probably a good guideline. When people switch to more local, seasonal food, many find they become more adventurous in their cooking and eating habits. If you unpack a local box scheme delivery, for example, you may well find an unrecognized fruit or vegetable that you have to discover the best way to prepare, and hopefully you will look forward to preparing and eating it again when it comes back into season. Or you may become interested in learning how to preserve them – a more traditional and low-impact way of extending the natural season of foods throughout the year.

> "IT IS NOT JUST WHAT ORGANIC FOOD CONTAINS, IT IS ALSO WHAT IT DOES NOT CONTAIN THAT IS IMPORTANT."

ORGANIC BENEFITS

Organic food is produced using environmentally and animal-friendly farming methods on organic farms. These methods are now legally defined in most countries of the world and any food that is sold as organic must be strictly regulated. Organic farming recognizes the direct connection between our health and how the food we eat is produced. Artificial fertilizers are banned and farmers develop fertile soil by rotating crops and using compost, manure, and clover in order. By contrast, modern intensive agricultural practices have led to the reduction of many minerals and vitamins in the food we eat; official food composition tables in the US and UK have shown that fruits, vegetables, meat, and dairy products all contain fewer minerals than they did in the past. As soils become depleted of minerals such as magnesium and zinc, for example, there is less for plants grown in this soil to draw up, and therefore less for us to absorb. Minerals that are particularly affected by these intensive farming methods are iron, zinc, copper, magnesium, and selenium, and their levels of depletion can be very significant. An early study in the Journal of Applied Nutrition in 1993 reported that organically and conventionally grown apples, potatoes, pears, wheat, and sweetcorn in a suburban area of the USA were analyzed and compared for mineral content. Weight-for-weight, average levels of essential minerals were much higher in the organically grown produce than in the conventionally grown foods. The organic produce was, on average, 63 per cent higher in calcium, 78 per cent higher in chromium, 73 per cent higher in iron, 118 per cent higher in magnesium, 178 per cent higher in molybdenum, 91 per cent higher in phosphorus, 125 per cent higher in potassium, and 60 per cent higher in zinc. More recent studies have confirmed this finding and interestingly, according to population studies, many people in the western world are becoming increasingly deficient in these same minerals, leading to problems such as anaemia, tiredness, sub-fertility, and poor immunity. Organic farming can help to halt this decline in mineral content. Levels of vitamin C, phenolic acids, and antioxidants also tend to be 60–80 per cent higher in organic produce. Just as important from a health point of view is the markedly more benign balance of omega-6 and -3 fatty acids in organic meat and dairy produce as compared to conventionally produced foods.

It is not just what organic food contains, it is what it does not contain that is important. Some synthetic chemicals commonly used in non-organic agriculture are now known to potentially disrupt the nervous, circulatory, endocrine, and reproductive systems of humans. This may be even more of a problem in babies and children, whose organs are developing fast. Although most countries now set safety levels for pesticide residues in food, these are based on individual chemicals, and don't take into account the cocktail effect of lots of pesticides, which are known to be more damaging in combination. Many food additives common in processed foods are also banned from organic food products; monosodium glutamate (MSG), Brilliant Blue, aspartame, and tartrazine, for example, are now being linked to health issues and behavioural problems in children. Organic standards also insist that animals are given plenty of space and fresh air to thrive and grow, guaranteeing that they are reared humanely and not routinely fed antibiotics to suppress disease or promote growth.

Organic is kinder to the environment, too. Organic farming works with nature, not against it, and research shows that it's better for birds, butterflies, and other wildlife. Organic farms are havens for wildlife and provide homes for bees, birds, and butterflies. In fact, plant, insect, and bird life is up to 50 per cent greater on organic farms. Biodiversity is something to encourage both in our environment and on our plate.

HOW ABOUT GM FOOD?

Genetically modified (GM) crops provide another potential health hazard. GM foods, which have had their genetic material (DNA) altered to achieve desired changes in their characteristics, have been developed by seed and chemical companies as one means of responding to climate change and a growing global population, although GM technologies have consistently underperformed. There is legitimate concern about how carelessly GM foods have been assessed for safety, and evidence that they may have risks to human health and wildlife. In a recent French study in 2012, rats fed a lifelong diet of a bestselling strain of genetically modified maize developed more and bigger breast tumours, and experienced kidney and liver dysfunction. In the US, GM foods don't have to be labelled, in spite of overwhelming public support for such a requirement in a country where GM-adulterated food is so prevalent. In most countries in Europe, farm animals are fed GM foodstuff, but actual GM foods for human consumption are not yet accepted. Crops that can be grown as GM varieties include soya beans, corn, rice, and tomatoes.

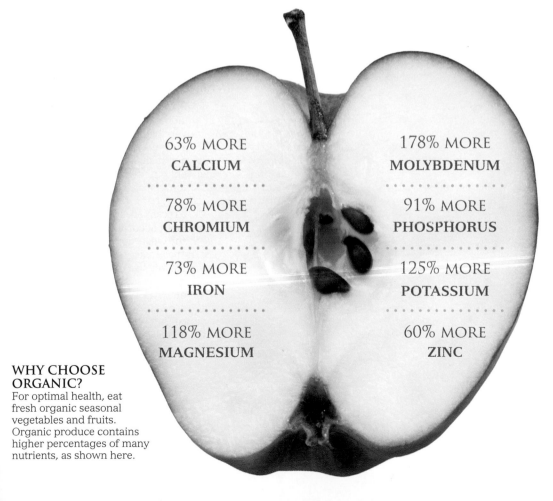

63% MORE
CALCIUM

178% MORE
MOLYBDENUM

78% MORE
CHROMIUM

91% MORE
PHOSPHORUS

73% MORE
IRON

125% MORE
POTASSIUM

118% MORE
MAGNESIUM

60% MORE
ZINC

WHY CHOOSE ORGANIC?
For optimal health, eat fresh organic seasonal vegetables and fruits. Organic produce contains higher percentages of many nutrients, as shown here.

LET FOOD BE YOUR MEDICINE

Food is the bedrock upon which a healthy life is based, and is the body's buffer against the stresses, strains, and the onslaughts of an increasingly toxic environment. Science has consistently shown that food can be used to support long-term heath as well as treat acute conditions. Ginger, for example, is a traditional remedy for nausea, honey can be as effective as conventional medicines at soothing night-time coughs, saffron contains antioxidants that protect against age-related vision loss, garlic helps thin the blood, thus lowering the risk of stroke, and a diet rich in tree nuts can support heart health and even men's fertility. As the cost, and acknowledged side effects, of conventional medical treatments rise exponentially, we owe it to ourselves to eat the most nutritionally dense, best-quality foods. Good food is everybody's right, and in our view the best way to democratize good food is through the widespread use of organic farming and a greater attention to the concepts of local and seasonal. In re-establishing the fundamental link between food and health and exploring the benefits of traditional diets we are not looking backwards, rather we are taking the best of our inherited knowledge about food and farming and applying it to a modern future.

For example, Chinese and Ayurvedic traditions have for thousands of years followed the concept that different foods have specific, healthy properties. Some foods, such as quail eggs, are considered energizing and full of concentrated life force while others, such as barley, are more soothing to the energies of the body. Traditional approaches to food also acknowledge the seasons: of recommending warming foods like oats and spices like cinnamon in winter; cleansing foods such as nettle or dandelion in spring; cooling foods like lettuce and cucumber in summer; and sustaining foods such as pumpkin and carrots in autumn.

The first half of this book will help you to identify foods that have both stood the test of time as healing foods and are shown by modern research as being particularly relevant for helping to improve a health issue. The second half contains recipes, inspired by traditional cultural practices, that benefit various parts of the body or internal systems. We hope that this information will both encourage and help you affirm the connection between food and health and make food choices for yourself and your family that lead to lifelong optimal health.

Food as medicine

NAUSEA

GINGER
has a recognized ability to quell feelings of nausea.

COUGHS

HONEY
is an ancient remedy for soothing coughs and other throat complaints.

HEART

GARLIC
can help your body to fight free radicals and lower blood pressure.

LIVER

BRUSSELS SPROUTS
are a good source of sulphur, which enhances liver function.

MEMORY

BERRIES
contain antioxidants, which can help to stave off mental decline.

CHOLESTEROL

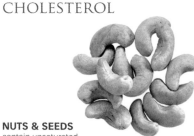

NUTS & SEEDS
contain unsaturated fats, which can lower cholesterol.

SUPPLEMENTS

A balanced diet is where health begins, but there are times when your diet may not provide all the nutrients you need. A Western diet and lifestyle can also leave us vulnerable to nutritional deficiencies including iron, calcium, magnesium, folic acid, vitamins B6, B12, C, and D. Most governments produce scientifically developed recommended dietary allowances (RDAs) to cover broadly healthy people of any age or gender. These are the basis for the Reference Daily Intake (RDI) values, which regulators use to create Daily Value (DV) packaging labels. RDAs are based on the lowest levels of nutrients required to prevent deficiency diseases such as scurvy and rickets and do not, as our tables on pages 338–41 illustrate, reflect the higher levels required for optimum health. This is why supplement nutrient levels are often much higher than RDA levels.

Who will benefit most from supplements?

Even in healthy people, multivitamins and other supplements may help to prevent vitamin and mineral deficiencies. They also provide more nutrients than diet can alone, so they may help to protect against, or manage, certain diseases. However, the following categories highlight those people who can most benefit from taking daily supplements:

● People who have lost weight, who may be deficient in a wide range of vitamins and minerals.

● Vegetarians, who are more likely to be deficient in vitamin B12, iron, vitamin D, zinc, iodine, riboflavin, calcium, and selenium.

● Vegans, who are even more likely than vegetarians to be low in protein, selenium, and B12.

● People living a typical "student lifestyle" and anyone not eating a balanced diet is likely to benefit from a multivitamin supplement.

● Elderly people living in their own homes, who are often deficient in vitamin D, vitamin A, vitamin E, calcium, and zinc, and occasionally vitamin B1 and vitamin B2.

● Smokers, who are most likely to be deficient in vitamin C and zinc.

● Pre-menopausal women, who have often been found to consume low amounts of calcium, iron, vitamin A, and vitamin C.

● Pregnant women are often advised to take a folic acid supplement, and studies have shown that taking a multivitamin supplement before and during pregnancy leads to a healthier pregnancy and a healthier baby.

● Anyone living in a colder climate who does not get regular sun exposure is likely to be deficient in vitamin D, which can lead to, among other problems, an increased incidence of breast cancer, bowel cancer, depression, osteoporosis, Parkinson's and heart disease.

● Anyone who is under stress is likely to benefit from taking additional B vitamins.

● Many men and women experiencing problems with low fertility are deficient in zinc.

Are supplements safe?

Generally speaking, taking nutritional supplements from reputable companies is extremely safe, but this doesn't mean all supplements are appropriate for everyone. It is worth doing some research to find out about the potential benefits and risks of taking a supplement. There are many sources of information available to help you become well-informed. If you are suffering from a specific disease, it is advisable to talk to a knowledgeable healthcare professional before taking a supplement. If you are pregnant or breastfeeding, only take those supplements specifically recommended for you to take during this time.

While many vitamins, minerals, and herbs are known to safely prevent or treat a variety of diseases, they work by altering your body chemistry – just like any medicine. So before you take a supplement, make sure you know about how it might interact with any medications you may be already taking.

Before you turn to supplements, bear in mind that using the information in this book may help you to replace depleted nutrients by eating more of a certain food. For example, if you need to replace lost potassium, you may choose to eat more bananas or drink coconut water, or eat more fresh berries to increase your vitamin C intake.

FOODS THAT HEAL

TAKE ADVANTAGE OF THE ENORMOUS **VARIETY** OF FOODS THAT HAVE INCREDIBLE **HEALTH** **BENEFITS** AND STAND AS A TESTIMONY TO "LET FOOD BE THY **MEDICINE**".

APPLES

 HELPS BALANCE BLOOD SUGAR LEVELS

 TACKLES DIARRHOEA AND CONSTIPATION

 HELPS STRENGTHEN BONES

 HELPS LOWER CHOLESTEROL

Available in many varieties, juicy, crunchy apples have been celebrated since antiquity for their health benefits. They are **high in pectin**, a fibre, and **slow-release sugars** that help to improve **heart health** and regulate the body's **blood sugar levels**. They also contain many important vitamins and minerals, and substances that promote, among other things, strong, healthy bones.

GREEN APPLES
Like other apples, green apples contain malic acid, a useful digestive aid.

RED APPLES
Antioxidants, which can protect against neurological damage associated with conditions such as Alzheimer's disease, are higher in red apples than in some other varieties.

YELLOW APPLES
The pectin in yellow and all other apples helps lower the body's absorption of excess dietary fats.

WHAT IS IT GOOD FOR?

BLOOD SUGAR REGULATION Fructose and antioxidant polyphenols in apples improve the metabolic balance and slow the rate at which sugar is absorbed into the bloodstream.

CONSTIPATION AND DIARRHOEA Pectin has an amphoteric action: paradoxically, it can provide relief from both constipation and diarrhoea, depending on the body's needs.

PROTECTING BONES The flavonoid phlorizin, found in apple skin, may help prevent bone loss associated with menopause, as it fights the inflammation and free-radical production that lead to bone loss.

REDUCES CHOLESTEROL Pectin and other constituents such as antioxidant polyphenols reduce levels of "unhealthy" (LDL) cholesterol, and slow down its oxidation – a risk factor for atherosclerosis (hardening of the arteries). Polyphenols also prevent free-radical damage to heart muscles and blood vessels.

HOW DO I GET THE BEST FROM IT?

THE WHOLE FRUIT Every part is edible. Supermarkets coat apples with wax to give a shine and keep them fresh over long periods, so always wash these apples before eating.

GO ORGANIC AND LOCAL Buy organic, and from sources as local as possible, for the freshest fruit without chemical contamination.

KEEP THE SKIN ON Peeling can remove more than half an apple's fibre, vitamin C, and iron.

HOW DO I USE IT?

A SIMPLE FOOD FOR CONVALESCENTS Grate 1 apple and allow to brown slightly to release the juices, making it easier to digest. Take 1–2 large spoonfuls every hour or as needed.

BAKED APPLES Core large apples, stuff with nuts, dried fruits, and spices such as cinnamon, and bake in a moderate oven until soft.

APRICOTS

 **PROMOTES CLEAR SKIN**    **HELPS PROTECT EYE HEALTH**    **PROMOTES BOWEL REGULARITY**    **PROTECTS AGAINST FREE-RADICAL DAMAGE**

Native to eastern Asia, apricots were cultivated by the Chinese for thousands of years before they reached the rest of the world. Low in calories yet **high in fibre** and many key vitamins, apricots can be eaten fresh or dried, and the leaves and kernels can all be used. Medicinally, they can help **improve digestion**, promote **clear skin**, and protect **vision**.

WHAT IS IT GOOD FOR?

EYE AND SKIN HEALTH Its high beta-carotene content is beneficial for ageing eyes. Studies also show a regular high intake of nutrients such as vitamins C and E, zinc, and copper – all found in apricots – can reduce the risk of macular degeneration by 25 per cent. They are also good for maintaining healthy skin.

DIGESTIVE HEALTH Its high fibre content aids bowel regularity, which can help prevent constipation and even bowel cancer.

ANTI-CANCER EFFECTS Its antioxidants can protect against free-radical damage linked to cancer and other diseases. The kernels also contain vitamin B17 (laetrile), shown in laboratory studies to kill cancer cells

HOW DO I GET THE BEST FROM IT?

EAT FRESH AND DRIED Both are rich in fibre, vitamins A, C, and E, and other key nutrients. Buy dried apricots without added sulphites.

APRICOT KERNEL The seed inside the stone is edible. As well as its anti-cancer properties, it helps remove toxins and strengthens the body's defences against disease.

KERNEL OIL Use the oil, which is rich in monounsaturated fats and vitamins A, C, and E, for cooking and salad dressings.

HOW DO I USE IT?

TO COUNTERBALANCE FATTY MEATS Pair with rich duck or goose meat, or include the dried fruits in stuffings or chopped into lamb stews.

LIGHTLY POACHED Poach fresh apricots in a light syrup of 1 part honey and 3 parts water. Add 6 crushed cardamom pods and ½ vanilla bean pod, and simmer until just tender.

PICKLED APRICOTS Japanese umeboshi, or pickled plums, are actually apricots. Eaten with rice, they stimulate digestion and prevent nausea, including nausea from hangovers.

Flesh
The very high levels of vitamin A in apricot promote healthy eyes and skin

Kernel
The kernel inside the stone is a source of a healthy oil rich in vitamin B17 (laetrile), known for its cancer-fighting properties

PEACHES AND NECTARINES

 **HELPS PREVENT METABOLIC SYNDROME**

 **FIGHTS FREE-RADICAL DAMAGE TO SKIN**

 **HELPS MAINTAIN WATER BALANCE**

Peaches originate from China, where they are considered an **uplifting**, **rejuvenating** fruit. Like other stone fruits, peaches and nectarines (a close relative) contain a balance of phenolic compounds – anthocyanins, chlorogenic acids, quercetin derivatives, and catechins – that work synergistically to **combat metabolic syndrome** (a group of risk factors that can lead to diabetes and heart disease).

PEACHES
These contain beta-carotene, lycopene, and lutein, which protect the heart and eyes.

NECTARINES
They have red, yellow, or white flesh and are a source of vitamins A and C and beta-carotene.

WHAT IS IT GOOD FOR?

WEIGHT MANAGEMENT Their phenolic compounds are known to have anti-obesity, anti-inflammatory, and anti-diabetic properties, and regular consumption of both can help prevent metabolic syndrome.

SKIN HEALTH Both are good sources of vitamin C, an essential component in the body's production of collagen. They are also a good source of the antioxidant lutein, which helps fight free-radical damage and supports healthy skin (and eyes).

DIURETIC Rich in potassium, phosphorus, and magnesium, peaches and nectarines are an antidote to a high-sodium diet and can help remove excess water from the body. They are also mildly laxative.

ANTI-CANCER Laboratory tests show that breast cancer cells – even the most aggressive type – died after exposure to peach extract.

HOW DO I GET THE BEST FROM IT?

EAT IN SEASON Eat ripe stone fruits as soon as possible after buying; they can quickly become over-ripe and lose their nutritional benefits, and tend to bruise easily.

PRESERVE FOR LATER Both peaches and nectarines make delicious jams and preserves.

HOW DO I USE IT?

ANTIOXIDANT ICED TEA Slice 2 ripe peaches into a pan, add 500ml (16fl oz) water, and bring to the boil. Remove from the heat, add 8 green tea bags, and steep for 5 minutes. Gently squeeze the teabags as you remove them. Add a further 240ml (8fl oz) water and a little honey to sweeten, if you like. When cool, serve over ice with a mint garnish.

BREAKFAST BAGEL Top a toasted bagel with soft goat's or kefir cheese and nectarine slices. A little freshly ground black pepper on top will bring out the sweetness of the fruit.

PEARS

 LOW-ALLERGY FOOD

 HAS A MILD LAXATIVE ACTION

HELPS CALM THE NERVES

 **HELPS KEEP JOINTS SUPPLE**

Dozens of different varieties of pear are now available; most have paper-thin skins and a similar shape, although some, such as the Chinese pear, look a little different. A cooling, uplifting, low-allergy fruit and an excellent source of **water-soluble fibre**, pears also contain useful amounts of **beta-carotene** and B vitamins, as well as traces of copper, phosphorus, potassium, and other essential elements.

WHAT IS IT GOOD FOR?

ALLERGY RELIEF Less allergenic than many other fruits as it is low in salicylates and benzoates. It is often recommended in exclusion diets for allergy sufferers, and pear juice is sometimes introduced as a first juice to infants. Also a good choice for convalescents.

CONSTIPATION Most of its fibre is insoluble, making it a good bulking laxative.

NERVOUS EXHAUSTION Considered to be a cooling and soothing food. Vitamin C also triggers the production of norepinephrine and serotonin, neurotransmitters that can help to lift your mood.

RHEUMATIC CONDITIONS Contains a combination of potassium, pectin, and tannins that help dissolve uric acid, making it ideal for those with rheumatic conditions, such as gout and arthritis.

HOW DO I GET THE BEST FROM IT?

KEEP THE SKIN ON Most of its vitamin C and dietary fibre is contained within its thin skin.

RIPEN AT HOME Pears bruise easily when ripe. Buy them slightly under-ripe and let them ripen at home.

DRIED Like most dried fruits, pears are high in sugar but are a good source of natural fibre. Eat just a few for a sustained energy lift.

JUICE THEM Fresh pear juice is cooling and uplifting if you are feeling hot and bothered.

HOW DO I USE IT?

UPLIFTING DRINK Boil dried pears in water for 15 minutes. Strain and reserve the hot liquid, allow to cool, then drink to relieve nervous exhaustion and symptoms of PMS.

POACH THEM Cook fresh pears gently in a light sugar syrup or wine; add a little grated ginger or cinnamon, if you like. Serve while warm, sprinkled with toasted almonds.

CONFERENCE PEAR
Fresh pears like these have higher levels of fructose, glucose, and levulose – the sweetest of all natural sugars – than in any other fruit.

RED ANJOU PEAR
Red-hued pears such as Red Anjou and Red Bartlett have more antioxidant anthocyanins than green, yellow, and brown varieties.

CHINESE PEAR
These pears may sound exotic but there is no nutritional difference between these and regular varieties.

PLUMS

⊙ **HELPS PROTECT EYE HEALTH**

≣ **HAS A LAXATIVE ACTION**

⚖ **HELPS BALANCE BLOOD SUGAR LEVELS**

◍ **SUPPORTS HEALTHY LIVER FUNCTION**

Plums, or gages, are members of the rose family and there are more than 2,000 varieties, including the greengage, Mirabelle, and damson. Plums have good **antioxidant** and **detoxifying** properties, are a **metabolic stimulant**, and contain chromium, potassium, selenium, and other minerals, as well as **vitamin C** and **beta-carotene**. Dried plums, or prunes, are a traditional treatment for constipation.

PURPLE PLUMS
Dark-skinned varieties with a red flesh are richer in beneficial antioxidants called anthocyanins than other varieties.

GREENGAGES
Like all plums, greengages are rich in potassium, beta-carotene, and fibre.

VICTORIA PLUMS
The antioxidants in these and other plums aid skin health.

PRUNES
Dried plums can help ease constipation.

WHAT IS IT GOOD FOR?

PROTECTS EYESIGHT Its antioxidants can help prevent age-related macular degeneration (a major cause of loss of vision).

CONSTIPATION Rich in stool-bulking fibres, especially pectin, fructose, and sulphur, which help food to move effectively through the colon. Together with substances such as sorbitol and isatin, these fibres are responsible for the fruit's well-known laxative effect.

METABOLIC STIMULANT Contains useful amounts of calcium, potassium, magnesium, and the antioxidant beta-carotene. These nutrients help regulate heart rate, blood pressure, blood sugar levels, and water balance. Damsons in particular, are noted for their ability to stimulate appetite and digestion if eaten before a meal.

DETOX Can initiate detoxification and help improve liver function. As well as improving internal health, its detoxifying properties can help promote healthy skin.

HOW DO I GET THE BEST FROM IT?

DRIED FRUIT Prunes are a good way to reap the benefits of plums all year round. They contain both soluble and insoluble fibre, which help promote bowel regularity and balance blood sugar levels.

KEEP THE SKIN ON The skin is where most of its beneficial antioxidants concentrate.

HOW DO I USE IT?

BAKE THEM Slice some plums in half, remove the stones, and bake in a moderate oven (180°C/350°F/Gas 4) until they are wrinkled. Eat as is or drizzle with a little honey-sweetened yogurt before serving.

SWEETEN A RICE SALAD Add chopped plums and pistachios to a cold brown rice salad. Dress with extra virgin olive oil and a fruity vinegar, such as blackberry or raspberry.

KIWI FRUIT

 **PROMOTES COLLAGEN SYNTHESIS**

 **HAS A MILD LAXATIVE ACTION**

 **REDUCES TRIGYLCERIDES IN THE BLOOD**

 **PROTECTS AGAINST COLDS AND FLU**

Native to China, and sometimes called a Chinese gooseberry, this unusual-looking fruit is now grown all over the world in sunny climates. There are some nutritional differences between the two varieties, green and gold, but both are good for **digestion** and **heart health**. Their high vitamin C content also promotes **skin health** and boosts the **immune system**, fighting off any inflammation.

WHAT IS IT GOOD FOR?

GREAT SKIN Vitamin C contributes to the formation of collagen and hastening the repair from sun and wind damage.

HEALTHY DIGESTION Its mild laxative effect is linked to its fibre content. Two kiwis provide 20 per cent of the daily recommended amount of fibre, and can aid digestion and maintain colon health. Also contains actinidin, an enzyme that aids the digestion of protein.

HEART DISEASE Studies show that the high levels of flavonoids and vitamins C and E in kiwis can reduce triglycerides (a type of fat) in the blood and the build-up of plaque in the arteries (atherosclerosis). The tiny black seeds contain vitamin E and omega-3 fatty acids, which act as natural blood thinners.

IMMUNITY Vitamin C boosts immunity, fights off colds and flu, and combats inflammation.

HOW DO I GET THE BEST FROM IT?

EAT RAW ON ITS OWN Eat with a spoon, as you would a boiled egg. The actinidin in green, but not gold, kiwis makes them incompatible with some foods such as dairy produce, which they cause to curdle.

GET COLOURFUL Green kiwis contain larger amounts of fibre, while gold kiwis contain higher levels of vitamin C and potassium.

HOW DO I USE IT?

A SUMMERY SMOOTHIE Blitz the flesh (seeds removed) of ¼ watermelon, 2 peeled kiwi fruit, and a peeled banana in a blender.

DETOX SOUP For a cold soup for 2, blend until smooth the flesh of 1 melon (galia or honeydew) cut in half, 1 kiwi fruit, and 1 ripe pear (all seeds removed), a handful of green grapes, grated fresh root ginger (optional), and 200ml (7fl oz) aloe vera juice. Chill in the refrigerator, pour into the empty melon shells, and garnish with chopped kiwi and fresh mint.

GREEN KIWI
Contains significantly more fibre than gold kiwi fruit.

GOLD KIWI
Gold kiwi contains large amounts of vitamin C, vital for boosting immunity.

FIGS

 REGULATES HEART RATE AND BLOOD PRESSURE

 HELPS STRENGTHEN BONES

 **PROMOTES BOWEL REGULARITY**

Figs are a lovely, sweet, seasonal fruit, generally available from July to September that can be enjoyed fresh or dried. Although each has its own benefits, both fresh and dried figs are beneficial foods for **blood pressure** thanks to their high potassium levels, and are also good for maintaining a good **digestive system** and improving **bone health**.

PURPLE FIGS
These figs are a good source of fibre, helping promote bowel regularity and reducing the risk of bowel cancer.

WHITE FIGS
Like purple figs, this white variety is a rich source of fibre, calcium, potassium, and other trace elements.

DRIED FIGS
Dried figs retain and concentrate all the nutritional benefits of the fresh fruit, although they are lower in beta-carotene.

WHAT IS IT GOOD FOR?

BLOOD PRESSURE Fresh and dried figs contain large amounts of potassium, which is crucial for the smooth functioning of muscles and nerves, balancing fluid levels in the body, and regulating the heart rate and water balance. Figs are an ideal healthy food to eat if you have high blood pressure.

BONE HEALTH A good source of calcium, with one serving providing 10 per cent of the daily recommended amount. Calcium is important in promoting the health and growth of bones. The potassium content of figs also helps reduce calcium lost through urine, meaning the body absorbs more calcium.

DIGESTION AND CONSTIPATION A fantastic source of fibre. Regularly including fibre in your diet is vital for maintaining a healthy digestive system, which in turn reduces the chances of constipation.

HOW DO I GET THE BEST FROM IT?

FRESH Compared to their dried counterparts, fresh figs are lower in calories and sugar. They are also higher in beta-carotene, which converts to vitamin A in the body.

DRIED Dried figs are available all year round. Compared to fresh figs, they contain more fibre, protein, calcium, potassium, magnesium, and phosphorus. They are also a great source of pectin, a form of soluble fibre, which is good for reducing blood sugar levels. They are, however, higher in calories and sugar.

HOW DO I USE IT?

AS THEY ARE Dried figs make a great sweet snack. Eat instead of sweets or chocolate, especially if you are trying to lose weight.

WITH CEREAL The health benefits of figs make them a fantastic addition to your breakfast. Adding chopped figs to muesli or porridge is a tasty way to include them in your diet.

QUINCE

 SOOTHES STOMACH UPSETS

 **CONTAINS ANTI-CANCER SUBSTANCES**

 **FIGHTS INFLAMMATION AND INFECTION**

 **HELPS MAINTAIN HEALTHY ARTERIES**

Quince is an ancient fruit native to the Middle East that is slowly finding its place again in the modern world. It boosts the **immune system** and benefits **heart health**, while its juice is used to treat diarrhoea and as a mouthwash and gargle to maintain **gum health** and treat **mouth ulcers**. This deeply fragrant fruit is too sour to be eaten raw, but cooking helps bring out its flavour and nutritional benefits.

WHAT IS IT GOOD FOR?

STOMACH SOOTHER Has an astringent quality that makes it a good general tonic for the digestive system. It is also mildly diuretic.

ANTI-CANCER Laboratory studies have shown the leaf and fruit contain substances that inhibit the growth of colon and kidney cancer cells.

FIGHTS FREE RADICALS Rich in antioxidant vitamins A, C, and E and unique phytonutrients, shown to have strong free-radical scavenging properties (free radicals are implicated in heart disease, diabetes, inflammatory conditions, and cancer).

HEART HEALTH Rich in potassium, which promotes a regular heartbeat and helps remove excess water from the body. Its fibre and antioxidants can contribute to healthy arteries and the regeneration of arterial walls.

HOW DO I GET THE BEST FROM IT?

BUY IN SEASON From September to November look for large firm fruits with a yellow skin. Paradoxically for such a hard fruit, quinces can bruise easily so avoid any fruits with signs of damage or decay. Don't store for long periods, and enjoy the fragrance they impart while it lasts.

MIX WITH WATER Several laboratory studies have shown that quince steeped in hot water has an immunity-boosting effect, and may help ease symptoms of allergic dermatitis.

HOW DO I USE IT?

GOES WELL WITH APPLES Add chunks of tart quince to apple sauce, pies, or crumbles to lift their texture, flavour, and aroma.

SWEETEN YOUR TEA Add a spoonful of quince jelly or preserve to green tea to sweeten, add scent, and further boost its antioxidant effect.

A VERSATILE PRESERVE Quinces are high in pectin so they make wonderful preserves.

Seeds
A decoction of the seeds produces a viscous substance which is a traditional Middle Eastern remedy for sore throats and coughs

Leaves
Studies have shown that the leaves and fruit contain properties that can inhibit the growth of certain cancer cells

Fruit
An astringent fruit that has a general tonic effects. Its juice can be used to treat diarrhoea and even as a mouthwash and gargle to maintain gum health and treat mouth ulcers

CHERRIES

 HELPS PROMOTE SLEEP   **HELPS INCREASE INSULIN PRODUCTION**   **REDUCES POST-EXERCISE INFLAMMATION**   **CAN HELP PREVENT GOUT**

Cherries – if you pick the correct kind – can rightly be called one of today's superfoods. Montmorency cherries have the most medicinal value as they are rich in **antioxidants**, are a good **anti-inflammatory**, and are useful in the prevention and **treatment of gout**. They are also one of very few fruits to contain melatonin, which can help treat insomnia and jet lag and can **encourage good sleep**.

DARK RED CHERRIES
Sweet cherries contain a significant amount of perillyl alcohol (POH), a chemical that may help slow or halt certain cancers.

MONTMORENCY CHERRIES
Studies show this sour, bright red variety is around 10 times more active at relieving pain than aspirin.

YELLOW AND RED CHERRIES
A very sweet variety with useful levels of vitamin C and the antioxidant beta-carotene.

WHAT IS IT GOOD FOR?

A GOOD NIGHT'S SLEEP Sour cherries are one of the few foods to contain significant amounts of melatonin, a hormone produced naturally by the body as part of our sleep–wake cycle. Studies show that a glass of sour cherry juice before bedtime can promote sound sleep.

ANTI-DIABETIC Tart cherries may be useful in treating diabetes. Their abundant antioxidant anthocyanins can increase insulin production, helping to regulate blood sugar levels.

ANTI-INFLAMMATORY Rich in potent antioxidants that can help fight inflammation. Drinking tart cherry juice has been shown to reduce post-exercise pain and inflammation in athletes and distance runners.

ARTHRITIC CONDITIONS Gout, an inflammatory condition related to arthritis, is caused by an excess accumulation of uric acid in the blood. Both sour and sweet cherries have been found to reduce levels of urates in the blood, and to reduce the risk of contracting gout.

HOW DO I GET THE BEST FROM IT?

CHOOSE FRESH IN SEASON Buy organic, in season, and as local as possible for the most nutrients. Alternatively, pit and freeze the fresh fruits to use through the year, or choose cherry concentrates and extracts.

PICK SOUR OVER SWEET Sour cherries have higher antioxidant levels than other cherries.

HOW DO I USE IT?

DRIED CHERRIES Dried cherries can be added to cereals and yogurts.

MAKE A CHERRY PIE Cherries don't lose their medicinal value when cooked. This makes them an ideal ingredient for jams and pies, strudels, and other desserts.

ADD TO SMOOTHIES Sweet, pitted cherries are a great addition to a fruit smoothie.

GRAPES

 HELPS REDUCE THE RISK OF CANCER

HELPS PREVENT HARDENED ARTERIES

HAS A MILD DIURETIC ACTION

HELPS BALANCE BLOOD SUGAR LEVELS

For thousands of years every part of the grape plant, including the sap in the vines, has been used as medicine. Grapes, a **natural diuretic**, contain a variety of **antioxidants**, especially oligomeric proanthocyanidin complexes (OPCs), which contribute to everything from **glowing skin** to protection from **heart disease** and **free-radical damage**. OPCs are especially concentrated in grape seeds.

WHAT IS IT GOOD FOR?

ANTI-CANCER The high levels of flavonoids, anthocyanins, stilbenes, and many other antioxidants, especially in dark-skinned grapes, have been found to reduce the risk of cancers of the breast and prostate caused by free-radical damage. Grape antioxidant dietary fibre (GADF) also helps to lower the risk of colon cancer. The seeds in particular are high in the antioxidant resveratrol, which has anti-cancer and anti-ageing properties.

CARDIOVASCULAR HEALTH Contains a wealth of antioxidants shown to prevent and reverse the effects of atherosclerosis (hardening of arteries). Red wine or grape juice is also high in resveratrol, which protects the heart.

DETOX AND WATER BALANCE Contains high levels of potassium and very little sodium, which encourages the body to flush out excess water and toxins.

STEADYING BLOOD SUGAR LEVELS Contains slow-release carbohydrates that assist with blood glucose control. Its antioxidant and fibre mix can also help reduce the threat of metabolic syndrome (a group of risk factors that can lead to diabetes and heart disease).

HOW DO I GET THE BEST FROM IT?

CRUNCH THE SEEDS Choose seeded varieties and eat the seeds – where OPCs, vitamin E, and linolenic acid all concentrate.

DRIED FRUIT When dried, fructose converts into a soluble fibre, fructan, which absorbs and removes cholesterol from the blood, and helps feed good bacteria in the gut.

HOW DO I USE IT?

IN A RICE DISH OR SALAD Raisins add flavour and nutrition to a rice dish while grapes add a touch of sweetness to a green salad.

FREEZE THEM A cooling snack, frozen grapes have the same nutritional benefits as fresh.

RED GRAPES
Anthocyanins are the most abundant antioxidant in red and black grapes. They protect the heart and have anti-cancer properties.

Leaves
The leaves are rich in antioxidant polyphenols, beta-carotene, and vitamin K, and are a traditional remedy for pain and inflammation .

WHITE GRAPES
Flavonoid antioxidants known as catechins – which also give cocoa its medicinal power – are most abundant in white varieties.

RAISINS
Dried white grapes are an effective prebiotic, feeding good bacteria in the gut.

BLACKBERRIES

 **HELPS REPAIR SUN-DAMAGED SKIN**

 **HELPS REMOVE TOXINS FROM THE GUT**

 **HELPS LOWER BLOOD PRESSURE**

 **CONTAINS ANTI-CANCER SUBSTANCES**

Blackberries are high in antioxidants, of which anthocyanins are responsible for their deep purple colour. Anthocyanins also fight **free-radical damage** in the body and address a range of modern conditions including **hypertension**, diabetes, cancer, vision loss, poor liver function, and **declining mental faculties**. The berries also have detoxifying properties and promote gut health.

Fruit
These berries are a source of salicylic acid, which helps lower blood pressure

Leaves
Reserve the leaves and brew as a tea to treat stomach upsets and boost mouth health

WHAT IS IT GOOD FOR?

SKIN HEALTH The berries are a great source of the antioxidant ellagic acid, which can help reduce damage done to skin from over-exposure to sun. Ellagic acid also prevents the breakdown of collagen, the "scaffolding" that supports firm skin and prevents inflammation.

HEALTHY GUT Contains both insoluble and soluble fibre, helpful for bowel regularity and removing toxins from the gut.

HEART PROTECTIVE Blackberries contain salicylic acid, a compound with properties similar to aspirin (also known as acetylsalicylic acid), which could help protect against heart disease and lower blood pressure.

ANTI-CANCER PROPERTIES Ellagic acid has been shown to stop the growth of cancer cells in laboratory tests.

HOW DO I GET THE BEST FROM IT?

FRESH IS BEST The nutrients deteriorate quickly so eat freshly picked or within a few days of purchase. Eat at room temperature.

LEAVES The leaves contain tannin and gallic acid, a natural antibiotic. Brewed in a tea, they are a traditional remedy for acute diarrhoea, mouth ulcers, and bleeding gums.

HOW DO I USE IT?

ADD TO A CRUMBLE Add to an apple crumble for added flavour and antioxidant benefits.

MAKE A VINEGAR Blackberry vinegar adds a real lift to salad dressings, marinades, and stir-fries. Mixed with a little water, the vinegar is also a useful remedy for sore throat and fever. Cover fresh blackberries in white wine or apple cider vinegar and store in a cool dark place for 3 weeks. Strain the vinegar into a pan, add 450g (1lb) caster sugar for every 600ml (1 pint) of strained liquid, and boil gently for 5 minutes. Decant into sterilized, tightly sealed bottles and use within a year.

BLACKCURRANTS

 HELPS REGULATE BLOOD PRESSURE

 PROTECTS AGAINST NEURO-DEGENERATION

 HELPS PROTECT AGAINST CATARACTS

 FIGHTS URINARY TRACT INFECTIONS

High in vitamin C, with useful levels of **potassium** and phosphorus, blackcurrants also contain a range of different anthocyanins, **antioxidants** that protect against **heart disease**, cancer, and neurological disorders such as **Alzheimer's disease**. The fruits also have antibacterial properties and promote **better vision**. Too sour to eat fresh on their own, they make good cordials, syrups, and jams.

WHAT IS IT GOOD FOR?

HEART HEALTH Its potassium content helps maintain a regular heartbeat, and acts as a diuretic and blood-pressure regulator. Its antioxidants also help prevent damage to blood vessel walls that can lead to atherosclerosis (hardening of the arteries).

BRAIN FOOD Anthocyanins, which give the berries their colour, help protect the brain from the free-radical damage associated with dementia and Alzheimer's disease.

BETTER NIGHT VISION Antioxidants in the fruit have been shown to improve night vision, relieve eyestrain, and help prevent cataracts.

URINARY TRACT INFECTIONS Has a similar antibacterial action to cranberries: regular consumption of the juice can help fight urinary tract infections (UTIs).

IMMUNITY-BOOSTING TONIC Its mixture of vitamin C and antioxidants is good as a general tonic to help protect and boost immunity, and heal wounds more quickly.

HOW DO I GET THE BEST FROM IT?

ADD SUGAR Turn into preserves or add the fresh fruits to other sweeter fruits in desserts.

A HEALTHY SEED OIL The oil is rich in vitamin E and several unsaturated fatty acids such as alpha-linolenic acid and gamma-linolenic acid. Regular consumption may help skin conditions, such as eczema and dermatitis.

USE THE LEAVES A tea made from the leaves can be used to treat coughs and sore throats.

HOW DO I USE IT?

SYRUP Turn the fruit into a sweet syrup or cordial, which retains its antioxidants and other immunity-boosting phytochemicals.

TEA Put a small handful of leaves in a teapot, pour over boiling water, leave to infuse for a few minutes, strain, and drink as required.

Fruit
Weight-for-weight, blackcurrants contain three times as much vitamin C as oranges. Too sour to eat raw, make them into sweetened cordials to enjoy their benefits

Leaves
Add the leaves to boiling water to make a tea that can help treat coughs and sore throats

BLUEBERRIES

 SLOWS THE GROWTH OF PROSTATE CANCER

 HELPS PREVENT COGNITIVE DECLINE

 EFFECTIVE AGAINST GASTROENTERITIS

 HELPS PROTECT EYE HEALTH

Native to North America, blueberries have long been valued for their nutritional and medicinal properties. They contain **antibacterial** compounds that fight off stomach bugs and **antioxidants** to **prevent eye damage** and improve both **eyesight** and **memory**. They also promote **prostate health**. Much sweeter than many small berries, they can be eaten fresh on their own to reap all the benefits.

Berries
Studies show that blueberries have some of the highest levels of active antioxidants per serving of any food

Leaves
Tea made from the leaves can be used to prevent urinary tract infections and regulate blood sugar levels

WHAT IS IT GOOD FOR?

PROSTATE HEALTH A rich source of concentrated proanthocyanidin compounds, which can slow the growth and spread of various cancers. Recent laboratory studies show that blueberry extract also significantly slows the growth of prostate cancer cells.

IMPROVED MEMORY It may have a positive effect on the nervous system. Also studies show it can increase levels of dopamine – a vital neurotransmitter – thus improving memory. May also alleviate cognitive decline.

HEALTHY GUT Contains anthocyanins, antibacterial antioxidants effective against causes of gastroenteritis, such as *E. coli*. Also combats the bacteria that cause diarrhoea.

SUPPORTING VISION Anthocyanins can help improve eye health by protecting against retinal degeneration. They may also help to prevent the eye condition glaucoma due to their collagen-enhancing properties.

URINARY TRACT INFECTIONS Recent studies confirm its usefulness in treating urinary tract infections (UTIs).

HOW DO I GET THE BEST FROM IT?

BUY ORGANIC Blueberries belong to a "dirty dozen" list of fruits that generally have the most pesticide residues. Eating organic is the only way to avoid chemical contamination.

LEAVES The leaves contain similar levels of antioxidants to that of the fruit. Use to prevent UTIs and regulate blood sugar levels.

HOW DO I USE IT?

FOR BREAKFAST Add to cereal or yogurt, or freeze to preserve them for longer and include them in a breakfast shake or smoothie.

LEAF TEA Pour boiling water on the leaves, infuse, strain, and drink as a tea that contains antibacterial and hypoglycaemic properties.

To freeze blueberries, spread them in a single layer on a large freezerproof tray, and place in the freezer overnight. When completely frozen, transfer the berries to a freezer bag; force as much air out of the bag as possible. Return to the freezer for storage.

CRANBERRIES

 FIGHTS URINARY TRACT INFECTIONS

 HELPS FIGHT GUM DISEASE

 HELPS ALLEVIATE HEAVY PERIODS

 HELPS PREVENT STOMACH ULCERS

Native to North America, these rather sour red berries are packed with **antioxidants** and have a number of health benefits. They are both **astringent** and **antibacterial**, helping, among other things, to promote good **gum health**. Beyond that they contain a unique substance that helps prevent infections from taking hold in the urinary tract, kidney, and bladder.

Fruit
Cranberries were used by Native Americans to treat bladder and kidney infections

Juice
To get the best from cranberry juice, look for brands low in sugar

Dried cranberries
Adding the dried fruit to cereals and muesli is a simple way to include more antioxidants in your diet

WHAT IS IT GOOD FOR?

URINARY TRACT INFECTIONS Contains non-dialyzable material (NDM) that prevents infections of the urinary tract (UTIs), bladder, and even kidneys.

PROTECTING TEETH The antioxidant proanthocyanidin, which gives the berries their bright red colour, can inhibit enzymes associated with plaque build-up, acid formation in teeth, and receding gums.

TONING AND ASTRINGENT Its astringent and slightly antiseptic nature helps alleviate heavy periods, diarrhoea, stomach upsets, sore throats, and laryngitis.

DIGESTION Preliminary research suggests that NDM may also prevent *Helicobacter pylori* bacteria attaching to stomach walls, giving it a useful role in preventing stomach ulcers.

HEALTHY HEART Its high vitamin C and anti-inflammatory antioxidant can protect against inflammation and heart disease by reducing oxidative stress caused by free radicals in the body.

HOW DO I GET THE BEST FROM IT?

JUICE Fresh juice gives you the overall benefits of the fruit. Choose unsweetened, unpasteurized versions, as sugar feeds bacteria that cause urinary tract infections. Better yet, juice the berries yourself.

DRIED Eat the dried berries to enjoy most of the fruit's benefits throughout the year. Only the vitamin C content is heavily diminished.

HOW DO I USE IT?

MAKE A TEA Add 1 heaped dsp dried berries to 600ml (1 pint) water. Simmer over a low heat for 10–15 minutes, strain, and drink.

IN BETWEEN BRUSHES Chew the dried berries thoroughly to release their gum-protecting properties and to give gums a gentle massage.

ELDERBERRIES

 HELPS FIGHT COLDS AND FLU

 **HAS A MILD DIURETIC ACTION**

Elderberries are the fruit of a woodland tree common throughout Europe, North America, and Asia. It was once regarded as a **complete medicine chest**, as all parts of the plant can be used medicinally. The fruits and flowers, which are most commonly consumed today, have **immunity-boosting** and **diuretic effects**. The raw berries are an acquired taste, but cooking makes them more palatable.

WHAT IS IT GOOD FOR?

STRENGTHENING IMMUNITY The flowers are a traditional remedy for relieving lung congestion. They promote sweating and can cool fevers. They are also anti-inflammatory. Syrup made from the berries is a well-proven way to boost immunity at any time, but especially in winter against colds and flu.

DETOX The fruits are known to have a mild diuretic and laxative action.

HOW DO I GET THE BEST FROM IT?

PRESERVE THE FRUITS Raw elderberries are too sour for some tastes. Turning them into jams, preserves, compotes, and syrups is the best way to get the most benefit from them.

FLOWERS The flowers can be used to make everything from a lightly sparkling elderflower "champagne" to a useful gargle to soothe sore throats. Chemicals in the flowers may also help to reduce swelling in mucous membranes in the sinuses.

HOW DO I USE IT?

A HEALING SYRUP Add 600ml (1 pint) strained juice from the berries to 450g (1lb) honey and mix together well. For colds and flu, take 10ml (2 tsp) as needed.

ELDERFLOWER TEA Add 2–4 fresh flower heads (or 2 tsp dried herb per cup) to a teapot, pour in boiling water, leave to infuse for a few minutes, strain, and drink as a tea to fight coughs and catarrhal conditions.

MAKE A CORDIAL Place 900g (2lb) berries in a pan with 1 cup of water and simmer over a low heat until the berries release their juice. Crush and strain, reserve the juice, and return to the pan with 250g (9oz) caster sugar and 2.5cm (1in) grated fresh root ginger (optional). Simmer for 1 hour. Strain and store in a tightly sealed sterilized bottle. Refrigerate and use within 3 months. To drink, dilute to taste.

BERRIES
Elderberries get their colour from antioxidant flavonoids that help prevent damage to the body's cells.

FLOWERS
The flowers (and berries) may help relieve nasal congestion.

Goji Berries

 HELPS MAINTAIN MUSCLE STRENGTH

 **SUPPLIES OXYGEN TO CELLS**

 **HELPS PROMOTE PEACEFUL SLEEP**

 **PROTECTS EYES FROM FREE-RADICAL DAMAGE**

These berries belong to the broader nightshade family that includes chilli peppers and tomatoes. Also called wolfberries, they are rich in a combination of **antioxidant** nutrients that benefit **cardiovascular health**, muscle health, and vision. They also contain a variety of **carotenoids**, including beta-carotene, known to boost **metabolic processes** and promote **good sleep** and **memory**.

FRESH WOLFBERRIES
Wolfberries don't store or travel well, which is why we eat them dried as goji berries.

DRIED GOJI BERRIES
The anti-ageing effects attributed to goji berries are due to their high antioxidant capacity.

What Is It Good For?

MUSCLE HEALTH Contains betaine, a nutrient that helps build muscle, and beta-sitosterol, which helps prevent the inflammation that causes sore muscles.

METABOLIC SUPPORT Pyridoxine (vitamin B6) is involved in numerous metabolic processes, aids the production of energy, and boosts the oxygen-carrying capacity of red blood cells. One serving of the berries contains nearly half the daily requirement of pyridoxine.

NEUROLOGICAL SUPPORT Betaine, used by the liver to produce choline, helps to soothe nerves, promote restful sleep, and has a role to play in enhancing memory.

VISION Abundant in lutein and zeaxanthin, antioxidants that have a proven ability to protect and maintain eye health.

ANTIOXIDANT BOOST Contains around 10 times the antioxidant capacity of blueberries, contributing to cardiovascular- and immune-system health. It may also protect against degenerative and inflammatory diseases, such as diabetes and arthritis. Its high antioxidant levels also mean it is a healthy skin food.

How Do I Get The Best From It?

DRIED Wolfberries deteriorate quickly once harvested. Dehydrating them preserves their nutritional benefits. Choose sulphite-free organic varieties to ensure a low toxic load.

JUICE Choose goji berry juice if you don't enjoy the dried fruit: it contains all the health benefits of the dried fruit except the fibre.

How Do I Use It?

AS THEY ARE Eat as a snack during the day to boost energy or satisfy cravings.

BREAKFAST FRUIT Soak in water and add to muesli, porridge, fruit, yogurt, and smoothies, or bake into home-made breakfast bars.

MULBERRIES

 **HELPS RESTORE VITALITY**

 **RELIEVES TIRED EYES**

 **SOOTHES NERVES, PROMOTES SLEEP**

 **HELPS EASE BLOATING AND CONSTIPATION**

Mulberries are an ancient fruit with a long tradition of use as a medicine, including as a **tonic** for the whole body. All parts of the plant, from root to tip, can be used medicinally, though these days we tend to concentrate only on the fruit and leaves, which are high in **antioxidant** anthocyanins and **cancer-fighting** resveratrol and vitamin C. They also protect against **eye damage** and act as a **sedative**.

WHAT IS IT GOOD FOR?

STRENGTHENING TONIC Can be used as a general tonic to restore vitality. The berries contain a useful amount of iron to benefit the kidneys, liver, and blood, and also resveratrol (also found in grape seeds), which has anti-cancer properties. Their high antioxidant content helps prevent heart disease and diseases associated with chronic inflammation.

EYE HEALTH The fruit and leaves contain zeaxanthin, which helps protect eyesight. Traditionally, mulberry was used to combat "dry conditions", such as dry skin and eczema, and a dry mouth and throat; its moistening properties can ease dry, strained eyes.

SEDATIVE A tea made from the fresh fruit or a teaspoon of the fruit preserve steeped in water is a traditional remedy for insomnia.

DIGESTIVE HEALTH Strengthens the digestive tract and can ease bloating and constipation.

LOWERS FEVERS A cooling food, it can be useful for treating fevers and heatstroke.

HOW DO I GET THE BEST FROM IT?

EAT DRIED Fresh mulberries don't store well, so enjoy their benefits in dried form – a good substitute for raisins.

MAKE A TEA FROM THE LEAVES The leaves, harvested after the first frosts of autumn, have antibacterial properties.

BE GENTLE Picked fresh from the tree, the berries are a healthful treat, but they are more fragile than other berries so pick carefully.

HOW DO I USE IT?

ADD THE LEAVES TO A SALAD The young, tender leaves can be eaten raw in salads.

MAKE A JAM The berries are high in pectin and so make an excellent jam.

A NATURAL SWEETENER Add dried berries to regular or green tea to add extra nutrients.

BLACK MULBERRIES
These dark berries have antiviral properties that are shown to be effective against the HIV virus. The fruit ripens to black.

RED MULBERRIES
Native to North America, these berries have antibacterial properties and can help fight urinary tract infections (UTIs). Despite the name "red", the berries turn a deep purple, almost black, at their ripest.

Leaves
Used to strengthen the liver and lungs, and treat fevers, colds, and eye infections. The leaves are antibacterial and anti-diabetic

DRIED WHITE MULBERRIES
Native to China, and the preferred food of silkworms. The fruit has a neuroprotective effect in humans.

RASPBERRIES

 **MINIMIZES THE ABSORPTION OF FAT**

 HELPS TONE THE UTERUS

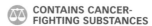 **CONTAINS CANCER-FIGHTING SUBSTANCES**

Recent studies confirm that raspberries contain a vast array of **antioxidants** with a host of potential benefits in **regulating metabolism** and **fighting diseases**. One of these antioxidants is the anti-inflammatory compound, ellagic acid, which is **cancer-protective**. The leaves can be used medicinally as a **tonic in pregnancy**, and in particular, preparing the uterus for a birth.

RED RASPBERRIES
Raspberries are high in beta-carotene, vitamin C, and folate.

Leaves
The astringent leaves are traditionally taken as a tea in late pregnancy

BLACK RASPBERRIES
Laboratory studies have proven that black raspberries have anti-cancer properties.

WHAT IS IT GOOD FOR?

METABOLIC AID Preliminary research suggests rheosmin, a phenolic compound, can suppress the digestion and absorption of fat, and stimulate the metabolism. Another compound, tiliroside, has a similar action, and may also help regulate blood sugar levels.

PREGNANCY AID The leaves are rich in tannins that may help tone and strengthen the uterus. However, only drink raspberry leaf tea during the last two months of pregnancy.

CANCER FIGHTER Phytonutrients in red and black berries may inhibit the development of certain cancers. Particular studies have focused on the potential of black raspberries to protect against DNA mutations and inhibit the growth of tumours. In laboratory tests, black raspberries have halted the development of oesophageal and colon cancer. The anti-inflammatory compound, ellagic acid, which is cancer-protective, may also help with bowel conditions.

HOW DO I GET THE BEST FROM IT?

EAT ORGANIC Recent research on organic raspberries has shown the organic fruits to be significantly higher in their total antioxidant capacity than non-organic berries.

MAKE SURE THEY ARE RIPE Studies show that fully ripe raspberries contain significantly more antioxidants than unripe fruits.

HOW DO I USE IT?

MAKE A JAM Extend the short season of raspberries by preserving them as jam.

MAKE A LEAF TEA Put 1 tsp dried leaves (or 2 tsp fresh) per 175ml (6fl oz) water in a teapot, pour over boiling water, leave to infuse for 10 minutes, strain, and drink as required. Raspberry leaf tea should only be drunk in the last 2 months of pregnancy; avoid it completely in the first 2 trimesters.

STRAWBERRIES

 HELPS PREVENT BLOOD VESSEL DAMAGE

 SOOTHES STOMACH UPSETS

 CONTAINS ANTI-CANCER SUBSTANCES

Fresh strawberries are a high **antioxidant** food: as well as being a rich source of **vitamin C**, they contain manganese, folate, potassium, B vitamins, and the beneficial **flavonoids**, quercetin and kaempferol. In addition, they have **heart-healthy** properties, benefit the **digestive system**, and are the only fruit to have seeds – a source of small amounts of omega-3 fatty acids – on their exterior.

WHAT IS IT GOOD FOR?

HEART HEALTH Apart from vitamin C, the berries are rich in quercetin and kaempferol, both of which can prevent "unhealthy" (LDL) cholesterol in the blood oxidizing and damaging artery walls (atherosclerosis).

DIGESTION A tea made from the leaves is a traditional remedy to soothe acid indigestion. Fibre in the fruit can aid a sluggish bowel.

ANTI-CANCER Contains the antioxidant compound ellagic acid that scavenges for, binds to, and helps to neutralize cancer-causing chemicals in the body.

HOW DO I GET THE BEST FROM IT?

EAT SEASONALLY Strawberries are grown all over the world and are available through the year, but they do not store well and quickly lose their nutrients once picked. They are most delicious and nutritious when eaten fresh in season.

GO ORGANIC Most strawberries are treated with high amounts of pesticides and fungicides. Eating organic is the only way to avoid this chemical contamination.

HOW DO I USE IT?

STRAWBERRY AND CUCUMBER SALAD Try this unusual and detoxifying combination: hull and halve 450g (1lb) strawberries and cut 1 cucumber into thin slices. Toss in a bowl and season with freshly ground black pepper (which brings out the flavour of the berries). Blueberries make a nice additional ingredient so add a few, if you like.

MAKE A TEA Tummy-soothing strawberry tea is best made from just-picked young strawberry leaves. Place a handful of fresh leaves in a teapot. Pour boiling water over the leaves and allow to steep for 5 minutes. Add honey if you like, strain, and serve. If fresh leaves aren't available, use dried.

Leaves
Fresh or dried strawberry leaves can be used to make a tea that can soothe upset stomachs

Berries
Nutrients in strawberries help prevent cholesterol from damaging artery walls

CITRUS FRUITS

 **HELPS PREVENT KIDNEY STONES**

 **HELPS LOWER CHOLESTEROL**

AIDS HEALTHY DIGESTION

 **HELPS REMOVE ACCUMULATED TOXINS**

This family of juicy fruits not only includes lemons, limes, oranges, and grapefruit, but also tangerines, mandarins, and less widely eaten fruits, such as pomellos and kumquats. Their **vitamin C** content is legendary, and regular consumption can help reduce the risk of **heart disease**, **kidney stones**, and **infections** of all kinds. They also boost **good digestion** and have alkalizing and **detoxifying** properties.

LEMONS
Lemons have antibacterial properties proven to fight the Vibrio species of bacteria, responsible for cholera.

LIMES
The vitamin K in limes is essential for healthy blood clotting.

ORANGES
Orange juice may help prevent kidney stones (calcium oxalate stone formation).

GRAPEFRUITS
High in vitamin C, these fruits can help reduce the severity of inflammatory conditions, such as asthma.

WHAT IS IT GOOD FOR?

KIDNEY STONES Lemons have the highest concentration of citrate; consuming dilute lemon juice or unsweetened lemonade daily has been shown to decrease the rate of stone formation. Orange juice may also help.

HEART HEALTH Contain hesperidin, which can reduce symptoms of hypertension, and pectin (fibre) and limonoid compounds, which can slow atherosclerosis (hardening of the arteries) and reduce "unhealthy" (LDL) cholesterol in the blood. Antioxidant flavones can also lower the risk of strokes in women.

RELIEVES INDIGESTION Mixed with hot water, lemon juice can relieve heartburn, nausea, acid indigestion, and stomach ache. It may also have an anti-parasitic effect.

ALKALIZING AND DETOXIFYING Lemons are a natural diuretic and can help reduce swelling, inflammation, and oedema (water retention). Also antibacterial, they flush out the bacteria that cause urinary tract infections (UTIs).

HOW DO I GET THE BEST FROM IT?

USE THE PEEL Citrus peel is full of beneficial antioxidants and has a high concentration of the fruit's limonoids. Modern science shows citrus peel fights free radicals, balances blood sugar levels, and supports thyroid health.

FOOD SYNERGY The vitamin C in citrus fruits helps the body absorb non-haem iron, a form of iron from plant sources such as vegetables.

HOW DO I USE IT?

A JEWELLED SALAD Peel and chop the fruit of 5 large oranges and place in a bowl. Add the seeds of 1 pomegranate and its juice. Add the juice of 1 orange, 3 tbsp olive oil, chopped fresh mint, and pepper, and mix gently.

MIX WITH WATER Start the day with a glass of warm water and lemon juice to alkalize and cleanse your system.

BANANAS

 HELPS STRENGTHEN BONES

 PROTECTS AGAINST ULCERS

 CONTAINS SLOW-RELEASE SUGARS

 LOWERS RISK OF HEART DISEASE AND STROKE

Bananas are an extremely versatile and healthy fruit. They are **rich in potassium**, which is essential for **maintaining blood pressure** at healthy levels, and are **natural antacids**, which makes them a soothing and healing choice for **upset stomachs** and **ulcers**. The ripe fruit consists of nearly 90 per cent natural **slow-release sugars** – ideal for athletes and busy people alike.

WHAT IS IT GOOD FOR?

BONE HEALTH Its potassium content slows the urinary calcium loss associated with a modern diet high in salt. Also contains prebiotic compounds that feed good bacteria in the gut. A healthy gut increases the body's ability to absorb key nutrients such as calcium – crucial for bone health.

SOOTHING THE STOMACH Has antacid effects that protect the stomach from ulcers. Also helps activate cells that build the stomach lining, and eliminates the bacteria that cause stomach ulcers. These antacid effects are also good for easing heartburn.

ENERGY BOOSTER The fruit contains both quick-release glucose and slow-release fructose, so it supplies energy in 2 ways.

CARDIOVASCULAR HEALTH An extremely good source of potassium and fibre. Studies show that potassium- and fibre-rich diets reduce the risk of stroke and heart disease. Potassium is also essential for the maintenance of blood pressure.

FOR CONSTIPATION Its high fibre content helps bowel regularity and eases constipation

HOW DO I GET THE BEST FROM IT?

EAT RIPE FRUIT To get the most antioxidants, eat when the skin is yellow with a few brown or black spots, and the flesh is ripe, almost to the point of spoilage.

HOW DO I USE IT?

IN THE BLENDER Banana is a good base for a fruit smoothie, as it works well with many flavours and is a natural thickener.

TO SWEETEN CEREALS Add to your cereal or porridge as a natural sweetener and as an extra source of fibre.

A FROZEN TREAT Bananas can be frozen and eaten as an alternative to ice lollies, or puréed and served as an alternative to ice cream.

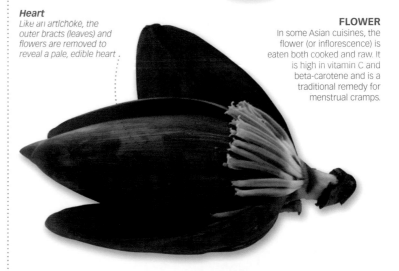

FRUIT
The potassium in bananas lowers blood pressure and insures against brittle bones.

Heart
Like an artichoke, the outer bracts (leaves) and flowers are removed to reveal a pale, edible heart .

FLOWER
In some Asian cuisines, the flower (or inflorescence) is eaten both cooked and raw. It is high in vitamin C and beta-carotene and is a traditional remedy for menstrual cramps.

DATES

 **PROMOTES BOWEL REGULARITY**

 **CONTAINS SLOW-RELEASE SUGARS**

 **HELPS MAINTAIN A REGULAR HEARTBEAT**

 **SOOTHES COUGHS AND SORE THROATS**

The date palm, one of the oldest trees cultivated by man, has its origins in the desert around the Persian Gulf. **Immunity-boosting** dates are high in **potassium**, supply **slow-release sugars**, and provide a range of other **essential nutrients**: they are a **good source of fibre**, **protein**, **minerals** including magnesium, manganese, selenium, and zinc, and trace elements, such as boron and zinc.

FRESH DATES
When ripe, the berries of the date palm tree are sweet and have the texture of a firm pear.

SEMI-DRIED DATES
Semi-dried dates are not as sweet as dried dates, but retain all the gut-friendly fibre and nutrients.

DRIED DATES
These dates provide all the benefits of the fresh berries in a concentrated form.

WHAT IS IT GOOD FOR?

SUPPORTING DIGESTION A great source of soluble and insoluble fibre, aiding digestion and promoting bowel regularity. Also contains tannins, which have an astringent quality that is useful for treating stomach upsets and intestinal troubles.

BALANCING BLOOD SUGAR Although high in sugar, dates defy the dogma that all sugar is bad. They benefit blood sugar control as their sugar is released slowly. Their soluble fibre content also aids blood glucose regulation.

HEART HEALTHY A very good source of potassium, an essential mineral that maintains proper muscle contractions, including those of the heart. Potassium also promotes a healthy nervous system and efficient metabolism by the body. The soluble fibre in dates also helps to lower "unhealthy" (LDL) cholesterol levels in blood.

COLDS AND FLU As an infusion, decoction, syrup, or paste, dates are a traditional remedy for sore throats, colds, and bronchial catarrh.

HOW DO I GET THE BEST FROM IT?

DRIED The drying process concentrates all the nutrients so just a few dates will supply good amounts of nutrients and fibre. Look for dates that have not been treated with sulphites.

FRESH Fresh dates are usually only available for a few weeks in late summer, often from speciality food shops. They contain much more vitamin C than the dried fruit.

HOW DO I USE IT?

IN CEREALS AND BREADS Adding chopped dates to muesli makes a great healthy breakfast. Dates are also a staple ingredient of sweet breads such as date and nut bread.

A SWEET SUBSTITUTE Dates are a delicious sweet yet healthy snack, and can be eaten as a replacement for sweets or chocolate.

MANGOES

 FEEDS GOOD BACTERIA IN THE GUT

 CONTAINS ANTI-CANCER SUBSTANCES

 **HELPS PROTECT EYE HEALTH**

 **PROTECTS AGAINST COLDS AND FLU**

Throughout Asia, the mango has both spiritual and medicinal significance. It is the national fruit of India, Pakistan, and the Philippines, and the national tree of Bangladesh. Mangoes are high in the antioxidants **beta-carotene** and **vitamin C** and so are good for boosting the **immune system**, protecting **eyesight**, and aiding **digestion**. They also help neutralize **free-radical damage** in the body.

WHAT IS IT GOOD FOR?

DIGESTION Contains enzymes that aid the breakdown and digestion of protein, and also fibre, which keeps the digestive tract working efficiently. Dietary fibre has more long-term benefits as well, lowering the risk of developing colon cancer, heart disease, type-2 diabetes, and diverticular disease.

ANTI-CANCER EFFECTS Laboratory tests show the triterpene compound lupeol, a kind of plant hormone found in mangoes, is effective against both prostate and skin cancers.

EYE HEALTH Rich in beta-carotene, a powerful antioxidant that helps to reduce the effects of free-radical damage in the body, including the skin and eyes. It also helps to prevent age-related macular degeneration (loss of vision).

IMMUNITY An average-sized mango contains up to two-thirds of the daily recommended intake of vitamin C, which plays a key role in boosting the immune system and so helps to reduce the incidence of colds and flu.

HOW DO I GET THE BEST FROM IT?

KEEP IT FRESH Eat as fresh as possible. Mangoes bruise easily, so unless you are using them immediately, buy hard fruits and allow to ripen at home. When you can't find fresh, dried mango is a good substitute.

ADD DAIRY Studies suggest the bioavailability of beta-carotene in the fruit improves by 19–38 per cent if combined with a little dairy.

HOW DO I USE IT?

QUICK MANGO SMOOTHIE Blitz 2 peeled, chopped mangoes, 250ml (9fl oz) cold milk or yogurt, and 1½ tbsp honey until smooth.

MANGO SALSA Dice and mix 1 ripe mango, ½ red onion, ½ sweet red pepper, 1 small cucumber, 1 small finely chopped jalapeño chilli and 3 tbsp each lime juice and chopped fresh coriander. Season and serve with fish.

Mango flesh
Contains prebiotic dietary fibre, which helps feed good bacteria in the gut

Green mango
In southeast Asia, green mango is used shredded in salads. Green mangoes have more vitamin C and more pectin than ripe mangoes, but have a very sour taste

MELONS

 **HELPS PROTECT EYE HEALTH**

HELPS KEEP BLOOD VESSELS SUPPLE

HELPS SPEED WOUND HEALING

Aromatic melons are, perhaps surprisingly, members of the gourd family that includes cucumber and squash. They were first cultivated in Persia and northern Africa nearly 4,000 years ago, and later by ancient Greeks and Romans. Rich in **beta-carotene**, **vitamin C**, and assorted **antioxidants**, they are good for **immune support**. They also contain potassium, which normalizes **blood pressure**.

HONEYDEW
It has the highest sugar content of any melon, but also contains vitamin C, folate, and potassium.

WATERMELON
Red-fleshed watermelon is a rich source of the plant pigment lycopene, which helps lower the risk of heart disease.

CANTALOUPE
This is the most nutrient-dense melon: a single serving provides around half your daily vitamin C and A needs.

WHAT IS IT GOOD FOR?

EYESIGHT Melons derive their bright colour from the antioxidant beta-carotene, important for skin and bone health and for preventing age-related macular degeneration (loss of vision). Cantaloupes also contain lutein and zeaxanthin, which are good for eye health.

BLOOD FLOW Citrulline, an amino acid in the rind and flesh of watermelon, can stimulate the production of nitric oxide, which relaxes and expands blood vessels, lowering blood pressure and enhancing blood flow.

BLOOD PRESSURE Contains a useful amount of potassium, a natural diuretic that helps to normalize blood pressure. Watermelons are rich in lycopene, which helps lower the risk of heart disease.

WOUND HEALING The citrulline in watermelon plays a role in the production of the amino acid arginine, which boosts immune function and speeds wound healing.

HOW DO I GET THE BEST FROM IT?

DETOX Melons are an excellent food for light detox days. Their water content (around 95 per cent) is highly mineralized, and has an alkalizing and diuretic effect.

GENTLE ON YOUR TUMMY Easy to digest, it also provides useful carbohydrates for energy.

EAT THE SEEDS The dried seeds contain healthy unsaturated fats and fibre, and make a nutritious addition to savoury dishes.

HOW DO I USE IT?

SPICE UP YOUR CANTALOUPE Sprinkle a little ground black pepper over cantaloupe slices to enhance their flavour.

RAINBOW SALAD Slice watermelon, kiwi, and soft goat's cheese into cubes, serve on bed of rocket or watercress, dress with balsamic vinegar, and sprinkle with sesame seeds.

PAPAYA

 CONTAINS NATURAL DIGESTIVE ENZYMES

 HELPS FIGHT INFECTIONS

 **HELPS LOWER CHOLESTEROL**

 REDUCES CATARACT AND GLAUCOMA RISK

Also called paw paw or tree melon, papaya has become a commercial crop that is now widely available. It is known to have **antibacterial** properties and promotes good **digestion**, and almost every part of the plant can be used. In the West, we tend to focus only on its brightly coloured orange flesh, which is a good source of **antioxidant** carotenoids, such as **beta-carotene**, that protect **eyesight**.

WHAT IS IT GOOD FOR?

DIGESTION Contains the enzymes papain and chymonpapain. Both have been shown to aid digestion, prevent constipation, and, in combination with the fruit's natural fibre, cleanse the colon. Papain is also helpful in healing and preventing stomach ulcers.

FIGHTS "BUGS" The seeds are effective against salmonella, *E. coli*, and staphylococcus infections. They can be used to support liver function and have an anti-parasitic function that helps to rid the body of intestinal parasites.

HEALTHY FIBRE Its natural fibre helps to control blood pressure and regulate levels of "unhealthy" (LDL) cholesterol in the blood. Its dietary fibre is also important in preventing diseases such as bowel cancer.

EYE HEALTH The beta-carotene and vitamins C and E in papaya help reduce the risk of cataracts, glaucoma, and age-related macular degeneration (loss of vision).

HOW DO I GET THE BEST FROM IT?

DON'T THROW THE SEEDS AWAY The seeds are edible either fresh or dried. They have a peppery flavour and can be used in cooking.

JUICE IT Papaya juice helps restore the good bacteria in the stomach – especially important after an illness or taking antibiotics.

GO GREEN Papain, a beneficial digestive enzyme, is found in greatest abundance in green, unripe papayas.

HOW DO I USE IT?

MAKE A CHUTNEY To benefit from the high concentration of papain in unripe papaya, make a spicy chutney for meats and cheeses.

PRAWNS AND PAPAYA Arrange cooked king prawns and papaya slices on a bed of lettuce. Drizzle with a dressing of walnut oil, lime juice, Dijon mustard, honey, salt, and pepper.

Ripe fruit
Contains vitamins E and C and beta-carotene, giving it potent antioxidant properties

Seeds
Papaya seeds are rich in fatty acids and papaya oil. They have a sharp, spicy taste and can be used in place of pepper

Unripe fruit
The highest concentrations of the beneficial digestive enzyme papain are found in the unripe fruits

POMEGRANATE

  **REDUCES THE RISK OF PROSTATE CANCER**

 **HELPS KEEP BLOOD VESSELS SUPPLE**

BLOCKS ENZYMES THAT DESTROY CARTILAGE

 PROVIDES ANTIVIRAL PROTECTION

Native to modern-day Iran and Iraq, pomegranate has been used as a folk medicine for thousands of years. The juice contains substances that support a **healthy prostate** and **antioxidants** to maintain the elasticity of the **arteries**. All parts of the plant are used as medicine in the Ayurvedic traditions; in the West, the arils (seeds) and their juice are most valued for their **antiviral** and **antibacterial** properties.

Seeds
Oil from the seeds contains isoflavones similar to those found in soya

Rind
Pomegranate rind is used in many medicinal traditions for making teas and gargles. Recent studies show it contains chemicals which are antibiotic and have cancer-fighting properties

WHAT IS IT GOOD FOR?

MEN'S HEALTH Drinking a glass of the juice every day has been shown to lower levels of prostate-specific antigen (PSA) in men. (The higher a man's PSA level is, the greater his risk of death from prostate cancer.)

HEART PROTECTIVE Its polyphenol compounds keep arteries elastic and so help lower blood pressure and the risk of heart disease and stroke. It also stops free radicals oxidizing "unhealthy" (LDL) cholesterol in the blood and causing plaque build-up on artery walls (atherosclerosis).

JOINT HEALTH Antioxidant flavonols have been shown to significantly reduce the activity of proteins that cause inflammatory conditions such as arthritis. Preliminary studies show that pomegranate extract (equivalent to one glass of juice) can block the production of an enzyme that destroys cartilage in the body.

FIGHTS INFECTION The juice has antiviral properties, and studies show that extracts of the fruit are effective against dental plaque.

HOW DO I GET THE BEST FROM IT?

EAT THE SEEDS The fruit is a high-fibre food, but only if you eat the seeds, which also contain unsaturated fats, beneficial isoflavones (plant hormones similar to those found in soya), and other micronutrients.

POMEGRANATE MOLASSES This concentrated form of the syrup includes all the nutritional values of pomegranate.

HOW DO I USE IT?

AS A "VINEGAR" Pomegranate molasses is a delicious substitute for balsamic vinegar in dressings, marinades, and glazes.

SUPERFRUIT SALAD Combine pomegranate seeds with pear, pineapple, and orange segments, chopped fresh mint, and lettuce. Drizzle with a honey-sweetened dressing.

A drizzle of pomegranate molasses brings a tangy, sweet-sour flavour and an antioxidant boost to a simple salad dressing of olive oil, lemon, and black pepper.

PINEAPPLE

 EASES SYMPTOMS OF INFLAMMATORY BOWEL

 ENHANCES SPERM QUALITY

 SPEEDS RECOVERY FROM SPORTS INJURIES

Thirst-quenching and cooling, pineapple is a good source of **manganese**, which can boost men's fertility, and contains significant amounts of **vitamin C**. The core contains the proteolytic enzyme bromelain, a powerful **anti-inflammatory** used to treat bowel and joint problems. Its anti-inflammatory and **astringent** quality makes it a good choice for **treating sore throats**.

Flesh
An excellent source of vitamin C, fibre, and manganese, an essential cofactor (chemical compound) in cellular energy production

Core
Contains enzymes that alleviate the pain of a sore throat and loosen congestion of the sinuses

WHAT IS IT GOOD FOR?

INFLAMMATORY BOWEL The juice can ease the symptoms of colitis, an inflammatory bowel condition marked by abdominal pain and bloating, diarrhoea, gas, and dehydration. Although most bromelain is concentrated in the core and stem, researchers have found that the juice provides enough of the enzyme to have a medicinal effect.

MEN'S FERTILITY Its high manganese content helps restore vitality and can help boost fertility by improving sperm motility.

STAYING FLEXIBLE Bromelain has shown promise in treating and preventing inflammatory conditions, such as arthritis, and may facilitate recovery after sports injuries.

DIGESTION Bromelain extract is an effective digestive aid, while using the juice as a marinade for meat dishes helps tenderize them, making them more easily digestible.

HOW DO I GET THE BEST FROM IT?

FRESH IS BEST The nutrients and enzymes disappear quickly once cut or cooked. When ripe, almost to the point of spoilage, the fruit's antioxidant levels are at their highest.

EAT THE CORE Bromelain concentrates in the fibrous core of the fruit.

JUICE IT The juice can help lower fever, ease sore throats, and acts as a natural expectorant.

HOW DO I USE IT?

A TANGY SORBET Juice 1 large pineapple, pour 250ml (9fl oz) into a large pan, and add 150g (5oz) caster sugar. Boil to a syrup and allow to cool. Add the pineapple pulp from the juicer and the juice of 3 large oranges. Pour into a plastic container. Freeze, removing it occasionally to give the sorbet a stir.

SALSA Dice and mix pineapple, chilli, red onion, garlic, fresh coriander, and lime juice.

COCONUT

 FIGHTS BACTERIA, VIRUSES, AND FUNGI

 ENHANCES METABOLISM

 PROVIDES ENERGY FOR THE BRAIN

 INCREASES "HEALTHY" (HDL) CHOLESTEROL

We may think of coconut as a nut, but it is a fruit, or drupe, similar to peaches and plums. It is native to the Indo-Pacific region, where it is the "tree of life". Its medicinal properties, which benefit among others the heart, brain, and stomach, stem from its unique **healthy fat content**, antibacterial effects, and **balance of sugar**, **dietary fibre**, proteins, antioxidants, **vitamins**, and minerals.

WHAT IS IT GOOD FOR?

A NATURAL ANTIBIOTIC Lauric acid – a fatty acid in coconuts – helps the body combat a wide spectrum of bacteria and viruses that cause colds, flu, herpes, gum disease, ulcers, and urinary tract infections, among others. The fruit also contains caprylic acid, found to be a potent anti-fungal that can fight disorders, such as candidiasis, thrush, and athlete's foot.

METABOLIC BALANCE The oil is high in medium-chain triglycerides (MCTs), healthy fats that help lower the risk of heart disease. MCTs can help with weight management by reducing appetite, boosting metabolism, and increasing the activity of fat-burning cells.

FEEDING THE BRAIN Studies show that the brains of Alzheimer's sufferers can utilize the ketones produced when MCTs are metabolized as an alternative energy source. This may help mediate some symptoms of the disease.

IMPROVING CHOLESTEROL RATIOS MCTs increase "healthy" (HDL) cholesterol without raising "unhealthy" (LDL) cholesterol levels.

HOW DO I GET THE BEST FROM IT?

CHOOSE THE RIGHT OIL Virgin coconut oil is not chemically treated (refined, bleached, and deodorized), so its MCTs remain intact.

IN YOUR COOKING Coconut oil is very heat stable so use for roasting and in savoury dishes.

HOW DO I USE IT?

AN ALTERNATIVE TO SPORTS DRINKS Hydrating coconut water from the immature fruit is a superior drink for restoring electrolyte balance during and after sport.

NOURISHING SALAD DRESSING Coconut oil, which is solid at room temperature, enhances the absorption of fat-soluble nutrients such as carotenoids. Mix with other more "liquid" ingredients, such as vinegar, honey, or thinner oils to make an excellent dressing.

COCONUT FRUIT
Contains less fat than many seeds and nuts, such as almonds, and less sugar and more protein than popular fruits, such as bananas, apples, and oranges.

Coconut water
A pure and perfect balance of electrolytes (It was given intravenously to soldiers during the Second World War when regular IV saline solution ran out)

COCONUT OIL
Coconut oil is high in healthy fats that help lower the risk of heart disease.

COCONUT MILK
Coconut milk, obtained primarily by extracting the juice from the white kernel, is rich in beneficial fats.

AVOCADO

 **HELPS KEEP JOINTS SUPPLE**

 **HELPS LOWER BLOOD PRESSURE**

 **HELPS IMPROVE FERTILITY**

The avocado has the distinction of being the fruit with the highest fat content. This may sound unhealthy, but its **beneficial monounsaturated oils**, which can lower blood pressure and lubricate joints, have earned it the title "the olive oil of the Americas". The flesh and oil contain **antioxidants** and are **anti-inflammatory**, helping to lower the risk of diseases such as **arthritis** and to boost women's fertility.

AVOCADO
The flesh contains a favourable balance of potassium and sodium that can help lower blood pressure.

AVOCADO OIL
The oil is pressed from the flesh of the avocado, not the seed, and is known for its ability to protect the heart and fight free-radical damage.

WHAT IS IT GOOD FOR?

ANTI-INFLAMMATORY The fats of this fruit are unique. They include phytosterols, plant hormones such as campesterol, beta-sitosterol, and stigmasterol, that help to keep inflammation under control. It also contains polyhydroxylated fatty alcohols (PFAs), which are anti-inflammatory. Also a source of omega-3 fatty acids, which help lubricate joints and reduce arthritic symptoms.

LOWERING BLOOD PRESSURE A good source of potassium and low in sodium. As a result, it can reduce the risk of high blood pressure and stroke. Also very rich in antioxidants and monounsaturated fats, which offer protection from heart disease and stroke.

FERTILITY BOOST The healthy fats have been shown to dramatically boost fertility and increase the success of IVF treatment.

HOW DO I GET THE BEST FROM IT?

PEEL WITH CARE The majority of the avocado's nutrients concentrate in the dark green flesh near the skin. Quick or careless peeling means you lose these benefits. Cut the fruit lengthways into quarters and peel off the skin in sections like you would a banana.

A RICH OIL The oil makes an excellent base for salad dressings and marinades, and can be used in sautés and as a dipping oil.

HOW DO I USE IT?

A COLOURFUL SALAD Add avocado to a salad to increase the absorption of key fat-soluble antioxidants, such as lycopene and beta-carotene, in the other vegetables.

GUACAMOLE This classic Mexican dip is quick and easy to make, and is also great as a healthy accompaniment to fish dishes. Mash 1 avocado, a couple of diced tomatoes, and a squeeze of lime juice into a paste, and add chopped fresh coriander to taste.

BROCCOLI

 PROMOTES PROSTATE HEALTH

 **PROMOTES COLLAGEN SYNTHESIS**

 **HELPS STRENGTHEN THE IMMUNE SYSTEM**

 **HELPS PROTECT EYE HEALTH**

This cruciferous vegetable has been widely studied for its medicinal properties, which include antibacterial and **immunity-boosting** activities. It is rich in **vitamin C** and **fibre** and has the highest level of **carotenoids** – particularly eye-healthy lutein – of all brassicas. It is also an excellent source of indole-3-carbinol, a chemical that boosts **DNA repair** in cells and appears to block the growth of cancer cells.

WHAT IS IT GOOD FOR?

PROSTATE HEALTH Diets high in broccoli are associated with a lower risk of aggressive prostate cancer.

SKIN FOOD Contains abundant pantothenic acid, beta-carotene, and sulphur compounds, all of which encourage great skin. It is also rich in vitamin C, which aids the formation of collagen and helps to repair damaged tissue.

IMMUNITY BOOST Higher in vitamin C than many citrus fruits, and rich in beta-carotene antioxidants, broccoli is an ideal food to eat to maintain a healthy immune system.

EYE HEALTH Has a useful amount of lutein, an antioxidant that promotes eye health and may also benefit the heart and circulation.

HOW DO I GET THE BEST FROM IT?

STEAM IT Eat raw or steam lightly to retain its vitamin C, iron, and chlorophyll content.

TRY A CHANGE OF COLOUR Purple sprouting broccoli generally contains more antioxidants and more of the phytochemical sulphoraphane, which gives broccoli its detoxifying and anti-cancer reputation.

SPROUT THE SEEDS The sprouts are lower in nutrients that the vegetable, but higher in sulphorophane, thought to help prevent cancer.

HOW DO I USE IT?

HEART-HEALTHY MEAL Stir-fry with soba (buckwheat) noodles. The rutin content of buckwheat, the vitamin C in broccoli, and the healthy fats in olive oil together can lower cholesterol levels.

SALAD BOOSTER The raw leaves and sprouts can add a serious nutritional boost to salads.

ADD TOMATOES Eating broccoli together with tomatoes can slow prostate cancer growth more effectively than eating either vegetable on its own.

PURPLE SPROUTING BROCCOLI
Contains more antioxidants than green varieties, but is more prone to nutrient loss when cooked.

GREEN BROCCOLI
Higher in vitamin C than many citrus fruits.

BROCCOLI SPROUTS
Higher than mature broccoli in the anti-cancer antioxidant sulphoraphane.

Leaves
These contain more beta-carotene than the flower or stalks

CABBAGE

 HELPS HEAL ULCERS

 **SUPPORTS HEALTHY LIVER FUNCTION**

 **FIGHTS FREE-RADICAL DAMAGE TO SKIN**

Many people don't consider cabbage a "love to eat" vegetable nowadays, but before we lost the habit of eating bitter foods it was revered as a warming, calming, **balancing**, and grounding food. It is now known to **clear the blood**, boost **skin health**, and is a remarkable remedy for **ulcers**. Its bitterness stimulates gastric juices to digest food more effectively, and it is also a mild **diuretic**.

GREEN CABBAGE
Contains a broad spectrum of nutrients including vitamin U – a potent ulcer remedy.

RED CABBAGE
Contains 2–8 times more vitamin C than other cabbages, and is rich in additional antioxidant anthocyanins.

BRUSSELS SPROUTS
These sprouts are higher in anti-cancer glucosinolates than other cabbages.

BOK CHOI
A good source of beta-carotene and vitamins C and B6.

WHAT IS IT GOOD FOR?

HEALS ULCERS Contains ample amounts of vitamin U, or S-methylmethionine. Vitamin U heals stomach and duodenal ulcers quickly.

SUPPORTS LIVER FUNCTION It stimulates the production of glutathione, the body's most important internally produced antioxidant, which plays a role in liver detoxification.

HEALTHY SKIN Contains vitamins C and K, and antioxidants that protect skin from free-radical damage. Its sulphur content may be useful in healing acne and eczema.

ANTIPARASITIC Its high sulphur content helps to maintain a gut free from parasites. It is also fibre-rich and promotes bowel regularity.

HOW DO I GET THE BEST FROM IT?

COOK IT LIGHTLY Cabbage retains more of its nutritional and medicinal benefits if lightly cooked or eaten raw.

TRY BOK CHOI Lighter in texture and taste, bok choi is also rich in vitamins A, B6, and C, beta-carotene, calcium, potassium, and fibre.

GET COLOURFUL Purple cabbage has more vitamin C and antioxidant anthocyanins, which help lower the risk of heart disease, diabetes, and certain types of cancer.

USE THE OUTER LEAVES The outer leaves contain more vitamin E and around 30 per cent more calcium than the inner leaves.

HOW DO I USE IT?

WRAPS The large leaves make ideal wraps. Use like tortillas and fill with ingredients, such as rice, pulses, and other vegetables.

JUICE IT The juice is especially good for skin and ulcers. If you find the taste too strong, try mixing it with celery juice.

FERMENT IT Eating sauerkraut is a great way to cleanse the digestive tract and encourage healthy gut flora.

KALE

 HELPS STRENGTHEN BONES

 **HELPS FIGHT INFLAMMATION**

 **HELPS LOWER CHOLESTEROL**

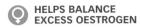 **HELPS BALANCE EXCESS OESTROGEN**

Kale's popularity has grown in recent years, as science has revealed it to be rich in beta-carotene, **vitamins C and K**, and **folate**. It is an exceptional source of **chlorophyll**, and its calcium and iron content are highly bioavailable (easily absorbed). It helps balance **hormones** and lower **cholesterol**, and its **antioxidants** and omega-3 fatty acids give it strong **anti-inflammatory** properties.

WHAT IS IT GOOD FOR?

BONE BUILDING Its high calcium, magnesium, and vitamin K content helps strengthen bones, benefitting those with osteoporosis.

ANTIOXIDANT BOOST Contains multiple antioxidants, including kaempferol and quercetin, which are responsible for anti-inflammatory benefits in diseases such as diabetes, arthritis, stroke, and heart disease.

LOWERS CHOLESTEROL Its fibre binds with cholesterol to remove it from the blood, lowering the risk of heart disease and stroke.

HORMONE BALANCING Contains indoles, natural substances that boost DNA repair and have an anti-oestrogen effect that can protect against and arrest the spread of oestrogen-dependent cancers, such as breast cancer.

HEALING ULCERS The juice is rich in sulphur, which can aid the healing of stomach and duodenal ulcers.

DIGESTIVE STIMULANT Its bitter flavour aids digestion and eases lung congestion.

HOW DO I GET THE BEST FROM IT?

ADD LEMON Serving kale with a lemon dressing or another acidic citrus fruit as part of a meal boosts the absorption of its iron and calcium content.

COOK BRIEFLY The less you cook kale, the more nutrients you retain. Cooking lightly also leaves the plant's cholesterol-lowering properties intact.

HOW DO I USE IT?

ADD TO JUICES Blend kale juice with spicy ginger and apple juice, or try a cleansing mix of celery, kale, and coconut water.

KALE PESTO Replace the basil and pine nuts in a pesto recipe with 400g (14oz) kale leaves, ribs removed, and 300g (10oz) toasted walnuts. Add to soups, stews, hot pasta, or dressings.

CURLY KALE
The antioxidants kaempferol and quercetin, which help fight inflammation, top the list of kale's beneficial properties.

CAVOLO NERO
This deep blue-green variety is rich in chlorophyll and folate.

PURPLE KALE
Purple varieties contain more anthocyanins – antioxidant red pigments – than green.

HORSERADISH

 **ANTIBIOTIC AND ANTIBACTERIAL**

HELPS REMOVE TOXINS FROM THE BODY

 HAS A DIURETIC ACTION

 HELPS CLEAR CONGESTION

This pungent root contains an array of nutrients in small amounts, but it is its volatile oils that are responsible for its **medicinal** effects. Its potent oil, allyl isothiocyanate, boosts **metabolism** and gives it **antibiotic** and **antibacterial** properties against food-borne pathogens. This is why, in the days before refrigeration, horseradish was eaten with fish or meats as a kind of insurance policy.

HORSERADISH ROOT
Its volatile oils can fight food-borne pathogens, such as *listeria* and *E. coli*.

HORSERADISH LEAVES
The young leaves, which can be eaten raw, contain oils that aid digestion.

WASABI
Sometimes called Japanese horseradish, wasabi is not true horseradish but a root with similar properties.

WHAT IS IT GOOD FOR?

ANTIBIOTIC AND INSECTICIDAL Laboratory tests have shown horseradish to be active against a variety of harmful bacteria, such as *listeria*, *E. coli*, and *staphylococcus*. Allyl isothiocyanate is also effective against intestinal worms.

DETOX As a stimulating food it can aid digestion, boost circulation, and help lower fevers by promoting perspiration.

BENEFITS THE URINARY SYSTEM Traditionally it has been used to help treat water retention, urinary infections, and kidney stones.

COMBATS SINUS INFECTIONS Stimulates the flow of mucous, and opens and cleanses the sinuses in much the same way as chilli peppers. Try taking horseradish at the first signs of cold, flu, or coughs.

HOW DO I GET THE BEST FROM IT?

FRESH AND RAW If grated and left to stand too long, or cooked for long periods, it loses its potency, so eat it fresh and raw.

EAT THE LEAVES The small tender leaves have a pleasant flavour with just enough "bite" to lift an everyday salad. The older leaves can be cooked and used as you would spinach or kale.

SERVE WITH VEGETABLES Studies show that serving vegetables such as broccoli with a little horseradish or wasabi can increase the amount of nutrients absorbed by the body.

HOW DO I USE IT?

ADD TO CONDIMENTS Freshly grated, it mixes well with mayonnaise, soured cream, yogurt, or cream cheese with fresh herbs and seasoning.

FOR HOARSENESS Infuse 2 tbsp grated horseradish root and 1 tbsp cider vinegar in 75ml (2½fl oz) boiling water for 1 hour. Strain and add 300ml (10fl oz) honey. Take 1 tbsp hourly until the condition eases.

Sweet Peppers

 PROMOTES COLLAGEN SYNTHESIS

 HELPS PROTECT AGAINST CATARACTS

 MAINTAINS HEALTHY BLOOD VESSELS

 CONTAINS ANTI-CANCER SUBSTANCES

Part of the nightshade family, which includes tomatoes, potatoes, and aubergines, peppers are rich in **antioxidants** to benefit **heart** and **eye health**. Their vitamin C content boosts **collagen** levels and they may also help to prevent **lung cancer**. They don't contain the beneficial compound capsaicin found in chillies, but weight-for-weight they contain more essential nutrients, as you can eat more of them.

What Is It Good For?

SKIN AND BONES Contains vitamin C, necessary for the synthesis of collagen, the main structural protein in the body that maintains the integrity of blood vessels, skin, and bones.

EYE HEALTH Possibly due to a combination of beta-carotene, vitamin C, lutein, and zeaxanthin, peppers have been shown to be protective against cataracts and age-related macular degeneration (loss of vision).

HEART HEALTH Antioxidant levels, including beta-carotene, capsanthin, quercetin, and luteolin, may vary between varieties, but all have been shown to prevent the oxidization of cholesterol, the cause of free-radical damage to the heart and blood vessels. Diets high in antioxidants can also help prevent blood clot formation and reduce the risk of stroke.

LUNG CANCER Beta-cryptoxanthin, found mostly in red peppers, may help prevent lung cancer in those at risk.

How Do I Get The Best From It?

RED BENEFITS Red peppers have significantly higher nutrient levels than green, including lycopene, which helps to protect against cancer of the prostate, cervix, bladder, and pancreas and lowers the risk of heart disease.

COOK THE RIGHT COLOUR Cooking lowers vitamin C levels in green peppers, but increases their beta-carotene content; in red peppers it increases vitamin C levels and lowers its beta-carotene. Yellow peppers are high in vitamin C, so may be the best choice if you want more of this vitamin, but overall, cooked red peppers are more nutritious.

How Do I Use It?

EAT RAW Slice and use as crudités with dips or salsas, or simply add to fresh salads.

STUFFED PEPPERS Fill with rice, mushrooms, other vegetables, and fresh herbs.

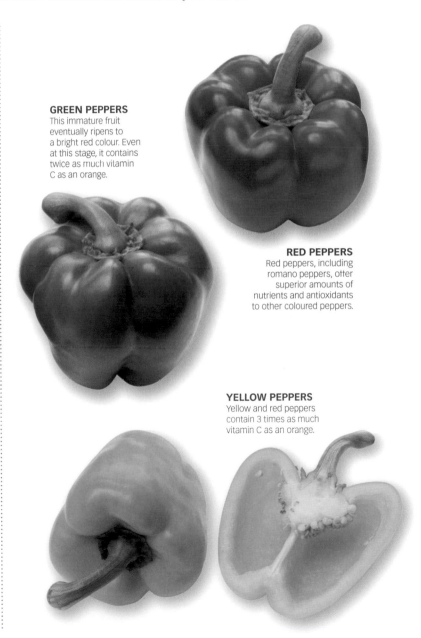

GREEN PEPPERS
This immature fruit eventually ripens to a bright red colour. Even at this stage, it contains twice as much vitamin C as an orange.

RED PEPPERS
Red peppers, including romano peppers, offer superior amounts of nutrients and antioxidants to other coloured peppers.

YELLOW PEPPERS
Yellow and red peppers contain 3 times as much vitamin C as an orange.

CHILLIES

 HELPS REMOVE TOXINS FROM THE BODY

 HELPS LOWER CHOLESTEROL

 CAN REDUCE APPETITE AND CRAVINGS

 HELPS CLEAR CONGESTION

The chilli pepper, the hottest member of the capsicum family, is a fruit pod from the plant belonging to the nightshade family. Its volatile oils, particularly capsaicin, account for its strong, spicy, pungent character and **antioxidant** and **anti-inflammatory** effects, which give chilli its **cholesterol-lowering**, **blood-sugar balancing**, and **appetite-suppressing** properties. Capsaicin can also aid **detoxification**.

Piri piri
Hot

FRESH CHILLIES
Some varieties are hotter than others, but the heat can vary enormously even between peppers of the same variety.

Jalapeño
Mild

Scotch bonnet
Super hot

DRIED CHILLI
The dried seeds and flakes make a useful seasoning. The seeds contain the highest amounts of capsaicin.

CAYENNE POWDER
Unlike standard chilli powder, which can be a mixture of spices, ground cayenne comprises pure hot chillies.

WHAT IS IT GOOD FOR?

DETOX The heat in capsaicin can help remove toxins by promoting increased sweating.

KEEPS ARTERIES CLEAR Studies show that capsaicin can help reduce "unhealthy" (LDL) cholesterol levels in obese individuals.

WEIGHT MANAGEMENT Hot chillies in quantities normally used for seasoning can stimulate digestion, reduce hunger and cravings, and boost metabolism.

CLEARS CONGESTION Hot chillies increase mucous secretion in the lungs and nose.

ANTI-DIABETIC There is evidence that hot chillies can help regulate blood sugar levels.

HOW DO I GET THE BEST FROM IT?

AS HOT AS YOU DARE For an occasional spicy meal, use the hottest chillies you can stand to get the most from their capsaicin content.

DRIED SEEDS Most of us throw the seeds away, yet they contain the most capsaicin. Dry the seeds, combine with seasonings, such as salt and garlic, and grind to a coarse powder to add a quick zing to any savoury dish.

CONTROL THE HEAT The heat of fresh chillies can vary. If you want to control how much heat you include in a dish, try using dried hot cayenne or milder chilli powder blends instead, which are still rich in capsaicin.

HOW DO I USE IT?

AS A THERAPY FOR COLDS Add chilli pepper and garlic to chicken soup as a therapeutic meal for colds, sinusitis, and bronchitis.

AS A MEDICINAL KICK IN DISHES Add chilli and cayenne powders to salsas, chutneys, marinades, and rubs for an additional kick.

PICK THE FRESHEST PRODUCE Choose fresh chillies with bright, deep colours and glossy, firm, taut skins. Buy only as much as you need and use it up quickly.

Whichever jewel-coloured chilli variety you select, the heat and beneficial capsaicin is concentrated in the seeds and white membrane inside.

CUCUMBERS

 DETERS OESTROGEN-BASED CANCERS

 HAS A DIURETIC ACTION

 CLEANSES AND TONES THE INTESTINES

 PROMOTES A HEALTHY DIGESTIVE TRACT

The watery composition of this member of the gourd family is packed with bioavailable (easily absorbed) **minerals**, **vitamins**, and **electrolytes**, making it an ideal way to top up your daily nutrients. Cucumber also contains **phytoestrogens** and digestive enzymes to **benefit the gut**, and is well known for being a classic cooling food, helping to maintain the body's **water balance** on hot days.

RIDGE CUCUMBERS
Keep the skin on to retain all the beneficial nutrients.

SMOOTH CUCUMBERS
Although 98 per cent water, cucumber contains a highly available mix of vitamins and minerals.

WHAT IS IT GOOD FOR?

HELPFUL PHYTOESTROGENS Contains lariciresinol, secoisolariciresinol, and pinoresinol – three lignans (plant hormones) that help reduce the risk of cardiovascular disease and several types of cancer including breast, uterine, ovarian, and prostate.

MAINTAINS WATER BALANCE Its ability to balance water in the body makes cucumber important for heart and kidney problems. It also has a mild diuretic action and can help prevent constipation.

SUPPORTS URINARY FUNCTION The caffeic acid in cucumber helps prevent water retention. Other nutrients it contains help dissolve uric acid accumulations and can aid in the treatment of kidney and bladder stones.

PROMOTES A HEALTHY GUT Contains erepsin, a digestive enzyme that helps break down protein. It also acts as an anti-parasitic and helps cleanse and tone the intestines.

LOWERS CHOLESTEROL Contains beneficial plant sterols that can help lower "unhealthy" (LDL) cholesterol levels.

HOW DO I GET THE BEST FROM IT?

EAT THE SEEDS The seeds have diuretic properties and so are worth consuming.

EAT THE SKIN The skin is a good source of silicon, chlorophyll, and bitter chemicals that aid digestion. It also contains the highest concentration of cholesterol-lowering sterols.

HOW DO I USE IT?

MAKE A COOLING DIP Grate a cucumber and mix with Greek yogurt, minced garlic, lemon juice, olive oil, and fresh mint for a tzatziki, or spices and natural yogurt for an Indian raita.

DRINK IT Juice with other vegetables, add slices to a cold jug of water, or brew the skin as a tea to alleviate swollen hands and feet.

Winter Squashes

 **HELPS FIGHT INFLAMMATION**

 **LOWERS RISK OF HEART DISEASE AND STROKE**

PROMOTES BOWEL REGULARITY

 **SUPPORTS A HEALTHY PREGNANCY**

Their bright orange flesh signals that all squashes have similar nutritional and medicinal benefits. They are good sources of healthy **carbohydrate**, **magnesium**, and antioxidant **carotenoids**, and are known to improve **cardiovascular health**, **digestion**, and benefit **pregnant women**. Unlike watery summer squashes, these squashes (which store well through winter) usually have tough rinds.

What Is It Good For?

HEALTHY CARBOHYDRATE About half its carbohydrate content is in the form of complex carbohydrates, or polysaccharides (including pectin). This makes it anti-inflammatory and antioxidant. It also has insulin-regulating properties.

CARDIOVASCULAR HEALTH Its wide range of nutrients, such as alpha- and beta-carotene, vitamin C, manganese, and magnesium, are all heart-healthy, helping protect against stroke and normalize blood pressure. Its folate content reduces homocysteine levels which, when too high, are a risk factor for heart disease.

BOWEL HEALTH Squashes are high in fibre, which promotes bowel regularity.

PREGNANCY Contains large amounts of folate so it is a good choice if you are pregnant. While folate deficiency isn't the sole cause of birth defects, adequate levels of this B vitamin can help protect against neural tube defects.

How Do I Get The Best From It?

SEEDS All squash seeds are edible and contain healthy fats, protein, and fibre. They have long been used in traditional medicine for prostate and urinary problems, and their high-fat, low-carbohydrate content is useful for heart health.

EAT THE SKIN Choose thin-skinned varieties, such as butternut. Cook with the skin on to make the most of the nutrients it contains.

BUY ORGANIC Squashes absorb heavy metals and other toxins from the soil, so buy organic.

How Do I Use It?

ROASTED SEEDS Rinse the seeds and bake on a baking tray for 15 minutes in a cool oven to preserve their beneficial fatty acids.

BAKED SQUASH Cube, toss in olive oil, season, and bake in a medium oven for 35–40 minutes.

BUTTERNUT SQUASH
This is a creamy squash with a thin, edible skin.

PUMPKIN
This squash is high in fibre and tastes sweeter than other varieties.

ACORN SQUASH
Small and round, this squash has a firm texture and slightly sweet taste.

COURGETTES

 AIDS WATER BALANCE

 **HELPS REDUCE AN ENLARGED PROSTATE**

 LOWERS CHOLESTEROL AND STROKE RISK

 SUPPORTS EFFICIENT METABOLISM

Related to melons, cucumbers, and other squash, courgettes and marrows are from the same plant – a marrow is more mature. Both contain a high volume of **water**, are **low in calories**, are an ideal light, **cleansing** food, and can **ease prostate conditions** in men. Their **vitamin C** and potassium levels are higher than in other squash, and they also contain **beta-carotene**, phosphorus, and folate.

GREEN COURGETTE
Nutrients such as folate and vitamin C are concentrated in the skin.

Courgette flower
The edible flower is high in folate and potassium

YELLOW COURGETTE
Particularly rich in antioxidant carotenes, such as lutein and zeaxanthin.

WHAT IS IT GOOD FOR?

DIURETIC AND LAXATIVE Their phytonutrients promote bowel regularity and aid water balance. They may also be useful in easing the symptoms of enlarged prostate in men.

LOWERS CHOLESTEROL The combination of fibre, vitamin C, and beta-carotene that courgettes contain help regulate blood sugar levels.

HEART HEALTH Contains magnesium, a mineral proven to reduce the risk of heart attack and stroke. Also contains folate, which breaks down homocysteine, a substance that raises the risk of heart attacks and stroke.

METABOLIC BALANCE Useful amounts of manganese can help the body metabolize protein and carbohydrates and digest fat, contribute to sex hormone production, and lower blood pressure.

HOW DO I GET THE BEST FROM IT?

EAT THE WHOLE PLANT From their skins to their seeds, courgettes and marrows are almost entirely edible. As cooling, sedative foods, they are useful for treating tired adrenals and frayed nerves. They can't be stored for long, so eat quickly while fresh.

EAT THE SKIN Important nutrients – including lutein and zeaxanthin, which promote healthy eyes – are concentrated in their skins.

JUICE THEM Their water content is highly mineralized and bioavailable (easily absorbed). Juice for a quick mineral boost.

HOW DO I USE IT?

TRY IT RAW Try adding julienne strips to your regular salad, or eat as crudités with dips.

STUFFED MARROW Slice the marrow in half lengthways, remove the seeds, and fill with grains, pulses, and/or vegetables. Bake in a medium oven until tender.

CORN

 FIGHTS AGE-RELATED VISION LOSS

 **HELPS REDUCE AN ENLARGED PROSTATE**

PROMOTES A HEALTHY DIGESTIVE TRACT

Much corn is now genetically modified, and modern yellow varieties are bred for their high sugar content. However, heirloom varieties, particularly blue corn, have a **high nutritional value** that can balance **blood sugars**, boost **eye health**, soothe the **urinary tract**, and can be bought as organic and GM-free. Yellow corns contain more **beta-carotene**, while red and blue contain more **anthocyanins**.

WHAT IS IT GOOD FOR?

EYE HEALTH Carotenoids, such as zeaxanthin and lutein support eye health and prevent age-related macular degeneration.

PROSTATE HEALTH Partly due to its significant potassium content, corn silk can soothe urinary tract irritation, is a useful diuretic, and can treat an enlarged prostate.

DIGESTIVE HEALTH Corn contains soluble dietary fibre that regulates the flow of waste material through the digestive tract. Soluble fibre also helps to control blood sugar levels.

HOW DO I GET THE BEST FROM IT?

POPCORN Without added butter, sugar, and salt, popcorn is a great high-fibre, low-calorie food. Try using organic blue and multi-coloured heirloom corn for extra benefits.

CORNMEAL Ground from dried maize, cornmeal is available in fine to coarse grades. Drying the corn improves the availability of B vitamins such as niacin, thiamine, pantothenic acid, and folate. Stoneground varieties are higher in nutrients and flavour.

EAT RAW OR LIGHTLY COOKED Add baby corn or raw kernels to salads or stir-fries.

HOW DO I USE IT?

MAKE A TEA Make a medicinal tea by steeping ¼ cup fresh corn silk in boiling water for 5 minutes. Strain and drink as a mild diuretic.

POLENTA Boil ground cornmeal in water or stock to create a thick porridge. Allow to cool and firm up, then bake in a medium oven or slice and grill it.

MAKE A CORN CHOWDER Strip the kernels from 6 cobs and simmer in boiling water until tender. Sauté some onions and garlic, put them in a blender with the kernels and some of the broth, and blitz until smooth. Serve topped with fresh corn kernels and coriander leaves.

Corn silk
The silky threads inside the husk are a useful diuretic and can relieve prostate enlargement

Fresh corn on the cob
Good source of skin- and eye-healthy beta-carotene and lutein

BLUE CORN
Contains 30 per cent more protein than yellow corn. Beneficial antioxidants include protocatechuic acid (which gives green tea its healthy properties).

BABY CORN
Harvesting corn while young means the cob, with its beneficial soluble fibre, can be eaten.

ARTICHOKE

 HELPS BALANCE BLOOD SUGAR LEVELS

 HELPS LOWER CHOLESTEROL

 AIDS THE DIGESTION OF FAT

 A MILD LAXATIVE AND DIURETIC

This edible member of the thistle family is among the top 10 highest **antioxidant-rich** foods. It is high in **dietary fibre**, and was traditionally eaten by the Greeks and Romans to maintain a **healthy gut**, promote **bowel regularity**, and **alleviate stomach upsets**. It also has a reputation for "cleaning the blood" by **detoxifying** the liver and gall bladder, reducing **cholesterol**, and balancing **blood sugars**.

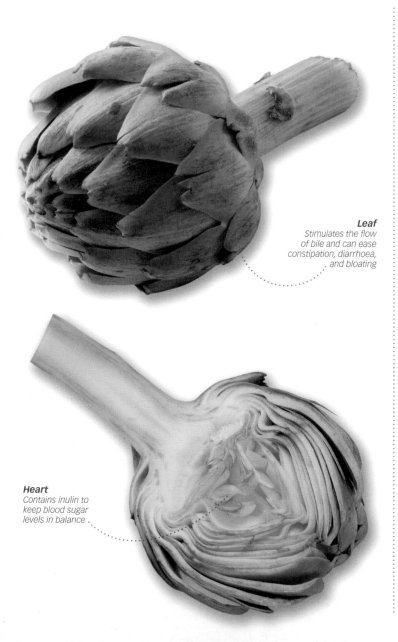

Leaf
Stimulates the flow of bile and can ease constipation, diarrhoea, and bloating

Heart
Contains inulin to keep blood sugar levels in balance

WHAT IS IT GOOD FOR?

BALANCES BLOOD SUGAR LEVELS The leaves and heart contain plant fibres including inulin (a prebiotic that feeds healthy gut flora) which helps maintain steady blood sugar levels.

REDUCES CHOLESTEROL The antioxidant flavonoid silymarin helps reduce "unhealthy" (LDL) cholesterol and raise "healthy" (HDL) cholesterol levels. It also protects the liver.

EASES INDIGESTION The leaves and hearts contain cynarine, a phytochemical that stimulates bile, helps digest fat, and prevents indigestion. May be particularly useful in cases of irritable bowel syndrome.

AIDS DETOXIFICATION A mild laxative and diuretic that supports kidney and liver health.

ENCOURAGES HEALTHY GUT Acts as a prebiotic food that encourages the growth of bifidobacteria in the gut.

HOW DO I GET THE BEST FROM IT?

LEAVES AND HEARTS Easy to digest, both leaves and hearts have similar nutritional and medicinal properties that benefit the liver.

MAKE A TEA Boil the fresh or dried leaves to make an antioxidant-rich, heart-healthy tea with a clean, slightly sweet taste.

HOW DO I USE IT?

CHOOSE SMALLER PRODUCE Look for smaller globes with dark, thick, fleshy leaves. Larger vegetables can be tough and tasteless.

HOW TO COOK IT Cook by boiling until tender. Dip the leaves into melted butter (or an olive oil and lemon dressing) and pull off the flesh at the base of the leaves with your teeth. Gently clear away the prickly thistle to reach the tender edible heart at the centre.

MARINATED HEARTS Artichoke hearts marinated in healthy olive oil are delicious in salads, as part of a dip, or by themselves.

Toning, strengthening artichokes are best served simply. Cut away the spiky top and tough outer leaves, and boil or steam until just tender. Marinate in olive oil, lemon slices, parsley, freshly ground black pepper, and salt.

AUBERGINE

 PROTECTS THE HEART AND BLOOD VESSELS

 **HELPS BALANCE BLOOD SUGAR LEVELS**

 HELPS REMOVE TOXINS FROM THE BODY

Aubergines, which grow on vines, are part of the same nightshade family that includes peppers and potatoes, and there are several varieties ranging in size, shape, and colour. They all contain beneficial amounts of **antioxidants** as well as potassium, folate, magnesium, **beta-carotene**, and **fibre**, while their medicinal properties include balancing **blood sugar** levels and boosting **gut health**.

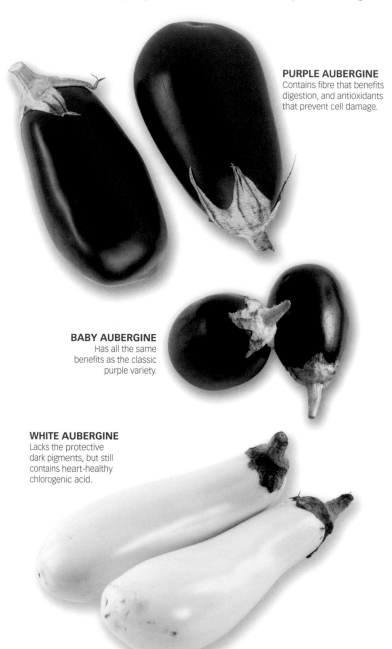

PURPLE AUBERGINE
Contains fibre that benefits digestion, and antioxidants that prevent cell damage.

BABY AUBERGINE
Has all the same benefits as the classic purple variety.

WHITE AUBERGINE
Lacks the protective dark pigments, but still contains heart-healthy chlorogenic acid.

WHAT IS IT GOOD FOR?

HEART HEALTH Dark purple varieties are particularly rich in the antioxidant polyphenol, chlorogenic acid, as well as caffeic acid and flavonoids, such as nasunin that protect the heart from oxidative stress caused by free radicals in the body.

BALANCES BLOOD SUGAR LEVELS The antioxidant chlorogenic acid also helps slow the release of glucose into the bloodstream after a meal.

DETOX Beyond promoting bowel regularity and water balance, some studies have shown that aubergine can help remove harmful chemical substances from the body.

HOW DO I GET THE BEST FROM IT?

CHOOSE CAREFULLY Aubergines spoil fairly quickly so choose firm, glossy examples. Ideally, eat within a day of buying.

LEAVE THE SKIN ON Aubergine's antioxidants concentrate in the skin, which tenderizes as you cook it. Some white varieties have a tougher skin that may need to be peeled before cooking.

HOW TO COOK IT Bake, roast, or fry. When fried, its spongy texture will soak up oil; to prevent this, first sprinkle aubergine slices with salt and leave in a colander to drain. Rinse well, press firmly to remove excess water, and cook.

HOW DO I USE IT?

BABA GANOUSH This classic dish is made from aubergine fried or baked until soft, and puréed with lemon juice, garlic, and olive oil. Spread on bread or use as a vegetable dip.

STUFFED AUBERGINE For a satisfying main meal, slice an aubergine in half lengthways, hollow out, and stuff with a mix of healthy grains, such as quinoa, wild rice, or bulgur wheat and vegetables.

TOMATOES

 HELPS REMOVE TOXINS FROM THE BODY

 **HELPS KEEP BLOOD VESSELS SUPPLE**

 **REDUCES THE RISK OF PROSTATE CANCER**

Although strictly a fruit, tomatoes are widely used as a vegetable in savoury dishes. They are rich in **beta-carotene**, vitamin C, and **lycopene** – a superstar of medicinal food substances and the source of their vibrant red colour. Lycopene has been found to reduce the risk of **prostate** and **breast cancer**, lower **cholesterol**, protect **eyes and skin**, and boost **immunity**.

WHAT IS IT GOOD FOR?

DETOX Tomatoes are abundant in potassium, which reduces water retention. They are also a good source of glutathione, which helps the body to remove fat-soluble toxins.

HEART HEALTH Contains large amounts of vitamins C and E and beta-carotene, all of which support heart health. However, lycopene is most important: it helps strengthen the walls of blood vessels and remove cholesterol from the blood.

PROSTATE CANCER Many cancers are linked with oxidative stress caused by free radicals in the body, and antioxidant foods, such as tomatoes, are known to be preventative. Research into prostate cancer shows that regularly eating raw or cooked tomatoes can reduce its development and spread.

HOW DO I GET THE BEST FROM IT?

JUICE One glass of tomato juice can contain 74 per cent of your recommended daily vitamin C intake, other key vitamins, such as K, B1, B2, B3, B5, and B6, and minerals, such as potassium, manganese, and iron.

COOKED When cooked, the lycopene content in tomatoes increases by 5 or 6 times.

KEEP THE SKIN ON The highest concentration of carotenoids is found in the skin.

HOW DO I USE IT?

SALSA Finely chop tomatoes, 1 small onion, and 2 chillies. Add finely chopped fresh coriander, lime juice, 1 tsp water, and salt to taste and mix well before serving.

HOMEMADE TOMATO JUICE Put 1.5kg (3lb 3oz) roughly chopped tomatoes in a pan. Add 1 chopped onion and 1 chopped celery stick, 2 tbsp sugar, and 1 tsp salt. Add some black pepper and, if you like, a few drops of chilli sauce. Cook gently until soup-like. Strain and refrigerate before drinking.

GREEN TOMATOES
Low in lycopene, but contain beta-carotene in amounts comparable to red tomatoes.

RED TOMATOES
Contain all four major carotenoids: alpha- and beta-carotene, lutein, and lycopene.

PURPLE TOMATOES
Scientists boast of "creating" purple tomatoes by genetic modification, but these anthocyanin-rich fruits already exist in nature.

YELLOW TOMATOES
Low in lycopene, but they contain more niacin and folate than red tomatoes.

LETTUCE

 HAS NATURAL SEDATIVE PROPERTIES

 HELPS EASE BLOATING AND DISCOMFORT

 STRENGTHENS HEART AND BLOOD VESSELS

We may think of lettuce as simply a base for more flavourful foods, but it is a useful source of **folate** and **soluble fibre** in the form of pectin. How rich it is in other nutrients depends on the variety: deeply coloured lettuces have greater stores of **beta-carotene**. It is also considered to be **cooling**, **diuretic**, and **calming** for the nerves: the milky juice in darker, bitter varieties contains a **sedative**, lactucarium.

RED LETTUCES (RED OAKLEAF)
The deep colour signals extra beneficial antioxidants, such as carotenes and anthocyanins.

LEAF LETTUCE (COS)
Darker, more bitter leaves aid digestion and contain substances that calm the nerves.

HEAD LETTUCE
These generally thick leaves contain mostly water, but their minerals are easily assimilated by the body.

WHAT IS IT GOOD FOR?

SEDATIVE Wild lettuce is a traditional herbal sedative. The dark, bitter lettuces contain lactucarium, which can relax nerves, reduce palpitations, and induce sleep.

DIGESTIVE AID AND DIURETIC Contains useful amounts of fibre and can help soothe gassy or griping pains. The watery nature of lettuce also helps to flush toxins from the body.

HEALING HAEMORRHOIDS The astringent nature of lettuce can help strengthen blood vessels and may help treat haemorrhoids.

HOW DO I GET THE BEST FROM IT?

CHOOSE LARGE LEAVES Large, loose lettuce leaves are richer in essential nutrients, especially chlorophyll, iron, beta-carotene, and vitamin C, than paler, tightly packed head lettuces, such as iceberg (mostly water).

BEYOND GREEN Ancient lettuce varieties were a rich array of colours. Red lettuces contain extra antioxidant pigments that enhance your daily intake of nutrients.

FRESH AND CRISP Its nutritional value depends on the variety, time of year, and how long it has been stored. To get the best out of lettuce and other salad leaves, buy what is in season and always choose fresh heads, leaves, or "living salad" leaves over pre-washed, bagged varieties of lettuce.

HOW DO I USE IT?

MIX IT UP Its watery texture and neutral, refreshing taste makes lettuce a good partner for fresh fruit.

MAKE A CALMING TEA Tea brewed from lettuce leaves is a useful night-time sedative. Simmer 3–4 large, deeply coloured lettuce leaves and 1 or 2 mint leaves in 300ml (10fl oz) water for 15 minutes. Remove from the heat, strain, and drink.

SPINACH

 **HELPS STRENGTHEN BONES**

 **CONTAINS ANTI-CANCER PROPERTIES**

 **HELPS FIGHT INFLAMMATION**

 **HELPS PREVENT ATHEROSCLEROSIS**

Packed with **vitamins** and **minerals**, spinach contains more than a dozen different **antioxidant** flavonoid compounds that have **anti-inflammation properties** that protect against **heart disease** and help to **neutralize the free radicals** that compromise the immune system and are linked to cancer. Its considerable vitamin K content also helps to **protect bones**.

WHAT IS IT GOOD FOR?

BONE HEALTH A single serving provides more than twice the daily recommended intake of vitamin K, which is important for maintaining healthy bones. It is especially good at protecting the elderly from bone fractures.

REDUCED CANCER RISK Studies have shown it can help to reduce the risk of certain cancers. Specifically, the antioxidant kaempferol appears to be protective against prostate and ovarian cancer risk.

ANTI-INFLAMMATORY Its high levels of antioxidants, particularly neoxanthin and violaxanthin, have anti-inflammatory effects.

HEART HEALTH Its vitamin C and beta-carotene work together to prevent the oxidization of "unhealthy" (LDL) cholesterol, which can lead to hardening of the arteries.

HOW DO I GET THE BEST FROM IT?

COOKED VS RAW While raw spinach is nutritious, cooked spinach is even more so, as its iron content is more available and it provides considerably larger amounts of beta-carotene, lutein, vitamins, and minerals.

SERVE WITH CITRUS FRUITS Contains oxalic acid that prevents our bodies absorbing all its iron and calcium. If eating raw, serve with a lemon dressing or a glass of orange juice to increase absorption of these vital minerals.

HOW DO I USE IT?

CITRUS SPINACH SALAD Toss 2 generous handfuls of spinach leaves, ½ finely chopped red onion, 1 orange peeled and separated into segments, and 2 tbsp toasted pine nuts in a bowl. For the dressing, mix 2 tbsp each of orange juice, white vinegar, olive oil, honey, and Dijon mustard with 1 tbsp chopped fresh coriander. Season and serve.

SPINACH PESTO Substitute basil leaves with spinach in any pesto recipe.

SPINACH
Among the many nutrients in spinach, the carotenoids lutein and zeaxanthin can help to protect the eyes.

MICROGREENS
These contain more antioxidants and other nutrients than the mature leaves.

WATERCRESS

 **CONTAINS ANTI-CANCER SUBSTANCES**

 **PROMOTES CLEAR SKIN**

 **AIDS OPTIMAL DIGESTION**

HAS A DIURETIC ACTION

This salad leaf is a member of the cruciferous vegetable family, which includes cabbage and broccoli. Its numerous health benefits include reducing the risk of certain **cancers**, aiding **digestion**, maintaining the body's **water balance**, and acting as a **natural antibiotic** to **boost immunity**. It doesn't have a particular growing season and so can be grown and harvested all year round.

Leaves
Contain digestive enzymes and are rich in vitamins C and K, iron, beta-carotene, and B vitamins

WHAT IS IT GOOD FOR?

REDUCED CANCER RISK A great source of the antioxidants vitamin C and beta-carotene, which help fight free radicals. Studies have found that regularly eating cruciferous vegetables can help reduce the risk of cancers of the colon, rectum, and bladder.

SKIN DETOX Rich in sulphur, which aids protein absorption, blood purification, and cell building, and promotes healthy skin and hair.

DIGESTIVE AID The chlorophyll that gives watercress its green colour is rich in digestive enzymes that help the body fully utilize the nutrients in any meal.

MAINTAINS WATER BALANCE A natural diuretic and diet aid as it is rich in potassium.

FIGHTS COLDS AND FLU The volatile oils that give it its peppery taste are a good remedy for coughs, colds, flu, and bronchial ailments.

HOW DO I GET THE BEST FROM IT?

JUICE A natural antibiotic. Add to freshly prepared juices to detox and boost clear skin.

BUY ORGANIC If watercress is not grown in controlled conditions, it runs the risk of being contaminated with harmful bacteria. Buying organic means it will contain neither the bacteria nor any pesticides.

EAT FRESH Aim to consume within 5 days of buying it, as it quickly loses its nutrients.

HOW DO I USE IT?

WATERCRESS SOUP A traditional remedy for inflammatory conditions including achy joints, swollen gums, and mouth ulcers. Simmer 225g (8oz) each of watercress and sliced carrots in water or vegetable stock until the watercress reduces to one-third of its original volume. Blend and season to taste before serving.

SALAD INGREDIENT The perfect base to any salad; use instead of, or with, lettuce.

MUSTARD GREENS

 HELPS REMOVE TOXINS FROM THE BODY

 CONTAINS ANTI-CANCER SUBSTANCES

 **HELPS LOWER CHOLESTEROL**

 **HELPS FIGHT INFLAMMATION**

Pungent, peppery mustard greens are the leaves of a mustard plant. They range from bright green to deep purple and are high in **antioxidants** and **anti-inflammatory** properties, and can help **detoxify** the body and lower "unhealthy" (LDL) **cholesterol**. The plant also produces hot, bitter-tasting brown seeds that are used to make Dijon mustard, and which are frequently used in Indian cooking.

WHAT IS IT GOOD FOR?

DETOX The antioxidant beta-carotene and vitamins C and K help to neutralize toxins and remove them from the body, providing effective detox support.

CANCER PREVENTION A combination of antioxidant, detoxification, and anti-inflammatory properties contribute to cancer prevention. Mustard greens are also rich in sulphurous chemicals called glucosinolates, which break down into cancer-fighting isothiocyanates. Studies have linked the leaves to the prevention of bladder, colon, breast, lung, prostate, and ovarian cancers.

LOWERS CHOLESTEROL Rich in natural substances called sulphoraphanes, which help remove the "unhealthy" (LDL) cholesterol that increases the risk of heart disease.

BROAD SPECTRUM ANTIOXIDANT Contains key antioxidants including hydroxycinnamic acid, quercetin, isorhamnetin, and kaempferol, which help lower the risk of inflammation and oxidative stress caused by free radicals in the body.

HOW DO I GET THE BEST FROM IT?

HOW TO COOK IT Cooking decreases the availability of its anti-cancer properties so add raw to salads. However, light steaming boosts its cholesterol-lowering properties.

SPROUT THE SEEDS The seeds, rich in volatile oils, can be sprouted. Add to salads or soups.

HOW DO I USE IT?

HEALTHY SAUTÉ Sauté chopped onions and garlic until tender in a few tablespoons of broth or stock. Add roughly chopped mustard greens and cook until barely wilted. Toss with sesame oil and season to taste before serving.

PASTA SAUCE Chop tomatoes and mustard greens and mix with pine nuts, goat's cheese, and a little olive oil. Stir through hot pasta.

DEEP GREEN
Sulphurous chemicals support the heart and tissues, and aid detoxification.

PURPLE LEAF
Has the same nutritional value as green leaves, but also contains extra antioxidant pigments.

MIZUNA
These spidery leaves can be grown in the garden or bought at farmers' markets.

ROCKET

 **SUPPORTS HEALTHY LIVER FUNCTION**

 **PROTECTS AGAINST INFECTIONS**

 **HELPS PROTECT EYE HEALTH**

 **HAS ANTI-ULCER PROPERTIES**

Once used mainly for its **energizing** medicinal qualities in stimulating **digestion** and protecting against **stomach ulcers**, rocket is now prized as a unique peppery, **low-calorie, detoxifying** salad leaf. The rocket plant is a relative of broccoli and cabbage and has many of the same benefits, including boosting the **immune system** and maintaining **eye and skin health**.

Leaves
A stimulating salad leaf that aids digestion and strengthens the liver.

WHAT IS IT GOOD FOR?

DETOX Sulphurous chemicals in rocket stimulate circulation, strengthen the liver, and have mild diuretic and laxative properties.

IMMUNE HEALTH Rocket leaves contain very high levels of vitamin C and beta-carotene. These nutrients have proven immunity-boosting properties and help the body to defend itself against infections. During digestion it releases isothiocyanates, which are protective against cancer.

HEALTHY EYES Rocket leaves contain large amounts of eye-healthy lutein and zeaxanthin. Including these nutrients in your diet can reduce the risk of age-related macular degeneration (loss of vision).

DIGESTIVE HEALTH Studies show rocket can stimulate digestion and also help protect against stomach ulcers.

HOW DO I GET THE BEST FROM IT?

REPLACE OTHER SALAD LEAVES Unlike spinach, its iron and calcium levels are highly available due to its low levels of oxalate.

EAT RAW AND FRESH Rocket begins to lose its nutrients soon after picking. Heat can further degrade its nutritional value. For this reason it is best to buy it fresh and use as quickly as possible after purchase.

HOW DO I USE IT?

ROCKET PESTO Blend 4 generous handfuls of rocket, 3 crushed cloves of garlic, 3 tbsp pine nuts, and 4 tbsp olive oil in a blender. Gradually add 45g (1½oz) pecorino cheese. Blend until smooth, then stir through hot pasta or mix with hot new potatoes.

SUPER SIMPLE SALAD As rocket is best eaten fresh and raw, use it as the base of a salad. Combine with lycopene-rich tomatoes and dress the salad with a simple olive oil dressing for an antioxidant-rich meal.

DANDELION

 SUPPORTS HEALTHY LIVER FUNCTION

 **HAS A MILD DIURETIC ACTION**

 **HELPS BOOST IMMUNITY**

 **PROMOTES HEALTHY SKIN**

Think of the dandelion as a superfood rather than a weed: it is a **nutritional powerhouse**, and can be used as a **diuretic** and **liver cleanser**. Every part can be used: collect the leaves before the familiar yellow flowers emerge to ensure the least bitter taste, and gather the flowers once they turn yellow. Never collect wild plants from chemically treated lawns or gardens.

WHAT IS IT GOOD FOR?

LIVER CLEANSER Helps clear inflammation and congestion of the liver and gall bladder.

DIURETIC A natural source of potassium, making it a safe, gentle diuretic.

IMMUNE SUPPORT Rich in antioxidants that help fight infection and speed wound healing.

HEALTHY SKIN A good source of vitamin C which supports collagen formation – the foundation of youthful skin and healthy gums.

HOW DO I GET THE BEST FROM IT?

LEAVES These supply all the major antioxidant vitamins, including vitamins C and E.

FLOWERS Dandelion flowers contain useful amounts of beta-carotene, vitamin C, iron, and other nutrients. The colourful petals contain antioxidant flavonoids, which help to lower blood pressure and boost immunity.

ROOTS The root, which can be dried and used as a caffeine-free coffee substitute, has a mild laxative and diuretic effect. It also has antiviral properties and contains inulin, a prebiotic that encourages healthy gut flora.

HOW DO I USE IT?

MAKE A PESTO Use the leaves on their own or combine with nettles and blend to a paste in a food processor with pine nuts, garlic, Parmesan cheese, and olive oil to make a springtime alternative to classic pesto.

DANDELION TEA Fresh or dried, all parts of the plant can be brewed into a refreshing tea that has diuretic properties.

ADD TO SALADS AND STIR-FRIES Add the yellow flower petals to salads and stir-fries, or pickle the flower heads in vinegar to preserve their nutritional benefits beyond the period they are in season.

ROAST THE ROOTS Cook like parsnips. They taste sweetest from autumn to early spring.

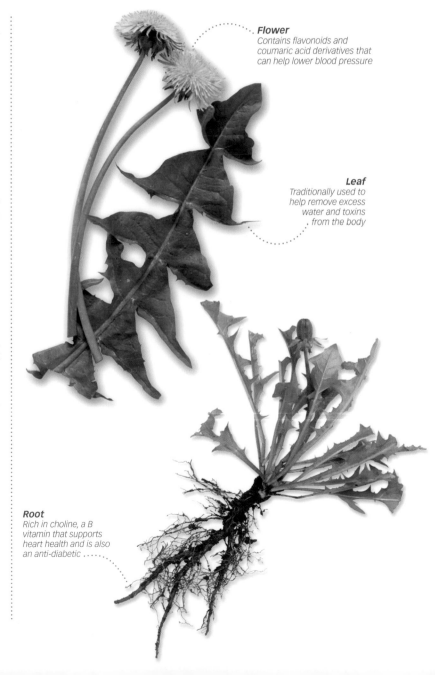

Flower
Contains flavonoids and coumaric acid derivatives that can help lower blood pressure

Leaf
Traditionally used to help remove excess water and toxins from the body

Root
Rich in choline, a B vitamin that supports heart health and is also an anti-diabetic

NETTLES

 HAS A POWERFUL DIURETIC ACTION

 HELPS REDUCE AN ENLARGED PROSTATE

 BOOSTS IRON STORES TO COMBAT FATIGUE

 HELPS BALANCE BLOOD SUGAR LEVELS

Many gardeners consider stinging nettles to be a weed, but they have long been used to **treat painful muscles** and joints, eczema, **arthritis**, gout, and **anaemia**. Today, they are used to benefit the blood, treat **urinary tract infections**, urinary problems during the early stages of an **enlarged prostate**, hay fever, or in compresses or creams to treat joint pain, sprains and strains, tendonitis, and **insect bites**.

Leaves
The vitamin C in the leaves allows their iron content to be more easily absorbed

Stems and leaves
The stems and leaves contain natural anti-inflammatory substances that work like conventional antihistamine. Herbalists believe that including nettle leaves in your diet in spring can help "inoculate" against seasonal allergies

WHAT IS IT GOOD FOR?

DIURETIC It keeps water flowing through the kidneys and bladder, washing bacteria away and stopping urine crystals forming into kidney stones.

HEALTHY PROSTATE Nettle root is comparable to finasteride (a commonly prescribed medication) for reducing the symptoms of prostate enlargement. Unlike finasteride, it doesn't decrease prostate size, but does improve urinary flow, post-urination dripping, and the urge to urinate.

BLOOD BUILDER Its iron content makes it a wonderful blood builder, and its vitamin C ensures better iron absorption. It is also a good source of vitamin K, which aids clotting.

DIABETIC CONDITIONS Nettle tea can help balance blood sugar levels.

RHEUMATIC CONDITIONS It can eliminate uric acid from joints. Studies suggest that nettle extract can help those with rheumatoid arthritis to lower their NSAID (nonsteroidal anti-inflammatory drug) use.

HOW DO I GET THE BEST FROM IT?

PICK FRESH PLANTS Avoid nettles treated with pesticides. Young nettle tops are full of nutrients and have a mild, pleasant flavour.

AS A TEA Steep fresh or dried nettles in hot water for 10–15 minutes for a detoxifying, diuretic tea. For prostate health, drink several cups of nettle root tea a day.

HOW DO I USE IT?

SPRING DETOX SOUP Sauté nettles, onion, leeks, and celery in butter, purée in a blender or food processor with stock and a little yogurt, and season to taste before serving.

YOUNG NETTLE PESTO Substitute basil leaves with nettles in any pesto recipe. Young spring leaves are more palatable and more potent.

CHICORY

- **PROMOTES A HEALTHY DIGESTIVE TRACT**
- **HAS A MILD DIURETIC ACTION**
- **HELPS REMOVE TOXINS FROM THE BLOOD**
- **HAS NATURAL SEDATIVE PROPERTIES**

Blanched white chicory, green-leafed chicory, and red-leafed varieties known as radicchios are the most familiar types of this bitter leaf. Grown in the dark, the popular white chicory lacks the usual array of vitamins, but it retains the **volatile oils** and other substances that **aid digestion,** and acts as a **detoxifier** and a mild diuretic. Chicory contains natural sedative compounds to **ease stress and pain**.

WHAT IS IT GOOD FOR?

INTESTINAL HEALTH Rich in mucilaginous (gum-like) fibre, which helps lubricate the intestines and soften stools.

BETTER DIGESTION Its bitter constituents stimulate bile production, increase appetite, and aid digestion. Chicory can also help combat excessive wind and indigestion.

AIDS DETOXIFICATION It is a natural diuretic and mildly laxative. As a good source of dietary fibre, it helps removes toxins from the blood and tissues.

MILD SEDATIVE Both chicory and radicchio contain the substance lactucopicrin, which contributes to its bitter taste and has sedative and analgesic properties.

ANTIOXIDANT Although it lacks most other vitamins, chicory is rich in the useful antioxidant beta-carotene, which can help protect against cancer.

HOW DO I GET THE BEST FROM IT?

EAT IT RAW While it can be eaten lightly braised, you will receive more of chicory's vitamin C, folate, and beta-carotene content if you eat it raw.

EAT IT FRESH Both chicory and radicchio are relatively fragile and only keep for a few days in the refrigerator crisper before wilting.

HOW DO I USE IT?

A NATURAL SCOOP Use the leaves of the witloof chicory, also know as Belgian endive, which have a natural curved shape, as crudités with dips, or fill with toppings or a rice and vegetable stuffing and serve as a finger food or starter.

ENLIVEN STIR-FRIES AND SALADS The mildly bitter flavour of chicory and radicchio gives a pleasant edge to salads and stir-fries.

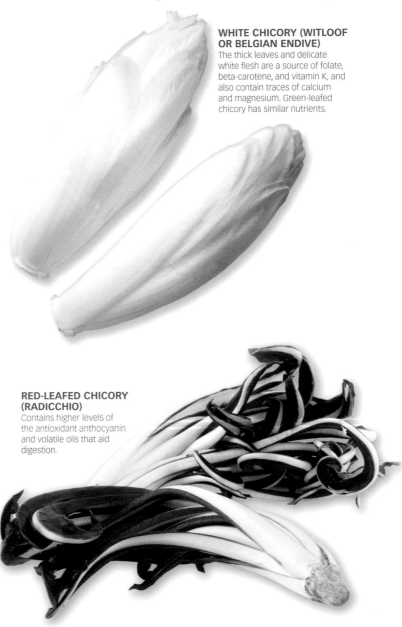

WHITE CHICORY (WITLOOF OR BELGIAN ENDIVE)
The thick leaves and delicate white flesh are a source of folate, beta-carotene, and vitamin K, and also contain traces of calcium and magnesium. Green-leafed chicory has similar nutrients.

RED-LEAFED CHICORY (RADICCHIO)
Contains higher levels of the antioxidant anthocyanin and volatile oils that aid digestion.

Green Beans

 **PROVIDES CELLULAR ENERGY**

 **STRENGTHENS CONNECTIVE TISSUE**

 **HELPS BUILD STRONG BONES**

 **PROTECTS AGAINST FREE-RADICAL DAMAGE**

Fresh green beans, which are the same species as the dried versions we use in chilli con carne and baked beans, are edible pods picked early in the plant's growth cycle; as they mature, the pods become tough, fibrous, and inedible. The beans are a **good source of vitamin C** and folate, and have useful amounts of **calcium** and **protein**. This makes them **heart-protective** and **anti-inflammatory**.

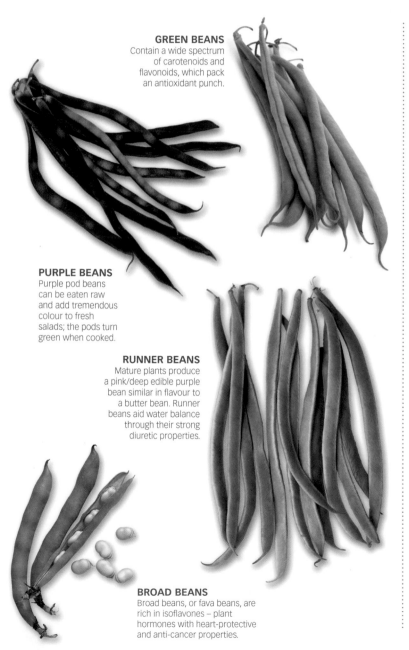

GREEN BEANS
Contain a wide spectrum of carotenoids and flavonoids, which pack an antioxidant punch.

PURPLE BEANS
Purple pod beans can be eaten raw and add tremendous colour to fresh salads; the pods turn green when cooked.

RUNNER BEANS
Mature plants produce a pink/deep edible purple bean similar in flavour to a butter bean. Runner beans aid water balance through their strong diuretic properties.

BROAD BEANS
Broad beans, or fava beans, are rich in isoflavones – plant hormones with heart-protective and anti-cancer properties.

What Is It Good For?

ENERGY BOOSTING Contains twice the amount of iron as spinach, so it's a good way to make up iron loss during menstruation. Iron is a component of red blood cells that transport oxygen from the lungs to cells throughout the body. It is also is a key element in making energy and the body's metabolism.

SKIN, HAIR, AND NAILS Provides an easily absorbed type of silicon, important for the formation of healthy connective tissues and strengthening nails.

BONE HEALTH Abundant in vitamin K, which activates osteocalcin, the main non-collagen protein found in bones that locks calcium molecules together inside the bone.

FIGHTS FREE RADICALS Levels of the antioxidants lutein, beta-carotene, violaxanthin, and neoxanthin are comparable to those in carotenoid-rich vegetables, such as carrots.

DETOX Beans have strong diuretic properties and help to speed the elimination of toxins from the body.

How Do I Get The Best From It?

DON'T CUT THEM Where you can, just top and tail the beans and cook whole to preserve their nutrients.

HOW TO COOK THEM Cook until "al dente" (slightly crunchy), or steam briefly to ensure their vitamin C content is retained.

How Do I Use It?

VERSATILE Add to salads, soups, and stews, or serve as a side dish. Pair tender varieties with lighter meats, such as poultry, and more robust, coarser varieties, such as runner beans, with red meats.

GET BEYOND BUTTER Serve with a dressing of olive oil, lemon, and garlic to bring out their flavour and boost their nutritional value.

OKRA

 HELPS BALANCE BLOOD SUGAR LEVELS

 AIDS DETOXIFICATION SYSTEM

 HELPS PROTECT EYE HEALTH

 PROMOTES A HEALTHY PREGNANCY

Okra, also known as bhindi and lady's fingers, is a flowering plant that belongs to the mallow family. It has a unique, slightly peppery taste somewhere between an aubergine and asparagus. Its main medicinal value lies in its extraordinary mix of **soluble and insoluble fibre**, which helps lower **blood sugar** levels, cleanse the **intestines**, and feed **good gut bacteria.**

WHAT IS IT GOOD FOR?

ANTI-DIABETIC A rich source of many nutrients, including fibre, vitamin B6, and folate. B vitamins slow the progress of diabetic neuropathy and reduce levels of homocysteine, a risk factor for this disease. The soluble fibre also helps to stabilize blood sugar levels.

BRILLIANT DETOX Abundant in both soluble and insoluble fibre. Soluble fibre absorbs water and helps bulk up stools, and helps lower "unhealthy" (LDL) cholesterol in the blood. Insoluble fibre helps keep the intestinal tract healthy, binding to toxins and aiding their removal. This decreases the risk of some forms of cancer, especially colorectal cancer.

PROTECTING VISION In addition to having good amounts of beta-carotene, it contains zeaxanthin and lutein. These compounds are essential for maintaining good vision.

FOLATE-RICH Okra is a good source of folate, a nutrient that enriches red blood cells, protects the heart, and lowers the risk of birth defects in babies.

HOW DO I GET THE BEST FROM IT?

LEAVE IT WHOLE The more you slice okra, the more it exudes a gelatinous substance that some find off-putting. Avoid this by trimming just the ends without puncturing the inner pod, and don't overcook it.

HOW TO COOK IT Cook lightly and quickly by steaming, grilling, or adding to a stir-fry to preserve its essential nutrients.

HOW DO I USE IT?

ADD TO A SALAD If you are tired of the same lettuce, tomato, and cucumber salad, try slicing whole grilled okra into a salad and drizzle with a chilli and lime dressing.

ADD TO STEWS Use in soups and stews and curries as a thickener.

GREEN OKRA
Okra is high in fibre in the form of mucilaginous gums and pectins. If you find purple okra it will have the additional cancer-protective antioxidant anthocyanin.

Seeds
Oil pressed from okra seeds is rich in heart-friendly polyunsaturated fats and is often used in African cooking

PEAS

 **PROMOTES A HEALTHY DIGESTIVE TRACT**

 BOOSTS IRON STORES TO COMBAT FATIGUE

 HELPS FIGHT INFECTION

 PROMOTES HEALTHY SPERM

While neither exotic nor rare, this naturally sweet legume has a nutrient content that guarantees it a place in the medicinal food world. Peas are rich in **vitamin K**, **manganese**, and **vitamin C**, and are a good source of **folate** and **trace elements**. Their **insoluble fibre content** is good for the gut and also helps to reduce the risk of **heart disease** and **stroke**.

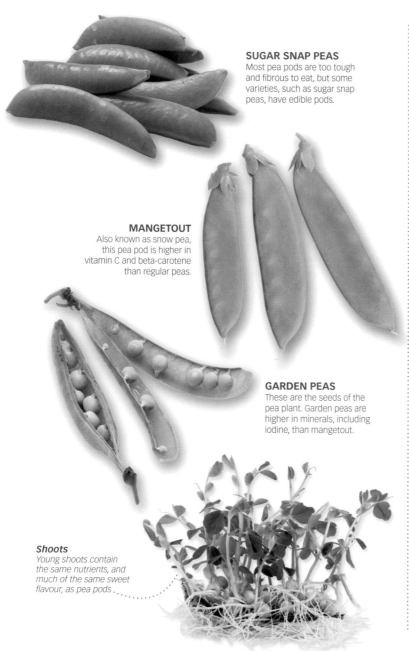

SUGAR SNAP PEAS
Most pea pods are too tough and fibrous to eat, but some varieties, such as sugar snap peas, have edible pods.

MANGETOUT
Also known as snow pea, this pea pod is higher in vitamin C and beta-carotene than regular peas.

GARDEN PEAS
These are the seeds of the pea plant. Garden peas are higher in minerals, including iodine, than mangetout.

Shoots
Young shoots contain the same nutrients, and much of the same sweet flavour, as pea pods

WHAT IS IT GOOD FOR?

DIGESTION Its fibrous content makes it useful for maintaining a healthy digestive tract.

ENERGY BOOST A good source of iron, which helps prevent anaemia and combats fatigue.

IMMUNITY Rich in vitamin C; a single serving of peas or mangetout supplies half your daily needs. Peas, especially pea shoots, also contain phytoalexins, an antioxidant that can inhibit *H. Pylori*, the bacterium that causes stomach and duodenal ulcers, and stomach cancer.

MEN'S HEALTH Glycodelin-A, a substance found in mangetout, can help strengthen sperm and improve their ability to fertilize a female egg.

EYE HEALTH The carotenoid pigment in green peas is lutein, which is well known for reducing the risk of cataracts and macular degeneration (loss of vision).

HOW DO I GET THE BEST FROM IT?

EAT RAW Get the best flavour and nutrients by eating fresh peas straight from their pods.

FROZEN OR DRIED The sugar in fresh peas quickly turns to starch with storage. Frozen peas are processed immediately after picking, which is why they tend to taste sweeter. Dried peas come in green and yellow varieties (usually sold split), and you can also buy dried wild peas. All are great for enjoying the benefits of peas beyond their summer season.

HOW DO I USE IT?

AS AN ALTERNATIVE TO LETTUCE Swap salad leaves for pea shoots in a stir-fry or salad.

MANGETOUT WITH CASHEWS Heat 1 tsp coconut oil in a frying pan. Add 3 handfuls of mangetout and the zest of ½ orange and cook on a low heat for 3–4 minutes. Season and serve with a handful of cashews sprinkled over the top for a skin-nourishing dish.

ASPARAGUS

 **HAS A MILD LAXATIVE ACTION**

 **REMOVES ENERGY-DRAINING TOXINS**

 **HELPS STRENGTHEN THE IMMUNE SYSTEM**

 **HELPS KEEP BLOOD VESSELS SUPPLE**

Asparagus is a member of the lily family. It has been prized for millennia for its unique flavour, succulent texture, and medicinal qualities: it has **detoxifying properties** and contains **antioxidants** that strengthen the heart and blood vessels. Traditional Chinese medicine also suggests it can benefit people with **respiratory illnesses** and **ease menstrual problems**.

WHAT IS IT GOOD FOR?

SUPPORTS THE GUT Asparagus contains inulin, a prebiotic that encourages healthy gut flora. Also has mild laxative and diuretic properties.

BOOSTS ENERGY Aspartic acid neutralizes excess ammonia in the body, which could otherwise result in a sense of feeling drained and lacking in vigour.

ANTI-INFLAMMATORY Contains rutin and glutathione, which protect cells against oxidative stress by free radicals in the body, promote a healthy immune response, and can strengthen blood vessels.

PROTECTS THE HEART AND MORE A great source of B vitamins, especially folate, which may help control homocysteine, a substance that promotes heart disease, cancer, and cognitive decline. Increased folate intake during pregnancy can help fight birth defects.

SKIN HEALTH A combination of detoxifying properties and beta-carotene in asparagus has a purifying effect on the skin.

HOW DO I GET THE BEST FROM IT?

BUY IN SEASON To get the most nutrients, always buy it in season. The asparagus season lasts from February to June.

USE IT QUICKLY Asparagus deteriorates quickly when stored. Buy and use within a couple of days to get the maximum benefit.

HOW TO COOK IT Grill or steam for 3–5 minutes (avoid boiling). Or braise quickly in a little vegetable broth to ensure the maximum flavour and retention of nutrients.

HOW DO I USE IT?

IN SALADS Add cooked cold asparagus to a colourful salad to make a delicious light meal.

AS A SPECIAL INGREDIENT Cook and serve with hot pasta, cooked fresh fish and chicken, or add to vegetable tarts.

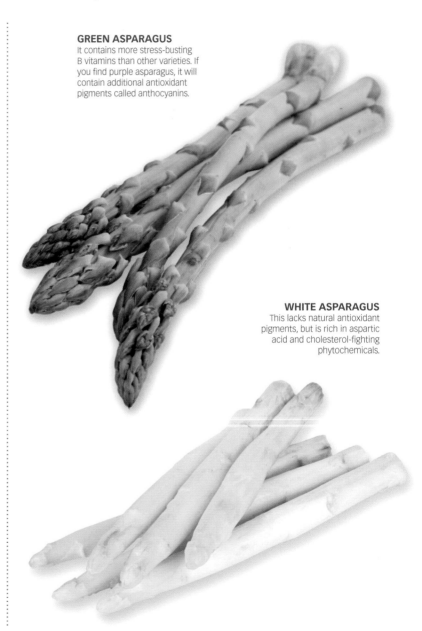

GREEN ASPARAGUS
It contains more stress-busting B vitamins than other varieties. If you find purple asparagus, it will contain additional antioxidant pigments called anthocyanins.

WHITE ASPARAGUS
This lacks natural antioxidant pigments, but is rich in aspartic acid and cholesterol-fighting phytochemicals.

CELERY AND CELERIAC

 **HELPS LOWER BLOOD PRESSURE**

 **HAS A DIURETIC ACTION**

PROMOTES FEELING OF FULLNESS

 **PROMOTES HEALTHY JOINTS AND MUSCLES**

There is more to bitter, aromatic celery than a pleasant crunch; in Eastern medicine, both the stalks and roots are used to **treat high blood pressure**. Celery and its close cousin celeriac are mildly **diuretic** and help reduce levels of the **stress hormone** cortisol. They are also rich in **B vitamins**, trace elements, **fibre** and **circulation-supporting coumarins**. Its taste and nutritional quality are highest when in season.

SEEDS
Rich in volatile oils and essential fatty acids.

STALKS
The water and fibre content can aid weight control.

CELERIAC CORM
High in phosphorus, which benefits the nervous, lymphatic, and urinary systems.

WHAT IS IT GOOD FOR?

LOWERS BLOOD PRESSURE Contains coumarins, which help lower blood pressure and aid water balance, and phthalides, anti-coagulants that reduce the risk of blood clots and stroke and lower stress hormone levels.

A DIET AID Celery is mostly water and fibre – two things that can aid weight control. Adding celery to your meal may help you to eat more slowly and chew more thoroughly, and therefore increase a feeling of fullness.

SOURCE OF SILICON It contains good amounts of silicon as well as vitamin K, which is not only beneficial for skin and hair but also for joints, bones, muscles, arteries, and connective tissues.

HOW DO I GET THE BEST FROM IT?

STALKS Low in calories and high in fibre, the stalks (and leaves) have, in addition to their other benefits, diuretic and laxative properties.

SEEDS Rich in volatile oils, traditionally used as a diuretic and sedative, and to reduce inflammation and treat menstrual discomfort. Studies show they may help lower blood pressure and "unhealthy" (LDL) cholesterol. Use as a seasoning or brewed as a tea.

HOW DO I USE IT?

COMBINE WITH FRUIT Celery is one of the few vegetables that combine well with fruit. Slice some into a fruit salad for extra crunch.

ADDS FLAVOUR The phthalides in celery and celeriac have no flavour of their own but can act as a natural flavour enhancer in meals.

AS A COLD REMEDY Combine celery juice with a little lemon juice to help treat the feverish symptoms of cold and flu.

JUICE IT Both stalk and corm yield an alkalizing, revitalizing, and detoxifying juice that helps regulate the body's water balance.

FENNEL

 EASES STOMACH CRAMPS

 **CONTAINS ANTI-INFLAMMATORY OILS**

 **A GENTLE HORMONE REGULATOR**

 **HAS A DIURETIC ACTION**

Aromatic fennel looks like a larger version of its relative dill, but has a distinct aniseed flavour. Since Roman times it has been valued for its ability to soothe **digestive troubles.** It also helps to relieve **water retention** and regulate **female hormones**. A low-calorie source of **vitamin C**, dietary fibre, and potassium, it also contains a range of **antioxidants** and **anti-inflammatory** volatile oils.

WHAT IS IT GOOD FOR?

STOMACH SOOTHER It encourages healthy digestion and eases stomach cramps. Can be effective against worms and parasites due to the volatile oil anethole, which gives fennel its characteristic aniseed flavour.

EASING COUGHS AND COLDS A syrup made from the juice is traditionally used to thin mucous and make coughs more productive.

HORMONE REGULATION Its oestrogenic qualities may help bring hormonal balance to females of all ages – from young mothers to women in menopause.

MAINTAINING WATER BALANCE Fennel can relieve water retention and bloating.

HOW DO I GET THE BEST FROM IT?

HOW TO COOK IT The tender stems can be added to soups or roasted in oil. Fennel can also be eaten raw in salads.

MAKE USE OF THE SEEDS A mild, cooled tea made from the seeds and sweetened with a touch of honey is a time-honoured way of settling the stomach and easing colic in babies.

HOW DO I USE IT?

BREW A TEA Boil 1 tsp of fennel seeds in a cup of water or milk and drink as required.

HEALING SYRUP To make a syrup from fennel juice as a traditional remedy for coughs, juice the whole plant – or steep the seeds in a little boiling water to make a strong decoction – and mix with lemon juice and honey to taste.

LIGHTLY ROAST Slice the bulb into wedges, put in an ovenproof dish, season, dot with butter, add a generous handful of fresh thyme, and bake in a medium oven until tender.

MAKE A SOUP To ease menstrual symptoms, cook equal quantities of fennel, asparagus, and fresh parsley in a broth of water and milk until soft. Purée, season to taste, and serve.

SEEDS
Contain concentrated volatile oils that sooth upset stomachs.

BULB AND LEAVES
Contain anti-inflammatory and antioxidant substances including rutin, quercetin, kaempferol glycosides, and anethole.

RHUBARB

 HELPS STRENGTHEN BONES

 PROTECTS AGAINST NEURO-DEGENERATION

 HELPS LOWER CHOLESTEROL

 HELPS PROTECT EYE HEALTH

Although we think of rhubarb as a fruit, it is actually a vegetable and a member of the buckwheat family. It is too sour to eat raw, but even cooked it contains a number of beneficial properties, including helping to **strengthen bones** and protect against **neurological damage**. It is also a good source of **fibre** and is known to help reduce "unhealthy" (LDL) **cholesterol** levels in the blood.

OUTDOOR RHUBARB
Field rhubarb has bright green leaves and is less tender than the forced variety, but has a better flavour.

FORCED RHUBARB
Forced rhubarb is grown in the dark, but it has all the same healing properties.

WHAT IS IT GOOD FOR?

BONE HEALTH Contains calcium and notable amounts of vitamin K, especially important for protecting against bone fractures as we age.

PROTECTING THE BRAIN Adequate vitamin-K levels can protect against the neurological damage linked to Alzheimer's disease. Vitamin K is also a useful clotting agent for blood, so may protect against bleeding and stroke.

HEART HEALTH Studies show that including rhubarb in your diet can help reduce an overbalance of "unhealthy" (LDL) cholesterol levels in the blood. It is also a good source of fibre and has moderate levels of vitamin C.

EYE HEALTH Contains useful amounts of lutein, which can reduce the risk of age-related macular degeneration (loss of vision).

HOW DO I GET THE BEST FROM IT?

RED IS BETTER THAN GREEN Red stalks contain more beta-carotene than green varieties. They also contain small amounts of poly-phenolic flavonoid compounds such as zeaxanthin and lutein.

MAKE SURE IT'S RIPE Rhubarb contains oxalic acid, which prevents the absorption of nutrients, such as iron and calcium. Most oxalic acid concentrates in the leaves, but it can be especially high in unripe stalks too. Look for stalks that are deeply coloured.

COOK IT The stalks are sour and considered inedible raw, so always cook before eating.

HOW DO I USE IT?

SPICE IT UP Sauté garlic and onions in olive oil, add chopped rhubarb, root vegetables, and pre-soaked lentils, add a little stock, season with pungent curry spices, and simmer until tender. Serve over rice.

AS A FRUIT Use in compotes, jams, muffins, and fruit pies instead of cherries and berries.

ONION FAMILY

 HAS A POWERFUL ANTIBIOTIC ACTION

 **HELPS LOWER CHOLESTEROL**

 **FEEDS GOOD BACTERIA IN THE GUT**

The onion family is part of the allium family, which also includes garlic. The Chinese, East Indians, Ancient Greeks, Romans, and even Egyptians all revered onions, and modern science has proved them right: onions contain dozens of medicinal chemical compounds that have **antibacterial** and **anti-inflammatory** actions in the body and promote good **heart** and **gut health**.

WHAT IS IT GOOD FOR?

ANTIBACTERIAL ACTION The sulphur compounds in onions – including thiosulphinates, sulphides, and sulphoxides – are responsible for their powerful antibacterial and antiviral action, and unique taste.

HEART HEALTH A good source of heart-healthy quercetin. This flavonoid helps avoid heart disease by preventing blood clots and cholesterol sticking to arterial walls. Over time, quercetin can also help raise levels of "healthy" (HDL) cholesterol in the blood.

HEALTHY GUT Contains a fibre called inulin and a range of other fructo-oligosaccharides. These compounds are known as prebiotics as they provide the right food to encourage the growth of healthy bacteria in the gut. This may be why including more onions in your diet has a role to play in preventing bowel cancer.

HOW DO I GET THE BEST FROM IT?

RAW IS BEST Its benefits are mostly lost when cooked. To enjoy at its medicinal best, use raw or braise lightly in stock or broth.

USE STRONG VARIETIES Highly flavoured onions contain the most healthful compounds.

HOW DO I USE IT?

A SIMPLE COLD REMEDY Mix onion juice with honey and take 2–3 tsp daily when you are fighting a cold or feel one coming on.

A VARIETY OF TASTES Onions and shallots add punch and bite to omelettes, soups, and stews, while leeks lend a rich, creamy flavour. Spring onions are ideal in stir-fries or with steamed fish, and can enliven mashed potato.

SPROUT THE SEEDS Add sprouting onion seeds to salads, sandwiches, and other dishes.

ONION SCAPES These immature flowering stalks, available in late spring/early summer, are delicious in a spring detox salad.

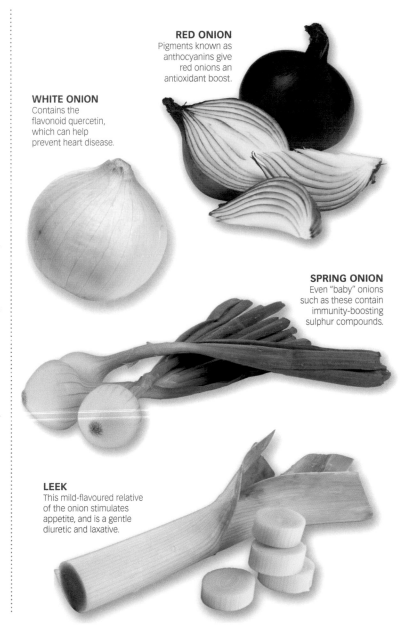

RED ONION
Pigments known as anthocyanins give red onions an antioxidant boost.

WHITE ONION
Contains the flavonoid quercetin, which can help prevent heart disease.

SPRING ONION
Even "baby" onions such as these contain immunity-boosting sulphur compounds.

LEEK
This mild-flavoured relative of the onion stimulates appetite, and is a gentle diuretic and laxative.

GARLIC

 **A NATURAL ANTI-COAGULANT**

 **HELPS STRENGTHEN THE IMMUNE SYSTEM**

 **REMOVES TOXINS AND POLLUTANTS**

 **CONTAINS ANTI-CANCER SUBSTANCES**

The main beneficial ingredients of this member of the allium family are allicin and diallyl sulphides – sulphurous compounds that are **antibacterial** and **antifungal**. Garlic is universally recognized for its health-promoting benefits: **aiding the circulatory** and **digestive** systems, boosting the **immune system**, lowering **blood pressure**, and fighting **heart disease**. It even helps to **eliminate toxins**.

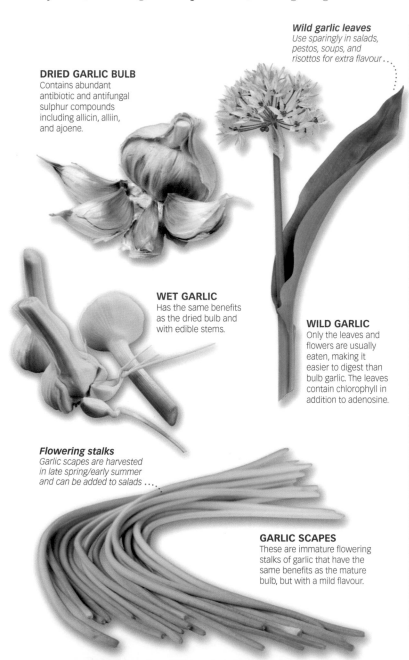

Wild garlic leaves
Use sparingly in salads, pestos, soups, and risottos for extra flavour

DRIED GARLIC BULB
Contains abundant antibiotic and antifungal sulphur compounds including allicin, alliin, and ajoene.

WET GARLIC
Has the same benefits as the dried bulb and with edible stems.

WILD GARLIC
Only the leaves and flowers are usually eaten, making it easier to digest than bulb garlic. The leaves contain chlorophyll in addition to adenosine.

Flowering stalks
Garlic scapes are harvested in late spring/early summer and can be added to salads

GARLIC SCAPES
These are immature flowering stalks of garlic that have the same benefits as the mature bulb, but with a mild flavour.

WHAT IS IT GOOD FOR?

HEART HEALTH The sulphur in garlic stimulates nitric oxide production in blood vessels. This relaxes and improves their elasticity, helping lower blood pressure and reducing the risk of stroke and atherosclerosis (hardening of the arteries).

IMMUNITY Its volatile oils are antibiotic and can be used to treat colds and coughs.

DETOXIFYING Contains sulfhydryl, which works by helping to remove toxic substances such as heavy metals from the body.

CANCER Garlic is recognized for helping to prevent numerous types of cancer, including bowel, breast, and lung cancer. It purportedly also helps treat prostate and bladder cancer.

REGULATES BLOOD SUGAR LEVELS A regular intake of garlic lowers the amino acid homocysteine, a risk factor in diabetes and heart disease.

HOW DO I GET THE BEST FROM IT?

FRESH IS BEST Choose fresh rather than bottled in water or oil, as its healthful allicin compounds degrade dramatically.

TRY BLACK GARLIC Fermented black garlic has a treacly balsamic flavour, twice the amount of antioxidants of white garlic, and gives no trace of bad breath.

HOW TO COOK IT Cooked garlic doesn't have the same levels of allicin as raw, but it does retain other compounds. Let it stand for 10 minutes after crushing or slicing to allow the allicin to develop before being heated. Microwaving kills off nearly all its benefits.

HOW DO I USE IT?

WET GARLIC Cook the stems like leeks or slice and use in soups and omelettes or as a garnish for salads.

EAT RAW Scatter raw over cooked vegetables.

BEETROOT

 HAS A LIVER-CLEANSING ACTION

 **LOWERS THE RISK OF HEART ATTACK**

 **IMPROVES BLOOD'S OXYGEN UPTAKE**

 **HAS AN ANTI-DIABETIC EFFECT**

They may look tough, but beetroots are a delicate vegetable with a unique group of **antioxidants** known as betacyanins. These pigments give beetroots their strong colour and are the source of their medicinal benefits: **supporting the liver**, **improving circulation**, and **purifying the blood**. Eaten raw, they have a crunchy texture; once cooked, they taste soft and buttery. Their leaves **aid digestion**.

WHAT IS IT GOOD FOR?

SUPPORTS THE LIVER Its phytochemicals stimulate the production of glutathione, a detoxifying antioxidant that combines with an array of antioxidant pigments to aid liver function and neutralize and excrete toxins.

STRENGTHENS THE HEART Its antioxidants lower cholesterol and blood pressure, while the B vitamins improve nerve function, helping to maintain a strong regular heartbeat.

NOURISHES THE BLOOD A combination of iron and antioxidants helps feed and purify the blood while improving its oxygen uptake, making beetroot a useful remedy for anaemia.

ANTI-INFLAMMATORY Contains choline, a B vitamin that supports heart health and is also anti-diabetic.

HOW DO I GET THE BEST FROM IT?

EAT FRESH Grated in a salad, it adds crunchy texture, lively colour, and is a nutrient boost.

USE THE LEAVES Beetroot greens are even more nutrient-packed than the root and are rich in bone- and blood-healthy vitamin K and beta-carotene, which is great for skin and eyes, among other things.

HOW TO COOK IT Lightly steamed or roasted is best. The freshest beetroots will cook faster, helping to retain essential nutrients.

HOW DO I USE IT?

JUICE IT The juice can lower blood pressure within an hour of drinking. Regular intake can lower the risk of heart disease, and is used as part of an anti-cancer regime in some clinics.

COMBINE IT Eat with carrots in salads (or as a juice) to boost energy, improve appetite, and aid hormone regulation during menopause.

LEAFY SALAD Use the leaves raw in salads as a slightly bitter digestive aid or lightly steam it like spinach.

RED BEETROOT
Liver-healthy betacyanins are the dominant antioxidant pigments in this root.

Leaves
Sometimes called chard, beetroot leaves of all varieties are rich in protein, fibre, vitamins, and minerals

Root
Cook with the skin and trimmed stems on to prevent the beneficial pigments bleeding away

GOLDEN BEETROOT
Immunity-boosting betaxanthins, particularly vulgaxanthin, are the main antioxidant pigments in this variety of beetroot.

CARROTS

 AIDS DIGESTION AND A FEELING OF FULLNESS

 **HELPS LOWER CHOLESTEROL**

 **POWERFUL ANTIOXIDANT**

 **HELPS MAINTAIN GOOD EYESIGHT**

The benefits of carrots are hinted at in their name; they are rich in beta-carotene (from which the body makes vitamin A). A diet high in carotenes is associated with significant decreases in the incidence of **some cancers**. Carrots also aid **digestion**, help **weight control**, contain silicon, which benefits skin and nails, and promote **eye health** due to their beta-carotene, lycopene, and lutein content.

ORANGE CARROTS
Contain beta-carotene and the eye-healthy antioxidants lutein and lycopene.

PURPLE CARROTS
Contain extra antioxidant pigments that may benefit diseases such as arthritis and heart disease.

WHAT IS IT GOOD FOR?

WEIGHT CONTROL High fibre promotes a feeling of fullness and aids bowel regularity.

CHOLESTEROL FIGHTING Contain a form of calcium easily assimilated by the body that may help lower "unhealthy" (LDL) cholesterol levels.

SKIN CONDITION In addition to beta-carotene, lutein, and lycopene, carrots contain silicon, which promotes healthy skin and nails.

SEEING CLEARLY Lutein and lycopene help maintain good eyesight and night vision.

HOW DO I GET THE BEST FROM IT?

EAT IT RAW A raw carrot a day can reduce the risk of cancers of the oesophagus, stomach, intestines, and prostate. The essential oils in carrots protect against intestinal parasites.

FRESH IS BEST As soon as a carrot is picked, its beta-carotene content begins to decline. Buy loose carrots rather than those in plastic bags and consume as quickly as possible.

DON'T THROW THE GREENS AWAY Carrot tops are edible and rich in protein, minerals, and vitamins. Use in small amounts in salads and dressings, as a garnish instead of a fresh herb, or brew into an antiseptic, diuretic tea.

HOW DO I USE IT?

A GREAT BASE FOR JUICE Juicing gives the highest concentration of beta-carotene. It makes a good base ingredient for fruit and vegetable juice mixes.

CHILDREN'S LUNCH PACKS A few carrot sticks a day can help strengthen and clean children's teeth, and may also help encourage lower jaw development and avoid overcrowded teeth.

PURÉE INTO A SOUP Use as a healing, strengthening dish for tummy upsets or if you have poor digestion.

A tea made from chlorophyll-rich carrot tops makes a delicious, detoxifying drink. Choose organic carrots with leaves that haven't been treated with chemicals.

RADISHES

 SUPPORTS HEALTHY LIVER FUNCTION

 **HELPS LOWER BLOOD PRESSURE**

 **TREATS CONGESTION AND INFLAMMATION**

Belonging to the cruciferous family of vegetables, fiery-tasting radishes grow in a variety of sizes, shapes, and colours, and are available all year. Both the roots and leaves are rich in **vitamin C**, potassium, magnesium, **B vitamins**, and trace elements, which help to fight **hypertension**. Its pungent essential oils help support a **healthy liver** and fight inflammation and congestion.

BLACK RADISHES
A very hot radish that is high in bowel-protective antioxidants.

RED, PURPLE, AND WHITE RADISHES
Essential oils in the flesh of all varieties have antiseptic properties.

DAIKON RADISHES
In Chinese medicine, the daikon radish is considered cooling and is used to soothe coughs, bronchitis, and laryngitis.

WHAT IS IT GOOD FOR?

DETOX The radish is a useful tool for fat digestion as it stimulates the flow of bile. It also has a cleansing, decongesting action on the gall bladder, liver, and blood. Traditionally, radishes have been used to help break up gallstones and kidney stones. They also have a diuretic and laxative action.

FIGHTS HYPERTENSION Radishes are high in potassium, which helps keep blood pressure low.

CLEARS CONGESTION The high vitamin C content in radishes can help treat colds and flu. The juice pressed from grated, fresh radish root is a traditional remedy for coughs, inflamed joints, and gall bladder problems.

HOW DO I GET THE BEST FROM IT?

USE THE GREEN TOPS Radish leaves contain 6 times more vitamin C than the roots, and also supply calcium.

LOOK FOR DAIKON RADISHES The daikon radish, a staple of Eastern cooking, is high in the enzyme myrosinase: it both aids digestion and during the digestive process and produces isothiocyanates, an antioxidant that has anti-cancer benefits.

HOW DO I USE IT?

JUICE IT Make a fiery detox drink by juicing apples, celery, and radishes. As a cold remedy, try mixing equal parts of radish juice and honey. Take 1 tbsp 3 times a day.

A SIMPLE SIDE DISH Gently braise radishes in butter and vegetable stock. Turn off the heat, add some fresh watercress, season, and serve.

ENERGIZING SALAD Make a salad from thinly sliced radish, a soft leaf lettuce (e.g. butterhead), and ruby grapefruit segments. Dress with a mustard vinaigrette containing some of the grapefruit juice.

POTATOES

 HELPS FIGHT INFLAMMATION

 **HELPS LOWER BLOOD PRESSURE**

 HELPS CALM THE NERVES

Potatoes are a surprisingly good source of vitamin C, potassium, fibre, B vitamins, copper, tryptophan, manganese, and even lutein. Their alkaline nature helps to **detoxify** and balance excess **acidity** in the body and relieve the **inflammation** and pain of **ulcers**. They are a **natural sedative** and encourage healthy **blood circulation**, and the skin contains chlorogenic acid, which helps prevent cell mutation.

WHAT IS IT GOOD FOR?

REDUCING INFLAMMATION Alkalizing and anti-inflammatory, potatoes soothe stomach and duodenum ulcers and reduce stomach acidity. They may also relieve the inflammation associated with arthritis.

HIGH BLOOD PRESSURE Potatoes are high in chlorogenic acid and anthocyanins, chemicals that help to lower blood pressure. The polyphenol in purple potatoes may also help.

CALMING THE NERVES Potatoes contain tryptophan, an amino acid with natural sedative properties.

HOW DO I GET THE BEST FROM IT?

USE THE JUICE Drinking the juice is a quick way to benefit from its anti-inflammatory properties. Wash and grate several red-skinned potatoes, put in cheesecloth, and squeeze to remove the juice. Drink as needed.

KEEP THE SKIN ON Potatoes lose a great deal of their nutritional value if they are peeled before boiling, as the nutrients leech into the cooking water. When buying potatoes, avoid those that are already washed, as the washing process destroys their natural protective coating, making them more vulnerable to bacteria and thus decay. Buy organic potatoes to ensure the skins are free from toxins.

HOW DO I USE IT?

POTATO AND NETTLE ROSTI Boil potatoes until al dente (still slightly firm). When cool, roughly grate, blend with a handful of chopped nettles, season, shape into small flat cakes, and shallow-fry. Drain and serve.

POTATO SALAD Use red-skinned potatoes in a potato salad for an extra dose of antioxidants.

CRUSHED POTATOES AND WILD GARLIC Cook new potatoes until just tender and crush rather than mash them together with a handful of wild garlic and butter or oil.

White flesh
The sedative tryptophan in potatoes makes them a good choice if you are stressed

Red skin
Contains antioxidant anthocyanins, which are good for the heart

NEW POTATOES
New potatoes are eaten with the skin on, which is rich in nutrients.

PURPLE POTATOES
In Korea, the purple potato is eaten as a way to lose weight.

SWEET POTATOES

 HELPS BALANCE BLOOD SUGAR LEVELS

 **FIGHTS FREE-RADICAL DAMAGE TO SKIN**

 **PROTECTS AGAINST INFECTION**

They may look uninteresting, but sweet potatoes are a superfood. A single sweet potato contains more than a day's-worth of **beta-carotene** and nearly all your daily **vitamin C** requirements. They help combat **free radicals** in the body, benefit **skin health**, and support the **immune system**. Due to their high level of slow-release carbohydrates, they can also help maintain **steady blood sugar levels.**

YELLOW FLESH, BROWN SKIN
High potassium levels regulate heart rate and help combat the effects of stress.

PURPLE SKIN AND FLESH
Rich in anthocyanin pigments, which support and protect the gut.

PURPLE SKIN, YELLOW FLESH
This colourful variety contains the highest amount of beneficial antioxidants.

WHAT IS IT GOOD FOR?

GLUCOSE CONTROL Sweet potatoes are a traditional treatment for diabetes. They contain slow-release carbohydrates and the hormone adiponectin, a combination that helps keep blood sugar levels steady.

BEAUTIFUL SKIN Its high levels of beta-carotene mean it benefits skin by fighting the free radicals that cause skin ageing.

IMMUNE BOOSTING As it is high in beta-carotene and vitamin C, regular consumption can strengthen the immune system and help develop resistance to infection. It may also provide anti-cancer benefits.

HOW DO I GET THE BEST FROM IT?

KEEP THE SKIN ON The skin is healthy and contains nutrients similar to that of the flesh underneath. To get your full complement, eat sweet potatoes with their skins on.

HOW TO COOK THEM Steaming or boiling rather than roasting preserves their slow-release carbohydrates and essential nutrients.

ADD SOME FAT Eat with a little butter or oil to ensure all the antioxidants, such as beta-carotene, are fully absorbed.

THINK PURPLE The purple-fleshed sweet potato is rich in antioxidant and anti-inflammatory anthocyanins – primarily peonidins and cyanidins – that can protect against irritable bowel and ulcerative colitis.

HOW DO I USE IT?

POTATO MASH Peel and cut roughly into chunks. Boil for 30 minutes or until soft, mash with butter and serve. Add brown sugar, cinnamon, and/or nutmeg for extra flavour.

AS A SALAD Add steamed (or leftover) sweet potatoes and sliced red peppers to rocket or spinach. Dress with a balsamic vinegar dressing. Add goat's cheese too, if you like.

TURMERIC

 **HELPS RELIEVE ARTHRITIC PAIN**

 **HELPS PREVENT HARDENED ARTERIES**

 **FIGHTS FREE-RADICAL DAMAGE TO BRAIN**

 **CONTAINS ANTI-CANCER SUBSTANCES**

Known to be extremely beneficial for health, turmeric is a key ingredient in almost any curry, and can be used fresh or as a powder. Its main healthy constituent is curcumin, a well-researched **antioxidant** and powerful **anti-inflammatory** that helps to fight **free-radical damage** and prevent and treat **arthritis**, **cardiovascular health**, **diabetes**, and even **neurological conditions**.

WHAT IS IT GOOD FOR?

ANTI-INFLAMMATORY Contains potent volatile oils with anti-inflammatory properties and, perhaps most importantly, curcumin, which gives it its vibrant colour. Curcumin has a medicinal effect comparable to drugs such as hydrocortisone and phenylbutazone, and can be used to provide relief from rheumatoid arthritis, treat inflammatory bowel disease, protect against diabetes, and avoid heart disease and stroke by preventing the build-up of plaque in the arteries.

ALZHEIMER'S PROTECTION Curcumin reduces the build-up of the protein amyloid-b in the brain. Amyloid-b causes oxidative (free radical) damage and inflammation in the brain and is one of the main causes of Alzheimer's disease. Antioxidants in turmeric help to fight this free-radical damage.

CANCER PROTECTION In laboratory studies, curcumin has been shown to stop the growth and spread of cancer cells.

HOW DO I GET THE BEST FROM IT?

FRESH OR DRIED The fresh root can be used in place of ginger in most meals. The powder is a key component in most Indian curries.

LEAVES The leaves can be used to flavour dishes, such as curries, or to wrap around food during cooking.

DON'T FORGET THE OIL Curcumin is better absorbed in the presence of oils, such as coconut, olive, ghee, and butter. Heating it slightly aids absorption.

HOW DO I USE IT?

AN ANTIOXIDANT DRINK Stir 1 tbsp turmeric powder into warm full-fat or semi-skimmed milk to treat painful joints or eczema.

A SPICY RICE DISH Enliven brown rice with cashews and raisins and season with turmeric, cumin, and toasted coriander seeds.

Root
Its vibrant yellow colour is due to curcumin – a powerful antioxidant and anti-inflammatory.

Leaves
The leaves also contain curcumin, along with trace amounts of vitamins and minerals. They have a less pungent flavour than the root and can be brewed as a medicinal tea

GINGER

 **HAS POWERFUL ANTI-INFLAMMATORY OILS**

 **HELPS ALLEVIATE ARTHRITIC PAIN**

 **REDUCES SYMPTOMS OF NAUSEA**

This pungent root is known for its ability to settle **stomach upsets** and **alleviate nausea**. Its active constituent, gingerol, is a relative of capsaicin and piperine, found in hot chillies. Studies show that its volatile oils have **anti-inflammatory** properties similar to those of NSAIDs (non-steroidal anti-inflammatory drugs) so it can ease the symptoms of **colds and flu, headaches**, and **menstrual pains.**

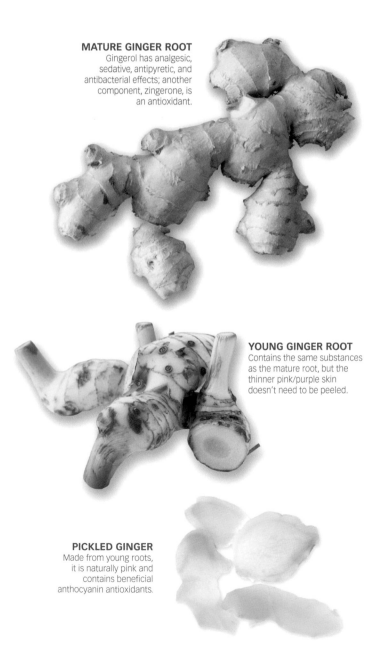

MATURE GINGER ROOT
Gingerol has analgesic, sedative, antipyretic, and antibacterial effects; another component, zingerone, is an antioxidant.

YOUNG GINGER ROOT
Contains the same substances as the mature root, but the thinner pink/purple skin doesn't need to be peeled.

PICKLED GINGER
Made from young roots, it is naturally pink and contains beneficial anthocyanin antioxidants.

WHAT IS IT GOOD FOR?

FIGHTS INFLAMMATION Reduces inflammation, lessens pain, and can lower medication intake in cases of osteoarthritis.

NAUSEA Studies show it can ease morning sickness, motion sickness, and nausea caused by cancer chemotherapy and post-surgery.

DIGESTIVE HEALTH Protects and heals the gut, hastens the movement of food through the gastrointestinal tract, and reduces gas, bloating, and cramping. It also awakens the taste buds and gets digestive juices flowing.

HOW DO I GET THE BEST FROM IT?

PEEL IT CAREFULLY The richest resins and volatile oils concentrate in and near the skin so peel carefully. The best way to peel ginger is with a teaspoon. Gently scrape the skin off rather than using a peeler.

EAT FRESH Whenever possible, choose fresh ginger since it is not only superior in flavour to dried but contains higher levels of active constituents, such as gingerol and zingibain. Store in a dry place.

LOOK FOR YOUNG ROOTS Most supermarkets sell the mature roots, though Asian supermarkets often sell the younger pale pink roots, which don't need peeling, are juicier, and have a milder taste.

HOW DO I USE IT?

SOOTHING SYRUP For sore throats or congestion, make a syrup of 2 tsp each ginger juice, turmeric, and black pepper, 1 tsp each honey and vinegar, and 3 tbsp water. Use as needed. An easy way to collect the juice is to grate the root and squeeze the juice from the shreds.

MAKE A TEA Mix 1 tsp freshly grated ginger, the juice of ½ lemon, and 1 tsp honey. Top up with boiling water. Take at the first signs of a cold or chill, or for indigestion or nausea.

MUSHROOMS

 **CLEANSING AND ANTI-INFLAMMATORY**

 **FEEDS GOOD BACTERIA IN THE GUT**

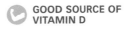 **GOOD SOURCE OF VITAMIN D**

 **CONTAINS ANTI-CANCER SUBSTANCES**

Most commercial mushroom varieties are actually the same mushroom at different stages of growth, and share common medicinal traits. Others, such as shiitake, rei-shi, and wild wood ear, are "super" mushrooms with extraordinary **healing powers**. All types contain varying degrees of **fibre**, protein, **B vitamins**, and **vitamin D**. They are also known to have **anti-inflammatory** and **antibacterial** effects.

WHAT IS IT GOOD FOR?

ANTIOXIDANT All mushrooms are considered "cleansing", and all except oyster and maitake contain ergothioneine, an amino acid that can help reduce inflammation. They also contain germanium, which improves cellular oxygenation and enhances immunity.

A PREBIOTOIC Eaten raw, mushrooms contain higher levels of prebiotic oligosaccharides, such as chitin and beta-glucan, which feed friendly bacteria in the gut.

A GOOD SOURCE OF VITAMIN D Common white mushrooms are one of the few non-animal sources of vitamin D – essential to bone health, hormone balance, immune defence, and as a cancer preventative.

ANTI-CANCER PROPERTIES Shiitake contains lentinan, which has anti-cancer, antiviral, and antibacterial properties. It also boosts the immune system by stimulating the production of white blood cells.

HOW DO I GET THE BEST FROM IT?

CLEANING MUSHROOMS Most store-bought mushrooms have been cleaned, while foraged mushrooms benefit from a brief wash or brush. Their nutrient quality is not affected.

HOW TO COOK IT Cooking mushrooms increases their starch, fibre, and fat content, and frees more antioxidants including carotenoids and ferulic acid, but does destroy some of their vitamin C content.

HOW DO I USE IT?

DRIED EXOTICS Dried mushrooms have an intense flavour. To reconstitute, soak in boiling water. Reserve the water, which will have leeched some nutrients out of the fungi, to use as a broth or as a stock for soups and stews.

AS A MEAT SUBSTITUTE Mushrooms give a meaty texture when cooked that can help to make a meal more satisfying.

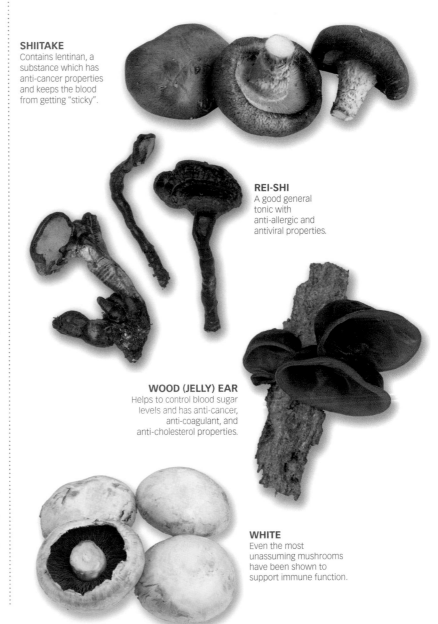

SHIITAKE
Contains lentinan, a substance which has anti-cancer properties and keeps the blood from getting "sticky".

REI-SHI
A good general tonic with anti-allergic and antiviral properties.

WOOD (JELLY) EAR
Helps to control blood sugar levels and has anti-cancer, anti-coagulant, and anti-cholesterol properties.

WHITE
Even the most unassuming mushrooms have been shown to support immune function.

NUTS

 FIGHTS INFLAMMATORY DISEASES    **HELPS LOWER CHOLESTEROL**    **HELPS KEEP JOINTS SUPPLE**

Some of the highest **antioxidant** levels of all plant foods are found in nuts. Antioxidants are vital for helping to **fight inflammation** and **cell and tissue damage** caused by free radicals (toxic byproducts of metabolism). Nuts are also **rich in fibre**, healthy fats, **vitamins**, and minerals, and research shows they help to **lower cholesterol**, **improve blood vessel function**, and **benefit muscles and joints** too.

Almonds

ALMONDS

WHAT IS IT GOOD FOR?

LOWERS CHOLESTEROL Almonds are a good source of the minerals zinc, magnesium, and potassium, and are very rich in antioxidant vitamin E, which supports the brain, the cardiovascular and respiratory systems, and helps keep skin healthy. They are especially rich in cholesterol-lowering monounsaturated fatty acids, such as oleic and palmitoleic acids. Their high fibre content also helps regulate blood sugar levels.

HOW DO I USE IT?

A VERSATILE INGREDIENT Eat with their skins on, as the flavonoids in the skins work synergistically with the vitamin E to more than double their antioxidant power. Use ground almonds as a low-starch, gluten-free flour in baking or to make almond milk, a useful alternative to dairy.

Cashew nuts

CASHEW NUTS

WHAT IS IT GOOD FOR?

GOOD FOR BONES A good source of monounsaturated oleic acid and omega-3 alpha linolenic acid (ALA), which are both healthy fats that help protect against heart disease and cancer. Cashew nuts also contain calcium, magnesium, iron, zinc, and folate, making them an excellent source of minerals that contribute to bone health. These nutrients also help with the formation of collagen, which is essential for supporting healthy skin and body tissues.

HOW DO I USE IT?

SWEET AND SAVOURY Cashew nuts contain starch so are useful for thickening water-based dishes, such as soups, meat stews, and some Indian milk-based desserts. Cashew cream made from blended soaked cashew nuts can be used as a healthy alternative to dairy cream.

Chestnuts

CHESTNUTS

WHAT IS IT GOOD FOR?

PROTECTS THE HEART Chestnuts can be classed as the only really low-fat nut, as they contain a fraction of the calories of other types of nuts. However, they are high in fibre, beta-carotene, and folate, and are also the only nuts that contain a significant amount of antioxidant vitamin C. In addition, they contain high levels of palmitic acid and oleic acid, the heart-healthy fatty acids found in olive oil.

HOW DO I USE IT?

AN ALTERNATIVE TO WHEAT Eat boiled, puréed, or roasted and added to pastries, soups, poultry, stuffings, casseroles, and appetizers. Chestnut flour is gluten-free and is used in many Italian dishes, such as polenta, gnocchi, sweet breads, and biscuits.

Hazelnuts

What Is It Good For?

RICH IN ANTIOXIDANTS High in monounsaturates, which protect the heart and help lower "unhealthy" (LDL) cholesterol levels in the blood, and vitamins E and K. Also a rich source of folate and the B vitamin biotin, which promotes healthy skin and hair, and copper, which helps build red blood cells, protects cells from free-radical damage, and strengthens connective tissues. Eaten with their skins on, hazelnuts contain 3 times as much antioxidant proanthocyanidin, which helps prevent free radicals from damaging organs and cells, as other nuts.

How Do I Use It?

AS A GARNISH Crush and sprinkle over baked fruit, muesli, crumble toppings, and savoury dishes.

Hazelnuts

Pine Nuts

What Is It Good For?

A GOOD SOURCE OF PROTEIN Contains more vitamin K, which protects bones and arteries, than other nuts. A good source of magnesium and potassium, which help maintain a steady heartbeat, lower blood pressure, and improve circulation. Although higher in fat than other nuts, they are richer in phytosterols, plant hormones that lower "unhealthy" (LDL) cholesterol levels in the blood, reduce the risk of certain types of cancer, and enhance immune function.

How Do I Use It?

ADD A HANDFUL Pine nuts added to a meal can help to create a feeling of fullness and satisfaction. Toss into hot pasta or pilaf or add to stuffed tomatoes, courgettes, or aubergines.

Pine nuts

Pistachio Nuts

What Is It Good For?

ANTI-INFLAMMATORY Their vibrant colour indicates a high antioxidant content. Pistachios are also high in beta-carotene and the compound oleanolic acid, both potent anti-inflammatories, and phytosterols, a type of anti-inflammatory plant hormone associated with improved immune function, lower levels of "unhealthy" (LDL) cholesterol, and a reduced risk of cancer. They contain valuable minerals, such as potassium, calcium, zinc, iron, and magnesium.

How Do I Use It?

KEEP IT COOL Heat can reduce their nutritional value so use as a garnish, sprinkle on probiotic yogurt, or combine with nettles, dandelion leaves, and Parmesan cheese to make a detoxifying springtime pesto sauce.

Pistachio nuts

Walnuts

What Is It Good For?

SUPPORTS A HEALTHY HEART A rich source of alpha-linolenic acid (ALA), an omega-3 fatty acid. ALA helps lower "unhealthy" (LDL) cholesterol levels and keeps arteries healthy. Walnuts also contain the antioxidants ellagic acid and a mix of tocopherols (the vitamin-E complex) including alpha, delta, and gamma tocopherol, which help reduce the risk of cancer and heart disease and maintain skin and tissue health. In addition, they contain serotonin, a brain chemical that can help lift depression.

How Do I Use It?

COOKED OR RAW Use in stuffings, baked goods, as a topping for fruit and yogurt, or in salads.

Walnuts

SEEDS AND SPROUTS

 **PROMOTES HEALTHY SKIN AND HAIR**

 **HELPS REMOVE TOXINS FROM THE BODY**

 **SUPPORTS HORMONE BALANCE**

 **PROTECTS THE HEART AND BLOOD VESSELS**

Though tiny, seeds are packed with nutrients such as **protein**, **fibre**, **iron**, **vitamins**, and **omega-3** fatty acids that help promote **healthy skin and hair**, **remove toxins**, **balance hormones**, and support **cardiovascular health**. Sprouting seeds converts their starch to slow-release carbohydrates, releases enzymes that **aid digestion**, and makes their nutrients more **bioavailable** (easily absorbed).

Sesame seeds

SESAME SEEDS

WHAT IS IT GOOD FOR?

HELPS IMPROVE SKIN A good source of vitamin E, which helps improve the condition of the skin as well as strengthen the heart and the nervous system. Also contains the plant hormones sesamin and sesamolin, which have been shown to lower blood pressure and protect the liver from toxic damage. Sesame seeds are very high in calcium, which is necessary for healthy bones and teeth. All varieties – white, brown, and black – are suitable for eating raw or soaking and sprouting.

HOW DO I USE IT?

A VERSATILE SEED Sprinkle the seeds on steamed vegetables, and add the sprouts to salads, stir-fries, baked goods, sandwiches, and quiches. Ground sesame seeds are the basis of tahini, a sesame paste that can be used in hummus recipes or salad dressings, or simply spread on toast with honey or miso drizzled over.

Sunflower seeds

SUNFLOWER SEEDS

WHAT IS IT GOOD FOR?

MAINTAINS HEALTHY HAIR AND SKIN An excellent source of vitamin E, an antioxidant that helps maintain healthy hair and skin, protects cells from damage, and has anti-cancer properties. The seeds are an excellent source of B vitamins too, especially folate, which helps support a healthy pregnancy and aids the immune system. They are also rich in protein and heart-healthy fats. Eat raw, or soak and sprout.

HOW DO I USE IT?

AS A SNACK OR IN DISHES Eat a handful as a snack or add to salads, stir-fries, baked goods, and trail mixes. Soaking and sprouting the seeds produce a substantial microgreen (smallest edible plant) that is very nutritious.

Pumpkin seeds

PUMPKIN SEEDS

WHAT IS IT GOOD FOR?

MEN'S HEALTH High in zinc, they are useful for promoting men's fertility and preventing prostate problems.

CARDIOVASCULAR HEALTH A good source of B vitamins, magnesium, iron, and protein. The seeds have high levels of essential fatty acids that help maintain healthy blood vessels and lower "unhealthy" (LDL) cholesterol in the blood. Eat raw or dry-roasted; they are nearly impossible to sprout, but soaking them for 1–2 hours helps release their nutrients.

HOW DO I USE IT?

SOAK THEM Eat the raw, dry-roasted, or soaked seeds on their own as a snack, and use in baking, cooking, as a soup garnish, and with muesli.

LINSEEDS

WHAT IS IT GOOD FOR?

HEART HEALTH Also known as flax seeds, linseeds are a great source of soluble mucilaginous (gum-like) fibre that can lower "unhealthy" (LDL) cholesterol in the blood, balance blood sugar levels, and act as a hunger suppressant. Their high omega-3 fatty acid content can help lower undesirable fats (triglycerides) in the blood, reducing the risk of stroke and heart attack, and is also beneficial to the eyes, joints, and brain health. Linseed shells are hard so either grind or sprout the seeds, or buy them ready-cracked, to benefit from their nutrients.

HOW DO I USE IT?

GRIND OR SPROUT If you buy whole linseeds, grind as needed and add to yogurt, oatmeal, cereal, smoothies, casseroles, and baked goods. Sprouting linseeds releases more of their protein and omega-3 fats.

Linseeds

POPPY SEEDS

WHAT IS IT GOOD FOR?

PROTECTS THE HEART The seeds contain both polyunsaturated and monounsaturated fatty acids, which can help protect the heart. They also contain iron, phosphorus, and fibre, as well as an array of B vitamins.

A GENERAL TONIC In traditional Ayurvedic medicine, poppy seeds are considered a general tonic and a remedy for diarrhoea. A tea made from the seeds is a age-old remedy for anxiety and nervous tension. Like hemp, most culinary-grade poppy seeds have been sterilized to prevent germination (into the opium poppy), although you cannot get "high" from eating poppy seeds. Since they are too small to chew thoroughly, grind the seeds before use to release their beneficial fats and nutrients, or soak and sprout them.

HOW DO I USE IT?

GRIND OR SPROUT Sprinkle the dried seeds on yogurt and use in savoury dishes, such as pasta, fish, and baked goods. If you are able to find unsterilized seeds, soak and sprout them; the sprouts can be eaten raw or incorporated into other foods, such as breads and cakes.

Black poppy seeds

White poppy seeds

HEMP SEEDS

WHAT IS IT GOOD FOR?

BOOSTS HEART HEALTH Contains a perfect balance of omega-3, 6, and 9 fatty acids, which help boost brain and heart health. They are also a source of complete protein and fibre that benefit gastrointestinal and heart health, and a source of phytosterols (plant hormones) that help lower cholesterol and promote hormonal balance in the body.

ANTI-INFLAMMATORY Hemp seeds also reduce inflammation, and keep skin and joints in good condition. In some countries, selling "live" hemp seed is illegal because the hemp plant is a member of the cannabis family. In these countries, the seeds are sterilized to prevent sprouting. You cannot get "high" from eating hemp seeds or sprouts.

HOW DO I USE IT?

LIVE SEEDS Try sprinkling hemp seeds over a salad, or use as a topping for yogurt, cereal, or desserts. Where you can buy live seeds, hemp sprouts make a nutritious addition to baked goods and smoothies, as well as to salads and sandwiches.

Hemp seeds

SEEDS AND SPROUTS CONTINUED

Alfalfa seeds

ALFALFA SEEDS

WHAT IS IT GOOD FOR?

DETOXIFIER Rich in nutrients and antioxidants, particularly chlorophyll, which helps remove toxins from the blood. Alfalfa seeds also have a natural diuretic action, which maintains water balance and helps lower blood pressure. In addition, they contain coumarin, a blood thinner that is useful for maintaining good blood circulation and preventing stroke. They also contain betaine, an enzyme that helps to break down proteins and fats and so aids good digestion.

WOMEN'S HEALTH Alfalfa seeds are a good source of phytoestrogens and are often used to promote better hormonal balance in women.

HOW DO I USE IT?

HELPS DIGEST PROTEINS Add alfalfa sprouts to any meal to assist digestion. Combine with other diuretic or digestive herbs, such as dandelion, for a synergistic effect.

Chia seeds

CHIA SEEDS

WHAT IS IT GOOD FOR?

HEALTHY HEART High in omega-3 fatty acids, which help lower the undesirable fats (LDL cholesterol and triglycerides) in your blood that can cause heart disease and stroke.

STRONG BONES Chia seeds are high in calcium and magnesium, which promote healthy bones and teeth, and in iron, folate, and soluble fibre.

HEALTHY GUT The mucilaginous (gum-like) fibre in the sprouted seeds promotes bowel regularity and helps stabilize blood sugar levels. Briefly soaking the seeds for 1 hour releases more of their beneficial fibre, or leave to soak for longer and sprout like other seeds.

HOW DO I USE IT?

SOAKED OR SPROUTED Add soaked seeds to yogurt, cereal, and muffin recipes, or sprinkle on a salad. They are also delicious stirred through warm oatmeal. Chia sprouts can be used like any salad green or sprout. Try adding them to soups or stews as a natural thickening agent. They also add flavour and nutrition to baked goods such as breads, muffins, and home-made crackers.

Red clover seeds

RED CLOVER SEEDS

WHAT IS IT GOOD FOR?

WOMEN'S HEALTH These seeds are perhaps best known as a source of phytoestrogens (plant hormones) that can help relieve menopausal symptoms such as hot flushes, water retention, and anxiety. They are also a source of calcium and so can promote strong bones and teeth.

CARDIOVASCULAR HEALTH Contains vitamins C, B-complex, and K, and beta-carotene – all helpful in lowering high blood pressure, improving blood circulation, and reducing the risk of heart disease. Similar in taste to alfalfa seeds, red clover seeds are exclusively for sprouting, not for eating raw.

HOW DO I USE IT?

HEALTHY ADDITION Red clover sprouts add flavour and crunch to food without overloading it with calories. They are best eaten raw, but can be used to add a distinctive flavour to soups and stir-fries.

Sprout seeds for a concentrated source of nutrients all year round. You can sprout in almost any kind of container, but a glass jar with a sprouting mesh or muslin cloth on top enables easy rinsing and draining.

MEDICINAL HERBS

There are fewer distinctions between **culinary** and medicinal herbs than we sometimes think; in fact, most medicinal herbs can be incorporated into our daily diet. Their **healing benefits** are most concentrated as a **tincture** or **tea**; they are subtler when used in **smaller ratios** for cooking. Prolonged exposure to heat is not recommended for any herb, however, so add towards the end of cooking.

Astragalus

ASTRAGALUS

 HELPS IMPROVE ENERGY LEVELS

WHAT IS IT GOOD FOR?

IMMUNITY ENHANCER A tonic that can help raise your energy levels if you are feeling run down or are convalescing. Astragalus is also useful for enhancing the function and number of white blood cells and increasing resistance to viral infections, as it has natural antibiotic properties. It is full of antioxidants that protect cells against free-radical damage, and is a natural diuretic.

HOW DO I USE IT?

ADD TO SOUPS AND STOCKS Astragalus is a healthy ingredient in soups. Try combining 10–15g (¼–½oz) of the herb with shiitake mushrooms, onions, garlic, miso, and carrots, or use as a base for a stock in which to cook rice. To make a tea, steep 2 tsp fresh or 1 tsp dried herb in 175ml (6fl oz) of boiling water for 5 minutes.

Valerian root

VALERIAN ROOT

 HELPS CALM THE NERVES AND PROMOTE PEACEFUL SLEEP

WHAT IS IT GOOD FOR?

RELIEVES NERVOUS CONDITIONS Used to treat a variety of conditions including insomnia, anxiety, and nervous restlessness. Sometimes described as "nature's tranquillizer", it has been extensively researched in recent years. Test results suggest it works in a similar way to prescription tranquillizers by increasing gamma aminobutyric acid (GABA) – a substance that has a calming effect on the nervous system – in the brain. Other uses include treating digestive problems, nausea, liver problems, and urinary tract disorders.

HOW DO I USE IT?

TAKE AS A TEA Considered inedible raw, valerian root is best taken as a soothing hot tea; combine in equal parts with fresh ginger root as a good circulation booster too.

Chamomile

CHAMOMILE

 HAS NATURAL SEDATIVE PROPERTIES

WHAT IS IT GOOD FOR?

RESTORES CALM A classic remedy for anxiety and sleep disturbances. It is excellent for children, easing colic, teething, restlessness, and hyperactivity. Soothes gastrointestinal cramps, and also inflammation in mucous membranes and the skin. Its antibacterial action helps fight infection, while its sedating qualities benefit the immune system by helping to lower levels of immune-compromising stress hormones.

HOW DO I USE IT?

IN COOKING Its sweet, apple scent makes it a pleasant garnish for salads, rice, or fish dishes. Chop and add to butter or soured cream to top baked potatoes. For bread and cakes, replace the water with a chamomile infusion and add 3 tbsp each of dried chamomile and lavender flowers.

Schisandra

INVIGORATES THE MIND AND BODY

What Is It Good For?

RESPONDS TO THE BODY'S NEEDS An adaptogen, it stimulates or calms the body according to its needs. It can help improve physical, mental, or spiritual energy and is a renowned aphrodisiac for men and women.

It supports kidney and lung function and helps improve circulation, which in turn provides benefits for the heart and skin, and may help revive a poor memory and build stamina.

How Do I Use It?

SAVOURY AND SWEET A common ingredient in traditional Chinese and Korean cuisines. Add the berries to rice dishes, soups, vegetable patties, jellies, jams, and even drinks.

Schisandra

Marshmallow Root

HELPS HEAL STOMACH ULCERS

What Is It Good For?

SOOTHES IRRITATION Rich in mucilaginous (gum-like) fibre, it acts to soothe irritation and inflammation of the mucous membranes, stomach, and intestines. It may be particularly useful for gastric ulcers and irritable bowel syndrome. It can also help heal

respiratory and urinary disorders. Its mild laxative effect makes it useful for treating occasional constipation.

How Do I Use It?

DRINK IT Make into a medicinal drink: soak 30g (1oz) of root in 600ml (1 pint) of cold water overnight and strain. The liquid will be very viscous and may need further dilution. Drink small servings throughout the day.

Marshmallow root

Milk Thistle

SUPPORTS HEALTHY LIVER FUNCTION

What Is It Good For?

SUPPORTS THE LIVER A powerful antioxidant that helps heal the liver and support its ability to break down and metabolize fats and proteins. It is considered a good treatment for gall-bladder inflammation, and any premenstrual and menopausal

symptoms which are related to liver function. It can also help increase breast milk production.

How Do I Use It?

A SOOTHING BREW Grind 1 tsp of seeds in a coffee grinder and steep in 175ml (6fl oz) of boiling water for 5–10 minutes. Or peel fresh stalks, soak overnight to remove bitterness, boil until just tender, and add butter.

Milk thistle

St John's Wort

HELPS LIFT DEPRESSION

What Is It Good For?

FIGHTS DEPRESSION It can help treat mild-to-moderate, but not severe, depression. In many studies it has been shown to work as well as conventional antidepressants. It is also a remedy for seasonal

depression, PMS, and depression and anxiety in menopause. Less well known are the herb's antibacterial, anti-inflammatory and antiviral properties, which make it a useful wound healer when used externally.

How Do I Use It?

USE INSTEAD OF WATER Take as a tea or, like chamomile, substitute water with a strong infusion of the herb in baking or savoury broths and stocks.

St John's wort

CULINARY HERBS

Traditionally, culinary herbs were used not only to add subtle flavour but to **preserve** and **enhance** the **healthful properties** of foods; many have been shown to be concentrated sources of **antioxidants** and medicinal oils with **antibacterial** effects. Eaten regularly, herbs can work synergistically with other foods to boost health in many ways, including **enhancing digestive health** and **detoxification.**

Basil

Coriander

Parsley

BASIL

 AIDS HEALTHY/OPTIMAL DIGESTION

WHAT IS IT GOOD FOR?

EASES DIGESTION Basil fortifies the digestive and nervous systems, and can be a good remedy for headaches and insomnia. Eugenol, a constituent of the oil in the basil leaf, has an anti-inflammatory effect on joints and the digestive tract. It is also a mild diuretic. In addition, it contains a range of natural antioxidants, which can help protect body tissues against free-radical damage.

HOW DO I USE IT?

EAT FRESH Use fresh basil and wait until the last moment to add the leaves to a dish. Scatter over tomato salads, soups, and egg, rice, and mushroom dishes. Make a pesto sauce or put some fresh leaves into olive oil for a pungent salad dressing (don't worry if they turn black).

CORIANDER

 HELPS REMOVE TOXINS FROM THE BODY

WHAT IS IT GOOD FOR?

DETOXIFYING Also known as cilantro. Contains detoxifying, antibacterial, and immune-enhancing oils. Can help remove heavy metals from the body. It also aids digestion, fights nausea and stomach cramps, balances blood sugar levels, and is mildly laxative.

ANTIOXIDANT The plant's green tops contain a higher concentration of antioxidants – such as quercetin, kaempferol, and apigenin – than the seeds. These substances are known to have cancer-fighting properties.

HOW DO I USE IT?

DON'T COOK IT Cooking destroys coriander's flavour and essential oils. Use instead as a garnish on rice dishes, salsas, and stir-fries, or juice with celery, cucumber, and carrot in a juicer for a quick detox drink.

PARSLEY

 SUPPORTS HEALTHY KIDNEYS AND BLADDER

WHAT IS IT GOOD FOR?

DIURETIC AID Parsley has a diuretic action and is rich in antioxidants that can help relieve congestion and inflammation in the kidneys and bladder. It is also an effective treatment for constipation. It has numerous other medicinal uses, including as a general tonic for the body and as a digestive aid. It is also rich in vitamin K, which helps support healthy bones.

HOW DO I USE IT?

A VERSATILE ADDITION Stir into omelettes and vegetable and rice dishes, or mix with butter, spread on crusty bread, and grill briefly for a quick snack. Add to mashed potato, fish cakes, or meat patties. Chew at the end of a meal to aid digestion and sweeten the breath.

ROSEMARY

 HELPS FIGHT INFLAMMATION

WHAT IS IT GOOD FOR?

A NATURAL ANTISEPTIC Contains caffeic and rosmarinic acids, both potent antioxidant and anti-inflammatory agents that also have strong antiseptic properties. Its antioxidant action can help reduce inflammation, thereby helping to lower the risk of asthma, liver disease, and heart disease. If used in a tea or gargle, it can help fight gum disease and relieve sore throats. It also contains a number of volatile oils, which have a sedative effect that help calm the nerves and ease stomach upsets.

HOW DO I USE IT?

A MEDITERRANEAN STAPLE Use to infuse meats such as lamb before or as they cook, add to potatoes to be roasted, to vegetables such as green beans, peas, and mushrooms, or use to make flavourful salad oils and vinegars. You can even use rosemary to flavour custard. For a medicinal tea, brew 1 tsp dried or 2 tsp fresh rosemary in 175ml (6fl oz) of boiling water for 5 minutes.

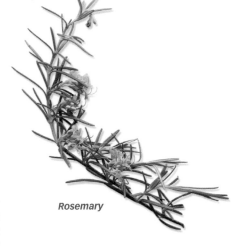

Rosemary

SAGE

 AIDS HORMONAL BALANCE

WHAT IS IT GOOD FOR?

WOMEN'S HEALTH Traditionally used to "normalize" the female reproductive system, sage is useful for helping to treat heavy or irregular periods and relieving menopausal symptoms. Eaten raw, it can also be effective in helping to treat rheumatic conditions, catarrh, excessive sweating, and stomach upsets. In laboratory tests, its antioxidants have shown potential for helping to improve memory and concentration levels in both healthy individuals and those with dementia. It also has a mild diuretic action.

HOW DO I USE IT?

MAKE SAGE HONEY Make a uniquely flavoured honey by packing a jar with fresh sage and covering with honey (both are antibacterial). Leave to infuse for 2–3 days or longer. Use in herbal teas and sweet dishes for a therapeutic boost. Add the fresh herb to salads, soups, and stuffings for rich meats, such as pork and goose. Make a seasoning by grinding dried sage leaves with coarse sea salt to use on almost any savoury dish.

Sage

Thyme

THYME

 HELPS FIGHT COLDS AND FLU

WHAT IS IT GOOD FOR?

A COLD REMEDY Can help loosen and expel mucous, making it a good choice if you have asthma, bronchitis, a cold, cough, flu, or sinus headache. A general tonic, antioxidant, and aid to digestion, it is also useful for treating colic in babies and excess gas in children and adults. Thymol, a constituent of thyme's essential oil, is an antibacterial that is effective against *Streptococcus mutans*, *E. coli*, *Staphalococcus aureus*, and *Bacillus subtilis*. When made into a tea, thyme can be used to treat sore throats and gum disease.

HOW DO I USE IT?

GREAT WITH MEAT Thyme is best used fresh in marinades, sauces, stocks, stuffings, and slow-cooked stews and casseroles. Its high iron content enriches the nutritional value of meat dishes and makes them more digestible. The crushed leaves make excellent herb oils and vinegars. For a medicinal tea, brew 1 tsp dried or 2 tsp fresh thyme in 175ml (6fl oz) of boiling water for 5 minutes.

CULINARY HERBS CONTINUED

Dill

DILL

 HAS A POWERFUL DIURETIC ACTION

WHAT IS IT GOOD FOR?

ANTIBACTERIAL Dill is a natural diuretic and antibacterial that can be effective against cystitis and bladder infections. Its essential oil constituents have a calming, anti-inflammatory effect on the digestive tract, which is why it has long been used as a treatment for stomach upsets and colic. Studies on animals suggest it may also have a useful role to play in helping to regulate blood sugar and cholesterol levels.

HOW DO I USE IT?

SPRINKLE LIBERALLY Both the seeds and fresh herb have similar benefits. The minty, aniseed flavour of fresh dill goes well with seafood, especially salmon, and makes a pleasant tea, or sprinkle on salads, new or baked potatoes, and steamed vegetables. Add the seeds to soups or casseroles, or sprinkle over vegetables and rice.

Mint

MINT

 SOOTHES STOMACH UPSETS

WHAT IS IT GOOD FOR?

RELIEVES INDIGESTION Menthol, the active oil in mint, is responsible for the antiseptic and antibacterial properties that make mint a good choice for relieving indigestion, irritable bowel syndrome, and soothing stomach upsets. Its adaptogenic properties mean it can help balance the body in whatever way is needed, so it can be both invigorating and mildly sedative. It also fortifies the nervous system and helps to relieve headaches.

HOW DO I USE IT?

ALL-ROUNDER It is a traditional sauce for lamb and helps aid digestion of the meat. Mix into dressings, or chutney or yogurt to serve with spicy foods like curries. Sprinkle over new potatoes or peas or, for a tasty salad, mix with cooked bulgur wheat. For tea, steep 1 tsp dried or 2 tsp fresh mint in 175ml (6fl oz) of boiling water for 5 minutes. Drink hot or cold.

Oregano

OREGANO

 PROTECTS AGAINST FREE-RADICAL DAMAGE

WHAT IS IT GOOD FOR?

ANTIBACTERIAL Contains the volatile oils thymol and carvacrol, which have an antioxidant effect, helping to protect against the oxidative stress caused by free radicals in the body. These volatile oils have been shown to also inhibit the growth of bacteria, including *Pseudomonas aeruginosa* and *Staphylococcus aureus*, as well as inhibiting the growth of the *Candida albicans* fungus. An analgesic, oregano can ease menstrual cramps and other abdominal pain. It is also a useful diuretic and appetite stimulant and helps clear mucous, so it can be helpful in cases of colds, flu, headaches, and respiratory illness.

HOW DO I USE IT?

A CLASSIC INGREDIENT Use in pasta sauces and salad dressings, in vegetable, fish, and chicken recipes, or in dishes with eggs and/or cheese. It is a good addition to stews, but add it towards the end of cooking to keep its beneficial oils and resins intact.

Tie a selection of herbs into a bouquet garni to flavour dishes while they cook, and remove the bundle before serving. The classic combination is thyme, parsley, and bay leaf, although you can add other herbs.

AMARANTH

HELPS LOWER CHOLESTEROL **SUPPORTS CELLULAR METABOLISM** **HELPS PROTECT AGAINST POLLUTION** **HELPS FIGHT INFLAMMATION**

Like buckwheat and quinoa, amaranth is actually the seed of a broad-leafed plant rather than a grass. It has been cultivated for 8,000 years, and was a staple of the Aztec diet. Today, both the grain and the leaves, which are high in **antioxidants**, are used in medicinal cooking as a source of **high-quality protein**, **cholesterol-lowering phytosterols**, and **anti-inflammatory phytochemicals**.

Grains
The grains contain phytosterols, plant hormones that help to lower cholesterol

Greens
Nutritionally similar to Swiss chard and spinach, but higher in calcium and 3 times higher in niacin, amaranth greens are worth seeking out in specialist Oriental shops

WHAT IS IT GOOD FOR?

HEART HEALTH Regular consumption of the seeds (or oil) can help reduce blood pressure and "unhealthy" (LDL) cholesterol levels, and improve immunity. Unlike other grains, it is not its fibrous content that protects the heart, but its levels of phytosterols and squalene.

TISSUE GROWTH AND REPAIR A good source of amino acids. In particular, it has good amounts of lysine, an essential amino acid found in limited amounts in other grains and plant sources. Amino acids are the building blocks for proteins in the body. They also aid metabolism and tissue growth and repair.

DETOX Squalene is a strong antioxidant that can help reduce the impact of toxic substances, such as pollution and industrial chemicals, on body systems. It can also improve the symptoms of chronic fatigue.

ANTI-INFLAMMATORY Contains lunasin, an anti-inflammatory substance. In addition to fighting inflammation, lunasin has been shown to halt the growth of cancer cells.

HOW DO I GET THE BEST FROM IT?

SPROUT IT The small size of the grains makes them fiddly and difficult to chew thoroughly; whether raw or cooked, a substantial number may pass undigested through the digestive tract with their nutrients unutilized. Instead, sprout them to get all their benefits.

USE THE LEAVES The leaves are a good source of vitamins K and C, iron, calcium, and folate.

HOW DO I USE IT?

ADD TO SALADS Add the sprouted amaranth grains to salads and sandwiches.

FOR BAKING Amaranth flour is gluten-free. On its own it is somewhat bitter, and most recipes recommend that amaranth should comprise no more than 10–15 per cent of the total weight of flour in any baked recipe.

QUINOA

HELPS PREVENT HARDENED ARTERIES

STRENGTHENS CONNECTIVE TISSUES

PROTECTS AGAINST FREE-RADICAL DAMAGE

EASY TO DIGEST AND GLUTEN-FREE

Easily digestible quinoa (pronounced keen-wah) grains are cooked in the same way as rice, and have a sweet, grassy flavour and texture. Quinoa is a complete **source of protein** and a **good source of anti-inflammatory**, **monounsaturated**, and **omega-3 fatty acids.** A heart-healthy grain, it is known to reduce "unhealthy" (LDL) cholesterol, and contains high levels of **antioxidants**.

WHAT IS IT GOOD FOR?

HEART HEALTH Unlike many other grains, quinoa contains oleic acid, a monounsaturated fatty acid and alpha-linolenic acid (ALA; an omega-3 fatty acid) in useful amounts. This combination can help to reduce "unhealthy" (LDL) cholesterol levels in the blood and fight inflammation that can lead to hardening of the arteries (atherosclerosis).

GOOD SOURCE OF PROTEIN Considered a complete protein because it contains all the essential amino acids; it is particularly high in lysine, important for tissue growth and repair.

ANTIOXIDANTS In addition to a spectrum of E vitamins including alpha-, beta-, gamma-, and delta-tocopherol, quinoa contains two antioxidant flavonoids, quercetin and kaempferol, which fight free radicals and are present in concentrations equal to or higher than high-flavonoid berries, such as cranberries.

DIGESTION Quinoa is easy to digest and doesn't contain gluten, making it suitable for anyone on a gluten-free diet.

HOW DO I GET THE BEST FROM IT?

WHOLE GRAIN The grains cook quickly, usually in 15 minutes, and are ready when translucent and the white germ on each grain has partially separated like a little white tail.

SPROUT IT Sprouting activates the beneficial enzymes in quinoa and boosts its nutrient content. Sprouted quinoa can be used in salads and sandwiches just like alfalfa sprouts.

HOW DO I USE IT?

INSTEAD OF RICE For a nutritious side dish, serve quinoa like pilau rice, cooked in stock and combined with vegetables. It is also good as a stuffing for marrows and peppers.

ENRICH YOUR BAKING Add cooked quinoa to muffins, breads, and even pancakes.

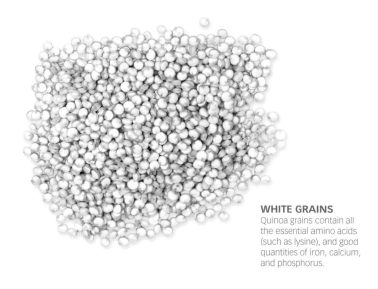

WHITE GRAINS
Quinoa grains contain all the essential amino acids (such as lysine), and good quantities of iron, calcium, and phosphorus.

RED GRAINS
The antioxidant pigment betacyanin, which also gives beetroots their colouring, is responsible for the bright red hue of this variety.

SPELT

 HELPS BALANCE BLOOD SUGAR LEVELS

 HELPS STRENGTHEN THE IMMUNE SYSTEM

 EASY TO DIGEST

An ancient variety of wheat with a subtle sweet, nutty flavour, spelt has a tough outer husk that makes it difficult to process. However, this protective husk helps the grain maintain its nutrient value. It is **high in fibre**, **B vitamins**, and **minerals** such as copper, iron, zinc, magnesium, and phosphorus. It also contains more **protein** than conventional wheat, and is highly **water-soluble** and **easier to digest**.

GRAINS
Spelt is a good source of B vitamins and certain minerals, and is higher in protein than conventional wheat.

SPROUTED SPELT
Sprouting breaks down indigestible starches into more easily digested sugars.

FLOUR
Though the reasons are not fully understood, some people sensitive to conventional wheat find they can tolerate spelt.

WHAT IS IT GOOD FOR?

METABOLIC SYNDROME Spelt and whole spelt flour offer more soluble fibre than both standard and durum wheat flours. Soluble fibre is particularly beneficial for lowering "unhealthy" (LDL) cholesterol and regulating blood sugar levels.

IMMUNITY It is higher in niacin (B3) than conventional wheat. Like other B vitamins, niacin aids in energy metabolism. It has additional functions, including antibacterial properties that help strengthen the body against disease. It also supports the adrenal glands and helps improve circulation.

DIGESTION Spelt is easily soluble in water and contains less gluten than conventional wheat, making it easier to digest. However, as spelt contains gluten, it is not suitable for coeliacs.

HOW DO I GET THE BEST FROM IT?

WHOLE GRAIN Add the whole grain to soups and stews in the same way you would barley, or cook it on its own as an alternative to rice.

FLOUR Spelt flour can be used wherever wheat flour is indicated, though its high water-solubility means you may need to use less liquid than with conventional flours. You can also buy sprouted spelt flour.

SPROUT IT Spelt sprouts are high in vitamins E, C, and B, phosphorus, magnesium, iron, calcium, amino acids, and protein. Select hulled spelt for sprouting.

HOW DO I USE IT?

SPELT RISOTTO Whole grains can be cooked on their own and used as a side dish or combined with vegetables, fresh herbs, and Parmesan cheese to make a risotto.

SPELT PASTA Pasta made from spelt is a delicious alternative to durum wheat pasta, and because of its easy digestibility it may leave you feeling less bloated.

RICE

 **HELPS LOWER CHOLESTEROL**

 **PROTECTS AGAINST COLON CANCER**

 **HELPS RELEASE CELLULAR ENERGY**

 **RELIEVES MENOPAUSAL SYMPTOMS**

Rice is a near-perfect food, and the predominant staple food for around half the world's population. This cholesterol-lowering food is is available in many varieties and colours and is a good source of thiamine, riboflavin, niacin, and **dietary fibre**. Certain rice varieties help to maintain stable **blood sugar levels**. Rice bran may also help to lower the risk of **bowel cancer**.

WHAT IS IT GOOD FOR?

LOWERS CHOLESTEROL The fatty acid content in whole brown rice has cholesterol-lowering properties. It is also rich in magnesium, which has been shown to lower the risk of diabetes.

HEALTHY GUT Brown rice contains fibre and selenium, which help protect the gut. Fibre helps remove waste products efficiently from the body, while the trace mineral selenium has been shown to substantially reduce the risk of colon cancer.

ENERGY RELEASE Rich in manganese, a trace mineral that helps produce energy from protein and carbohydrates. It is also involved in the synthesis of fatty acids, which are important for a healthy nervous system.

HORMONE BALANCE The phytosterols in rice bran oil have been shown to help relieve menopausal symptoms, such as hot flushes.

HOW DO I GET THE BEST FROM IT?

CHOOSE BY COLOUR White rice is nutrient-poor, but brown rice is an all-round healthy choice. Its minimal processing preserves the grain's nutritional value and healthy oils, much of which concentrates in the bran. Deeply coloured red or black rice has been proven to actively reduce the progress of atherosclerosis (hardening of the arteries).

RICE BRAN OIL This versatile oil is high in monounsaturates and contains the antioxidant y-oryzanol, as well as a range of tocopherols (the vitamin E family) and phytosterols (plant hormones). Heating does not appear to destroy its constituents. Use rice bran oil for cooking, marinades, and dressings.

HOW DO I USE IT?

EXOTIC COCONUT RICE Boil brown rice and grated fresh root ginger in unsweetened coconut milk and water. Serve garnished with finely chopped fresh coriander.

BROWN RICE
This minimally processed rice is one of the most nutritionally dense varieties.

WHITE RICE
Milled or polished white rice has had its hull and bran removed. It is a good source of protein, but most of its other nutrients are removed with the hull.

WILD RICE
Although not a true rice, wild rice is eaten just like one. It contains twice the amount of zinc and 8 times the amount of vitamin E as brown rice.

RED RICE
This variety has the highest iron and zinc content of all commercially available rice. Red rice contains a variety of anthocyanins that give its bran a red or deep purple colour.

BULGUR WHEAT

 **HELPS FIGHT INFLAMMATION**

 **PROMOTES BOWEL REGULARITY**

 **HELPS BUILD STRONG BONES**

 **HELPS BALANCE BLOOD SUGAR LEVELS**

Bulgur wheat is a low-fat whole grain **rich in dietary fibre**. It aids digestion, acts as an **anti-inflammatory**, and **protects against cholesterol** and **gallstones**. It has a characteristic crumbly texture, produced by pre-cooking, drying, and crushing whole grains, often from several varieties of wheat. This process prevents bulgur wheat, one of the world's earliest processed grains, from spoiling.

Wheat berries
In a process discovered 4,000 years ago, wheat berries are par-boiled, dried, and ground to produce bulgur wheat grains

Grains
Bulgur wheat is rich in manganese and magnesium, which help keep inflammation at bay and maintain metabolic balance. The grain is a healthy "fast food" that can be prepared in just 20 minutes

WHAT IS IT GOOD FOR?

ANTI-INFLAMMATORY The antioxidant betaine in bulgur wheat is a potent anti-inflammatory. Regular consumption of betaine-rich foods can help prevent the inflammation of joints and arteries by as much as 20 per cent.

DIGESTION AND CONSTIPATION High in insoluble fibre, which promotes bowel regularity, and aids the production of butyric acid, which fuels cells that maintain a healthy colon. The carbohydrates in bulgur wheat are absorbed slowly, helping to maintain steady blood sugar levels.

STRONG BONES Around half of all dietary magnesium is required for building healthy bones. As a result, this mineral needs to be constantly replaced and bulgur wheat is a good natural source. Magnesium also relaxes nerves and muscles and maintains the cardiovascular system.

METABOLIC BALANCE High in manganese, a trace mineral with an anti-inflammatory, antioxidant effect essential for most body systems. It supports healthy bones, maintains normal blood sugar levels, helps the body form tissue, and balances sex hormones.

HOW DO I GET THE BEST FROM IT?

A BETTER FAST FOOD Unlike many types of grain, bulgur wheat is quick to prepare. It is a fantastic alternative to rice and potatoes and can be a better choice than a sandwich to maintain energy throughout the day.

HOW DO I USE IT?

BOOST YOUR BREAD Enrich a bread recipe by substituting 75g (2½oz) of flour with the same amount of reconstituted bulgur wheat.

IN A SALAD Mix cooked bulgur wheat, puy lentils, sliced spring onions, radishes, and tomatoes, cumin, and mint and coriander leaves. Toss in an olive oil and lime dressing.

OATS

HAS NATURAL SEDATIVE PROPERTIES   **EASY TO DIGEST**   **HELPS CONTROL INSULIN SECRETION**   **HELPS LOWER CHOLESTEROL**

Long before we relied on an instant bowl of sugary cereal, breakfast often meant porridge cooked with oats; they can also be used in healthy cereals, snacks, biscuits, and breads. Oats contain **multiple nutrients** and a gummy, **water-soluble fibre**, beta-glucan, which helps **reduce "unhealthy" (LDL) cholesterol**. They are also known to be a **natural sedative**, and excellent for **easing indigestion**.

WHAT IS IT GOOD FOR?

SOOTHES NERVES Oats contain the alkaloid gramine, a natural sedative, which can treat depression, anxiety, and insomnia without side effects. Tea made from oat straw is a traditional remedy for anxiety and insomnia.

DIGESTION Oats are easy to digest and useful in diets for convalescents and for easing upset stomachs. The fact that oats contain more soluble fibre than any other grain also means that they are digested more slowly, creating an extended sensation of fullness.

DIABETES As well helping to prevent big spikes in blood sugar levels, the beta-glucan fibre has beneficial effects for diabetics. Useful amounts of magnesium in the grain also help regulate insulin secretion.

REDUCES CHOLESTEROL Oats, oat bran, and oatmeal contain a specific type of fibre known as beta-glucan, which can quickly help lower "unhealthy" (LDL) cholesterol levels. Studies show that including just 60–85g (2–3oz) of oats a day in a low-fat diet can reduce LDL cholesterol by 8–23 per cent. In addition, avenanthramides, antioxidant compounds unique to oats, help prevent free radicals from damaging LDL cholesterol, thus reducing the risk of cardiovascular disease.

HOW DO I GET THE BEST FROM IT?

RAW AND COOKED Oats deliver benefits whether eaten raw or cooked.

OAT MILK Made from soaked oat groats, this is a nutritious alternative to dairy milk.

HOW DO I USE IT?

BREW A TEA You can buy oat straw to make a soothing tea for adults and children.

SPROUTED OAT PORRIDGE Use sprouted oats and combine with chopped walnuts, dried fruit, such as raisins or dates, a little cinnamon, and a drizzle of maple syrup.

OAT STRAW
The immature tops of the oat plant can be dried to make a soothing tea that calms the nerves.

WHOLE OATS (FLATTENED)
Oats contain more soluble fibre than any other grain.

OAT GROATS
Oat groats are the hulled grains of oats.

OAT MILK
Oat milk naturally contains more calcium than cow's milk.

RYE

 REGULATES APPETITE AND BLOOD SUGAR

 PROMOTES A HEALTHY DIGESTIVE TRACT

 HELPS KEEP BLOOD VESSELS SUPPLE

A hardy, cold-climate grain, rye berries (also known as rye seeds) are a rich and versatile **source of dietary fibre**, especially arabinoxylan, which helps to **balance blood sugar levels** and **lower "unhealthy" (LDL) cholesterol**. They are also **nutrient-dense**, supplying high levels of iron, calcium, potassium, zinc, vitamin E, a variety of B vitamins, and an array of **antioxidant compounds**.

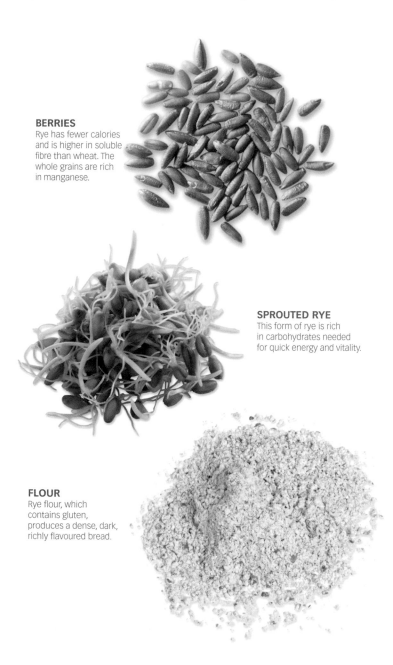

BERRIES
Rye has fewer calories and is higher in soluble fibre than wheat. The whole grains are rich in manganese.

SPROUTED RYE
This form of rye is rich in carbohydrates needed for quick energy and vitality.

FLOUR
Rye flour, which contains gluten, produces a dense, dark, richly flavoured bread.

WHAT IS IT GOOD FOR?

BLOOD SUGAR REGULATION A type of fibre in rye, arabinoxylan helps balance blood sugar levels, reducing the risk of type-2 diabetes and heart disease. Wholegrain rye bread is the best way of providing this fibre. It also regulates the appetite more effectively than wheat bread, and reduces the signs of inflammation more effectively than potato or wheat bread in people with metabolic syndrome (which can lead to diabetes and heart disease).

DIGESTION Contains mucilaginous (gum-like) fibre, which helps to lubricate the digestive tract and ease gastritis and stomach pain. Its lubricating action is also good for maintaining healthy skin and mucous membranes.

HEART HEALTH Its soluble fibre helps to maintain the elasticity of blood vessels, so lessening the risk of atherosclerosis (hardening of the arteries) and hypertension.

METABOLIC SIGNALLING Studies show that rye can actually switch off certain genes involved in metabolic syndrome, including those that regulate insulin, stress response, and overactive immune response.

HOW DO I GET THE BEST FROM IT?

SWITCH TO RYE BREAD Rye bread is a superb dietary aid, helping you feel fuller for longer and ensuring a steady supply of energy.

DRINK IT To make a mildly laxative and energizing drink, boil 2 tbsp of rye berries in 1 litre (1¾ pints) of water for 10 minutes. Allow to cool, then strain and add honey and lemon juice to taste.

HOW DO I USE IT?

RYE FLOUR Rye flour can be used for pancakes, muffins, and drop scones. Use it just as you would use wheat flour, or mix it 50:50 with wheat flour for a lighter result.

MILLET

 HELPS PROMOTE PEACEFUL SLEEP

 **HELPS PREVENT METABOLIC SYNDROME**

 HELPS PREVENT GALLSTONES

Once a staple grain of Africa and India, today millet ranks as the sixth most important grain in the world and sustains around one-third of the global population. It is a **nutritious**, **non-acid-forming** grain considered to be one of the **least allergenic** and **most digestible** grains available. It is **high in protein**, fibre, B-complex vitamins, iron, magnesium, phosphorus, and potassium.

WHAT IS IT GOOD FOR?

PEACEFUL SLEEP Contains substantial amounts of tryptophan, an amino acid that can help induce a good night's sleep.

CONTROLLING METABOLIC SYNDROME The B vitamins in millet, especially niacin (B3), can help lower "unhealthy" (LDL) cholesterol, while magnesium helps lower blood pressure and reduces the risk of heart attack, especially in people with atherosclerosis (hardening of the arteries) or diabetes. It also helps reduce the severity of asthma and the frequency of migraine attacks. Its high fibre content helps increase insulin sensitivity and reduce levels of blood fats (lipids).

HELPS PREVENT GALLSTONES Evidence shows that eating foods (such as millet) high in insoluble fibre can help prevent gallstones. Insoluble fibre helps to reduce the secretion of bile acids, excessive amounts of which contribute to the formation of gallstones.

HOW DO I GET THE BEST FROM IT?

UNHULLED MILLET Usually sold with the largely indigestible hull removed. Hulled millet can be used like any other grain.

A LITTLE PREPARATION Pre-soaking millet shortens its cooking time. Its flavour can be enhanced by lightly roasting the grains in a dry pan before cooking; stir for 3 minutes or until you detect a mild, nutty aroma.

SPROUT IT Millet can also be sprouted to use in salads and sandwiches. Soak the raw, untoasted grains for about 30 minutes, drain, and keep moist until they begin to sprout.

HOW DO I USE IT?

A BETTER BREAKFAST Millet can form the basis of a nutritional porridge. Serve with dried fruit and sliced almonds.

IN A SALAD Use cooked millet instead of rice or pasta in salads to add flavour and nutrition.

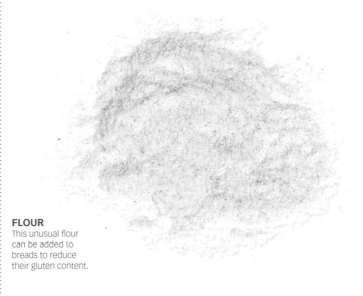

FLOUR
This unusual flour can be added to breads to reduce their gluten content.

WHOLE GRAINS
Millet seeds are antioxidant-rich and especially high in magnesium, necessary for maintaining healthy nerve and muscle function.

BARLEY

 HELPS FEED BACTERIA IN THE GUT

HELPS LOWER CHOLESTEROL

HELPS BALANCE BLOOD SUGAR LEVELS

Barley is a grain with a number of fantastic medicinal properties. Thanks to its **high fibre content**, it is great for **improving digestion** and **lowering cholesterol**, while its low glycemic index is one of a number of its properties that helps to **improve blood sugar levels** and **reduce the risk of diabetes**. It is also versatile, and can be served instead of rice, added to casseroles, or used in baking.

GRAINS
Studies show that wholegrain barley can help to maintain steady blood sugar levels for up to 10 hours after consumption – much longer than wholegrain wheat.

GRASS
Barley grass is an easily digested green food sprouted from barley seeds.

WHAT IS IT GOOD FOR?

DIGESTION AND CONSTIPATION Barley grain has a very high fibre content. One portion provides nearly half the daily recommended amount. Barley fibre feeds good bacteria in the gut, which in turn produce butyric acid, the primary fuel for intestinal cells, necessary for maintaining a healthy colon. In addition, barley grass juice has been shown to improve the symptoms of ulcerative colitis.

HEART HEALTH The high levels of soluble fibre in barley help to remove excess fat and cholesterols from the bloodstream, lowering the risk of hypertension and atherosclerosis (hardening of the arteries).

MANAGING BLOOD SUGAR Barley is a slow-release carbohydrate that helps maintain steady blood sugar levels. In addition, barley is abundant in magnesium and manganese, both of which are necessary for carbohydrate metabolism.

HOW DO I GET THE BEST FROM IT?

WHOLE BARLEY When selecting barley, choose whole barley, or pot barley, rather than pearl barley. The husk, which contains much of the grain's nutrients, remains intact in whole barley.

BARLEY GRASS To get the best from the antioxidants in barley grass, juice the young shoots when they are 3–7 days old.

HOW DO I USE IT?

BARLEY RISOTTO Don't simply add barley to casseroles. Whole barley grains make an excellent risotto; the sweet taste of the grain works especially well with mushrooms.

ENRICH YOUR BAKING Barley is low in gluten so use it in baking. Substitute up to half the quantity of regular wheat flour for barley flour. As well as reducing the gluten content, it adds extra flavour and texture.

BUCKWHEAT

 **PROTECTS THE HEART AND BLOOD VESSELS**

 **EASY TO DIGEST**

 **HELPS MAINTAIN ENERGY LEVELS**

Buckwheat is not a true cereal, but is instead related to rhubarb, sorrel, and dock. The grain contains both insoluble and soluble fibre, which help to **lower "unhealthy" (LDL) cholesterol**, **balance blood sugar levels**, and keep the **gut healthy**. Buckwheat is also rich in **antioxidant** flavonoids that help **protect the heart**, and is ideal for **gluten-free** diets, as it doesn't contain gluten.

WHAT IS IT GOOD FOR?

CIRCULATORY SYSTEM Contains important antioxidant flavonoids: quercetin, thought to have anti-inflammatory and anti-allergic properties; and rutin, which strengthens the capillaries and improves circulation, and can help protect against painful varicose veins.

DIGESTION AND CONSTIPATION Its gum-like mucilaginous fibre is lubricating and soothing to the digestive tract. Buckwheat also contains a type of indigestible fibre that acts like a prebiotic, feeding helpful bacteria in the gut.

ENERGY BALANCE The grain contains slow-release carbohydrates that help maintain steady blood sugar levels. It is abundant in magnesium and manganese, both of which are necessary for carbohydrate metabolism.

ANTI-CANCER Like most whole grains, it contains plant hormones called lignans, which can promote hormone balance in both men and women. One lignan, enterolactone, has been shown to protect against breast and other hormone-dependent cancers.

HOW DO I GET THE BEST FROM IT?

BUCKWHEAT SPROUTS Soak raw, untoasted seeds for 30 minutes, drain, and keep moist until they begin to sprout. (Toasted buckwheat has a golden brown colour, whereas raw buckwheat is white or light green.)

BUCKWHEAT FLOUR The flour is gluten-free and can be used in baking. Dark-coloured buckwheat flour contains the husk and a greater proportion of protein than the light flour, while sprouted buckwheat flour is even more nutrient-rich.

HOW DO I USE IT?

MAKE A PORRIDGE Soak and sprout the seeds to release their mucilaginous fibre and use to make "porridge" by combining with yogurt or nut milk and fruit.

GRAIN
Buckwheat contains 8 essential amino acids required by the body, as well as high proportions of manganese, magnesium, and fibre.

SPROUTS
Sprouting the grain makes its nutrients more available to the body and activates enzymes, which lower blood pressure.

PULSES

 **PROMOTES BOWEL REGULARITY**

 PROTECTS THE HEART AND BLOOD VESSELS

HELPS BUILD STRONG BONES

Including more pulses in your diet is a terrific way to **maintain digestive health**, **lower cholesterol levels**, and **regulate blood sugar levels** as they contain **protein** and **fibre**. Most pulses are good sources of **iron**, an integral component of red blood cells that transport oxygen from the lungs to every cell in the body. Pulses are also an excellent choice if you want to cut back on your meat intake.

Adzuki beans

ADZUKI BEANS

WHAT IS IT GOOD FOR?

HEART HEALTH Rich in soluble fibre, which is absorbed during digestion and helps maintain "healthy" (HDL) cholesterol levels in the blood. The beans contain potassium and magnesium, which are good for regulating blood pressure and improving blood flow, and essential B vitamins including B6, B2, B1, B3, and folate – all necessary for the cellular energy production that fuels metabolism. Also a good source of the trace element molybdenum, which aids liver detoxification.

HOW DO I USE IT?

ADZUKI BEAN PATTIES Combine cooked adzuki beans with rice, egg, garlic, onion, and fresh herbs; form into patties and shallow fry. Or add the beans to casseroles or soups for extra fibre, protein, and flavours, or sprout them and add to salads.

Black beans

BLACK BEANS

WHAT IS IT GOOD FOR?

BLOOD HEALTH Black beans are abundant in both iron and the trace element molybdenum. Iron is essential for carrying oxygen to our red blood cells, and for the production of haemoglobin, a primary component of red blood cells. Molybdenum is essential for healthy liver function and is a key component in chemical reactions that release iron in the body. In addition, the beans are a good source of fibre to help cleanse and protect the colon.

HOW DO I USE IT?

BLACK BEAN SALAD Mix cooked black beans, orange segments, sliced red onion, and cumin seeds with an oil and vinegar dressing. Eating pulses with vitamin-C-rich foods increases iron absorption, as the type of iron (non-haem) in plants is harder to absorb than iron in meat (haeme).

Butter beans

BUTTER BEANS

WHAT IS IT GOOD FOR?

BLOOD AND TISSUE HEALTH A milder, creamier relative of the broad bean, butter beans are a good source of potassium, iron, copper, manganese, and soluble fibre – all essential for a healthy cardiovascular system and digestive tract. They also contain molybdenum, which promotes liver health, and are high in tryptophan, an amino acid, and protein, which is necessary for building and repairing tissue and muscle in the body.

HOW DO I USE IT?

BUTTER BEAN HUMMUS Blitz cooked butter beans with sautéed onion and garlic, and lemon juice in a food processor or blender. Gradually add enough extra virgin olive oil until the mix reaches a thick but smooth consistency. Season to taste and serve.

CHICKPEAS

WHAT IS IT GOOD FOR?

BONE HEALTH Beyond their fibre content, chickpeas may also be good for bone health. They are rich in manganese, which helps build bones and is necessary for healthy bone structure, and calcium, phosphorus, and magnesium, which are also vital bone-healthy minerals. The fibre in chickpeas has been shown to help reduce levels of "unhealthy" (LDL) cholesterol and help regulate appetite and reduce food cravings.

HOW DO I USE IT?

CHICKPEA GAZPACHO Add chickpeas to gazpacho for a more satisfying dish. The antioxidant lycopene, found in abundance in tomatoes, also works synergistically with chickpeas to reduce oxidative stress (caused by free radicals in the body) on bones.

Chickpeas

KIDNEY BEANS

WHAT IS IT GOOD FOR?

DIGESTION AND BOWEL REGULARITY Kidney beans contain both soluble and insoluble fibre. Soluble fibre can help lower "unhealthy" (LDL) cholesterol; insoluble fibre helps to promote good digestive health and bowel regularity. Also high in blood-building iron, phosphorus – a co-factor in maintaining healthy bones and teeth – and vitamin K, which helps protect the nervous system from free-radical damage and may even have an anti-cancer effect.

HOW DO I USE IT?

RICE AND BEANS Cooked rice and kidney beans make a complete protein meal. Add sautéed chopped onion, garlic, peppers, and tomatoes and season with chilli powder, fresh coriander, thyme, salt, and black pepper to taste.

Kidney beans

LENTILS

WHAT IS IT GOOD FOR?

CARDIOVASCULAR HEALTH Lentils of all types are extremely high in molybdenum and iron, making them an excellent food for helping to oxygenate the blood and aid the release of cellular energy. The insoluble fibre they contain also helps to keep cholesterol at healthy levels. Lentils are also rich in vitamin B1 (thiamine), which helps to regulate the nervous system and maintain a steady heartbeat.

HOW DO I USE IT?

SPROUT IT Dried lentils are deficient in 2 essential amino acids, methionine and cysteine. However, sprouting them increases their levels of all amino acids, including these 2, and produces a food that is a complete protein in its own right.

Red lentils

MUNG BEANS

WHAT IS IT GOOD FOR?

DETOXIFICATION Green mung beans have long been used in traditional Chinese and Indian medicine to keep the body running smoothly due to their detoxifying properties and anti-inflammatory benefits. Mung beans are also rich in fibre and isoflavones and phytosterols (plant hormones) that can help lower cholesterol. In addition, they contain a useful amount of potassium, which can help lower blood pressure.

HOW DO I USE IT?

AS BEAN SPROUTS The beans can be added to stews, but they are usually eaten as bean sprouts. A staple of Chinese cooking, they can be added to any stir-fry, salad, or sandwich.

Mung beans

SPICES

Made from the bark, root, bud, or berry of a plant, spices are generally used **dried** rather than fresh, which means their **essential oil** content is highly concentrated and they have a more **pungent** taste. Research into many common spices has found that they possess **powerful antioxidant** and **antibiotic** qualities, and benefit **digestive health**.

Cardamom

CARDAMOM

 HELPS CLEAR CONGESTION

WHAT IS IT GOOD FOR?

METABOLIC BOOSTER A volatile oil constituent called cineol in cardamom can help break up chest congestion, making the spice a good choice for treating bronchitis, laryngitis, and colds. An effective digestive stimulant and diuretic, cardamom boosts the metabolism and helps the body burn fat more efficiently. It is also effective against *H. pylori*, the bacterium that causes ulcers. Studies also show it can help maintain healthy circulation and prevent the free-radical damage that can lead to stroke and atherosclerosis.

HOW DO I USE IT?

USE WHOLE SEEDS Buy the pods or whole green or bleached white seeds to use, lightly crushed, in rice dishes, curries, and meat stews. Freshly ground cardamom can give a surprisingly tangy lift to an everyday fruit salad. It can also be infused in milk to settle the stomach or to make a spicy custard or rice pudding.

CINNAMON

 HELPS BALANCE BLOOD SUGAR LEVELS

WHAT IS IT GOOD FOR?

ANTISEPTIC Cinnamon is a digestive aid that helps normalize levels of both glucose and triglycerides (a type of fat) in the blood, reducing the risk of diabetes and heart disease. It is also a first-class antiseptic that can help fight bacteria, viruses, and fungal infections. It is rich in antioxidants, which give it a mild analgesic and anti-inflammatory effect, and perhaps this is why it was traditionally used to aid recovery from colds and flu, sore throats, fevers, and headaches. Just smelling cinnamon is said to boost cognitive function and memory.

HOW DO I USE IT?

A VERSATILE FLAVOUR For a quick pick-me-up, use a cinnamon stick to stir tea, hot chocolate, or milky coffee. It is equally nice grated or crumbled into savoury dishes, such as stews, stuffings, vegetable bakes, pickles, and relishes as it is added to sweet dishes, such as stewed fruits, pies, and rice or milk puddings.

Cinnamon

Aromatherapy in your kitchen

Like all plant products, spices contain a wealth of vitamins, minerals, and trace elements. Unlike fresh herbs, spices are generally used in their dried form, and since we use dried spices in such minute amounts in cooking, we benefit less from these nutrients than we do their powerful essential oils, which are highly concentrated. If stored properly – in airtight containers away from light – spices can keep their beneficial properties for a very long time. Wherever possible, buy spices whole and grind or crush them as needed: their aroma will be stronger and their active ingredients more potent.

CORIANDER

 STIMULATES APPETITE AND AIDS DIGESTION

WHAT IS IT GOOD FOR?

LOWERS CHOLESTEROL Valued in traditional Ayurvedic medicine for its anti-inflammatory properties, modern research shows that coriander has cholesterol-lowering effects. It can stimulate appetite, help increase the secretion of gastric juices, and aid digestion. It is also a diuretic and an antibacterial shown to be effective against salmonella, *E. coli*, and MRSA. Recent studies suggest that the antioxidants in coriander may also have a role to play in protecting the nervous system from free-radical damage. This can help to lower the risk of neurodegenerative illnesses, such as Alzheimer's and Parkinson's diseases.

HOW DO I USE IT?

AN EVERYDAY SPICE The seeds can be used in curries, chutneys, stews, soups, rubs, and marinades. They blend well with smoked meats, game, and even fish. Ground coriander seeds also add an extra dimension to breads, desserts, and sweet pastries.

Coriander

CUMIN

 RICH IN ANTI-INFLAMMATORY ANTIOXIDANTS

WHAT IS IT GOOD FOR?

A POWERFUL ANTIOXIDANT A good general tonic, cumin is also antiseptic and antibacterial, and can help to improve blood circulation. It helps fortify the digestive tract, relieving nausea, bloating, and constipation. Laboratory tests suggest its antioxidant oil content can inhibit the growth of cancer cells. Ordinary cumin seeds are brown in colour and contain many beneficial properties. However, black cumin seeds, known as "black seed", have a much higher concentration of these medicinal oils.

HOW DO I USE IT?

USE THE WHOLE SEED Buy the whole seeds and use in pickles or preserves. Add the ground seeds to rubs or marinades, or make a spicy Eastern-style salad with tomatoes, green peppers, courgettes, and/or aubergines and sprinkle a little ground cumin on top.

Cumin

FENUGREEK

 SOOTHES AND PROTECTS THE GUT

WHAT IS IT GOOD FOR?

A METABOLIC BOOST The seeds are a good source of mucilaginous (gum-like) fibre that soothes and protects the digestive tract from free-radical damage. A tonic and antioxidant, fenugreek can also help boost the metabolism, and it is also a traditional remedy for stimulating the production of breast milk. The seeds are rich in diosgenin, a plant oestrogen that may boost women's vitality during the menopause by easing symptoms including hot flushes, anxiety, and insomnia. In laboratory tests, diosgenin has also demonstrated anti-cancer effects.

HOW DO I USE IT?

ADD SOME SPICE The seeds have a strong aroma that lifts pickles, dahls, curries, and vegetable and rice dishes. They can be sprouted like bean sprouts and used as a vegetable. A tea made from the seeds mixed with honey and lemon can help soothe flu-like symptoms.

Fenugreek

SPICES CONTINUED

Juniper

Liquorice

Nutmeg

JUNIPER

 HELPS STIMULATE INSULIN SECRETION

WHAT IS IT GOOD FOR?

A DIABETIC AID Stimulates insulin release, making it a useful aid if you are diabetic. It can also support and, where there has been no permanent damage, help to heal the pancreas. Traditionally, it has been used as a digestive aid, and an antiseptic for treating urinary infections and water retention. Chewing the berries is a traditional remedy for inflamed and infected gums. Essential oils in the berries contain active compounds that help to clear uric acid from the body, making it useful for rheumatic conditions such as gout.

HOW DO I USE IT?

USE THE FRESH BERRIES Crush the berries lightly and add to meat and game recipes. Combined with garlic and sea salt, they add a wonderful flavour to cabbage and other green vegetables. The fresh berries can also be used in stuffings, sauces, marinades, and pâtés.

LIQUORICE

 HELPS FIGHT BACTERIAL AND VIRAL INFECTIONS

WHAT IS IT GOOD FOR?

METABOLIC STIMULANT Its anti-diabetic and antioxidant properties aid the treatment of metabolic syndrome (a group of risk factors that can lead to diabetes and heart disease). It can help support liver health, and is an antiseptic that helps to calm the stomach. It is also an expectorant and decongestant that can help fight respiratory infections. There is some evidence that liquorice in small amounts can be used to decrease sugar cravings. In addition, it can be used as a treatment for cases of low blood pressure.

HOW DO I USE IT?

MAKE A TEA Boil the root to make a tea if you are feeling nauseous or starting a cold. Liquorice tea is also good for maintaining dental health; try garling with the tea once cooled. Liquorice and soy sauce, which marry well together, help counter the effects of stress and give a deep, delicious flavour to Oriental dishes.

NUTMEG

 FIGHTS THE EFFECTS OF STRESS

WHAT IS IT GOOD FOR?

HELPS YOU ADAPT As an adaptogen, it can be both a stimulant and a sedative, according to the body's needs. In times of stress, it can help lower blood pressure. Conversely, it can lift your mood and acts as a tonic and stimulant, making it beneficial if you are convalescing or over-tired. It is also a digestive that can soothe stomach-aches, ease wind, and help stop diarrhoea. Its volatile oils have anti-inflammatory properties that make it useful for treating joint and muscle pain. In traditional Indian medicine, it is used to calm respiratory problems such as asthma.

HOW DO I USE IT?

THE ORIGINAL COMFORT FOOD A great addition to cooking when you feel stressed. Use in milk and rice puddings and in white or cheese sauces. It can also transform mashed potatoes and other vegetable dishes. Sprinkle or grate over hot chocolate or warm milk for a quick pick-me-up.

PEPPERCORNS

 STIMULATES APPETITE AND AIDS DIGESTION

WHAT IS IT GOOD FOR?

DIGESTIVE AID Pepper aids digestion and stimulates the appetite. It has antioxidant and anti-inflammatory properties and is traditionally used to aid detoxification, ease lung and bronchial infections, and relieve shock and stress. In laboratory tests, piperine, a compound found in peppercorns, halted the growth of breast cancer cells. True peppers are green, black or white; pink "peppercorns" are actually from an unrelated species and do not have the same health benefits.

HOW DO I USE IT?

USE THE WHOLE SPICE Always buy whole peppercorns and grind as required; if pre-ground, they quickly lose their active properties. Use in stocks and marinades and grind liberally over hot vegetable dishes and salads. Crush the peppercorns roughly and use to completely coat meat before grilling, or add to oil and vinegar for a spicy dressing.

Pepper

SAFFRON

 FIGHTS AGE-RELATED VISION LOSS

WHAT IS IT GOOD FOR?

A POTENT ANTIOXIDANT Saffron is actually the dried stigmas of the saffron crocus. It contains the potent antioxidants crocin, safranal, and picrocrocin, which can help delay age-related macular degeneration (loss of vision), help prevent hardening of the arteries (atherosclerosis) and inhibit the growth of cancer cells. Taken in tea or milk, it can help treat insomnia and may help lift depression. Its anti-inflammatory properties may be helpful in treating asthma and allergies, and as a stimulant it can help improve the circulation.

HOW DO I USE IT?

USE SPARINGLY Saffron is expensive, but a little goes a long way. Use it to flavour and colour dishes such as paella, risotto, bouillabaisse, spicy lamb, chicken dishes, and even sweet desserts. Mixed with garlic, thyme, and oil it makes an excellent marinade for fish. Saffron can also be used in bread and cake baking.

Saffron

STAR ANISE

 PROTECTS AGAINST COLDS AND FLU

WHAT IS IT GOOD FOR?

ANTIVIRAL Although traditionally used to ease wind, hiccups, and water retention, star anise excels in helping speed recovery from viral infections. Its potent antiviral properties are effective against both the herpes virus and the flu virus – so much so that its constituents have been harnessed by pharmaceutical companies to produce flu medicines such as Tamiflu. Star anise also contains plant oestrogens that can stimulate breast milk supply and help increase vitality in women.

HOW DO I USE IT?

ADD SPICE TO DESSERTS Star anise has a spicy, liquorice-like taste that adds an edge to sweet dishes. The seeds go particularly well with figs. Try adding a little ground star anise to ground coffee before brewing, or to some vanilla-flavoured yogurt. Add the whole spice or the seeds to fish and vegetable dishes.

Star anise

FATS AND OILS

 **HELPS FIGHT INFLAMMATION**

 **A READY SOURCE OF ENERGY**

 **HELPS LOWER CHOLESTEROL**

A mix of different oils and fats in small amounts is crucial for optimal health, **energy**, and **metabolism**. They also help us absorb fat-soluble vitamins D, E, and K, and the carotenoids that we need to make vitamin A. A good balance of polyunsaturates, monounsaturates, and saturated fats (needed for the synthesis of vitamin D) has an **anti-inflammatory** effect and promotes **heart health**.

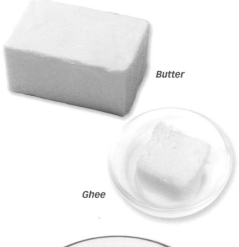

Butter

Ghee

BUTTER

WHAT IS IT GOOD FOR?

MAINTAINS ENERGY Butter and ghee, a form of clarified butter, have similar properties and are a source of energy. Both contain medium- and short-chain fatty acids, of which one, lauric acid, is a potent antimicrobial and antifungal substance. These fats are not associated with heart disease in the way that long-chain fatty acids (present in some vegetable oils) are, as they are used directly as energy by the body and not stored as fat. In addition to some saturated fats, butter contains other healthy fats, such as monounsaturates, that help us absorb fat-soluble nutrients. Organic butter has higher levels of these healthy fats.

HOW DO I USE IT?

VERSATILE INGREDIENT Use in moderation as a spread, in baking, and in sauces. Ghee is used in much the same way as butter in cooking.

Olive oil

OLIVE OIL

WHAT IS IT GOOD FOR?

LOWERS CHOLESTEROL Protects against heart disease by raising levels of "healthy" (HDL) cholesterol while keeping levels of "unhealthy" (LDL) cholesterol in check. Contains more monounsaturated fatty acids than any other natural oil. These fatty acids help normalize blood clotting and control blood sugar levels, making olive oil a good choice for helping prevent metabolic syndrome. The oil is easy to digest, which gives it a healing effect on stomach ulcers.

HOW DO I USE IT?

A GOOD ALL-ROUNDER Regular filtered olive oil is better for cooking, as it has a higher "smoke point", but has fewer nutritional benefits. Save cold-pressed extra virgin oil for uncooked dishes and dressings. Store away from heat and light.

Sunflower oil

SUNFLOWER OIL

WHAT IS IT GOOD FOR?

LOWERS BLOOD PRESSURE Low in saturated fats and high in vitamins E and D and beta-carotene. The best sunflower oils are pressed from plants naturally bred to provide more monounsaturated fat and omega-9 fatty acids, which can help reduce blood pressure, promote memory, and help prevent cancer; look for a product with a high oleic content. Avoid regular sunflower oil, which is low in monounsaturates and high in omega-6 fatty acids, making it pro-inflammatory.

HOW DO I USE IT?

ALTERNATIVE TO ANIMAL FATS Use in sweet and savoury recipes. Use the nutrient-rich unrefined oil for cold dishes; the refined oil has a higher smoke point that is better for cooking.

FLAXSEED OIL

WHAT IS IT GOOD FOR?

HEART HEALTH Flaxseed oil, which is extracted from linseeds, contains the essential fatty acid alpha-linolenic acid (ALA) that can help prevent heart attacks and stroke. Studies suggest ALA may reduce heart disease risk in a variety of ways, including reducing inflammation and excessive blood clotting, promoting blood vessel health, and reducing the risk of arrhythmia (an irregular heartbeat). The oil also contains polyunsaturated omega-3 and omega-6 fatty acids. Consumed daily, it can help improve the dry eyes associated with Sjogren's syndrome.

HOW DO I USE IT?

KEEP IT COOL Flaxseed oil doesn't keep well. Buy in a dark container and store away from light and heat. It's not heat stable, so use it cold. Drizzle on cottage cheese, or scoop out the flesh of a baked potato, mix with quark cheese and flaxseed oil, and replace in the potato skins. Add to juices and smoothies or use to enrich condiments such as ketchup, mayonnaise, and salad dressings.

Flaxseed oil

HEMP SEED OIL

WHAT IS IT GOOD FOR?

ANTI-INFLAMMATORY Hemp seed oil contains the highest percentage of essential fatty acids in any oil and contains the perfect ratio of omega-3, -6 and -9 fatty acids, which are crucial for healthy circulation, cell growth, and the immune system. Its high omega-3 content makes it a good vegetarian alternative to fish oil, and means it is both anti-inflammatory and an antioxidant. Including it in your diet will benefit your heart and nervous system as well as improving your skin and helping to maintain healthy joints. A good brain food, hemp seed oil can support memory and cognitive function and may help prevent dementia.

HOW DO I USE IT?

KEEP IT SIMPLE Store in a dark container away from heat and light. Look for oils that have not been bleached or deodorized. The oil is not suitable for frying or cooking at high temperatures and should be used cold to enjoy its benefits. Add to juices, smoothies, yogurts, cottage cheese, salad dressings, and steamed vegetables, or use a little on bread instead of butter.

Hemp seed oil

BLACK SEED OIL

WHAT IS IT GOOD FOR?

ANTI-INFLAMMATORY Studies show its anti-inflammatory and detoxifying effects can help treat arthritis and rheumatic conditions, and can relieve symptoms in cases of allergic rhinitis (hay fever), eczema, and asthma. It also contains a component called gamma linolenic acid (GLA), which has been shown to reduce the pain associated with diabetic neuropathy (damage to the nerves due to high blood pressure from diabetes). In addition, black seed oil can help raise levels of "healthy" (HDL) cholesterol in the bloodstream.

HOW DO I USE IT?

A HEALTHY ADDITIVE Makes a pungent addition to salad dressings and stir-fries. Mix with honey and garlic to treat allergies and coughs and ward off colds and flu. To treat diarrhoea, mix 1 tsp black seed oil with 225ml (8fl oz) of plain probiotic yogurt and eat as needed. Mix 1 tsp of the oil with a glass of orange juice as an energy boost to start the day.

Black seed oil

FERMENTED FOODS

 HELPS STRENGTHEN THE IMMUNE SYSTEM   **FEEDS GOOD BACTERIA IN THE GUT**   **CONTAINS ANTI-CANCER SUBSTANCES**

The biochemical process of fermentation in foods encourages the growth of friendly bacteria that help maintain a **healthy gut**. It is not an overstatement to say that a healthy gut – one that digests food and nutrients efficiently – is the basis of good health. Healthy and balanced intestinal flora is also a way of **preventing intestinal disorders**, from **irritable bowel syndrome** to **cancer**.

Sauerkraut

SAUERKRAUT

WHAT IS IT GOOD FOR?

INHIBITS CANCER CELLS Laboratory studies show that isothiocyanates, the antioxidant chemicals in fermented cabbage, or sauerkraut, can inhibit the growth of cancer cells

SUPPORTS HEALTHY GUT FLORA Cabbage naturally contains the friendly bacterium *Lactobacilli plantarum*. Fermenting promotes the growth of this organism, which can help balance intestinal flora and inhibit the growth of *E. coli*, salmonella, and candida. It can also help improve the general health of the digestive tract.

HOW DO I USE IT?

A BETTER PICKLE Use uncooked as a pickle. Add sauerkraut to a sandwich or bagel instead of lettuce, or serve to accompany rich meats and sausages. Mix 1–2 tbsp into stir-fried brown rice, scrambled egg, shiitake mushrooms, carrots, or onions, and drizzle a little soy sauce and sesame oil on top. Avoid pasteurized brands, which have fewer nutrients.

Kimchi

KIMCHI

WHAT IS IT GOOD FOR?

ANTI-CANCER BENEFITS An Oriental version of sauerkraut, kimchi is a pungent blend of fermented cabbage, radish, red chillies, garlic, and salt, and is the national dish of Korea. The anti-cancer and heart-healthy benefits in kimchi derive from the many nutrients in the cruciferous cabbage. The mixture of spices and beneficial bacteria in kimchi is also powerfully anti-microbial against harmful bacteria such as *Helicobacter pylori*, *Shigella sonnei*, and *Listeria monocytogenes*.

HOW DO I USE IT?

A SPICY SIDE DISH Kimchi can be served not only as a side dish with steamed rice, but also with tempeh, noodles, fish, meat, and vegetables. Use as you would a relish on burgers, roasted meat, and baked potatoes.

The benefits of brine

Vegetables can be preserved in brine using a natural process known as lacto-fermentation. The brine solution allows beneficial bacteria and enzymes to flourish while retarding the growth of harmful organisms. The result is a food with multiple health-giving properties for the digestive tract. However, unlike home-made pickles, most commercially available pickles are produced using a strong mixture of processed salt and industrial-strength vinegar. This added salt eliminates any health benefits, while the pasteurization (heating) process destroys precious enzymes.

SOY SAUCE

WHAT IS IT GOOD FOR?

SUPPORTS A HEALTHY GUT
Fermenting soya beans to make soy sauce creates unique carbohydrates, called oligosaccharides, which are probiotics that feed friendly bacteria in the gut. Although high in sodium, which could contribute to raised blood pressure in some individuals, recent research suggests that the peptides in soy sauce, created by the fermentation process, help to keep blood pressure low. Soy sauce is rich in antioxidants, which can help protect blood vessels and lower cholesterol. It also contains niacin (B3) and manganese, which help support an efficient metabolism.

HOW DO I USE IT?

BUY THE BEST QUALITY Look for properly fermented products. If you have a wheat sensitivity, try tamari soy sauce. Use to season sautéed vegetables or combine with garlic and ginger as a marinade for tempeh, fish, or chicken. Use instead of table salt to season foods. Avoid soy sauces containing MSG (monosodium glutamate, a synthetic flavour enhancer) which can cause headaches and rashes.

Soy sauce

MISO

WHAT IS IT GOOD FOR?

ANTI-CANCER PROPERTIES Rich in cancer-protective isoflavones, which protect the heart and aid hormone balance in both men and women. Evidence suggests that women who consume 3 or more bowls of miso soup daily have a significantly lower risk of breast cancer.

AIDS DIGESTION Miso is a high-antioxidant fermented food that feeds friendly bacteria in the gut, helping to enhance immunity and aid digestion. It is made from grains, such as barley and rice, or soy beans, and contains all the essential amino acids required by the body, which makes it a complete protein.

HOW DO I USE IT?

AS A VERSATILE PROTEIN Look for organic naturally aged, non-pasteurized miso sold as a thick paste. The longer it is aged, the darker its colour. Use dark miso in a vegetable-bean casserole to supply plenty of high-quality protein, or mix with water to make an energizing, alkalizing broth. Use a light-coloured miso as a substitute for milk, butter, and salt in creamed soups, or as a marinade to tenderize meat.

Miso

TEMPEH

WHAT IS IT GOOD FOR?

PHYTOESTROGEN-RICH High in phytoestrogens, tempeh helps protect against heart disease and cancer, regulates immune function, and may help relieve menopausal symptoms. Not to be confused with tofu (which is not fermented), tempeh is made from fermented, lightly cooked soya beans. Fermentation increases its antimicrobial benefits, providing protection against gastrointestinal upsets. Tempeh is rich in dietary fibre, which helps maintain a healthy digestive tract. This fibre also helps remove fats from the blood. It has also been shown to help lower levels of "unhealthy" (LDL) cholesterol while raising levels of "healthy" (HDL) cholesterol.

HOW DO I USE IT?

MEAT SUBSTITUTE Tempeh has a hearty, nutty flavour that makes it a popular meat substitute. It can be baked, sautéed, steamed, or marinated, and used in sandwiches, curries, and salads. Its relatively neutral taste means it absorbs whatever flavours it is cooked in.

Tempeh

MEATS

 PROMOTES TISSUE GROWTH AND REPAIR

 **HELPS RELEASE CELLULAR ENERGY**

 **PROMOTES HEALTHY SKIN AND HAIR**

Meat is an important source of nutrients and **bioavailable** (easily absorbed) protein that helps the body repair and **build tissue**, **generate energy**, and maintain **healthy skin and hair**. However, eating too much highly processed, intensively reared meat contributes to health problems such as heart disease and cancer. Organic meat has a much healthier nutrient profile, particularly in terms of fats.

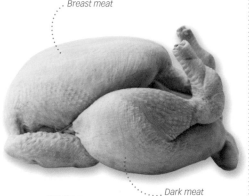

. Breast meat

. . . . . Dark meat

Chicken

CHICKEN

WHAT IS IT GOOD FOR?

IMMUNITY-ENHANCING Chicken contains all the B vitamins, which help the body produce energy and form red blood cells, and also help strengthen the nervous system. Chicken meat is particularly high in the heart-healthy vitamin B3 (niacin): the dark meat contains double the amount of zinc and iron of the light meat, giving it immune-boosting properties; while the white meat is higher in potassium and phosphorus, helping to build strong bones, teeth, and tissues.

HOW DO I USE IT?

CHICKEN SOUP Laboratory studies suggest that the synergistic action of nutrients in chicken may help halt the spread of infection and fight inflammation. If you have a cold or flu, a bowl of chicken soup may be your best medicine.

Beef silverside

BEEF

WHAT IS IT GOOD FOR?

METABOLIC BALANCE A source of high-quality protein, beef also contains B vitamins, which fuel cellular energy production. The iron in beef helps produce more red blood cells that carry oxygen around the body. Beef also contains zinc, which aids cell division and helps in the formation of protein.

CHOLESTEROL HEALTH Stearic acid, a saturated fatty acid that accounts for 50 per cent of beef fat, is converted by the body to monounsaturated oleic acid, the main fat in heart-healthy olive oil.

HOW DO I USE IT?

ADD GREEN VEGETABLES Beef can be harder to digest than white meat. Marinating or rubbing raw beef with spices such as rosemary, mustard, black pepper, garlic, onions, or horseradish can aid digestion and prevent the formation of carcinogenic heterocyclic amines – substances that form when red meat is cooked at a high temperature.

Healthy animals produce healthy meat

Outdoor-bred, pasture-fed, organic animals produce meat with lower total fat and higher levels of healthy fats such as omega-3 fatty acids; they are also less prone to contamination with E. coli and other bacteria. Meat does contain cholesterol, but this fat is also an essential nutrient that helps the body to synthesise steroid hormones, including those that regulate blood sugar, blood pressure, sex hormone balance. Eating meat with antioxidant-rich green vegetables, as opposed to starchy ones, can help prevent the free-radical damage to cholesterol that is associated with heart disease.

LAMB

WHAT IS IT GOOD FOR?

HEALTHY NERVOUS SYSTEM Lamb contains good amounts of B vitamins and is particularly rich in B12 and folate. These nutrients are necessary for a healthy central nervous system and aid the prevention of heart disease, mood disorders, and dementia, including Alzheimer's disease and vascular dementia in older people. Lamb is one of the few commercial meats that is still mostly pasture fed, which means it is naturally lower in cholesterol than some other meats and contains omega-3 and omega-6 fatty acids and conjugated linolenic acid (CLA).

HOW DO I USE IT?

NON-STARCHY VEGETABLES Animal protein meats, such as lamb, are healthiest and easiest to digest when eaten with non-starchy vegetables (rather than rice and potatoes). Choose vegetables such as green beans, broccoli, kale, collards, and spinach to serve with lamb.

Leg of lamb

PORK

WHAT IS IT GOOD FOR?

A SOURCE OF GOOD FATS Pork is unique in that it contains more monounsaturated and polyunsaturated fats than saturated fat. This means that, as part of a healthy diet, it has a role to play in lowering cholesterol levels and reducing the risk of stroke and hypertension. Unlike beef and lamb, it is not a source of vitamin A, but it does contain useful amounts of the minerals zinc and iron, which help regulate energy release. It also contains B vitamins, specifically B1, B2, and B3 (thiamine, riboflavin, and niacin), which are also necessary for energy regulation as well as muscle growth and repair.

HOW DO I USE IT?

FRESH CUTS We consume a lot of pork in the form of preserved meat. The link between these processed meats and bowel cancer is now well-established, so opt for fresh cuts you can cook yourself. Try eating pork with fermented vegetables, such as sauerkraut to aid digestion, and feed good bacteria in the gut.

Rolled pork leg joint

TURKEY

WHAT IS IT GOOD FOR?

CONTROLS INSULIN SECRETION Turkey belongs to a small group of high-protein animal foods (which also include tuna and egg whites) that can help keep post-meal insulin levels balanced for longer. The combination of B vitamins and tryptophan amino acid in turkey has a balancing effect on blood sugar levels, helps keep the nerves calm, avoids hypoglycaemia and low moods, and has an immune-enhancing effect. It also contains selenium, necessary for the efficient function of the immune system and thyroid. Selenium is an antioxidant that helps combat the oxidative stress caused by free radicals in the body.

HOW DO I USE IT?

EAT THE DARK MEAT As with chicken, there are benefits in choosing the darker meat of the leg and thigh, as it contains more metabolism-boosting iron, zinc, and B vitamins than the white meat. Use the dark meat as a filling for a sandwich or wrap with mango chutney and watercress.

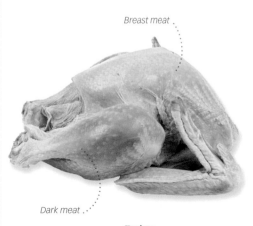

Breast meat

Dark meat

Turkey

MEATS CONTINUED

Venison

Quail

Wood pigeon

VENISON

WHAT IS IT GOOD FOR?

METABOLIC BOOST Venison is deer meat that is very low in fat: like other red meats, it is high in protein and iron – which is necessary for efficient metabolism – but is low in saturated fats. It is also rich in potassium, phosphorus, and zinc. Venison contains useful amounts of vitamins B1 and B3, which help keep the metabolism in good shape and aid the growth, repair, and detoxification of tissues and bones. It is also a good source of the heart-protective vitamins B6 and B12, which can help keep arteries healthy.

HOW DO I USE IT?

ANTIOXIDANT-RICH MEAL Many recipes recommend long, slow cooking, although venison is probably best served medium-rare. For an antioxidant-rich meal, cover the raw meat with a dry rub of pepper, paprika, garlic, onion, thyme, and crushed juniper berries, and serve with roasted beetroots, sweet potatoes, and apple sauce.

QUAIL

WHAT IS IT GOOD FOR?

LOW-FAT ENERGY BOOSTER Quail is lower in fat and higher in protein than chicken. The meat of this small bird has a sweet, delicate taste and is a great source of copper and iron, which are important nutrients for helping to generate energy. Quail also contains vitamin B-complex and vitamins C, E, and K, which help to strengthen the immune system. It is also a great source of iron, which helps transport oxygen throughout the body, and copper which, along with iron, helps prevent anaemia and is necessary for healthy joints, skin, hair and connective tissue.

HOW DO I USE IT?

KEEP IT SIMPLE Choose quail that hasn't been intensively farmed. A single quail provides around 85–140g (3–5oz) of meat – essentially a single serving; cook quickly in a moderate oven (180°C/350°F/Gas 4) for 10 minutes only to preserve its moisture and nutrients. Quail quickly absorbs the flavour from marinades, so don't let any strong mixtures overpower its delicate flavour.

WOOD PIGEON

WHAT IS IT GOOD FOR?

IMMUNE-BOOSTING A wild bird with a distinctly gamey flavour, wood pigeon is high in key immunity-boosting trace elements, such as iron, zinc, and selenium; zinc is particularly important for male prostate health. Wood pigeon also contains the highest levels of phosphorous – which is necessary for healthy bones, tissue repair, and hormone production – of all commonly consumed game. It is low in fat – containing less fat than lamb or duck – and is a better source of blood-building iron than beef.

HOW DO I USE IT?

COOK QUICKLY Pigeon has a deep crimson colour and great depth of flavour. It tastes wonderful in pies or on its own in a red wine sauce. As with quail, it benefits from quick cooking. Try serving hot on a bed of leafy greens or lentils, or in a salad with blackberry vinegar.

WATERFOWL

WHAT IS IT GOOD FOR?

GOOD FATS Duck and goose, known collectively as waterfowl, are particularly good for fuelling the metabolic processes. Both are rich in iron and B vitamins, and duck, in particular, can contain up to 3 times more iron than chicken. Although waterfowl is perceived as a fatty meat, both duck and goose have a fat profile that is similar to chicken and are high in heart-healthy monounsaturated and polyunsaturated fats. Both meats are also a good source of selenium, an antioxidant mineral that supports a healthy immune system.

HOW DO I USE IT?

NUTRITIOUS VARIETY Try cooking duck breasts instead of chicken breasts to provide variety and extra nutrition, or cook a goose as an alternative to seasonal turkey roast. Duck and goose fat are very heat-stable alternatives to using olive oil or lard in cooking.

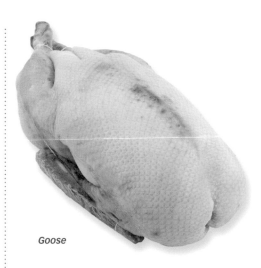

Goose

LIVER

WHAT IS IT GOOD FOR?

BLOOD BUILDER The liver is a storehouse of valuable nutrients for the body. All types of liver provide essential iron and B12 to support healthy blood. Whether from mammals or birds (or even fish), liver is also a tremendous source of protein and vitamin A, which is necessary for proper immune function as well as healthy skin, eyes, and mucous membranes. Lambs' and calves' liver are the richest sources of vitamin A, while chicken livers are a rich source of folate. As long as the animal it comes from was healthy and organic, all types of liver provide a major boost for the immune system, skin, eyes, and lungs.

HOW DO I USE IT?

A CLASSIC DISH Only eat organic liver, and enjoy it in patés or as a main meal. Marinating liver in lemon juice for 1–2 hours to draw out any impurities will give it a better texture. Lightly frying liver so it is still slightly pink in the middle, and serving on a bed of sautéed onions, is a classic way to enjoy this meat.

Pig liver

KIDNEYS

WHAT IS IT GOOD FOR?

ANTIOXIDANT-RICH Kidneys, most often from beef or lamb, are a good source of the antioxidant mineral selenium, which has a role to play in protecting against heart disease and cancer. They also contain moderate amounts of vitamin A, which promotes healthy skin, and large amounts of B vitamins, iron, and zinc. Men benefit from the zinc and selenium in kidneys, both of which help maintain fertility and a healthy prostate, while women of childbearing age will benefit from the iron, which can help replace what is lost during menstruation.

HOW DO I USE IT?

ADD TO CASSEROLES Kidneys add richness to beef and lamb dishes. Before cooking, marinate in lemon juice or brine for 1–2 hours to remove any trace of ammonia and improve their texture. Or cook simply with mushrooms and serve on toast.

Kidneys

OILY FISH

 PROTECTS THE HEART AND BLOOD VESSELS

 SUPPORTS A HEALTHY NERVOUS SYSTEM

 **HELPS LUBRICATE JOINTS**

 **PROMOTES EFFICIENT METABOLISM**

This group of fish are unique, as their **heart-healthy** fats are distributed through their flesh rather than concentrated in their liver, as with white fish. They are particularly high in certain **omega-3 fatty acids**, which protect the **cardiovascular** and **nervous systems**. The fat-soluble vitamins A, D, E, and K are also abundant, benefitting bone, joint, muscle, skin, and eye health, and metabolic balance.

Salmon

SALMON

WHAT IS IT GOOD FOR?

SUPPORTS HEALTHY AGEING Uniquely rich in the omega-3 fatty acids eicosapentaenoic acid (EPA) and decosahexaenoic acid (DHA). In combination with its abundant supply of selenium, these omega-3 fatty acids help lower blood pressure, "unhealthy" (LDL) cholesterol levels in the blood, and inflammation, reducing the risk of heart disease, stroke, and cancer. They also protect the eyes and joints and feed the brain, helping to prevent dementia and loss of mental functions. Salmon is also relatively low in the pro-inflammatory omega-6 fatty acids (already overabundant in the modern diet).

HOW DO I USE IT?

GO WILD Choose wild or organic, as farmed salmon can contain residues of veterinary medicines. Grill on a high heat to seal in nutrients.

Herring

HERRING

WHAT IS IT GOOD FOR?

HEART HEALTH A good source of eicosapentaenoic acid (EPA) and decosahexaenoic acid (DHA), fatty acids that lower hypertension, triglycerides (fatty deposits) in the blood, and inflammation, helping to reduce the risk of heart disease and stroke. It also contains vitamin D, calcium, and phosphorus, which are all important for bone health, and also vitamin B12, which aids the production of cellular energy.

HOW DO I USE IT?

A LIGHT BITE Smoked herring is known as kippers, a delicacy that can be eaten at any meal. Rollmops are pickled herrings. Make your own with subtly flavoured vinegar and serve with fresh bread, or cut into chunks and add to potato salad.

Mackerel

MACKEREL

WHAT IS IT GOOD FOR?

HEALTHY AGEING Contains an abundance of nutrients, including vitamins A, B-complex, C, D, E, and K, calcium, potassium, selenium, and magnesium, which help regulate the metabolism, including blood sugar and cholesterol levels, and support healthy heart, bones, teeth, nerves, and muscles. It is rich in anti-inflammatory omega-3 fatty acids that keep blood vessels elastic and reduce swollen joints, pain, and stiffness associated with arthritis.

HOW DO I USE IT?

A HEALTHY MEAL Serve warm with asparagus on a bed of noodles and a miso and ginger dressing, or serve cold on a bed of sprouted lentils or other sprouted pulses, walnuts, and chives. To make fish cakes, blend with spring onions, butter beans, mustard, parsley, and a little egg.

SARDINES

WHAT IS IT GOOD FOR?

LOWERS CHOLESTEROL Sardines are one of the most concentrated sources of the omega-3 fatty acids EPA and DHA, which have been found to lower triglycerides (fatty deposits) and "unhealthy" (LDL) cholesterol levels in the blood. They are an excellent source of vitamin B12 and a great source of vitamin D, which plays an essential role in bone health since it helps to increase the body's absorption of calcium.

HOW DO I USE IT?

QUICK AND CONVENIENT Canned sardines make a convenient and nutritious quick meal served on toast or pasta. Fresh sardines are delicious grilled or barbecued. Cooking them quickly in this way keeps their essential nutrients intact.

Sardines

TROUT

WHAT IS IT GOOD FOR?

A GOOD SOURCE OF PROTEIN Lower in fat than some other fish, but still contains good amounts of omega-3 fatty acids. Also a good source of protein, potassium, phosphorus, vitamin B12, and iron, which protect the heart and build healthy bones. Like most oily fish, semi-oily trout contains cholesterol, which is necessary for the synthesis of vitamin D and the production of vital hormones in the body, including the different sex hormones testosterone, progesterone, and oestrogen.

HOW DO I USE IT?

MIX WITH FRESH FLAVOURS When served with pulses, oily fish such as trout help increase the absorption of iron from the beans. Or cook with a lemon and almond crust or a rub of ground dried herbs and garlic mixed in a little olive oil. Grill on a high heat

Trout

SEA BASS

WHAT IS IT GOOD FOR?

IMMUNE ENHANCING An excellent source of high-quality protein and very rich in vitamins A, D, and E, which, with its omega-3 oils, are anti-inflammatory, immunity-enhancing, and may help protect against degenerative diseases and cancer. It is also high in phosphorus, potassium, calcium, magnesium, zinc, and selenium. A semi-oily fish, it contains a good balance of fats but in lower quantities than oily fish, so it's a good choice if you want to limit your consumption of total fats.

HOW DO I USE IT?

A LOW-FAT CHOICE Grill simply with lemon and garlic, or spice it up with ginger, chilli, and spring onions.

Sea bass

TUNA

WHAT IS IT GOOD FOR?

HEART HEALTH Like trout and sea bass, tuna is a semi-oily fish. It is an excellent source of protein, as well as selenium, magnesium, potassium, and omega-3 essential fatty acids. Tuna also contains the B vitamins niacin, B1, and B6, and folate; B vitamins help lower levels of homocysteine, which can cause atherosclerosis (hardening of the arteries due to the build-up of plaque).

HOW DO I USE IT?

THINK SMALL Tuna concentrates toxins like mercury. Smaller species such as skipjack are safest to eat, but limit consuming any type to once a week. Soy sauce and wasabi makes a good marinade for grilled tuna.

Tuna

ALGAE

 HELPS FIGHT INFECTION

 FEEDS GOOD BACTERIA IN THE GUT

 SUPPORTS AND PROTECTS THE LIVER

This group of aquatic plants is prized by Asian cultures as a delicacy and a rich **source of nutrients** and **antioxidants,** such as beta-carotene and zeaxanthin, **selenium**, zinc, and **vitamins C, E, and B-complex**. It is also rich in **protein** and **amino acids** that help the body to **fight infection,** and a beneficial type of **fibre** that encourages the growth of **good bacteria** in the gut and aids **detox.**

CHLORELLA
Chlorella is a green algae and is one of the richest sources of the detoxifying plant pigment chlorophyll.

SPIRULINA
The most commonly used type of blue-green algae, spirulina is a rich source of beta-carotene and amino acids.

AFA (APHANIZOMENON FLOS-AQUAE)
A unique blue-green algae found in Upper Klamath Lake in Oregon, USA. AFA contains phenylethylamine (PEA), which may help balance mood and improve mental clarity.

WHAT IS IT GOOD FOR?

BOOSTS IMMUNITY Chlorella contains "Chlorella Growth Factor" (CGF), which can enhance immune function and stimulate tissue repair. Laboratory studies suggest that blue-green algae can fight the viruses that cause herpes, HIV, and influenza, though evidence in human beings is still lacking.

PROBIOTIC Helps to promote the growth of friendly bacteria in the gut. It is a good choice after a course of antibiotics, which can kill both good and bad gut flora in the intestines.

DETOX Helps support and protect the liver, and has a laxative effect. Blue-green algae may protect the liver from toxic damage. Chlorella has been shown to help remove heavy metals (such as cadmium and mercury), pesticides, and industrial pollutants from the body.

ANTIOXIDANTS Green and blue-green algae can help fight inflammation and damage to tissues and organs caused by free radicals.

HOW DO I GET THE BEST FROM IT?

DRIED CONCENTRATE Fresh algae doesn't keep well so it is often sold as supplements in a dried, powdered form. Many algae are now farmed rather than wild-gathered; this is not a bad thing, as they can easily become contaminated with waterborne pollutants.

USE IN SMALL QUANTITIES The drying process concentrates the nutrients so a little goes a long way. Mega-dosing with algae can produce uncomfortable stomach cramps.

HOW DO I USE IT?

SALAD DRESSING To give your salad a boost, try mixing 1–2 tsp algae powder into an oil and vinegar salad dressing.

A HEALTHY ADDITIVE Dried algae are versatile and generally have a mild taste – ideal for mixing into soups, stir-fries, salsas, guacamoles, smoothies, and vegetable juices.

SEAWEEDS

 ASSISTS WEIGHT MANAGEMENT

 HELPS REMOVE TOXINS FROM THE BODY

 LOWERS RISK OF HEART DISEASE AND STROKE

 FIGHTS THE EFFECTS OF STRESS

Every type of seaweed has a unique taste and texture, but all possess broadly the same nutritional benefits. They are, for instance, **protein-rich** and a source of **iodine**, necessary for **metabolism**. They are also a good source of **fibre** and **chlorophyll**, which help **remove toxins** from the body, and **heart-healthy** magnesium and potassium, which **protect blood vessels** and fight the effects of **stress**.

WHAT IS IT GOOD FOR?

METABOLISM Its high iodine content helps support healthy thyroid function, which in turn helps regulate the metabolism of cells and assists weight management. Brown seaweeds such as kelp and wakame contain the antioxidant carotenoid fucoxanthin, which improves insulin resistance and helps metabolize fat more efficiently.

DETOX A source of detoxifying chlorophyll and mucilaginous (gum-like) fibre that helps maintain bowel regularity and binds to and removes toxins and fats from the body.

HEART HEALTH Contains high amounts of magnesium, which lowers blood pressure, and folate, which breaks down homocysteine, a risk factor for heart disease and stroke.

STRESS Magnesium, pantothenic acid, and riboflavin support the health of the adrenal glands, which play a critical role in our response to stress. Without this nutritional support, constant stress can exhaust the adrenal glands, resulting in chronic fatigue, lowered immunity, and mood changes.

HOW DO I GET THE BEST FROM IT?

FRESH OR DRIED Drying does not damage its nutritional content. If you can forage fresh seaweed, make sure you rinse it well.

VEGETABLE PROTEIN If you don't eat meat or want to cut back on animal protein, seaweed is a good source of quality vegetable protein.

HOW DO I USE IT?

FLAVOUR ENHANCER Use ground seaweed as a flavour enhancer instead of salt, to flavour and thicken stocks, or add to soups, broths, or miso for extra protein and vitamins.

ADD TO BREAD To balance blood sugar levels and add protein, replace half the flour with ground seaweed. Use water not milk, omit the salt, and add 1 extra tbsp oil or butter.

DULSE
High in protein, dulse contains all the essential trace minerals as well as the antioxidant beta-carotene and vitamins C, E, and B-complex.

KELP
A rich source of iodine and other important trace minerals.

NORI
Particularly high in protein, which makes up 50 per cent of its dry weight, and contains a comparable amount of fibre to spinach.

WAKAME
Contains a high amount of magnesium, which improves heart function and acts as a diuretic.

Aloe Vera

 PROVIDES ANTIVIRAL PROTECTION

 HELPS EASE BRONCHIAL COMPLAINTS

 HELPS BALANCE INTESTINAL FLORA

The sword-like leaves of aloe vera contain a clear mucilaginous gel with **detoxifying**, **antiseptic**, and **anti-inflammatory** properties that is used internally and externally to **treat respiratory complaints** and **aid digestion**. In some Asian countries, the whole leaf, which contains **immunity-boosting** and **antioxidant** beta-carotene and vitamins C, E, many B vitamins, and minerals, is cooked and eaten.

Leaves
The antiviral potential of aloe gel in the leaves has been shown to boost the effectiveness of HIV treatments

ALOE PLANT
Of the 200-plus species of aloe plants, only 2 – Aloe Barbadensis Miller and Aloe Arborescens – are grown commercially, with Aloe Barbadensis Miller being the most widely used.

PURE ALOE GEL
Unprocessed aloe gel contains aloin, a powerful laxative. Processed aloe vera juices contain much less of this substance.

What Is It Good For?

IMMUNITY STIMULANT Contains a substance called acemannan, an immune stimulant and an antiviral. It is effective against the herpes virus, and in HIV patients it may work synergistically with conventional medicines.

RESPIRATORY EASE Can help soothe coughs and bronchial asthma. Its antiseptic properties can help to heal colds and sore throats.

DIGESTION Helps balance intestinal flora. Can be useful in cases of irritable bowel syndrome, and is a laxative that is reputed to help expel parasites from the digestive tract.

ANTI-INFLAMMATORY Blocks the formation of histamine, which makes it a useful remedy for allergic conditions. Also contains natural salicylic acid, the base material for aspirin, so it is useful for general aches and pains and also conditions such as arthritis. As a gargle, it is also a beneficial treatment for gingivitis, an inflammatory condition of the gums.

How Do I Get The Best From It?

GROW YOUR OWN Aloe plants are relatively easy to grow, but they don't like cold weather. Plant in pots and bring indoors in winter.

PURE GEL Aloe is most effective if minimally processed. If you can't get fresh, look for 100 per cent aloe juice products and pure gels, not extracts from the macerated leaves.

How Do I Use It?

MAKE A FRESH JUICE Cut 1 aloe leaf (25–30cm/10–12in long) into manageable sections, peel like an avocado or mango, and scoop out the clear gel "fillet". Blitz in a food processor or blender with 240ml (8fl oz) apple juice and drink while very fresh.

MIX INTO HEALTHY JUICES Aloe juice can be bitter so mix with apple and cucumber juice or fresh pineapple juice and coconut water.

WHEATGRASS

 HELPS REMOVE TOXINS FROM THE BODY

 HELPS BUILD RED BLOOD CELLS

HEALS AND STRENGTHENS THE GUT

Before they form seed heads, young wheat shoots are known as wheatgrass, which consists of 70 per cent **chlorophyll**. It supports the **immune system**, removes **toxins** from the blood and body tissues, improves **digestion**, is **gluten-free**, unlike other forms of wheat, and is high in vitamins C, E, and B-complex, **beta-carotene**, calcium, magnesium, potassium, iron, natural enzymes, and amino acids.

WHAT IS IT GOOD FOR?

DETOXIFIER Chlorophyll aids detoxification and, along with other plant-based nutrients, is a natural chelator (a substance that helps to draw heavy metals out of the body). In women with breast cancer, wheatgrass juice has been shown to remove the toxic byproducts of chemotherapy from their blood. There is also evidence that chlorophyll helps to protect the liver from toxins.

BLOOD BUILDER Its vitamin C and folate may help treat anaemia resulting from deficiencies in these nutrients. Its high chlorophyll content assists in the formation of healthy red blood cells; studies show it reduces the transfusion requirements of people with thalassemia – a genetic disorder in which the body makes an abnormal form of haemoglobin.

DIGESTION Since it contains nutrients but little fibre, wheatgrass juice is a good way to supply nutrition to people with ulcerative colitis. There is also some evidence that daily ingestion of wheatgrass juice can help heal some of the symptoms of ulcerative colitis.

HEART HEALTH Animal studies have shown the juice can help lower total cholesterol and other blood fats, such as triglycerides (a type of fat in the blood), and which can specifically lower "unhealthy" (LDL) cholesterol levels.

HOW DO I GET THE BEST FROM IT?

RINSE WELL It is grown in moist conditions so is prone to mould; wash well before juicing.

ON ITS OWN It doesn't mix with food so take on an empty stomach 1 hour before eating.

HOW DO I USE IT?

AS A SHOT Serve in a shot glass with a slice of orange to help absorb its mineral content.

RECONSTITUTE IT The convenience and consistency of reconstituted dried powders can be a better option than fresh wheatgrass.

WHEATGRASS SHOOTS
Unlike other forms of wheat, wheatgrass does not contain gluten, and the juice pressed from it may help to heal symptoms of ulcerative colitis.

WHEATGRASS JUICE
A rich source of detoxifying and blood-building chlorophyll. It needs to be juiced to get the most benefit from its nutrients.

WHEATGRASS POWDER
Fresh wheatgrass juice does not store well. Dried powders have a longer shelf life and can be used as needed.

HONEY

 HELPS HEAL ULCERS    **FIGHTS RESPIRATORY INFECTIONS**    **HELPS SPEED WOUND HEALING**    **PROVIDES SEASONAL ALLERGY RELIEF**

Although honey is made up of mostly simple sugars and water, it has many medicinal properties, including its ability to help **heal skin wounds** and **ulcers**. Its effectiveness lies in its levels of **vitamins C, D, E, K, and B-complex**, and **beta-carotene**, minerals, enzymes, and essential oils. It's also a **natural antibiotic** and rich in **antioxidants**, making it effective at **fighting respiratory infections**.

HONEYCOMB
Raw honey extracted from the honeycomb is not sterilized or pasteurized, leaving its vitamins and enzymes intact and undamaged.

MANUKA HONEY
The antimicrobial properties of this honey (manuka is a wild shrub native to New Zealand) are well known and defined by the Unique Manuka Factor (UMF). A UMF of 10 and above is considered very beneficial.

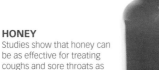

HONEY
Studies show that honey can be as effective for treating coughs and sore throats as conventional cough syrups.

WHAT IS IT GOOD FOR?

HEALS ULCERS Its antioxidants may help to heal the colon in cases of ulcerative colitis. Manuka honey contains, in addition to hydrogen peroxide, unique antibacterial substances that are useful against *Helicobacter pylori* bacteria, which causes stomach ulcers.

RESPIRATORY INFECTIONS Can be as effective as the cough suppressant diphenhydramine, and may help children sleep better. Types of honey shown to work well for coughs include buckwheat, eucalyptus, citrus, or labiatae (mint family) varieties. The antimicrobial properties of manuka honey make it a good choice if you or your child has a cold.

ANTISEPTIC Contains hydrogen peroxide, one reason why it may be effective at inhibiting bacterial growth in laboratory studies. Used topically, it can help speed wound healing.

ALLERGIES Unfiltered honey, rich in pollen, can relieve the symptoms of seasonal allergies.

HOW DO I GET THE BEST FROM IT?

COLOUR COUNTS Choose the darkest honey you can find, as it contains more nutrients. Buckwheat, avocado, sagebrush, and tupelo honeys are particularly good choices.

BEWARE OF FAKE HONEY Unpasteurized and unfiltered honey is the most nutritious. Avoid ultra-purified honey, which has had all traces of pollen removed, and cheap fake honeys (often pale in colour and sold in squeezy bottles) which have no medicinal benefit at all.

STORE CAREFULLY Store away from light at room temperature to preserve its properties.

HOW DO I USE IT?

SIMPLE COUGH SYRUP Take 1 tbsp of honey on its own or combine with a little lemon juice and/or fresh ginger root for a warming cough syrup that will boost your vitamin C intake.

Honey is a powerhouse of healing nutrients and enzymes and is one of the world's oldest natural remedies. The darker the colour of the honey, the more concentrated these substances will be.

STEVIA

 HELPS BALANCE BLOOD SUGAR LEVELS

 HELPS FIGHT BACTERIA AND VIRUSES

 PROTECTS THE HEART AND BLOOD VESSELS

 AIDS HEALTHY DIGESTION

Native to South America, stevia is prized for its naturally sweet taste and medicinal properties. Its leaves contain 2 "glycoside" molecules, stevioside and rebaudioside, which are 300 times sweeter than refined sugar, but contain **no calories** and **do not raise blood sugar levels or cause dental cavities**. These glycosides are also now available as a processed powder or concentrated liquid.

Leaves
Stevia leaves, which have a sweet taste reminiscent of aniseed, can be ground and used in cooking or added whole to teas

Granules
Since it does not contain sugar, stevia is a good alternative sweetener for diabetics

WHAT IS IT GOOD FOR?

ANTI-DIABETIC There is evidence to suggest that for some people it can improve insulin sensitivity and prevent a postprandial spike in blood sugar levels in type-2 diabetics.

IMMUNITY ENHANCER Inhibits the growth and reproduction of bacteria and other infectious organisms; it has been shown to be effective against *Streptococcus mutans*, *Pseudomonas aeruginosa*, and *Proteus vulgaris*. It is also good as an antiseptic mouthwash and gargle, and studies show regular use can help lower the incidence of dental cavities.

HEART HEALTH Helps strengthen the heart and vascular system. Stevioside, a chemical compound in stevia, is believed to be the active ingredient responsible.

BENEFITS DIGESTION Improves digestion and the overall health of the gastrointestinal tract.

HOW DO I GET THE BEST FROM IT?

AVOID ADDITIVES Look for stevia products with a minimum of additives. Many contain the sweetener maltodextrin or the alcohol sugar erythritol, and bulking and anticaking agents. Use for some, but not all, the same purposes as refined sugar (it won't caramelize and can't be used to make meringues).

FRESH LEAVES Add a fresh leaf to a cup of regular or herbal tea for a hint of sweetness.

HOW DO I USE IT?

MAKE AN EXTRACT Add 240ml (8fl oz) warm water to 60g (2oz) fresh, finely chopped stevia leaves. Leave to infuse for 24 hours, strain into a clean jar or bottle, refrigerate, and use to sweeten drinks. Consume within 1 month.

MAKE A GREEN POWDER Crush dried leaves to a powder in a pestle and mortar, coffee grinder, or herb blender. Store in a clean container to use in baking and other recipes that call for green stevia powder.

MAPLE SYRUP

 PROMOTES PROSTATE HEALTH

 **HELPS RELEASE CELLULAR ENERGY**

 **CONTAINS ANTI-CANCER SUBSTANCES**

 HELPS KEEP BLOOD VESSELS SUPPLE

This natural sweetener is gaining ground as an **energy-boosting**, healthy alternative to refined sugar. Recent studies have found it is rich in **phenolic compounds**, which have **anti-cancer, antibacterial,** and **anti-diabetic** properties, and manganese and zinc, making it a good choice for **heart health** and **boosting men's fertility**. In addition, it contains 15 times more calcium than honey, and less sodium.

WHAT IS IT GOOD FOR?

MEN'S HEALTH Zinc helps support men's reproductive health and protects against prostate enlargement. Its abundant manganese levels also help in the production of sex hormones in both men and women.

SUSTAINED ENERGY Manganese is essential for cellular energy production and the synthesis of fatty acids and cholesterol. Zinc aids cellular metabolism and protein synthesis.

ANTI-CANCER EFFECTS Laboratory studies show that its antioxidant polyphenols are better than broccoli, blueberries, carrots, and tomatoes at slowing the growth of prostate and lung cancer cells.

HEART The zinc in maple syrup is a useful antioxidant that protects artery walls from free-radical damage and helps prevent hardening of the arteries (atherosclerosis).

BETTER BLOOD SUGAR CONTROL Its antioxidant polyphenols, combined with its plant hormone, abscisic acid, have been shown to improve the body's sensitivity to the blood-sugar-regulating hormone insulin.

HOW DO I GET THE BEST FROM IT?

REAL AND ORGANIC Look for 100 per cent organic maple syrup; cheap products are simply corn syrup with maple flavouring.

CHOOSE YOUR COLOUR Lighter syrups have a mild flavour that suits cereals and coffee. Use dark syrup in baking, marinades, and sauces.

HOW DO I USE IT?

POUR IT ON Add to porridge or marinades – it goes well with ginger and soy sauce. Drizzle over broccoli or mix into sweet potato mash.

TO DETOX For a cleansing 1-day fast, mix 200ml (7fl oz) maple syrup, the juice of 3 small lemons, 2 tsp cayenne pepper, and 2 litres (3½ pints) purified water. Drink through the day.

MAPLE SYRUP
Four tablespoons of maple syrup have the same antioxidant capacity as a serving of broccoli or a banana.

MAPLE SUGAR
To make maple sugar, the sap is boiled for longer than it is boiled for making the syrup. It's about twice as sweet as refined sugar and retains most of the minerals of the syrup.

BLACKSTRAP MOLASSES

HELPS RELEASE CELLULAR ENERGY

HELPS STRENGTHEN BONES AND TEETH

HELPS BUILD RED BLOOD CELLS

HELPS EASE MENSTRUAL CRAMPS

Unlike refined sugar, corn syrup, and artificial sweeteners, which contain no nutrients and are linked to a variety of health problems, this viscous black-gold residue (produced when sugar cane is turned into refined sugar) is rich in **bone-building** calcium, iron to **enrich the blood**, potassium to **ease muscle cramps**, and B vitamins to fuel efficient **metabolism** and help strengthen the **nervous system**.

BLACKSTRAP MOLASSES
One tablespoon of it contains almost 26 per cent of your daily requirement of iron, 20 per cent of calcium, and 61 per cent of magnesium.

SUGAR CANE
Blackstrap molasses results during the third and final refinement process of boiling sugar syrup derived from sugar cane.

WHAT IS IT GOOD FOR?

ENERGY RELEASE Provides the same quick energy boost as refined sugar. Unlike sugar, it is a source of important nutrients including selenium, manganese, and the B vitamins pyridoxine (B6) and choline.

STRONG BONES A great source of calcium, which helps build and maintain strong bones and teeth. Calcium also promotes a healthy gut, helps maintain a steady heartbeat, and enhances the function of the nervous system.

HEART HEALTH Choline supports healthy nerve function, strengthens cell membranes, and prevents the build-up of homocysteine, a substance linked to heart disease and osteoporosis. Iron helps build the red blood cells that transport oxygen to all parts of the body, and is necessary for cellular energy production and metabolism.

WOMEN'S HEALTH It is a useful remedy during menstruation. Taking 2–3 tsp daily can help balance any iron lost.

HOW DO I GET THE BEST FROM IT?

IRON TONIC A useful iron supplement for those who cannot tolerate the constipation associated with iron tonics and supplements.

A MORNING ENERGIZER Since it is an energy-booster and a natural laxative, it is best taken first thing in the morning before food.

LOOK FOR UNSULPHURED MOLASSES True blackstrap molasses does not need sulphur as a preservative. If it contains sulphur, it is an inferior product without the nutrients.

HOW DO I USE IT?

GREAT FOR COOKING It gives baked goods, like gingerbread, a distinctive flavour. It is also used in barbecue sauces and baked beans.

MAKE A TEA Add 1 tsp to ginger tea as a remedy for menstrual or abdominal cramps.

CHOCOLATE

 LOWERS RISK OF HEART DISEASE AND STROKE   **PROTECTS AGAINST FREE-RADICAL DAMAGE**   **AN EFFECTIVE COUGH SUPPRESSANT**   **SOOTHES STOMACH UPSETS**

Scientific research into chocolate is turning up some intriguing possibilities about its healthful nutrients, including improved **immunity**, greater **longevity**, and **quicker recovery** from intense exercise. Dark chocolate without unhealthy additives and sugar has been shown to lower the risk of **cancer** and **stroke**, and lowers **blood pressure** as effectively as antioxidant-rich fruit and vegetables.

WHAT IS IT GOOD FOR?

HEART HEALTH Moderate consumption protects the heart by thinning the blood in much the same way as low-dose aspirin, while its beneficial flavanols protect artery walls and lower blood pressure and cholesterol.

IMMUNE SUPPORT Weight for weight it has the same amount of antioxidants as red wine. These support overall immunity and intestinal immunity by boosting the response of antibodies and T-helper cells (a type of blood cell that helps kick-start the immune response), and strengthening the intestinal lining against invading microorganisms.

EASES COUGHS One of the stimulants in cocoa, theobromine, has been shown to be more effective than codeine (a traditional cough suppressant) for soothing a sore throat.

DIGESTION Studies show substances in dark chocolate help ease gastrointestinal upsets.

HOW DO I GET THE BEST FROM IT?

CHOOSE ORGANIC At least 30 pesticides are used in conventional cocoa so opt for organic.

GO DARK For the most antioxidants, look for semi-sweet or dark chocolate with at least 70 per cent cocoa solids and less sugar. Milk chocolate contains much fewer antioxidants.

A LITTLE OF THE BEST Eating a small quantity of a quality chocolate will be more satisfying than a highly processed bar. Avoid bars with hydrogenated or partially hydrogenated oils.

HOW DO I USE IT?

RAW CACAO NIBS The minimally processed nibs contain all the cocoa bean's nutrients. Eat as they are or add to fruit salads or baking.

HOT COCOA Milk inhibits the absorption of cocoa polyphenols, so mix 2 tbsp good-quality cocoa powder with hot water and drink in a demitasse cup as you would an espresso.

COCOA POWDER
Plain unsweetened cocoa powder has twice the level of antioxidant polyphenols as processed dark chocolate, and 4 times that of milk chocolate (white chocolate contains no antioxidants).

COCOA BEANS
Catechin and epicatechin, the antioxidants found in cocoa beans and cocoa products, are the same as those that give green tea its anti-cancer properties.

CACAO NIBS
These are dried, roasted, and crushed cacao, or cocoa, beans that are used to make chocolate. Like cocoa powder, they are high in antioxidants.

DARK CHOCOLATE
Studies show that people who eat dark chocolate regularly have a lower risk of heart disease and stroke.

MILK

 HELPS KEEP BLOOD VESSELS SUPPLE

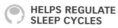 **HELPS REGULATE SLEEP CYCLES**

 **HELPS PREVENT METABOLIC SYNDROME**

Evidence shows milk has a place as a healthy food, despite being defamed by food faddists. Its **calcium** and **vitamin D** content helps the body **burn calories** more efficiently and maintain a **steady weight**, while its healthy fats help **lower blood pressure**. Organic and raw milks are higher in these **healthy fats** and **essential cofactors** than cheap milk and so are much better for you.

GOAT'S MILK
Nutritionally comparable to cow's milk, goat's milk is higher in B vitamins than either cow's or sheep's milk. If you are allergic to cow's milk, you may be able to tolerate goat's or sheep's milk.

SHEEP'S MILK
Milk from sheep is higher in fat than cow's and goat's milk, but has 40 per cent more protein than both. It is also marginally higher in phosphorus, magnesium, zinc, and iron, and is a comparable source of calcium.

COW'S MILK
A good source of protein and calcium, and is high in phosphorus and vitamin B12.

WHAT IS IT GOOD FOR?

HEART HEALTH Calcium may help reduce the risk of hypertension by keeping blood vessels elastic. Goat's and sheep's milks contain capric acid, a healthy fat that can help raise levels of "healthy" (HDL) cholesterol. Palmitoleic acid, another healthy fat, protects against insulin resistance and diabetes.

HEALTHY MIND A good source of B vitamins, especially B12, for the healthy functioning of the brain and nervous system, cell metabolism, and for helping to regulate sleep/wake cycles.

METABOLIC BALANCE Can significantly reduce your risk of metabolic syndrome (a group of factors that can lead to diabetes and heart disease) and even some cancers.

WEIGHT CONTROL Contains a novel form of vitamin B3 (niacin), which may help maintain a steady weight and improve energy expenditure. The calcium in dairy foods also increases the metabolism of fat.

HOW DO I GET THE BEST FROM IT?

HEALTHY FATS Half the fat in milk is saturated fat, but the other half has healthy fat, such as oleic acid (found in olive oil), palmitoleic acid, and conjugated linoleic acid (CLA). Sheep's and cow's milks are rich sources of CLA.

ORGANIC IS A MUST Milk from grass-fed cows contains CLA. Test tube studies indicate that CLA helps to kill skin, colorectal, and breast cancer cells. It may also help to lower "unhealthy" (LDL) cholesterol and prevent atherosclerosis (hardening of the arteries).

HOW DO I USE IT?

USE FULL FAT Full-fat milk contains only 4 per cent fat; take out the fat, and its fat-soluble vitamins A, D, E, and K are also reduced.

TRY RAW MILK Many nutritionists believe that pasteurizing milk impairs its nutritional value so try unpasteurized, or raw, milk in your diet.

YOGURT

 HELPS STRENGTHEN THE IMMUNE SYSTEM

 ASSISTS WEIGHT MANAGEMENT

 HELPS LOWER BLOOD PRESSURE

 SOOTHES STOMACH AND BOWEL UPSETS

The human intestines contain around 400 different species of bacteria, good and bad. Live yogurt, which is colonized by or cultured with certain types of "good" bacteria, can help keep things in balance; good bacteria help to turn organic acids into glucose, **lower cholesterol**, help **metabolize nutrients**, break down enzymes, proteins, and fibres in food, and help kick-start the **immune system**.

WHAT IS IT GOOD FOR?

IMMUNITY Probiotics in yogurt have a general immunity-boosting effect and inhibit a range of pathogenic bacteria and yeasts in the gut. Probiotics also show potential in preventing allergies, such as eczema, particularly in children. In older or immune-compromised people, yogurt may help increase resistance to bacterial and viral diseases.

WEIGHT MANAGEMENT Regular consumption of calcium-rich foods is linked to lower body weight in children and adults: yogurt helps reduce fat around the waistline and retain more lean muscle than diets that don't include it.

LOWERS BLOOD PRESSURE Calcium helps keep blood vessels more supple, enabling them to expand slightly when necessary to keep blood pressure low.

DIGESTIVE HEALTH Gut health is inseparable from the health of the rest of the body. Live cultures in yogurt can improve the microflora of the gut, which in turn helps ease symptoms of inflammatory bowel disease and lowers the incidence of ulcers.

HOW DO I GET THE BEST FROM IT?

CHOOSE LIVE Look for products that state specifically that yogurt is "live" or "probiotic".

KEEP IT NATURAL Avoid yogurts with artificial colours, flavours, thickeners, and sweeteners. Buy a good-quality organic, plain, live yogurt and add your own ingredients.

TRY ALTERNATIVES Sheep's and goat's milk yogurts may be easier for some to digest than cow's milk yogurts. Sheep's milk is richer in fat and is a particularly creamy alternative.

HOW DO I USE IT?

AN OMEGA-3 BOOST Stir 1 tbsp ground flaxseed into organic plain yogurt to add both fibre and healthy omega-3 fatty acids.

PLAIN YOGURT
Yogurt is made by culturing milk with a starter culture of friendly bacteria such as *Lactobacillus delbrueckii* subsp. *bulgaricus* and *Streptococcus salivarius* subsp. *thermophilus*. Other beneficial bacteria may be added during the culturing process.

YOGURT DRINK
Flavoured yogurt drinks have become a popular way to get concentrated daily "shots" of probiotic cultures, although beware of additives, such as sugar, in the drinks

GREEK-STYLE YOGURT
This yogurt is strained to remove some of the watery whey. This results in a thicker, creamier yogurt.

Kefir

 HELPS STRENGTHEN THE IMMUNE SYSTEM

 HELPS REDUCE BLOATING AND WIND

 CONTAINS ANTI-CANCER SUBSTANCES

 HELPS LOWER CHOLESTEROL

This probiotic and fermented food is made by culturing fresh milk with kefir "grains" – live colonies of bacteria and yeasts. Kefir is a good source of **calcium**, **protein,** and **potassium**, may have **anti-cancer** benefits, helps maintain the heath of the **digestive tract,** and **boosts immunity**. Kefir grains, which contain many more live bacteria than yogurt, remain alive indefinitely and can be used repeatedly.

KEFIR GRAINS
These small gelatinous nodules contain colonies of more than 30 bacteria and yeasts that are bound together in a stable, symbiotic relationship. After the grains have fermented milk, they can be filtered out and added to a new batch of milk.

KEFIR CHEESE
Cheese made from kefir contains all the beneficial probiotic microorganisms that kefir is famous for.

KEFIR MILK
Probiotics in kefir can control the growth of harmful bacteria and aid digestion, and some even manufacture vitamins in the gut.

What Is It Good For?

IMMUNE SUPPORT Kefiran, an indigestible fibre unique to kefir, has anti-inflammatory and immunity-supporting properties. Regular consumption may increase the activity of the body's natural killer cells and T-helper cells (a type of blood cell that helps kick-start the immune response). Kefir helps maintain the balance of healthy bacteria in the gut necessary to fight harmful fungi, viruses, and bacteria.

DIGESTION By breaking down lactose in milk, kefir may significantly reduce symptoms of lactose intolerance, including bloating and stomach pain, as well as speeding recovery from diarrhoea in infants. It may help with other food allergies too, such as those to eggs.

ANTI-CANCER POTENTIAL Its probiotic properties can have anti-cancer effects. Laboratory and animal studies have found that kefir can slow breast cancer cell growth.

HEART Various studies have shown that kefir may help lower "unhealthy" (LDL) cholesterol and blood pressure, though results are mixed.

How Do I Get The Best From It?

MAKE YOUR OWN Many kefir products are mixed with sugars and other additives and don't have the same medicinal benefits. Where possible, make your own kefir (p332).

How Do I Use It?

FOR VEGETARIANS Use kefir grains to ferment non-dairy milks, such as almond, soya, coconut, or oat milk.

A VERSATILE INGREDIENT Kefir can be made into a huge variety of products including cheese, spreads, and yogurt. It can also be used in baked goods, and is especially good as a sourdough starter.

TENDERIZES MEATS Kefir's mildly acidic nature can help tenderize meat. Added to sauces, it acts as a thickener.

EGGS

 **HELPS PROTECT EYE HEALTH**

 **HELPS STRENGTHEN BONES AND TEETH**

 **BOOSTS MENTAL PERFORMANCE**

 **HELPS PREVENT METABOLIC SYNDROME**

Eggs are an excellent source of quality **protein**. They contain **vitamin D** – necessary for healthy bones and teeth – and nutrients that help **balance blood sugar levels**, protect against **heart disease**, and support the healthy function of **nerves** and the **brain**. Although egg yolks contain cholesterol, studies show "unhealthy" (LDL) blood cholesterol is raised more by excess saturated fats than it is by eggs.

WHAT IS IT GOOD FOR?

AN ANTIOXIDANT BOOST Egg yolks contain the antioxidants lutein and zeaxanthine, which help protect eyes from age-related macular degeneration (loss of vision), and tryptophan and tyrosine, antioxidant amino acids that help prevent cancer and heart disease.

BONES One of the few food sources of vitamin D, and rich in phosphorus. This combination helps provide the body with the necessary building blocks for healthy bones and teeth.

BRAIN FOOD An excellent source of choline, other B-vitamins, and the mono- and polyunsaturated fats necessary to support a healthy nervous system and brain. Choline helps improve memory, and evidence shows a protein-rich breakfast, such as eggs, improves mental performance throughout the day.

METABOLIC BALANCE Evidence suggests that during digestion, egg proteins are converted into peptides that help lower blood pressure in the same way as conventional drugs such as ACE inhibitors. In addition, most of the fat in eggs is mono- and polyunsaturated, and other fatty acids called phospholipids help reduce the absorption of cholesterol.

HOW DO I GET THE BEST FROM IT?

FREE-RANGE AND ORGANIC Organic free-range eggs contain more vitamin A, omega-3 fats, and vitamin E than intensively formed eggs, and less saturated fat.

EASY ON THE HEAT As eggs lose nutritional value when cooked, try light methods of cooking, such as poaching or soft boiling.

HOW DO I USE IT?

A SIMPLE PROTEIN MEAL Add poached or soft-boiled eggs to salads for a healthy protein-enriched meal.

TRY QUAIL'S EGGS Substitute 3–4 quail's eggs for 1 large chicken's egg in salads or on toast.

CHICKEN'S EGGS
A good source of vitamin D, B-complex, and trace minerals that support cellular development and a healthy nervous system. They also contain less cholesterol than other types of egg.

QUAIL'S EGGS
These small eggs contain more phosphorus – essential for cell membranes and strong bones and teeth – than other commonly consumed eggs. They are also high in folate.

DUCK'S EGGS
Weight-for-weight, duck's eggs are higher in omega-3 fats, iron, folate, and choline than other types of eggs.

GOOSE EGGS
Contain a similar mix of nutrients to other commonly consumed eggs, but have a much higher omega-3 fat content.

TEA

 ANTIOXIDANT AND ANTIBACTERIAL

 HELPS LOWER CHOLESTEROL

 CONTAINS ANTI-CANCER SUBSTANCES

 HELPS BUILD STRONG BONES

The average tea leaf contains as much as 30 per cent **antioxidant** polyphenols, which help protect against **heart disease** and **cancer** and are **anti-inflammatory,** benefitting joints. Tea also contains **beta-carotene**, vitamins B2, C, D, and K, and potassium. Even the caffeine in tea, when taken in moderation, has health benefits: it helps **boost metabolism**, **burn fat**, and acts as a **mild diuretic**.

GREEN TEA
This delicate tea is produced by lightly steaming and then drying the freshly cut tea leaves. It is rich in a group of antioxidant polyphenols called catechins.

BLACK TEA
The dominant antioxidant polyphenols in black tea – theaflavins and thearubigins – have been shown to be as beneficial as those in green tea.

OOLONG TEA
Oolong is a semi-fermented sun-dried black tea rich in the antioxidant polyphenols called theaflavins.

WHITE TEA
Less bitter than green tea, white tea is minimally oxidized but contains similar catechins to green tea.

WHAT IS IT GOOD FOR?

IMMUNE SUPPORT Its powerful antioxidant catechins and theaflavins are antibacterial and antiviral. Studies show they can be effective against the flu virus and common causes of bacterial diarrhoea. The catechins in green and oolong teas may also have anti-allergy properties, and there is some evidence they can help reduce symptoms of eczema.

HEART Moderate consumption of black and green tea lowers "unhealthy" (LDL) cholesterol, reducing the risk of heart disease and stroke.

ANTI-CANCER A regular intake of green tea can protect against breast cancer, while tests suggest green and black tea help prevent cancer cells forming and will even kill bone, lung, stomach, and prostate cancer cells. The catechin epigallocatechin-3-gallate (EGCG) in green tea binds to certain carcinogens and helps remove them from the body.

HEALTHY BONES Consumption of green and black tea has been associated with higher bone mineral density in older adults, especially in the lumbar spine region.

ARTHRITIS Green tea polyphenols can prevent the breakdown of collagen and cartilage, so are a useful potential treatment for arthritis.

HOW DO I GET THE BEST FROM IT?

THE PERFECT CUP Use water that has boiled for no more than 10 seconds.

ORGANIC IS BEST Tea is treated with a vast number of pesticides. To avoid a toxic cup of tea, always choose organic.

HOW DO I USE IT?

DECAFFEINATE YOUR OWN TEA Pour boiling water over tea leaves, wait 30 seconds, and discard the liquid to remove roughly 60 per cent of the caffeine. Pour on more water and drink. (Waiting longer than 30 seconds destroys many vitamins, polyphenols, and flavour.)

ROSE

 PROTECTS AGAINST BACTERIAL INFECTION

 **HELPS EASE MENSTRUAL CRAMPS**

 HAS NATURAL SEDATIVE PROPERTIES

 **HELPS EASE JOINT PAIN**

A member of the same family as plums, cherries, apricots, and almonds, rose has many of the same benefits. The petals contain volatile oils that help **calm nervous tension** and are **antibacterial** – useful for treating **urinary tract infections** and **digestive upsets**. They are also rich in vitamins C, D, E, and B3, **beta-carotene**, and **antioxidants**, such as lycopene, lutein, and **anti-inflammatory** quercetin.

WHAT IS IT GOOD FOR?

ANTIBACTERIAL Its essential oils have proven antimicrobial properties.

WOMEN'S HEALTH The dried leaves and hips can be used to make an iron-rich tangy tea to make up for iron lost and as a tonic to soothe stomach cramps during menstruation.

STRESS Its scent has been proven to calm breathing and lower blood pressure, while its essential oils have a calming effect on frayed nerves and can lower feelings of anxiety.

ARTHRITIS Rosehips contain flavonoids, such as anthocyanins and quercetin, which have antioxidant properties. With their high vitamin C content, the hips can help decrease inflammation in arthritis and joint pain.

HEART Oil pressed from rosehip seeds is high in vitamin C and linoleic (omega-6) fatty acid and linolenic (omega-3) fatty acids. Eating hips from the *Rosa canina* (dog rose) for just 6 weeks helps reduce both blood pressure and "unhealthy" (LDL) cholesterol in the blood.

HOW DO I GET THE BEST FROM IT?

ORGANIC AND NATURAL Look for organic or wild-crafted sources to avoid a variety of toxic pesticides and fungicides. Choose 100-percent natural rose water, steam-distilled from rose petals and preservative-free.

ROSEHIP OIL Heart-healthy rosehip oil can be consumed, but it is too delicate to heat. It should make up no more than 20 per cent of the total oil content of a salad dressing.

HOW DO I USE IT?

MAKE A TEA For a calming, anti-inflammatory tea, steep rosehips and hibiscus flowers in equal amounts in boiling water for 5 minutes.

ROSEHIPS Can be eaten raw, though some may find the taste too tart so add to jams, jellies, syrups, fruit crumbles, and pies.

ROSEHIPS
These fruits are full of vitamin C, and their seeds yield a healthy oil that can help treat inflammation.

DAMASCENA ROSE
The oil from this rose is traditionally used to calm and uplift the mind. It is anti-inflammatory, cooling, and soothing.

ROSE WATER
An extraction of the essential oils found in rose petals, rose water retains the astringent, toning, soothing, and antiseptic properties of the whole plant.

DRIED ROSES
Rose tea is a traditional remedy for menstrual complaints.

Recipes That Heal

MANY FOODS WORK SYNERGISTICALLY TO BOOST **HEALTH** AND **VITALITY**. DISCOVER THE RIGHT COMBINATIONS WITH THESE **UNIQUE** RECIPES BASED ON THE PRINCIPLES OF TRADITIONAL **HEALING**. IF YOU ARE KEEN TO IMPROVE SPECIFIC HEALTH AREAS, TAKE **INSPIRATION** FROM THE SPECIALLY DESIGNED **A DAY OF...** EATING PLANS.

A Day Of... Heart Health

Many studies have shown that eating a healthy diet and increasing the amount of exercise you take can radically improve your heart health. These cholesterol-lowering recipes are packed with foods to improve your circulation and lower your blood pressure.

Cholesterol-busting Breakfast

Start your day with a steaming bowl of cooked oats, which are full of heart-healthy folate and potassium. This fibre-rich superfood can help to lower levels of "unhealthy" (LDL) cholesterol and keep arteries clear. For the tastiest porridge, soak the oats in water first, and stir in some freshly grated apple as it cooks.

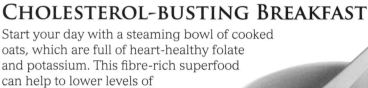

APPLE
Lowers "unhealthy" (LDL) cholesterol and is a source of vitamin C and heart-healthy antioxidants

PLAIN YOGURT
Yogurt is a natural source of calcium, and regular consumption can help prevent high blood pressure, and therefore, lower the risk of heart attack and stroke

PORRIDGE OATS
Cooking oats breaks down their phytate content, ensuring that you receive all the benefits of their nutrients

Omega-rich Lunch

Oily fish such as sardines are one of the most concentrated sources of the omega-3 fatty acids EPA and DHA, which help lower triglycerides and "unhealthy" (LDL) cholesterol levels.

TO PREPARE THE SARDINES

Mix together 1 tablespoon each of cooked and cooled short-grain rice, toasted pine nuts, and currants, a dash of lemon juice, and 1 teaspoon each of chopped parsley, mint, and dill. Divide between 6 whole, cleaned sardines, packing the stuffing inside each fish. Wrap a vine leaf around each fish to hold it together. Brush with olive oil and grill for 4–5 minutes, turning halfway through. Serve with lemon wedges.

SARDINES
Rich in numerous nutrients, including vitamins B12 and D, that have been found to support cardiovascular health

VINE LEAVES
A staple of heart-healthy Mediterranean cuisine; rich in vitamins and minerals

PINE NUTS
Contain an abundance of vitamins and minerals that help maintain normal metabolic functions

LEMON JUICE
Particularly high in magnesium, important for a healthy heart. Its pectin content and limonoid compounds also reduce cholesterol

PARSLEY
Particularly high in vitamin K for heart and circulatory health

HEART-PROTECTIVE DINNER

Pulses are known to lower the risk of heart attack and stroke, as they help lower "unhealthy" (LDL) cholesterol levels in the blood and balance blood sugar levels. Recent studies have also proven that shiitake mushrooms can help protect against cardiovascular diseases.

SEE BEANS BAKED IN A PUMPKIN POT RECIPE *p253*

SHIITAKE MUSHROOMS
Help keep blood vessels clear and prevent oxidative stress

RED AND YELLOW PEPPERS
Contain vitamins C, E, and K for heart and circulation health

BUTTER/LIMA BEANS
Very good source of cholesterol-lowering fibre

GARLIC
Cardioprotective by helping repair damage to blood vessels

OLIVE OIL
Provides healthy omega-3, -6, and -9 fatty acids

PUMPKIN
The carotenoids it contains help to protect the circulatory system

A Day Of... Good Digestion

In most cultures, good digestion is considered fundamental to general health. Try this plan of eating the right foods at the best time, using ingredients that boost digestive health. To encourage efficient absorption and elimination, don't rush your food, and chew thoroughly.

Balancing Breakfast

Breakfast is a good time to eat a balance of foods: fibre to keep your bowels regular, protein to sustain you, and carbohydrates to give you energy for the day ahead. Top this off with some antioxidant-rich fruit.

BERRIES
A delicious way to boost your vitamin and antioxidant intake

TOASTED FLAKES
Wholegrain wheat flakes provide B vitamins and fibre for roughage. To make, toast wholegrain flakes in an oven at 180°C (350°F/Gas 4) for 20 minutes, turning occasionally.

SUNFLOWER SEEDS
Good source of pantothenic acid, phosphorus, copper, and manganese

PUMPKIN SEEDS
Contain high levels of essential fatty acids and zinc

PLAIN YOGURT
A natural probiotic to keep gut flora healthy

LINSEEDS
Gentle bulk laxative that provides omega-3 and omega-6 fatty acids

Sustaining Lunch

Make lunch your main meal. Chicken provides a low-fat source of protein and assists healthy digestion; here it is rubbed with lime juice, grilled until cooked through, and served with a spicy sauce.

TO MAKE THE SAUCE

Sauté, in olive oil, crushed garlic cloves, a thumb of crushed fresh ginger root, chopped spring onions, and sweet potato, and a spice mix (turmeric, cumin, and coriander) for 10 minutes. Cook until the vegetables are tender. Add 300ml (10fl oz) of stock and some lime juice. Process in a blender.

CHICKEN
Rich in many nutrients including selenium and zinc

LIME JUICE
Excellent source of vitamin C, and can help relieve indigestion

SWEET POTATO
Easily digested source of carotenoids

CUMIN
Stimulates digestive enzymes

TURMERIC
Anti-inflammatory that helps prevent gas

EASILY DIGESTED DINNER

Soup can make an ideal light meal to enjoy in the evening: this carrot soup is easily digested, packed with nutrients, and you can make enough to last for a couple of days. In traditional Chinese medicine, cooked carrots are thought to improve digestion as they contain fibre, thus aiding bowel regularity. The fibre also promotes a feeling of fullness, good if you are trying to cut down on calories.

SEE CARROT AND COCONUT SOUP RECIPE *p213*

COCONUT
Helps fight off inflammation and unwanted bacteria

ONION
Provides a source of phytonutrients

CARROT
Easily digested source of carotenoids

CORIANDER
Promotes a healthy digestion

LIME
Source of vitamin C and a digestive tonic

A Day Of... Liver Health

The liver needs all the help it can get – it has the job of breaking down and eliminating every dietary and environmental toxin in our bodies. This 1-day plan will give you an idea of which foods can help stimulate the natural detoxifying processes in the liver and encourage regeneration.

Cleansing Breakfast

Grapefruit is an effective liver-cleansing and antioxidant-rich fruit. Combine it with a detoxifying, freshly juiced fruit and vegetable juice for an invigorating start to your day.

APPLE
Triterpenoids in the skin have potent protective activity for liver cells

CARROT
Its carotenoid content helps prevent oxidative damage inside the body

MINT
A herb with tonic and decongestant properties

GRAPEFRUIT
Contains enzymes that help the liver break down toxins more efficiently

LIVER-BOOSTING LUNCH

Cynarin, an active chemical constituent in globe artichokes, helps improve the proper functioning of both the liver and gall bladder – it causes increased bile flow and is an aid to digestion, making artichokes an ideal food to support the health of the liver.

LEMON
The ultimate liver-cleansing fruit, it is high in vitamin C and bioflavonoids

GLOBE ARTICHOKE
Contains bioactive phytonutrients for liver and gut health

OLIVE OIL
Stimulates activity in the liver, gall bladder, and bile duct

GARLIC
Activates liver enzymes that support detoxification

PARSLEY
A gently stimulating herb that encourages the elimination of toxins; also contains vitamins and minerals

TO MAKE THE HERB ARTICHOKES

Cut off each stalk but leave 2cm (¾in) at the top. Peel the remaining stalk, cutting away the tough exterior. Cut off the top of the cone and scoop out the hairy choke. Squeeze lemon juice into the cavity. Mix 2 chopped garlic cloves, 1 tablespoon of finely chopped mint, and a bunch of finely chopped flat-leaf parsley. Stuff the mix in the cavity. Simmer the artichokes in a pan of water over a medium heat for 30 minutes or until tender. Ensure they stay upright in the pan.

REGENERATIVE DINNER

In traditional Chinese medicine, the liver is strengthened by eating sour-flavoured foods and cleansed by green leafy foods. This dish is bursting with ingredients that help the body eliminate toxic substances, clear blood vessels, and enhance bowel movement and urine output.

SEE MUNG BEAN AND PURPLE SPROUTING BROCCOLI RECIPE *p248*

GREEN MANGO
Its sweet-sour flavour increases liver and gall bladder function

CARROTS
Contain antioxidants renowned to enliven the liver

PURPLE SPROUTING BROCCOLI
Contains sulphur compounds to support the liver's ability to detoxify chemicals in the body

MUNG BEAN SPROUTS
Abundant in minerals and fibre that are essential for detoxing

LIME
Source of healing vitamin C and liver tonic

CHICORY
Traditionally used to cool and cleanse the liver

A Day Of... Skin Health

Choosing foods that are packed with the vitamins and minerals your skin needs will, over time, actively nourish your skin and dramatically boost its appearance. Start with this day of delicious meals and build from there, selecting skin-friendly foods and turning them into tasty recipes.

Collagen-boosting Breakfast

Eggs are powerhouses of nutrients that are beneficial for the skin. They include collagen-building protein, vitamin A, omega fatty acids, and carotenoids to protect against UV ageing. Cook scrambled eggs with chopped fresh herbs to add valuable antioxidants.

CHIVES
Contain detoxifying sulphur and anti-inflammatory quercetin

TURMERIC
Excellent antioxidant properties to prevent free-radical damage

EGGS
Choline and lutein help promote skin elasticity and prevent wrinkles

MARJORAM
Popular Mediterranean herb with antiseptic and anti-inflammatory properties

Omega-rich Lunch

Oil-rich cold-water fish, such as salmon, are a real superfood when it comes to skin health: their anti-inflammatory properties help to improve dry skin and relieve eczema and psoriasis. Serving baked salmon in a salad with a yogurt dressing is a great way of getting many of the nutrients your skin needs.

TO MAKE THE SALAD DRESSING

Mix together the juice of 1 orange and ½ tablespoon each of chopped hazelnuts, sherry vinegar, plain yogurt, and hazelnut oil.

PLAIN YOGURT
Contains protein and zinc for skin health

HAZELNUTS
Good source of vitamins and minerals for healthy hair, skin, and nails

SALMON
Contains omega oils to keep skin elastic and prevent wrinkles

LAMB'S LETTUCE
Its antioxidants prevent free-radical damage

RADIANCE-BOOSTING DINNER

Eating fresh, young green vegetables regularly is a good way to cleanse the body and keep the complexion clear. Include asparagus, as it stimulates the digestion by acting as a prebiotic and contains compounds that have an anti-inflammatory effect and help to prevent the signs of ageing.

SEE STIR-FRIED SPRING VEGETABLES RECIPE *p259*

OLIVE OIL
High in polyphenols, known to help postpone ageing and boost cell repair......

ASPARAGUS
A storehouse of vitamins and minerals that can benefit the skin ...

MANGETOUT
Good source of vitamins A and C for skin health

SPINACH
Rich in iron and antioxidants that have anti-inflammatory effects

WILD GARLIC
Contains sulphur compounds to keep skin blemish-free

A Day Of... Healthy Joints

To reduce the inflammation and pain associated with arthritis and joint problems, switch to a diet that contains foods known to reduce inflammation and cleansing foods that help remove the toxins which aggravate the problem. Sample this 1-day plan to learn which foods to incorporate into your diet.

Easy-mover Breakfast

Fruit is a source of antioxidants that helps rid the body of cell-damaging free radicals and suppresses inflammation (avoid oranges, as they may make some arthritis pain worse). Apple (fresh or dried) is particularly good for joint problems, but keep its skin on, as this is what contains many of the best nutrients. Serve with buckwheat grains, toasted in a medium oven until golden, and plain yogurt.

PLAIN YOGURT
Provides calcium for healthy bones and joints

DESSERT APPLES
Contain inflammation-fighting antioxidants. Use dried apple rings for extra flavour

DRIED CRANBERRIES
Contain vitamin C to help reduce pain and inflammation

BUCKWHEAT
A highly nutritious, gluten-free grain. Contains quercetin, which has anti-inflammatory properties

DRIED APRICOTS
Good source of anthocyanidins

Joint-health Lunch

Cold-water salmon, tuna, herring, mackerel, and halibut contain omega-3 fatty acids, which are potently anti-inflammatory. Bake in the oven until cooked through and serve cold with an apple cider vinegar dressing.

TO MAKE THE DRESSING

A yogurt-based cider vinegar dressing is a great accompaniment to baked salmon. Mix together 2 tablespoons each of apple cider vinegar and finely chopped mint, and 4 tablespoons of Greek yogurt. Drizzle over the cold salmon.

LEMON
A source of vitamin C and bioflavonoids, and can help reduce inflammation

DILL
Good source of calcium to help reduce bone loss, and antioxidants

SALMON
High in protein to help build healthy connective tissue, and in anti-inflammatory omega-3 fatty acids

CUCUMBER
May improve inflamed joints since it helps eliminate uric acid and contains vitamin C

APPLE CIDER VINEGAR
Traditionally used to alkalize the body and relieve the pain of arthritis

Anti-inflammatory Dinner

This soup is packed with the powerful anti-inflammatory properties of turmeric and so can help relieve swelling and pain including rheumatic and arthritic pain. Use either dried turmeric or fresh turmeric root in your recipes.

SEE PUY LENTIL SOUP WITH FRESH TURMERIC RECIPE *p212*

DRINK

Apple cider vinegar and honey is a traditional remedy for arthritis, as the overall effect of apple cider vinegar and honey is alkalizing. To make, add 2 teaspoons each of honey and unpasteurized apple cider vinegar to a glassful of lukewarm water. Drink 2 or 3 times a day before meals.

PUY LENTILS
Vegetarian source of collagen-building protein

TURMERIC
Contains curcumin, a potent anti-inflammatory

GINGER
Zingibain suppresses substances that trigger pain and cause tissues to swell

ONIONS
Source of quercetin, which reduces inflammation

CORIANDER
Source of vitamins A, C, and K for healthy bones and joints

A DAY OF... BOOSTED ENERGY

Great energy comes from a good balance of rest, exercise, and eating foods that are packed with nutrients to strengthen reserves and provide vitality. This 1-day plan provides an introduction to some of the foods that are known to act as a tonic for the body.

POWER BREAKFAST

Quail's eggs are renowned in China for invigorating and strengthening the body. They are a rich source of protein, iron, potassium, and B vitamins, and taste delicious scrambled with lightly fried chopped tomatoes.

TOMATOES
A superfood containing antioxidants such as lycopene and vitamin C

PARSLEY
Contains energy-promoting iron and vitamins A, C, and K

QUAIL'S EGGS
Packed with 3–4 times the energy-boosting nutrients of a chicken's egg

BLACK PEPPER
Volatile oils stimulate digestion to promote the absorption of all nutrients from food

RYE BREAD
A rich source of magnesium, promoting enzymes involved in the body's use of glucose and insulin secretion

VITALITY LUNCH

Asparagus is packed with energy-promoting nutrients. Stir-fry with other vegetables, such as immune-boosting broccoli and carrots, adding the ones that need the most cooking to the wok first. Combine with protein-rich prawns and cleansing, anti-inflammatory fresh ginger root for an easy yet revitalizing feast.

RED PEPPER
A gently stimulating vegetable full of essential nutrients

PRAWNS
A warming, nourishing food high in protein and carotenoids, such as astaxanthin

CHIVES
A simple way to add stimulating qualities to a dish, chives also promote a healthy appetite

ASPARAGUS
A source of the essential energy nutrients potassium and B vitamins

BROCCOLI
Enhances detoxification, which helps enhance energy

CARROTS
Root vegetables help boost reserves of energy and are a source of beta-carotene

ENERGY-SUSTAINING DINNER

To support long-term energy, eat a light cooked meal in the evening. Wood pigeon meat is tasty, tender, and nutritious, and is regarded as an excellent kidney and energy tonic. Goji berries are added to give a metabolic boost.

SEE WOOD PIGEON BREASTS WITH GOJI BERRIES RECIPE *p260*

PIGEON
Excellent source of
iron and B vitamins
for energy

ONION
A warming and
nourishing source
of phytonutrients to
boost good health

CHILLI
Stimulating to taste buds
and improves energy levels

**SHIITAKE
MUSHROOMS**
Considered a good
general tonic that boosts
various body systems

GOJI BERRIES
A superfood packed
with essential nutrients

CARROTS
Good source of slow-
release energy

A Day Of... Stress Relief

Traditionally, many foods have been known to support the nervous system during times of stress. Today we understand that in fact these foods have an effect on neuro-transmitters in the body, such as the hormone serotonin, which is why they generate a "feel-good" factor.

Positive Breakfast

Eating a healthy breakfast can set the scene for a positive attitude through the day and sustained energy levels. This combination of granola, fresh fruits, and honey provides many nutrients to support the sense of well-being.

TO MAKE THE GRANOLA

Drizzle rolled oats with honey on an oiled baking tray and toast in the oven until golden. Remove and leave to cool. Mix with ingredients such as pine nuts, pumpkin seeds, dried fruits, corn flakes, and bran flakes to taste.

ROLLED OATS
A traditional remedy to support a stressed nervous system

BANANA
Contains potassium to regulate nerve function

PUMPKIN SEEDS
Full of stress-busting magnesium, B vitamins, and serotonin

SULTANAS
Good source of energy, vitamins, minerals, and antioxidants

HONEY
A sweet source of antioxidants to protect cells from oxidative damage

STRESS-BUSTING LUNCH

Sustain your body and mind with foods packed with the nutrients you need to fight stress, such as this fish soup, full of B vitamins, magnesium, and phytonutrient-rich herbs and spices.

MONKFISH
An excellent source of B vitamins, important for alleviating stress

CHILLI
A warming, stimulating source of nutrients for optimal health

TOMATOES
Source of carotenoids and potassium, for good nerve health

HADDOCK
Rich in magnesium, the anti-stress mineral

FENNEL
Strong antioxidant that contains cell-protective components

SAFFRON
Used in herbal medicine for its anti-depressant properties

TO MAKE THE SOUP

Fry 1 chopped onion in olive oil until soft. Add 1 crushed garlic clove and 1 finely chopped fennel bulb, and cook until the fennel softens. Stir in 1 finely chopped red chilli, a splash of white wine, 400g can of tomatoes, 900ml (1½ pints) of hot fish stock, and a pinch of saffron. Bring to the boil, then reduce to a simmer for 45 minutes. Blend to a smooth soup. Pour into a clean saucepan and add 300ml (10fl oz) of hot water. Simmer gently. Add 200g (7oz) cubes of monkfish and haddock loin and cook over a low heat for 6–10 minutes.

RECOVERY DINNER

Shiitake mushrooms are renowned for being adaptogenic, which means they help the body recover quickly from all kinds of stress. Marinated tofu, which is made from soya beans, is easy to digest.

SEE MARINATED TOFU WITH SHIITAKE AND NOODLES RECIPE *p258*

SESAME SEEDS
Rich in beneficial minerals

SHIITAKE MUSHROOMS
Potent phytonutrients increase resistance to stress and fatigue

MANGETOUT
Its B vitamins help produce the hormones necessary to fight stress

TOFU
A good source of tryptophan for stress-relief and better sleep

MUNG BEAN SPROUTS
Contain B vitamins and magnesium to manage stress symptoms

A Day Of... Men's Health

To enhance men's health, choose foods that improve vitality, support the body's energy levels, and are good for the heart and circulation. Men also benefit from a diet that is rich in antioxidants, essential fatty acids, strengthening minerals, and protein. Try this menu for a day of health-boosting benefits.

Fuel-up Breakfast

Start the day with a combination of fresh fruit, seeds, and yogurt – good for your vitamin and mineral intake – or try buckwheat pancakes or oat porridge with fresh fruit. Other suitable options for breakfast are eggs or fish.

BLUEBERRIES
An immune-boosting superfood packed with antioxidants for cancer-prevention

PUMPKIN SEEDS
An excellent source of zinc – essential for reproductive system and prostate health

SUNFLOWER SEEDS
A rich source of omega oils and B vitamins for both heart and brain health

PLAIN YOGURT
Good source of calcium, and enhances gut health

Active-life Lunch

Cold-water oily fish, such as salmon, mackerel, and herring, are rich in omega-3 and other essential fatty acids good for heart and brain health and for keeping joints flexible. Mix cured or pickled herring with cooked root vegetables such as potato (capable of building reserves of energy) and beetroot (particularly good for the heart and circulation).

TO MAKE THE DRESSING

Mix 150ml (5fl oz) of mayonnaise, 1 tablespoon of creamed horseradish, and 1–2 teaspoons of Dijon mustard with lemon juice.

HERRING
A very good source of protein, vitamin B12, selenium for longevity, and EPA and DHA

ONIONS
Phytochemical compounds allium and allyl disulphide have anti-cancer and blood-sugar-regulating properties, while quercetin helps prevent heart disease

BEETROOT
Highly nutritious source of magnesium, iron, and betaine for cardiovascular health

POTATOES
Good source of fibre, and rich in vitamins C and B6 and potassium

HORSERADISH
Naturally antibiotic and anti-catarrhal herb with decongestant properties

PROTEIN-PACKED DINNER

Quinoa provides important protein with essential amino acids and helps build muscle, while tomatoes contain lycopene, which aids healthy circulation. The addition of strength-building walnuts makes this a great meal for active men.

SEE SAVOY CABBAGE PARCELS RECIPE *p265*

CABBAGE
Good source of detoxifying and anti-cancer compounds

TOMATOES
Great source of lycopene for heart health

QUINOA
One of the best cereal-sources of protein

WALNUTS
Renowned in China for improving men's health and stamina

CRANBERRIES
Contain proanthocyanidins, which help cells resist bacterial infection

A Day Of... Women's Health

It's much easier to cope with the demands of modern life if you eat healthy meals that boost your energy levels and sense of well-being. Here are foods that are particularly suitable for women's health, and known for their anti-cancer, anti-stress, nourishing, and balancing benefits.

Balancing Breakfast

Choose a breakfast of ingredients that are full of essential nutrients such as iron, calcium, and the antioxidant vitamin C. Eating plenty of soluble fibre-rich dried fruits, such as prunes and apricots, will also help balance blood sugar levels and prevent constipation.

PLAIN YOGURT
Contains probiotics for gut health and calcium for bones

ORANGE
Excellent source of vitamin C and bioflavonoids to support the circulation

APRICOTS
Rich in fibre, vitamin A, carotenoids, and iron to to promote better digestion, improve eyesight, and build red blood cells

PRUNES
Source of fibre and antioxidant phytonutrients

Hormone-protective Lunch

Research has confirmed watercress as a true superfood. It contains an abundance of phytonutrients including substances renowned for their anti-cancer properties, and also iron and vitamin K to help prevent osteoporosis. Try this light yet filling watercress soup.

ONION
Its phytochemical compounds contribute to healthy skin and help prevent infections

WATERCRESS
Contains gluconasturtin with potent cancer-inhibiting properties

PEARS
Low in calories and high in dietary fibre and antioxidants

CRÈME FRAÎCHE
Good source of calcium for bone health

OLIVE OIL
Mediterranean diet staple containing omega-3, -6, and -9 fatty acids

HOW TO MAKE THE SOUP

Fry 1 onion in butter until soft, stirring to prevent burning. Add the stalks of a large bunch of watercress, 3 chopped pears, and 1 litre (1¾ pints) vegetable stock. Season and simmer for 15 minutes. Remove from the heat, add the watercress leaves, and blitz in a blender. Stir in 200ml (7fl oz) crème fraîche and the juice of ½ lemon. Serve garnished with Parmesan.

IMMUNITY-ENHANCING DINNER

Chicken is particularly suitable for women in terms of nourishment and rejuvenation, as it has immune-boosting properties and high B vitamin levels to help the body produce energy. Eat with stress-reducing potatoes and salad.

SEE GINGER CHICKEN RECIPE *p261*

CHICKEN
Low-fat protein and selenium for metabolic and thyroid health

GARLIC
Contains compounds to protect heart and prevent infection

LIME
Excellent source of vitamin C

HONEY
This antioxidant-rich elixir protects heart and waistline

GINGER
Improves digestion and protects against ageing

POTATOES
Source of vitamins B and C to protect against stress

A DAY OF... HEALTHY PREGNANCY

While you are pregnant, eat foods that are packed with as much nourishment as possible for you and for your growing baby. It is particularly important to concentrate on foods that contain abundant minerals, such as calcium and iron. Consume as few additives as possible, so eat organic if you can.

DIGESTION-FRIENDLY BREAKFAST

Ease yourself into the day with foods that are nourishing and easily digested. This smoothie of fresh fruits, crushed linseeds, and orange juice is the perfect choice. Eggs are also a good breakfast option.

APRICOTS
Good source of fibre, iron, and antioxidants

PAPAYA
Contains enzymes that assist the digestive system

ORANGE JUICE
Rich in vitamin C and bioflavonoids to help prevent varicose veins

LINSEEDS
Help prevent constipation and a good source of omega-3 fatty acids

OATCAKES
A slow-release carbohydrate to balance blood sugar levels, and easily digested

NUTRITIOUS LUNCH

Lunch is a good time to have a protein-rich meal to benefit you and your baby. Chicken contains B vitamins that help the body cope with stress, release energy, and form DNA. This lunch includes chicken shaken in a spicy toasted coconut mix, stir-fried, and served with a tropical salad.

TO MAKE THE SALAD

Put 2 tablespoons of toasted coconut, 1 teaspoon each of ground ginger and cinnamon, a pinch of ground nutmeg, and zest of ½ lemon in a large plastic food bag and mix. Add 1 chicken breast cut into strips. Season and shake well to coat the chicken. Stir-fry the chicken for 3–4 minutes in olive oil. Mix with the salad ingredients and add lemon juice.

GINGER
One of nature's best anti-nausea remedies, ginger also stimulates digestion

AVOCADO
Rich source of omega fatty acids, vitamin K, and fibre

COCONUT
Contains manganese and healthy essential fatty acids

ROCKET
Source of folate and antioxidant phytonutrients

CHICKEN
Source of protein and tryptophan to help the body cope with stress

MANGO
Prebiotic qualities, plus fibre, vitamins B6, and C

SUSTAINING DINNER

Sweet potatoes are both nourishing and easy to digest, making them a great food to eat in the evening. They are combined here with aubergine and sweet peppers – all good sources of phytonutrients that are known to be beneficial for the healthy development of new cells.

SEE VEGETABLE MOUSSAKA RECIPE *p278*

AUBERGINE
Anthocyanins in the skin of the aubergine help brain cell development

CHEESE
Good source of calcium to build strong bones and teeth, and for muscle and nerve function

RED PEPPERS
Contains carotenoids for healthy heart and eyes

SWEET POTATO
Contains nutrients that act as antioxidants, and are anti-inflammatory and blood-sugar regulating

COURGETTE
Source of B vitamins including folate

RECIPE CHOOSER

❤ HEART AND CIRCULATION

BREAKFASTS

SNACKS

SOUPS

LIGHT MEALS AND SALADS

Mushroom Frittata with Cherry Tomatoes and Basil p236

MAIN MEALS

SWEET TREATS

DIGESTION

Spicy Raw Vegetable Spaghetti p246

URINARY

RESPIRATORY

Sea Bass with Spinach and Mango p250

Quail's Egg and Chicory Salad p224

 DETOX

METABOLIC BALANCE

Chanterelles and Chillies with Pasta p267

Cherry Strudel p293

IMMUNE SUPPORT

⚡ ENERGY BOOST

Butternut Squash Soup p219

MUSCLES AND JOINTS

SNACKS

Butternut Squash and Walnut
Bites p200

Mushroom and Chestnut Bites p202

SOUPS

Puy Lentil Soup with Fresh
Turmeric p212

Carrot and Coconut Soup p213

Sweet Potato and Celeriac Soup p216

LIGHT MEALS AND SALADS

Mushroom Frittata with
Cherry Tomatoes and
Basil p236

MAIN MEALS

Savoy Cabbage Parcels p265

Grilled Mackerel with Chard p275

Grilled Sardines with Tomato
Salsa p276

Barlotto with Chestnut
Purée p281

SWEET TREATS

Nutty Sugar Loaf p289

Cherry Strudel p293

Baked Quince p294

Sesame Heart Cookies p299

DRINKS

Barley Grass and Barley
Lemonade p306

Sour Cherry Drink p308

Deep Cleansing Tea p322

OILS, DRESSINGS, AND EXTRAS

Flatbread with Sweet Potato
and Coriander p327

Sourdough Rye Bread p328

SKIN AND HAIR

BREAKFASTS

Feta and Oregano Squares p180

Almond Porridge with
Apricots p188

SNACKS

Sprouted Medley p204

Tomato Crackers p205

SOUPS

Carrot and Coconut Soup p213

LIGHT MEALS AND SALADS

Spinach and Ricotta Filo Rolls p230

Buckwheat Pancakes with Nettles
and Feta Cheese p238

Artichokes in a Sweet Spicy
Sauce p239

MAIN MEALS

Spicy Raw Vegetable Spaghetti p246

Chanterelles and Chillies with
Pasta p267

SWEET TREATS

Sesame Heart Cookies p299

DRINKS

Five-Flavour Juice p312

Marshmallow and Liquorice
Tea p320

Deep Cleansing Tea p322

Deep Nurture Tea p322

OILS, DRESSINGS, AND EXTRAS

Sourdough Rye Bread p328

Rose and Fennel Seed Oil p333

Rose and Raspberry Vinegar p334

Blackberry Vinegar p334

MIND AND EMOTIONS

BREAKFASTS

Poached Eggs and Spinach p182

Quail's Eggs on Rye Bread p184

Kefir Cheese with Linseed and
Berries p184

Oat Porridge with Goji Berries
and Cinnamon p187

Sweet Saffron Rice With
Cardamom p191

SNACKS

Butternut Squash and Walnut
Bites p200

Mushroom and Chestnut Bites p202

Spicy Crackers p207

SOUPS

Raw Tomato Soup p210

Quail Soup p217

Butternut Squash Soup p219

LIGHT MEALS AND SALADS

Nori Vegetable Roll p234

Fresh Coriander Leaf Pesto
with Pasta p241

Braised Red Chicory and Celery
Heart Salad p243

MAIN MEALS

Vegetable Hot Pot p256

Sauerkraut Parcels p264

Savoy Cabbage Parcels p265

Grilled Sardines with Tomato
Salsa p276

Fragrant Rice and Millet p283

SWEET TREATS

Fresh Fig Delight with Pear
and Red Wine Sauce p285

Almond and Raspberry Cake p286

Nutty Sugar Loaf p289

Warm Fruit Salad in Sweet
Wine Sauce p290

Cherry Strudel p293

Rose Petal and White Wine
Sorbet p295

Mediterranean Nut Squares in Rose
and Cardamom Syrup p298

Almond and Pistachio
Macaroons p300

Poppy Seed and Walnut Roulade p302

Dried Fruit and Nut Roll p303

DRINKS

Sour Cherry Drink p308

Alert and Joyful Juice p313

Valentine's Special p315

Rose Syrup p315

A Cup of Happiness p317

Mint and Friends Tea p318

Marshmallow and Liquorice
Tea p320

Deep Sleep Tea p321

Astragalus and Schisandra
Broth p324

Seaweed and Miso Broth p325

Venison Casserole with Cranberries p270

Blackberry Lemonade p306

BREAKFASTS

DON'T SKIMP ON THE MOST **IMPORTANT MEAL** OF THE DAY. FRESH FRUIT, WHOLE GRAINS, AND QUALITY PROTEIN SET THE TONE FOR YOUR DAY WITH **BALANCING AND SUSTAINING** MEALS THAT FEED YOUR **BODY AND MIND**.

BUCKWHEAT AND BLACKBERRY CREAM

◎ **PROTECTS THE HEART AND BLOOD VESSELS**

⚡ **CONTAINS SLOW-RELEASE SUGARS**

◎ **HELPS ALLEVIATE HEAVY PERIODS**

≡ **EASY TO DIGEST AND GLUTEN-FREE**

This is a quick, antioxidant-rich porridge recipe. Both blackberries and roasted buckwheat help strengthen the heart, lower cholesterol, and have haemostatic properties, meaning that they help reduce the flow of blood. This makes it a good choice for women who suffer from heavy bleeding during menstruation. It can also be beneficial for men with prostate discharge.

SERVES 4

8 tbsp buckwheat grains
1 litre (1¾ pints) almond milk
a large pinch of salt
4 tsp vanilla extract
400g (14oz) blackberries

1 To toast the buckwheat, preheat the oven to 180°C (350°F/Gas 4). Spread the buckwheat grains thinly over some baking trays and toast in the oven until they are golden. Shake the baking trays occasionally to stop the grains burning. Remove from the oven.

2 Place a handful of roasted buckwheat in a coffee grinder or a powerful food processor or blender, and blitz into a fine meal. Repeat with the rest of the roasted buckwheat. Pour the almond milk into a small saucepan and heat it gently over a low heat. Spoon in the buckwheat, add the salt and vanilla extract, and whisk thoroughly until the mixture is smooth. Cook for 5 minutes, adding more almond milk if necessary until you achieve the consistency you prefer.

3 Meanwhile, place the blackberries in the clean food processor or blender and blitz to a smooth sauce.

4 Remove the pan from the heat and pour the buckwheat cream into 4 serving bowls. Pour the blackberry sauce on top and serve.

Blackberries (p30) need to be fresh, as nutrients can deteriorate with age. They contain salicylic acid, which helps protect against heart disease.

BUCKWHEAT PANCAKES WITH FRESH BERRY SAUCE

 **HELPS KEEP BLOOD VESSELS SUPPLE**

 **PROMOTES A HEALTHY DIGESTIVE TRACT**

 **PROTECTS AGAINST FREE-RADICAL DAMAGE**

This antioxidant-rich breakfast dish is heart-healthy and full of beneficial fibre, and contains warming cinnamon, which has antiseptic properties. For the maximum nutrients, why not grind your own flour (see Tip below); use either raw buckwheat or roasted buckwheat grains. Raspberries, cranberries, and blueberries are ideal, either on their own or in combination.

SERVES 4–6

175g (6oz) fresh berries, such as raspberries, cranberries, and blueberries

225g (8oz) organic buckwheat flour

1 tsp baking powder

¼ tsp rou gui (Chinese cinnamon bark) or ½ tsp ground cinnamon

a pinch of salt

275ml (9½fl oz) rice milk (or milk if dairy is not an issue)

1 large egg

1–2 tbsp ghee

3 tbsp maple syrup, to serve

1 Place the fresh berries in a food processor or blender, and blitz until smooth (avoid puréeing blueberries, if using, as their flavour is lost when blended with other berries). If you want the sauce to be free from pips, strain it through a fine sieve. Set the sauce aside while you make the pancakes.

2 Mix together the buckwheat flour, baking powder, rou gui or cinnamon, and salt in a mixing bowl. In another bowl, whisk together the rice milk and egg. Gradually pour the egg mixture into the dry ingredients, whisking constantly as you do so, to form a smooth batter.

3 Heat a frying pan, brush the base and sides with a knob of ghee, then ladle a little of the pancake mixture into the pan to make a thin pancake. Fry for 2–3 minutes, then toss or turn the pancake and cook it on the other side. Keep the cooked pancakes hot by stacking them on a plate set over a bowl of very hot water while you repeat with the rest of the batter.

4 Stir the blueberries, if using, into the berry sauce. Drizzle the pancakes with maple syrup and serve with the berry sauce.

TIP: Grinding your own flour is always a healthier choice because once the grains are crushed, their nutrients begin to deteriorate quickly. As a result, whole grains have a much longer shelf life than ready-milled flour, which may already be up to 1 year old by the time you buy it. Buckwheat is a soft grain (it has had the hull, or bran, already removed), so it is easy to turn into flour. Simply blitz a few handfuls of grain at a time in a coffee grinder (or use a powerful food processor or blender).

Cassia bark or "rou gui" (Cinnamon cassia or Cortex Cinnamoni) is a pungent variety of Chinese cinnamon, with properties similar to culinary cinnamon (Cinnamon zeylanicum).

POACHED EGGS AND SPINACH

 BOOSTS IRON STORES TO COMBAT FATIGUE    **STRENGTHENS HEART AND BLOOD VESSELS**    **HELPS PROMOTE PEACEFUL SLEEP**

Organic, free-range eggs are quality foods that, when prepared correctly by poaching or soft-boiling, provide complete nutrition. Traditionally, egg yolks are considered nourishing to the liver, heart, and kidneys, and are known to contain antioxidant amino acids that protect against heart disease. They can also help combat anaemia, diarrhoea or constipation, and even insomnia.

SERVES 4

1 tbsp olive oil
4 shallots, finely chopped
1 chilli, deseeded and finely chopped
1 tsp ground turmeric
2 garlic cloves, crushed
4 tbsp coconut cream
200g (7oz) spinach, chopped
salt and freshly ground black pepper
1 tbsp white wine vinegar
4 chicken's or duck's eggs
4 slices of wholemeal toast, or some cooked millet, to serve
a bunch of coriander leaves, finely chopped, to garnish (optional)

1 Heat a tablespoon of water with the olive oil in a small saucepan. Add the shallots and chilli, and cook over a low heat until the vegetables are soft. Stir in the turmeric, then add the garlic and coconut cream. Cook until the coconut cream is heated through, and then add the spinach. Stir the mixture until the spinach wilts and remove from the heat. Add a pinch of salt and a sprinkle of black pepper.

2 Heat a wide, shallow pan filled with water until tiny bubbles appear on the bottom (don't allow the water to boil before adding the eggs). Add the vinegar to the water to help keep the egg protein from disintegrating (the acid in the vinegar acts as a coagulant). Give the water a few swirls with a spoon, which will keep the eggs in the centre of the pan. Crack each egg into a small plate or ramekin dish and slide into the water, just below the surface. The egg will sink to the bottom and rise as it cooks. Poach the eggs for about 3 minutes.

3 Place a piece of wholemeal toast on each plate, or fill a cook's ring with a 2cm (¾in) layer of cooked millet, and spoon some of the spinach on top. Remove the ring, if using. Place a poached egg on top of each stack and sprinkle some coriander leaves over it, if using. Season with a little black pepper and serve immediately.

Duck's eggs (p143) are traditionally believed to have a cooling, anti-inflammatory effect on the lungs, making them useful for asthma, dry coughs, and sore throats.

Quail's Eggs On Rye Bread

 **HELPS MAINTAIN ENERGY LEVELS**   **PROMOTES A SENSE OF WELL-BEING**

As a hearty breakfast or brunch on cold winter mornings, this recipe is ideal. Quail's eggs, which are considered to be an energizing food in traditional Chinese medicine, are combined here with peppers, chilli, garlic, and chives, which have warming properties. This dish is particularly beneficial if you need to regain your strength after a prolonged illness, surgery, or childbirth.

SERVES 4–6

2 tbsp olive oil

1 small onion, finely chopped

½ red chilli, finely chopped

1 large yellow pepper, deseeded, skinned (optional), and finely chopped

2 large tomatoes, skinned (optional), and finely chopped

1 garlic clove, crushed

salt and freshly ground black pepper

6 slices of rye bread

1 tbsp ghee, or clarified butter

6 quail's eggs

1 tbsp chopped chives

1 Heat the olive oil in a medium saucepan and sauté the onion and chilli over a medium heat for 2–3 minutes until the onions soften. Add the yellow pepper and continue stirring for 2–3 minutes, then add the tomatoes, crushed garlic, and 2 tablespoons of water, and cook over a low heat until the mixture thickens. Remove from the heat and season with salt and black pepper.

2 Meanwhile, toast the rye bread and heat the ghee in a medium frying pan. Break the eggs into the pan and fry them, removing them as soon as the whites are cooked and while the egg yolks are still soft.

3 Divide the slices of toast between 4 or 6 hot serving plates. Top each slice of toast with a spoonful of sautéed vegetables and an egg. Garnish with the chopped chives, and serve while hot.

Kefir Cheese With Linseed And Berries

 **HELPS FIGHT INFLAMMATION**    **HELPS IMPROVE CIRCULATION**    **PROMOTES A SENSE OF WELL-BEING**

This combination of quality dairy produce and anti-inflammatory, omega-3-rich linseed oil is a twist on a healing regimen, the Budwig Diet, which helps to counter the effects of modern diets that are high in unhealthy fats. The diet has been used to treat and help prevent heart disease, diabetes, arthritis, and even cancer. The probiotic kefir cheese also helps to boost immunity.

SERVES 2

4 tbsp linseeds

6 tbsp organic kefir cheese (p332), or use quark or cottage cheese

6 tbsp linseed oil

about 250g (9oz) soft berries

1 Place the linseeds in a food processor or blender and blitz briefly to crush them roughly.

2 Add the kefir cheese and linseed oil to the food processor and blitz again until combined. Transfer the mixture to 2 serving bowls.

3 Tip the berries into the food processor and blitz until smooth. Spoon the berry sauce over the kefir cheese mixture in the bowls, and serve.

MILLET AND QUINOA PORRIDGE WITH PLUM COMPOTE

 **PROMOTES BOWEL REGULARITY**

 **PROMOTES METABOLIC BALANCE**

 **SUPPORTS HEALTHY LIVER FUNCTION**

 **LOWERS RISK OF HEART DISEASE**

Plums are often used in the treatment of diabetes and liver conditions – and stewed plums also help relieve constipation – while millet and quinoa benefit the metabolic balance. Although millet is one of the most easily digestible grains, sprouting it and the other grains and seeds enhances their digestibility further, and therefore the body's ability to assimilate the nutrients they provide.

SERVES 4

4 tbsp quinoa, sprouted
4 tbsp millet, sprouted
450ml (15fl oz) organic rice milk
12 purple plums, cut in half with the stone removed
1 small cinnamon stick (optional)

1 Heat the sprouted quinoa and millet with the rice milk in a small saucepan over a medium heat. Bring to the boil, reduce the heat, and simmer for 10–12 minutes.

2 Meanwhile, place the plums and cinnamon stick, if using, in a separate pan, add water to cover, and simmer over a low heat for 10–12 minutes.

3 Remove the cinnamon stick and discard. Divide the porridge between 4 serving bowls, spoon the plum compôte on top, and serve.

MILLET AND PEARS WITH CARDAMOM

 **HELPS BALANCE BODY pH**

 **RELIEVES VOMITING AND DIARRHOEA**

 **SUPPORTS HEALTHY KIDNEY FUNCTION**

 **HELPS ALLEVIATE MORNING SICKNESS**

The soothing properties of millet, cooling pears, mind-enhancing cardamom seeds, and energy-boosting pistachios are joined in this comforting recipe. It's a perfect breakfast if you are suffering from acidosis (excessive acid build-up in the body), but you can enjoy its benefits any time. It is also a useful dish to eat in the days before embarking on a detox regime.

SERVES 4

500g (1lb 2oz) millet
a pinch of salt
3 pears, peeled, cored, and sliced
1 tbsp raisins
¼ tsp cardamom seeds
1 tbsp kudzu (an Asian thickener), or plain flour or cornflour
1 tsp vanilla extract
2 tbsp maple syrup
1 tbsp chopped pistachio nuts

1 Rinse the millet in cold water and drain thoroughly. Transfer to a frying pan and dry-fry over a medium heat until it releases a fragrant aroma.

2 Bring 750ml (1¼ pints) of water to the boil in a medium saucepan. Add the millet and salt, turn the heat down, and simmer for 10 minutes.

3 Add the pears, raisins, and cardamom seeds to the millet and cook for 15 minutes more over a low heat.

4 Dissolve the kudzu in 2 tablespoons of water and add to the millet. Stir in the vanilla extract and keep stirring until the mixture thickens. Divide between 4 serving bowls, drizzle with the maple syrup, scatter the pistachios on top, and serve.

OAT PORRIDGE WITH GOJI BERRIES AND CINNAMON

 **EASY TO DIGEST**  **HELPS MAINTAIN ENERGY LEVELS**  **PROMOTES A SENSE OF WELL-BEING**

Oats and goji berries are full of slow-release energy and fibre, and both contain nutrients to help support a healthy nervous system. They are also considered to be natural sedatives, helping to lift low moods and calm the nerves. The addition of cinnamon and black sesame seeds provides a warming quality that makes this an excellent dish if you are feeling weak or are convalescing.

SERVES 4

butter, for greasing
225g (8oz) medium oatmeal or porridge oats
700ml (1¼ pints) rice or cow's milk
1 tbsp maple syrup
25g (scant 1oz) goji berries
1 tsp ground cinnamon
60g (2oz) sunflower seeds
25g (scant 1oz) black sesame seeds
a pinch of salt

1 Preheat the oven to 190°C (375°F/Gas 5). Generously grease a glass or ceramic ovenproof dish with the butter. Place all the ingredients in the dish, mix well, and bake in the oven for 30 minutes. After 15 minutes, check the porridge and stir, adding some hot water or more milk, if it is sticking or becoming too thick and solid.

2 Remove from the oven, divide between 4 serving bowls, and serve with a small jug of warmed milk.

ALMOND PORRIDGE WITH APRICOTS

 **HELPS LOWER CHOLESTEROL**

 **PROMOTES HEALTHY SKIN AND HAIR**

 **REPLACES IRON LOST IN MENSTRUATION**

 **HELPS BALANCE BLOOD SUGAR LEVELS**

This simple breakfast is a good source of iron which helps build red blood cells, which then carry more oxygen around the body to benefit your heart, skin, hair, and general health. It is also good for replenishing iron lost during menstruation. If you don't want to prepare ahead and soak the almonds overnight first, simply blitz the dry raw nuts coarsely and use bought almond milk.

SERVES 4

125g (4½oz) raw almonds

1 tsp vanilla extract

12 apricots, halved, with stone removed

2 tbsp maple syrup

2 tbsp chia seeds

2 tbsp linseeds, crushed in a pestle and mortar

1 Rinse the almonds, tip into a bowl, and pour in twice the amount of water to cover, so the nuts can swell and still remain submerged. Leave to soak overnight.

2 Strain the soaked almonds, rinse, and place in a blender or food processor. Add 500ml (16fl oz) of water and the vanilla extract, and blitz until the ingredients turn into a milky liquid.

3 Strain the liquid through a sieve, reserving the almond milk and leaving the almond meal in the sieve to drip-dry.

4 Pour a little water into a medium saucepan to cover the base of the pan. Add the apricots and cook over a medium-high heat for 15–20 minutes or until they soften, adding a little more water if necessary. When the apricots are soft, but not mushy, add the maple syrup, stir to combine, and remove the pan from the heat.

5 To serve, put 2 tablespoons of almond meal into each serving bowl and sprinkle each portion with ½ tablespoon each of chia seeds and crushed linseeds. Put some of the apricots and maple syrup on top and pour in a little of the reserved almond milk before serving.

Linseed (p95) is a great source of soluble fibre that helps balance blood sugar levels and suppresses hunger.

Pre-soaked Barley Breakfast

 **HELPS MAINTAIN ENERGY LEVELS**    **HELPS EASE CONSTIPATION**    **HELPS MAINTAIN WATER BALANCE**    **LOWERS RISK OF HEART DISEASE**

Make this "instant" energizing breakfast cereal of toasted barley before you go to bed at night and it will be ready when you get up in the morning. It is a great way to set you up for an active day. Barley is often used as a traditional remedy for non-specific inflammatory conditions of the urinary system and, together with prunes, helps maintain bowel regularity and blood pressure.

SERVES 4

125g (4½oz) toasted barley
2 tsp vanilla extract
60g (2oz) soft prunes, chopped
4 tbsp maple syrup
4 tbsp toasted pumpkin seeds

1 Place the toasted barley in a large wide-mouthed flask (which can hold 750ml–1 litre/1¼–1¾ pints to accommodate the threefold increase in the volume of barley grains). Add the vanilla extract and pour 400ml (14fl oz) of boiling water over the barley. Seal the flask and leave overnight.

2 In the morning, empty the soaked barley into a mixing bowl, mix in the soft prunes, divide the mixture between 4 serving bowls, drizzle over the maple syrup, sprinkle with toasted pumpkin seeds, and serve.

Prunes (p24) *are renowned for promoting bowel regularity, but their high fibre content also helps to balance blood sugar levels.*

SWEET SAFFRON RICE WITH CARDAMOM

 **HELPS IMPROVE CIRCULATION**

 **FIGHTS AGE-RELATED VISION LOSS**

ENHANCES MEMORY AND SENSE OF WELL-BEING

This is a version of desi, a sweet rice eaten on the first morning of the new year by Buddhist communities to symbolize their hopes and expectations for a new cycle of life. Supported by cardamom, the yellow pigments in saffron aid memory retention and recall, help slow age-related macular degeneration, improve blood circulation, and impart a sense of well-being.

SERVES 4–6

150g (5½oz) jasmine or basmati rice

a pinch of salt

5cm (2in) piece of cinnamon stick

4 tbsp milk

a pinch of saffron strands

2 tbsp butter, melted

1 tbsp brown sugar

½ tsp cardamom pods, crushed

zest of 1 orange

1 tbsp raisins

3 tbsp pistachio nuts, plus a few extra to garnish

2 tbsp flaked almonds

1 Rinse the rice in a sieve under cold running water, then place in a bowl, pour in enough water to cover, and set aside to soak for 30 minutes.

2 Drain the rice, place it in a medium saucepan and add 300ml (10fl oz) of water, the salt, and the cinnamon stick. Bring to the boil, turn the heat down, and simmer for 10–12 minutes.

3 Meanwhile, place the milk and saffron in a separate saucepan and warm gently over a low heat. Add the melted butter and sugar and stir until the sugar dissolves. Add the cardamom pods and orange zest and allow all the ingredients to infuse for 2–3 minutes on a very low heat.

4 Using a thick-bottomed medium saucepan, toast the raisins over a medium heat for 1–2 minutes. Remove from the heat and set aside, then add the nuts, toast until golden, and remove from the heat.

5 When the rice is cooked and the water has been absorbed, add the toasted raisins and nuts and combine well. Pour in the infused milk, mix well, and cook over a low heat for 1–2 minutes until the aromas and saffron colour have suffused the rice.

6 Transfer to small serving bowls, heaping up the mixture to symbolize prosperity, and serve with few pistachios scattered on top.

Saffron threads (p119) have long been used in traditional medicines for their stimulating and mood lifting qualities.

WARM CHICKEN CONGEE

 **SOOTHES STOMACH UPSETS**

 **HELPS MAINTAIN ENERGY LEVELS**

Congee is a soothing, nourishing food for anyone convalescing from gastric upsets or recovering from exhaustion and illness. This Chinese dish is traditionally made by gently simmering rice and water on the lowest possible heat for up to 6 hours, stirring regularly to prevent it from sticking. This recipe is an adaptation of the original and cooks in half the time or less.

SERVES 4–6

1 organic free-range chicken, about 1.5kg (3lb 3oz)

200g (7oz) long-grain or basmati brown rice

5cm (2in) piece of fresh root ginger, grated

1 tbsp tamari soy sauce

1 tbsp sesame seed oil (toasted sesame seed oil is fine)

sea salt and freshly ground black pepper

2 tbsp finely chopped spring onions, to garnish

2 tbsp finely chopped coriander leaves, to garnish

1 Place the chicken, rice, and ginger in a large heavy-based saucepan with a lid. Cover the ingredients with water and bring to the boil. Then reduce the heat to low and gently simmer for 1½–3 hours or until the chicken meat is falling off the bones and the rice is soft. Add more water if necessary during cooking to prevent the congee from boiling dry. Congee should have a thick soup-like consistency.

2 Remove the pan from the heat, transfer the chicken to a plate, and carefully remove the bones and skin. Shred the chicken meat and return it to the pan. Add the tamari soy sauce, sesame oil, and sea salt and black pepper to taste, and stir to combine.

3 Divide the congee between 4 serving bowls, garnish with the spring onions and coriander leaves, and serve.

TIP: Tamari is a type of soy sauce that contains little or no wheat, making it a good, gluten-free choice.

SNACKS

WHY WASTE TIME ON EMPTY CALORIES? THESE **NUTRIENT-DENSE** NIBBLES ARE GREAT ON THEIR OWN OR FOR DAYS WHEN YOU NEED SOMETHING EXTRA TO **SUSTAIN YOU**. YOU COULD ALSO TRY THEM AS DELICIOUS SIDE DISHES.

EZZE

 **HELPS IMPROVE CIRCULATION**

 **AIDS HEALTHY/OPTIMAL DIGESTION**

 **HELPS STRENGTHEN THE IMMUNE SYSTEM**

This hot Bhutanese relish brings together the therapeutic properties of chillies, onions, garlic, coriander, and tomatoes to help stimulate blood circulation and enhance the digestive system. It is also a good food to eat in winter to bolster your immune system. The large chillies used here are not as hot as some smaller varieties, but if you prefer a milder relish, substitute them for bell peppers.

SERVES 4

3 large tomatoes

5 large red chillies, deseeded and finely chopped

5 large green chillies, deseeded and finely chopped

1 large red onion, finely chopped

3 garlic cloves, crushed

a small bunch of coriander leaves, chopped

juice of ½ lime

1 tbsp extra virgin olive oil

salt and freshly ground black pepper

1 Cut a cross on the top of each tomato with a sharp knife, then dip the tomatoes in a bowl of boiling water for 20 seconds. Remove with a slotted spoon and, when cool enough to handle, remove the skins and finely chop the flesh. Transfer to a large bowl.

2 Add the chillies, onion, garlic, coriander leaves, and lime juice to the mixing bowl. Pour in the olive oil, mix well, and season to taste with salt and black pepper. Serve with Cabbage Momos (p235), or with other snacks as a chilli sauce.

Chillies (p56) have antioxidant and anti-inflammatory properties, which means they can help lower cholesterol and balance blood sugar levels.

HUMMUS WITH CORIANDER

 **HELPS EASE CONSTIPATION**

 **HELPS BALANCE BLOOD SUGAR LEVELS**

 **HELPS REMOVE TOXINS FROM THE BODY**

The high-fibre chickpeas in hummus benefit gut health, while sesame seeds act as a general tonic. For the best flavour and the most antioxidants, choose a dark variety of dried chickpeas and soak and cook them yourself; otherwise canned chickpeas are fine. Store any leftover garlic purée under a layer of olive oil in a tightly sealed jar, refrigerate, and use within 2 weeks.

MAKES 450G (1LB)

400g (14oz) chickpeas, cooked, drained, and rinsed, or 400g can chickpeas, drained and rinsed

3 tbsp dark tahini paste

juice of ½ lemon

1 tsp coriander seeds, very finely crushed

½ tsp smoked paprika

1 tbsp extra-virgin olive oil

salt and freshly ground black pepper

2 tsp black sesame seeds (or use white sesame seeds instead)

1 tbsp pomegranate seeds, to garnish

a small bunch of coriander leaves, finely chopped, to garnish (optional)

For the garlic purée

2 large garlic bulbs, with each clove peeled

120ml (4fl oz) olive oil

1 tbsp white wine

½ tsp chopped thyme leaves

½ tsp chopped rosemary leaves

1 Preheat the oven to 170°C (325°F/Gas 3). To make the garlic purée, place the garlic cloves in a small baking dish, add the olive oil, wine, thyme, and rosemary, cover the dish with a lid or foil, and bake for 40 minutes or until the garlic cloves are soft. Blitz the softened mixture briefly in a food processor or blender to make a purée.

2 To make the hummus, put 1 tablespoon of the garlic purée and the rest of the ingredients except the sesame seeds in a food processor or blender, and blitz to a semi-coarse paste. Add the sesame seeds, taste the hummus, and add more seasoning and/or lemon juice if needed. If the mixture is quite dry, add a little water to loosen it. If you prefer a very smooth texture, use a hand-held stick blender and add the sesame seeds along with the rest of the ingredients. Serve in a bowl garnished with a sprinkle of pomegranate seeds and coriander leaves, if using.

BUTTERNUT SQUASH AND WALNUT BITES

 PROMOTES A SENSE OF WELL-BEING

 HELPS EASE BACK PAIN

AIDS HEALTHY DIGESTION

 **HELPS MAINTAIN WATER BALANCE**

Astringent walnuts and creamy butternut squash promote a sense of well-being, support bone and muscle health, and benefit the digestive and urinary systems. Tamari sauce – a Japanese dark soy sauce – helps give these bites a complex depth of flavour. You can turn this into a light meal for four people, if you like, by simply tossing the cooked bites in some salad leaves.

SERVES 8–10 (ABOUT 30 BITES)

60g (2oz) walnut halves

1 medium-sized butternut squash, peeled and deseeded

2 garlic cloves, finely chopped

2 tbsp olive oil

2 tbsp tamari soy sauce

1 Count how many walnut halves you have, then cut the squash into the same number of small cubes, making sure each cube is just big enough for a walnut half to sit on top of it. Place the cubed squash in a bowl. Add the walnuts, garlic, olive oil, tamari soy sauce, and 1 tablespoon of water, and mix well. Set aside to marinate for 1–2 hours.

2 Preheat the oven to 180°C (350°F/Gas 4). Transfer the marinated squash and walnuts to a baking dish arranging them in a single layer. Cover with foil and bake in the oven for 20–30 minutes.

3 Arrange the squash cubes on a serving tray, decorate each with a walnut half, and serve as a finger food with drinks.

Walnuts (p93) contain beneficial oils that promote healthy skin and hair.

MUSHROOM AND CHESTNUT BITES

 STRENGTHENS KNEES AND LOWER BACK

 **PROMOTES A SENSE OF WELL-BEING**

 **PROMOTES A HEALTHY DIGESTIVE TRACT**

These bites make great party canapés and are a tasty vegetarian alternative to sausage rolls. Chestnuts and hazelnuts are traditionally considered to be a tonic for the body, including muscles and joints. Shallots, oregano, and parsley bring the added benefit of helping to boost energy levels. Oregano and shallots can aid the body's digestion of the puff pastry in this recipe, too.

MAKES 24

1 tbsp olive oil, plus extra for greasing

5 small shallots, finely chopped

50g (1½oz) hazelnuts, toasted, finely chopped

110g (3½oz) chestnuts, cooked, peeled, and finely chopped

175g (6oz) button mushrooms, chopped

salt and freshly ground black pepper

1 tbsp chopped parsley leaves

½ tsp dried oregano

350g (12oz) ready-made puff pastry

1 egg, beaten

1 Preheat the oven to 200°C (400°F/Gas 6). Place the olive oil in a medium saucepan and heat gently. Add the shallots and cook over a medium heat until soft and translucent. Add the hazelnuts, chestnuts, and a dash of water and mix well.

2 In a separate saucepan, dry-fry the mushrooms, stirring constantly to prevent them sticking to the base of the pan and burning. This process help to dry them out and concentrates their flavour. When all the mushroom juices have been released and have evaporated, transfer the mushrooms to the shallot and nut mixture, season with salt and black pepper, add the parsley and oregano, and combine all the ingredients.

3 Roll out the puff pastry to roughly 5mm and cut it into 3 long strips, each 7.5cm (3in) wide. Spoon the mixture down the centre of each strip. Brush the edges with beaten egg, roll up the pastry strips lengthways to make long sausage shapes, and seal the edges well. Slash the top of each pastry roll with a sharp knife in criss-cross shapes and cut each roll into 8 pieces. Arrange the bites on an oiled baking sheet and bake in the oven for 10 minutes or until golden. Serve warm or cold.

Hazelnuts (p93) are a good source of biotin, a B vitamin that supports musculoskeletal health by strengthening connective tissues.

KALE CRISPS

 PROMOTES A HEALTHY DIGESTIVE TRACT    **HELPS LOWER CHOLESTEROL**    **HELPS REMOVE TOXINS FROM THE BODY**

Kale, which retains its vibrant colour when dried (rather than baked), supports the body's detoxification processes and helps to lower levels of "unhealthy" (LDL) cholesterol in the blood. Its high fibre content also improves digestion and benefits intestinal health. Drizzling lemon juice on the leaves and leaving them to stand enhances their concentration of phytonutrients.

MAKES 100G (3½OZ)

500g (1lb 2oz) kale, tough stems removed, and the leaves torn into bite-sized pieces

juice of 1 lemon

1 tbsp extra virgin olive oil

¼ tsp salt

½ tsp garlic powder

1 Place the kale in a large bowl, add the lemon juice, and set aside for 30 minutes. Add the olive oil, salt, and garlic powder and combine well.

2 If you have a dehydrator, set it to 40°C (104°F). Cover the silicone sheets with baking parchment and arrange the leaves on top, ensuring they don't touch. Dehydrate for 6–8 hours, turning them halfway through. When dry, store in an airtight jar and consume within 2 days.

3 Otherwise, preheat the oven to its lowest setting – 50°C (120°F/Gas ¼) or lower. Arrange the leaves on large rimmed baking trays, making sure they don't overlap. If they won't all fit, make the crisps in batches. Dry in the oven for 1–2 hours or until the leaves are dry and crispy, switching the baking trays from back to front and top to bottom halfway through, and turning the leaves over if needed.

COURGETTE CRISPS

 HAS A DIURETIC ACTION    **AIDS HEALTHY DIGESTION**    **HELPS PREVENT BLOOD VESSEL DAMAGE**

Courgettes, like other summer squashes, have cooling, refreshing properties, and are a mild diuretic. Here they are marinated first in warming, heart-friendly spices and then dried to make healthy snacks. The trick is to slice them thinly so that they dry out more quickly and turn crispy. Smaller courgettes with mild-tasting yellow skins are best, but any courgettes will work well.

MAKES 450G (1LB)

juice of 3 lemons

3 medium courgettes, thinly sliced

For the spice powder

1 tsp coriander seeds

1 tsp cumin seeds

¼ tsp ground turmeric powder

¼ tsp chilli powder

¼ tsp ground ginger

¼ tsp garlic powder

½ tsp Himalayan pink salt, or sea salt

1 For the spice powder, dry-fry the coriander and cumin seeds over a medium heat until their aromas develop. Transfer to a pestle and mortar, grind to a powder, and combine with the spice powders and salt.

2 Pour the lemon juice into a large bowl, add 1½ tsp of the spice powder, and mix to a thin consistency, adding more lemon juice if necessary. Add the courgettes and combine well. Set aside for 1 hour.

3 Cover silicone sheets or baking trays with baking parchment and arrange the courgette slices on top. If using a dehydrator, set it to 40°C (104°F) and dry the slices for 10–12 hours, turning them halfway through.

4 Otherwise, preheat the oven to its lowest setting – 50°C (120°F/Gas ¼) or lower – and dry the slices for 1–2 hours or until crisp, turning them halfway through. Store in an airtight jar and consume within 1 week.

SPROUTED MEDLEY

 **PROMOTES HEALTHY SKIN**

 **PROMOTES EFFICIENT METABOLISM**

 **HELPS MAINTAIN ENERGY LEVELS**

 **AIDS HEALTHY DIGESTION**

This healthy snack is full of enzymes, flavour, and vital nutrients: germinated seeds provide amino acids to support skin and cell regeneration in the body and boost energy levels and digestion. They may also help fight the signs and symptoms of premature ageing. For this dish, prepare a little ahead – 3 types of sprouts are used and they all take different amounts of time to sprout.

SERVES 6

1 tbsp alfalfa seeds
½ tbsp celery seeds
1 tbsp clover seeds
½ tbsp radish seeds
4 tbsp green or Puy lentils
4 tbsp mung beans
2 tbsp millet
2 tbsp wheat grain
2 tbsp quinoa
4 tbsp sunflower seeds

For the dressing

2 tbsp chopped lemon thyme leaves
3 tbsp toasted sesame oil
2 tbsp orange juice
1 tbsp tamari soy sauce
1 tsp honey

1 When you sprout each type of seed, legume, or grain, put it into a separate 1–1.5-litre (1¾–2¾-pint) wide-mouthed jar and cover with muslin or cheesecloth, securing the cloth in place with a rubber band. To drain the water from a jar, pour it out through the muslin cover. Pour fresh tepid water into the jar through the muslin, and drain in the same way.

2 Half-fill the jars of alfalfa, celery, clover, and radish seeds with tepid water and place them away from direct sunlight at room temperature for 5 hours. Drain, rinse, and drain again, then let the seeds stand without water for 8–12 hours. Rinse and drain the seeds twice a day for the next 6 days. On the seventh day, rinse and drain the seeds and stand the jars in broad daylight for 12 hours to increase their chlorophyll content. The sprouted seeds should have expanded to 8 times their original size.

3 Half-fill the jars of lentils and mung beans with tepid water, place the jars away from direct sunlight at room temperature, and leave to soak overnight. Drain, then rinse and drain twice a day for 3 days. The sprouted legumes will expand to 2–3 times their original size.

4 Half-fill the jars of millet, wheat, and quinoa with tepid water, place the jars away from direct sunlight at room temperature, and leave to soak overnight. Drain, then rinse and drain twice a day for 2 days, or until they sprout small "tails" no bigger than the grains themselves.

5 Half-fill the jar of sunflower seeds with tepid water, place the jar away from direct sunlight at room temperature, and leave to soak overnight. Drain, then rinse and drain the seeds twice at 6-hourly intervals. Sunflower seeds have a delicate film-like skin that detaches from the seed during sprouting. Remove the muslin cover and skim as many of these skins off the surface of the water as you can while you rinse the seeds, as they quickly spoil and can cause the sprouts to rot. Leave to sprout for 18 hours or until the seeds have a 5mm–1cm (¼–½in) long "tail" and a crunchy texture.

6 Mix all ingredients for the dressing together in a small jug. Drain the sprouts and serve them as 3 different medleys in separate serving bowls: alfalfa, celery, clover, and radish sprouts in the first; lentil and mung bean sprouts in the second; and sunflower, quinoa, wheat, and millet sprouts in the third. Combine each of these medleys with one-third of the dressing, and allow guests to help themselves.

TOMATO CRACKERS

 **HELPS KEEP BLOOD VESSELS SUPPLE**

 **PROMOTES HEALTHY SKIN AND HAIR**

 **AIDS HEALTHY DIGESTION**

These crackers are a great substitute for other savoury biscuits, and are full of health benefits. Linseed and tomatoes help improve blood circulation and maintain the health of blood vessels. They also help nourish the skin, help restore dull, unruly hair, and soften and strengthen dry, brittle nails. Chew the crackers well to benefit from the rich healing oil in the linseeds.

MAKES 50

250g (9oz) whole linseeds
1 tsp dried oregano
50g (1¾oz) cracked linseeds
65g (2oz) sun-dried tomatoes (not in oil)
300g (10oz) tomatoes
salt and freshly ground black pepper

1 Weigh 50g (1¾oz) of the whole linseeds, place them in a food processor or blender, add the oregano, blitz to a fine consistency, and empty into a bowl. Add the sun-dried tomatoes to the food processor, blitz to fine pieces, and transfer to the bowl. Add the rest of the whole and the cracked linseeds to the bowl and mix.

2 Add the fresh tomatoes to the food processor and blitz to a purée. Add the puréed tomatoes and seasoning to the dry ingredients and mix them together well with a wooden spoon.

3 Taste and adjust the seasoning as required, then set the mixture aside for 2–3 hours for the seeds to partly absorb the liquid. When the mixture has thickened and is sufficiently dry yet pliable, divide into 3 equal parts.

4 Spread the cracker mixture thinly (2–4mm/⅛–¼in thick) over 3 silicone sheets or sheets of baking parchment. Score the surface of the cracker mixture into small triangles, squares, or rectangles with a sharp knife to define the shape and size of the crackers.

5 If you have a dehydrator, set it to 45°C (113°F) and dry the crackers for 6–7 hours, turning them halfway through. Otherwise, preheat the oven to its lowest setting – 50°C (120°F/Gas ¼) or lower. Cover the top of the cracker layer with another sheet of baking parchment and bake for 2 hours. Carefully turn each cracker layer over, remove the baking parchment or silicone sheets, place the cracker sheets directly onto the oven racks, and bake for 1 hour more. Remove from the oven and allow to cool for 6–7 hours, turning the cracker sheets over halfway through so they dry out completely.

6 Once cool, break along the scored lines to make individual crackers. Store in an airtight container and consume within 1–2 weeks.

SPICY CRACKERS

 **PROMOTES BOWEL REGULARITY**    **PROMOTES A SENSE OF WELL-BEING**

Seeds are packed with protein for energy and fibre to boost digestive health. Here linseeds, chia seeds, and black and white sesame seeds (ingredients in furikake, a dried Japanese condiment) are enlivened by flavoursome tomatoes, spices, and herbs. Drying or baking the seed mixture on a very low heat to make "raw" crackers means the seeds retain more of their beneficial nutrients.

MAKES 50 CRACKERS

200g (7oz) whole linseeds

50g (1¾oz) cracked linseeds

50g (1¾oz) whole chia seeds

20g (¾oz) furikake (or black and white sesame seeds)

45g (1½oz) sun-dried tomatoes (not in oil) or tomato purée

salt and freshly ground black pepper

chilli flakes, to taste

1 tsp dried Italian seasoning (basil, thyme, and garlic powder), or similar mixed herbs

300g (10oz) tomatoes

1 Mix the seeds and furikake together in a bowl. Blitz the sun-dried tomatoes, if using, to fine pieces in a food processor or blender. Add the pieces or the tomato purée to the seeds and season with salt, black pepper, chilli flakes, and the dried mixed herb seasoning. Mix everything thoroughly, taste, and adjust the seasoning if necessary.

2 Place the fresh tomatoes in a food processor or blender and blitz to a fine purée. Gradually mix this fresh tomato purée into the dry seed blend with a wooden spoon.

3 Divide the cracker mixture into 3 equal lots and spread it thinly (2–4mm/¼–⅛in thick) over 3 silicone baking sheets or sheets of baking parchment. Score the surface of the seed mix into small triangles, squares, or rectangles to define the shape and size of the crackers.

4 If you have a dehydrator, place the crackers in it and dry at 45°C (113°F) for 6–7 hours, turning them halfway through. If you don't have a dehydrator, preheat the oven to 50°C (120°F/Gas ¼). If using baking parchment, cover the top of the cracker layer with another sheet of parchment. Place the crackers in their parchment or on silicone sheets on baking trays and bake for 2 hours. Remove the baking trays from the oven and carefully turn each cracker layer over to dry out the base. Remove the baking parchment or silicone sheets, place the cracker layers directly on the oven racks, and bake for a further 1 hour. Remove from the oven and allow to cool.

5 Once cool, break along the scored lines to make individual crackers. Store in airtight containers. They will keep for up to 2 weeks.

TIP: Rather than choosing sun-dried tomatoes stored in oil, look for ones that are packaged like dried fruit; they have a drier texture that is excellent for this recipe.

SOUPS

EVEN THE **SIMPLEST** INGREDIENTS CAN BE QUICKLY TRANSFORMED INTO EASY-TO-DIGEST SOUPS THAT STIMULATE, **PROTECT**, **DETOX**, AND **STRENGTHEN**. WARM YOURSELF UP – OR COOL YOURSELF DOWN – WITH THESE SATISFYING BLENDS.

Mung Bean And Spinach Soup

HELPS LOWER BLOOD PRESSURE

AIDS DETOXIFICATION SYSTEM

HELPS EASE CONSTIPATION

If you suffer from high blood pressure, headaches, or constipation, or are in need of a detox, try this soup. Mung beans contain lots of fibre and potassium, both of which help lower blood pressure. They also have detoxifying properties and are an anti-inflammatory, as is iron-rich spinach. Plan ahead and soak the beans overnight or sprout them for 3 days before cooking.

SERVES 4

200g (7oz) mung beans

5 small shallots, finely chopped

2cm (¾in) piece fresh ginger root, finely chopped

2 garlic cloves, finely chopped

½ tsp turmeric powder

½ tsp crushed coriander seeds

1 tbsp olive oil

1 litre (1¾ pints) vegetable stock, or your choice of broth (pp323–325), or water

100g (3½oz) baby spinach leaves

juice of 1 small lime

salt and freshly ground black pepper

2 tbsp chopped coriander leaves, to garnish

1 Soak the beans according to the packet instructions or sprout them for 3 days (p204).

2 Pour a thin layer of water into a medium saucepan, set over a medium heat, and bring to a simmer. Reduce the heat, add the shallots, ginger, garlic, turmeric powder, and coriander seeds, and cook over a low heat, stirring occasionally and adding a little more water if necessary. Meanwhile, drain and rinse the beans.

3 When the shallots have softened, add a dash of water, the olive oil, and the beans to the pan. Pour in the vegetable stock, increase the heat, and bring to a simmer. If you are using sprouted beans, let the soup simmer gently for 20–25 minutes or until the sprouts are soft. Otherwise, simmer for 30–40 minutes or until the cooked soaked beans fall apart. Stir in the baby spinach leaves and add the lime juice.

4 Serve the soup as is or blitz to a smooth consistency using a stick blender or in a food processor or blender. Add salt and black pepper to taste just before serving (adding salt to beans as you cook them makes them harder), then transfer to 4 serving bowls and garnish with the chopped coriander leaves.

Limes (p40) contain high levels of vitamin K, which stimulates the liver to support blood coagulation.

RAW TOMATO SOUP

 **HELPS LOWER BLOOD PRESSURE**

 **TONES AND CLEANSES THE LIVER**

 **HELPS CLEAR CONGESTION**

 **HAS AN UPLIFTING EFFECT**

Comprising more than 90 per cent water and rich in antioxidants, tomatoes cleanse the liver, purify the blood, and are cooling and hydrating. They are useful in treating high blood pressure, accompanied by red eyes and headaches. The freshly juiced basil in this recipe enhances digestion, helps clear respiratory congestion and phlegm, and can lift the mood.

SERVES 4

8 large ripe tomatoes
2 tbsp basil
8 celery sticks
1 red chilli, deseeded and finely chopped
2 small garlic cloves, roughly chopped
2 tbsp extra virgin olive oil
salt and freshly ground black pepper

1 Using a sharp knife, cut a light cross through the skin at the top of each tomato, then place the tomatoes in a bowl and cover with hot water. Let the water cool a little, then drain. Peel the skins off the tomatoes, cut into quarters, remove the seeds, dice the flesh, and place it in a blender or food processor.

2 Remove the basil leaves from their stalks and reserve the leaves as a garnish. Juice the basil stalks with the celery sticks in a juicer and add the juice to the blender, along with the chilli and garlic.

3 Blitz the ingredients until smooth. Add the olive oil, season to taste, and blitz once more. Pour the soup into 4 serving bowls. Garnish with the basil leaves, tearing them roughly with your fingers if they are large, or leaving them whole if they are small, and serve.

Basil (p100) has a reputation in traditional Chinese medicine for "restoring vital spirits, quickening the brain, and awakening joy and courage". Its oil has a powerful anti-inflammatory effect.

WILD GARLIC SOUP

 HELPS STRENGTHEN THE IMMUNE SYSTEM

 HELPS REMOVE TOXINS FROM THE BODY

 HELPS LOWER BLOOD PRESSURE

Sweet potato, wheatgrass, and wild garlic, all have anti-inflammatory and cleansing properties, so this is the perfect soup if you are feeling the cold or your immune system is sluggish after any winter bugs or illnesses. Wild garlic is only available in the spring, so if you want to make this soup at other times of the year, substitute it with a mixture of wild rocket and spinach.

SERVES 4

1 tbsp sunflower oil

4 medium shallots, chopped

1 medium sweet potato (about 400g/14oz), peeled and chopped into small cubes

700ml (1¼ pints) vegetable stock

1 tbsp wheatgrass juice or 1 tsp wheatgrass powder (optional)

4 tbsp crème fraîche or natural yogurt, to serve (optional)

200g (7oz) young wild garlic leaves

salt and freshly ground black pepper

1 Heat the sunflower oil in a medium saucepan over a low heat, add the shallots and a little water, and allow the shallots to soften. Add the sweet potato and sauté for 5 minutes. Pour in the hot vegetable stock, bring to the boil, and simmer for about 15 minutes until the sweet potato softens.

2 Meanwhile, if using the wheatgrass juice or powder, mix it with the crème fraîche or yogurt in a small bowl.

3 Remove the pan from the heat, pour the mixture into a blender or food processor and blitz until smooth. Add the wild garlic leaves and blitz again until smooth. Season to taste. Pour the soup into 4 individual serving bowls, swirl a tablespoon of crème fraîche or yogurt into each portion, and serve.

Wild garlic (p82) is a seasonal leafy food that is easy to digest and can be eaten cooked or raw.

SWEET POTATO AND CELERIAC SOUP

 PROMOTES A SENSE OF WELL-BEING

 HELPS MAINTAIN ENERGY LEVELS

 **HELPS IMPROVE CIRCULATION**

SUPPORTS HEALTHY KIDNEY FUNCTION

Root vegetables and spices are the essential ingredients in this comforting, warming, and healthy soup. These foods increase your energy levels, boost the circulatory system, aid digestion by promoting bowel regularity. They also strengthen the kidneys and enhance urine output. Turmeric also benefits muscles and joints and helps to alleviate any inflammation.

SERVES 6

1 tbsp ghee, or clarified butter

1 onion, finely chopped

1 garlic clove, chopped

1 tsp coriander seeds, crushed

½ tsp turmeric powder or ground turmeric root

½ tsp chilli flakes

2 sweet potatoes (250g/9oz total weight), peeled and diced

1 celeriac (400g/14oz total weight), peeled and diced

1.2 litres (2 pints) vegetable stock

salt and freshly ground black pepper

6 tbsp natural yogurt

2 tbsp pumpkin oil

a small handful of coriander leaves, chopped

1 Melt the ghee and a little water in a large, heavy-based saucepan with a lid over a medium heat, then add the onion and cook until soft. Add the garlic, coriander seeds, turmeric powder, and chilli flakes and stir. Add the sweet potato and celeriac, place the lid on, reduce the heat, and sweat them for 5 minutes, making sure they don't discolour. Add the stock and bring to the boil, then reduce the heat, place the lid on, and simmer for 30 minutes over a low heat or until the vegetables are tender.

2 Remove the pan from the heat, let the soup cool slightly, season with salt and black pepper to taste, and use an electric hand blender to blend to a smooth consistency. Alternatively, blitz the soup in several batches in a food processor or blender.

3 Transfer the soup to 6 serving bowls, stir a spoonful of yogurt into each portion, drizzle over a little pumpkin oil, scatter the coriander on top, and serve.

QUAIL SOUP

 BOOSTS IRON STORES TO COMBAT FATIGUE

 **HELPS IMPROVE CIRCULATION**

 **PROMOTES EFFICIENT METABOLISM**

 **HELPS STRENGTHEN THE IMMUNE SYSTEM**

This cold-weather soup is best eaten at lunchtime; quail meat, shiitake mushrooms, goji berries, and astragalus root are all well known for being traditional tonics that help boost energy levels and improve circulation. They can also support the lungs, spleen, and kidneys, building resistance to infections, lowering the rate of perspiration, and reducing water retention.

SERVES 4–6

2 quails

10g (¼oz) astragalus root, or astragalus root powder

6 shallots, topped and tailed with skins on

3 garlic cloves, with skins on

1 large carrot, sliced

10 black peppercorns

15g (½oz) goji berries, washed

200g (7oz) shiitake mushrooms, sliced

a large piece of wakame or nori seaweed, cut into small pieces

1 tbsp barley miso paste

50g (1¾oz) buckwheat noodles, to thicken

a large sprig of flat-leaf parsley, finely chopped

1 Place the quails in a large cooking or casserole pot with a lid, add the astragalus root, shallots, garlic, carrot, and peppercorns, cover with water, and bring to the boil. Turn the heat down, half-cover the pot with the lid, and simmer on a very low heat for 1½ hours.

2 Remove the pot from the heat, remove the quails, and set aside to cool slightly. Strain the soup through a sieve and reserve the liquid. Discard the astragalus root and carrot slices and reserve the rest of the ingredients in the sieve. Measure the soup and return it to the pot.

3 When the quails are cool enough to handle, carefully remove the meat from the bone, shred it with 2 forks, and return it to the pot. If the birds are from wild stock, look out for lead shot and discard any shot you find as you shred the meat. Squeeze the garlic cloves and shallots from their skins directly into the soup.

4 Adjust the quantity of soup by adding more water if needed to make 1 litre (1¾ pints) of soup. Bring the soup back to the boil, add the goji berries, and lower the heat to a simmer.

5 Add the shiitake mushrooms, followed by the wakame seaweed and barley miso paste. Let the soup simmer for 10 minutes, then add the buckwheat noodles and let them cook through for 5–7 minutes.

6 Pour into serving bowls, garnish with the parsley, and serve with some rye bread on the side.

QUAIL
copper and iron

SHIITAKE MUSHROOMS
*panthothenic acid
(vitamin B5)*

GOJI BERRIES
pyridoxine (vitamin B6)

INCREASE YOUR ENERGY
THESE THREE FOODS, ARMED WITH THEIR RESPECTIVE NUTRIENTS, HELP TO BOOST THE METABOLISM'S ABILITY TO GENERATE ENERGY.

BUTTERNUT SQUASH SOUP

 **AIDS HEALTHY DIGESTION**

 **SUPPORTS HEALTHY LUNG FUNCTION**

HELPS STRENGTHEN THE IMMUNE SYSTEM

 **PROMOTES A SENSE OF WELL-BEING**

Squash has fibre, which benefits the stomach and digestive system. It's a good choice if you suffer from allergies or food sensitivities, as it's a non-allergenic. Squash is also rich in beta-carotene to strengthen lungs, pancreas, and spleen. Combined with garlic, onions, and spices, this makes an immune-boosting meal. Both lemongrass and coconut milk add a mental and emotional uplift.

SERVES 6

2 tbsp olive oil

3 small onions, finely chopped

1kg (2¼lb) butternut squash, deseeded and cut into small chunks

1.5 litres (2¾ pints) vegetable stock

4 kaffir lime leaves

1 stalk lemongrass, bruised

2 garlic cloves

200ml (7fl oz) coconut milk

zest and juice of 1 lime

salt and freshly ground black pepper

a few sprigs of coriander leaves, to garnish

1 lime, cut into 6 wedges with a cut across the centre of each wedge, to serve

1 Heat the olive oil in a large saucepan, add the onions, and sauté over a low heat for 2–3 minutes until they are translucent. Add the squash and cook over a medium heat, stirring occasionally until the vegetables are softened at the edges. Add the stock, kaffir lime leaves, lemongrass, and garlic. Bring to the boil, then lower the heat and simmer for about 30 minutes or until the squash is cooked through, but still retains some shape.

2 Remove the kaffir lime leaves and lemongrass and discard. Add the coconut milk and bring back to the boil. Remove from the heat, add the lime zest, and season with salt and black pepper to taste. Pour the soup into a food processor or blender, and blitz to a smooth consistency. Add some fresh lime juice to taste, pour into bowls, and garnish with the fresh coriander. Just before serving, fix a lime wedge to the rim of every bowl for each person to add a little extra lime juice, if they like.

TIP: Keep the skin on the butternut squash to take advantage of the extra fibre, especially if it is a young one. Once cooked and blended the texture will become smooth.

Coconut milk *(p49) is rich in antioxidants, such as beta-carotene, and bowel-healthy fibre.*

ADZUKI BEAN SOUP

 HELPS MAINTAIN WATER BALANCE    **AIDS HEALTHY DIGESTION**    **HELPS MAINTAIN ENERGY LEVELS**

Tangerine peel is thought to aid digestion and so is excellent in combination with adzuki beans, which are also known to benefit digestive health, eliminate toxins, and reduce water retention, particularly in women who are menstruating. They also help sustain energy levels. This is an unblended, chunky soup, so it's up to you how small you want to chop the vegetables.

SERVES 4–6

1 tangerine or orange
115g (4oz) adzuki beans
2 tbsp olive oil
4 shallots, finely chopped
1 medium leek, chopped
2 carrots, finely diced
2 garlic cloves, crushed
2 celery sticks, finely diced
4 medium tomatoes, skinned and finely chopped
1 tsp tomato purée
750–900ml (1¼–1½ pints) chicken or vegetable stock
2 bay leaves
2 courgettes, finely diced
2 tbsp finely chopped parsley
salt and freshly ground black pepper
2 tbsp finely chopped basil leaves, to garnish

1 Using a potato peeler, remove the peel from the tangerine or orange and arrange it on a baking tray. Leave the tray in the oven at a low temperature (110°C/225°F/Gas ¼) for 1 hour or until the skin is dried. Grind the peel to a powder in a pestle and mortar, or leave whole and remove at the end of cooking.

2 If you are using dried adzuki beans, soak them according to the packet instructions, then drain, discarding the soaking water. Place the beans in a saucepan, cover with fresh water, bring to the boil, simmer for 15 minutes, and drain. If using canned, simply drain and rinse.

3 Meanwhile, heat the olive oil in another large saucepan and sauté the shallots over a low heat until they soften. Add the leek, carrots, and garlic, stir, and cook for 2–3 minutes. Add the celery, allow to soften, then add the tomatoes and tomato purée. Cook for 5–10 minutes until soft. Add the adzuki beans to the onion and tomato mixture.

4 Pour in the stock, add the bay leaves and dried tangerine peel, and bring to the boil. Reduce the heat immediately to a slow simmer for 30 minutes, then add the courgettes and parsley. Simmer for a further 10 minutes, then remove the bay leaves and whole peel, if using. Add salt and black pepper to taste, and serve in bowls garnished with the basil. Serve with rye bread on the side.

Light Meals And Salads

LIGHT DOESN'T HAVE TO MEAN INSUBSTANTIAL. ENJOY A FUSION OF **FRESH** INGREDIENTS, **THERAPEUTIC** HERBS, AND FLAVOURFUL SPICES THAT **HEAL** AND SATISFY YOUR NEED FOR **SUSTAINED ENERGY**.

RAW CURLY KALE SALAD

 **HAS ANTI-CANCER PROPERTIES**

 **HELPS REMOVE TOXINS FROM THE BODY**

 **PROTECTS AGAINST COLDS AND FLU**

 **HELPS IMPROVE CIRCULATION**

Kale is rich in antioxidant, anti-inflammatory, and anti-cancer nutrients. It also contains sulphur, making it an ideal food to help detox the body, and is known to help lower "unhealthy" (LDL) cholesterol levels in the blood. Leaving the dressed leaves to stand for 30 minutes softens them and makes cooking unnecessary, but if they are large and tough, steam them first for just 5 minutes.

SERVES 2

500g (1lb 2oz) kale, stems removed

juice of 1 lemon

2 tsp coriander seeds

¼ small lemon (with peel on)

2 avocados, peeled and stones removed

2 tbsp olive oil

salt and freshly ground black pepper

1 red chilli, deseeded and finely chopped

4 garlic cloves, finely chopped

1 Place the kale in a large bowl and sprinkle the lemon juice over it. Using your hands, coat the leaves thoroughly in the lemon juice. Set aside for 30 minutes for the kale to soften.

2 Place the coriander seeds and lemon quarter in a blender or food processor and blitz briefly. Add the avocados, olive oil, salt, and black pepper and blitz into a paste.

3 Transfer to the large bowl, add the finely chopped chilli and garlic, and stir until well combined and the kale is thoroughly coated. Set aside for 15–30 minutes for the flavours to develop fully and to enhance the availability of the nutrients. Serve.

Avocados (p50) contain healthy monounsaturated fat, which helps in lowering blood pressure and lubricating joints.

QUAIL'S EGG AND CHICORY SALAD

 **HELPS MAINTAIN
ENERGY LEVELS**

 **TONES AND CLEANSES
THE LIVER**

 **HELPS IMPROVE
CIRCULATION**

Known in the East as "animal ginseng", quail's eggs have a sweet flavour and are very nutritious. They are an excellent energy-giving food, helping to improve the circulatory system, which in turn strengthens muscles and bones. Here the eggs are combined with chicory leaves, which have a slightly bitter taste and act as a gentle stimulant and tonic for the liver.

SERVES 4

12 quail's eggs

salt and freshly ground black pepper

150g (5½oz) assorted lettuce leaves

1 medium avocado, peeled and sliced

2 medium heads of chicory, leaves separated

200g (7oz) cherry tomatoes, halved

a large handful of coriander leaves, roughly chopped

For the dressing

60g (2oz) feta cheese

4 tbsp extra virgin olive oil

1 large garlic clove, crushed

2 tbsp lemon juice

1 tsp green peppercorns in brine, drained, with a little extra brine

2 tbsp roughly chopped parsley leaves

1 To make the dressing, cut the feta cheese into small cubes and place them in a small bowl or screw-top glass jar. Pour over the olive oil, garlic, and lemon juice. Add the green peppercorns together with a little of their brine and the chopped parsley. Stir gently to combine well and leave for 3–4 hours for the flavours to develop.

2 Put the quail's eggs in a saucepan, cover with water, add a pinch of salt, and bring to the boil. Cook in the boiling water for 3 minutes, then drain and rinse under cold water to prevent the yolks from discolouring. Remove the eggshells.

3 Arrange the lettuce, avocado slices, chicory leaves, and cherry tomatoes on 4 serving plates. Slice the eggs in half and divide them between each portion. Spoon the feta cheese dressing over the salad, garnish with the chopped coriander leaves, season with salt and black pepper, and serve.

Quail's eggs *(p143) are high in phosphorus – essential for cell membranes, and strong bones and teeth.*

ADZUKI AND MUNG BEAN SALAD

 HELPS MAINTAIN WATER BALANCE

 **PROTECTS THE HEART AND BLOOD VESSELS**

HELPS REMOVE TOXINS FROM THE BODY

 **HELPS CONTROL BODY TEMPERATURE**

Both adzuki and mung beans have diuretic properties and can help to reduce water retention, particularly in the lower abdomen and legs. In addition, they can benefit the heart and vascular systems, and help the body eliminate toxins. Mung beans are also known to cool the body's internal temperature, so they are a useful food to eat if you are suffering from heatstroke.

SERVES 4

150g (5½oz) dried adzuki beans
150g (5½oz) dried mung beans
6 garlic cloves with skins on
1 lemon, sliced in half
2 bay leaves
200g (7oz) cherry tomatoes, sliced in half
a pinch of salt

For the dressing

2 garlic cloves, peeled
juice of ½ lemon
juice of ½ lime
5 tbsp extra virgin olive oil
a handful of basil leaves, coarsely torn into shreds
a handful of flat- leaf parsley leaves, chopped
a handful of mint leaves, chopped

1 Soak the beans according to the packet instructions, then drain and rinse in cold water. Transfer to a large saucepan and add the garlic, lemon, and bay leaves. Pour over plenty of water, bring to the boil, and simmer for about 1 hour over a low heat until the beans are cooked.

2 Meanwhile, preheat the oven to 180°C (350°F/Gas 4). Arrange the tomato halves on a greased baking sheet, sprinkle with a little salt, and roast in the oven for 15–20 minutes.

3 To make the dressing, pound the garlic with the lemon and lime juices using a pestle and mortar. Slowly add the extra virgin olive oil and herbs until all the ingredients are combined. Keep the dressing ready to pour over the hot beans as soon as they are cooked.

4 Drain the beans and remove the lemon, garlic, and bay leaves. Reserve the garlic cloves, if you like, and squeeze the softened garlic paste into the dressing. Discard the rest of the flavourings. Toss the hot beans in the dressing, add the tomatoes, and set aside until cool to serve as a light summer salad.

SUPPORT YOUR HEART

THE GARLIC CLOVES IN THIS RECIPE PROVIDE A HIGH DOSE OF THE COMPOUND ALLICIN, WHICH CAN HELP TO LOWER CHOLESTEROL AND PROMOTE HEART HEALTH.

Herring With Cucumber And Seaweed Salad

 HAS A DIURETIC ACTION   **HELPS REMOVE TOXINS FROM THE BODY**    **HELPS IMPROVE CIRCULATION**    **FIGHTS THE EFFECTS OF STRESS**

This dish offers the health-boosting properties of seaweed and oily fish. Seaweed has a diuretic effect, helping to detoxify the body, and also helps protect blood vessels and fight the effects of stress. The omega-3 fatty acids and vitamin D in herring benefit the heart and blood circulation, too. If you can't find a packaged seaweed mix, try using nori and dulse seaweeds.

SERVES 4

1 packet of dried mixed seaweed vegetables (approximately 25g/scant 1oz)

100ml (3½fl oz) dry white wine

juice of 2 limes

1 tsp coriander seeds, crushed

1 tbsp white wine vinegar

½ tsp salt

2 kaffir lime leaves

4 fresh herring fillets, about 100g (3½oz) each

1 cucumber, thinly sliced

100g (3½oz) red clover sprouts

1 carrot, peeled and julienned

4 lemon wedges, to garnish.

For the dressing

1 tbsp tamari soy sauce

1 tsp honey

2 tsp rice vinegar

2 tbsp finely chopped dill leaves, plus extra to garnish

1 Rinse the seaweed vegetables in a colander under running water, place in a bowl, and cover with tepid water. Set aside to reconstitute for at least 15 minutes or until soft, then drain.

2 Place the white wine, lime juice, coriander seeds, white wine vinegar, salt, kaffir lime leaves, and 100ml (3½fl oz) of water in a medium saucepan and bring to a slow boil. Turn the heat down low, let the ingredients simmer for 2–3 minutes, then turn the heat down again to its lowest setting, add the herring fillets, and let them poach for 10–12 minutes or until cooked through. The fish are cooked when their flesh is opaque. If you like, you can reserve the poaching liquid, thicken it with 1 tablespoon of kudzu (a popular Asian thickener) or plain flour or cornflour, and serve it as a warm sauce to pour over the fish and seaweed and vegetable salad.

3 Meanwhile, combine all the ingredients for the dressing in a small bowl or jug. Place the reconstituted seaweed, cucumber slices, red clover sprouts, and julienned carrot in a large bowl, pour over the dressing, and mix well.

4 Divide the salad between 4 serving plates and place a herring fillet on top of each. Garnish with a little more dill and the lemon wedges.

Swiss Chard And Sweet Potato

 **HELPS FIGHT INFLAMMATION**

 **HELPS MAINTAIN WATER BALANCE**

HELPS PROTECT EYE HEALTH

AIDS HEALTHY DIGESTION

Here's a different way of serving leafy, fibre-rich Swiss chard, which is high in vitamin K and antioxidant carotenoids. It's slightly bitter taste fades with cooking, and marries well with the sweet potato in a dish that helps relieve inflammation and dryness in the body, for instance in the mouth, skin, nose, and lungs, supports eye health, and improves digestion. This also makes a great side dish.

SERVES 4

1 tbsp olive oil, plus extra to drizzle

2 shallots, peeled and finely chopped

1 tsp coriander seeds, crushed

1 chilli, deseeded and finely chopped

2 garlic cloves, minced

2 large sweet potatoes, peeled and cubed

250g (9oz) Swiss chard, stalks removed and finely chopped, and leaves finely sliced

salt and freshly ground black pepper

1 Heat the olive oil with a tablespoon of water in a medium saucepan with a lid. Add the shallots and coriander seeds and cook over a low heat, stirring occasionally, until the shallots have softened.

2 Add the chilli and garlic, and cook for 1 minute. Add the sweet potato and cook over a medium heat for about 5 minutes, adding a dash of water if necessary. Then add the chopped chard stalks, cover with the lid, and cook for 10 minutes.

3 When the sweet potato is almost cooked, add the shredded chard leaves, cover, and let them wilt for about 3 minutes. Season with salt and black pepper, drizzle over a few drops of olive oil, and serve.

Swiss chard *is a good source of phytonutrients that help protect the pancreas and balance blood sugar.*

SPINACH AND RICOTTA FILO ROLLS

 **HELPS COMBAT ANAEMIA**

 **AIDS HEALTHY DIGESTION**

 **HELPS PROTECT EYE HEALTH**

 **HELPS RELIEVE DRYNESS AND ITCHING**

The primary therapeutic benefit of their iron-rich dish is to help build the red blood cells that carry oxygen throughout the body and help improve anaemia. It can also assist digestion and help moisten the lungs and colon. Spinach is often recommended in cases of night-blindness and hypertension while soft cheese also has a moistening effect on dry, itchy skin.

SERVES 4

500g (1lb 2oz) ricotta cheese

5 eggs

a pinch of salt

500g (1lb 2oz) young spinach leaves, roughly chopped

100ml (3½fl oz) crème fraîche

2 tbsp olive oil

1 packet ready-made filo pastry

thick or Greek-style yogurt, to serve

1 Preheat the oven to 200°C (400°F/Gas 6). In a large bowl, mix the ricotta cheese with the eggs and salt. Add the spinach and crème fraîche and mix well.

2 Grease a square baking dish with a little olive oil. Lay a large piece of baking parchment on a flat surface and place a sheet of filo pastry on it with one of the longer edges facing you. Sprinkle the pastry with a few drops of olive oil and spread a thin layer of the spinach, egg, and cheese filling over it. Roll up the pastry sheet into a neat roll, pushing it away from you, and using the parchment to help you. Transfer the roll to the baking dish, curving the ends up if the dish is smaller than the length of the pastry sheet.

3 Repeat with the rest of the pastry sheets and filling. Sprinkle a few drops of olive oil over the rolls and bake for 30–40 minutes or until the rolls are golden on top and the filling is cooked through. Serve with some thick yogurt on the side.

Spinach (p67) is famous for its iron content which is more easily absorbed by the body when cooked.

TROUT AND LETTUCE WRAPS

 **AIDS HEALTHY DIGESTION**    **HELPS REMOVE TOXINS FROM THE BODY**   **HELPS LOWER CHOLESTEROL**

This dish enhances digestion and can aid weight reduction. In addition, cooling lettuce has detoxifying properties and mangoes can help to relieve symptoms of motion sickness, while the omega-3 fatty acids in trout bring cardiovascular benefits. Using a bed of fresh rosemary, fennel, or dill leaves on which to grill the trout gives them a fragrant, smoky aroma.

SERVES 4

8 large lettuce leaves, such as romaine, butter, escarole, or iceberg, or use 12 leaves of Little Gem lettuce

2 trout (350g/12oz each), filleted

a bunch of rosemary sprigs

a bunch of fennel or dill fronds

a dash of olive oil

a pinch of salt

2 tbsp pumpkin seeds

For the filling

1 large mango, peeled, with stone removed, and cubed

a bunch of coriander leaves, chopped

3 tbsp spring onions, finely chopped

250g (9oz) cherry tomatoes, sliced in half

1 small chilli, deseeded and finely chopped

1 tbsp olive oil

½ tbsp lemon juice

salt and freshly ground black pepper

1 If using large lettuce leaves, remove any thick veins so they can be folded over without breaking.

2 Preheat the grill to high. Score the trout fillets with several diagonal cuts through the skin along their length to prevent them curling up while being grilled. Line the grill pan with sprigs of rosemary and large fronds of fennel or dill. Arrange the trout fillets skin-side up on top and drizzle with olive oil rubbing it in to the skins. Sprinkle the fish with salt and place under the hot grill. Grill for 4–5 minutes or until the skin is crisp and the flesh is cooked through and flakes when tested with a fork. Remove the fillets from the grill and allow to cool.

3 To make the filling, combine the mango cubes, coriander leaves, spring onions, tomatoes, and chilli in a bowl. Add the olive oil, lemon juice, and salt and black pepper, mix together gently, and set aside.

4 To toast the pumpkin seeds, heat a small saucepan over a medium heat. Add the pumpkin seeds and dry-fry for 2–3 minutes or until they darken slightly and give off a fragrant aroma. Shake the pan regularly and stir the seeds with a wooden spoon as you heat them. Cut the cooled trout fillets into squares and gently fold them into the filling.

5 To make the wraps, divide the filling between the lettuce leaves, placing a little in the middle of each leaf. Sprinkle some toasted pumpkin seeds on top and fold the edges of each lettuce leaf up and over the filling. Use a cocktail stick to secure each wrap. If using small leaves such as Little Gem lettuce, don't wrap them but use like scooped spoons with the filling resting within the curved stem. Arrange the wraps on a serving plate and serve.

STUFFED VINE LEAVES

 **AIDS HEALTHY DIGESTION**

 HAS A DIURETIC ACTION

Dark green vine leaves contain fibre, vitamins and minerals including vitamins C and K, folate, and manganese. These nutrients help reduce water retention and benefit the urinary system, and together with pine nuts, almonds, and mint they also benefit the digestive system. The leaves have a subtle acidic flavour and soft texture similar to spinach once cooked.

SERVES 4

30 vine leaves, or Swiss chard leaves, stalks removed

150g (5½oz) white or brown basmati rice

4 shallots, finely chopped

3 tbsp olive oil

2 tbsp pine nuts, toasted

2 tbsp almond flakes, toasted

2 tbsp raisins

2 tbsp finely chopped mild mint leaves

1 tsp pimentón dulce (smoked paprika)

salt and freshly ground black pepper

700ml (1¼ pints) vegetable stock or broth

1 tbsp tomato purée

1 tbsp lemon juice

thin lemon wedges, to serve

1 Preheat the oven to 180°C (350°F/Gas 4). Blanch the vine leaves by immersing them in a large saucepan of boiling salted water for 30 seconds, then quickly rinse in cold water to halt the cooking process, drain, and set aside. Cook the rice according to the packet instructions.

2 Heat a thin layer of water in a saucepan, add the shallots, and stir for about 5 minutes until they have softened. Stir in the cooked rice, olive oil, pine nuts, almond flakes, raisins, mint, and smoked paprika, and season with salt and black pepper. Remove from the heat and allow the mixture to cool before handling it.

3 Lay some of the vine leaves, vein side up, on a flat surface. Place a small ball of the filling at one end of each leaf, fold 3 sides of the leaf up over the filling and roll into a cylindrical parcel. Place each parcel, with the loose end of the vine leaf facing down, in an ovenproof dish with a lid. Repeat with the rest of the vine leaves and filling. Arrange the parcels tightly together to prevent them unfolding while cooking.

4 Heat the stock in a small saucepan, add the tomato purée and lemon juice, mix well, bring to the boil, and gently pour the hot stock over the stuffed vine leaves. Cover them with a small heatproof plate to keep them in place and cover with the lid. Cook in the oven for 1 hour or until all the liquid has soaked up. Transfer the stuffed vine leaves to a serving dish, decorate with lemon wedges, and serve.

Vine leaves are rich in antioxidants and are a traditional remedy for pain and inflammation.

NORI VEGETABLE ROLL

 HAS NATURAL SEDATIVE PROPERTIES

 PROMOTES BOWEL REGULARITY

 **HELPS MAINTAIN ENERGY LEVELS**

 **MAINTAINS HEALTHY BLOOD VESSELS**

Brown rice and red quinoa, which both have a nutty flavour, are known to have a calming effect on the nervous system. The high fibre content of brown rice also benefits digestion. Nori, like quinoa, is high in protein, keeping your energy levels higher for longer. It also helps strengthen blood vessels. This wholesome dish is a practical food to eat on the go or serve as a picnic snack.

SERVES 4–6

175g (6oz) shortgrain brown rice
175g (6oz) red quinoa
¼ tsp Himalayan pink salt or other natural salt
1 tbsp rice vinegar
1 tbsp mirin sauce
1–2 tbsp sesame seeds
6–8 sheets of nori, toasted
1–2 tbsp toasted sesame oil

For the dipping sauce

1 tbsp tamari soy sauce
juice of 1 orange

For the filling

1 large avocado, stone removed, peeled, and cut into strips
1 carrot, peeled and julienned
2cm (¾in) fresh ginger root, peeled and julienned
1 small chilli, deseeded and julienned
1 red pepper, deseeded and julienned
1 celery stick, julienned
1 small leek, white stalk only, julienned

1 Place the rice and quinoa in a large saucepan, add 800ml (1¼ pints) of water and bring to the boil. Reduce the heat, cover with a lid, and simmer for 1 hour or until the water is absorbed.

2 Remove the pan from the heat and add the Himalayan pink salt, rice vinegar, and mirin sauce. Combine well and set aside to infuse.

3 Meanwhile, toast the sesame seeds by dry-frying them in a saucepan until they turn golden, then set aside to cool. Combine the ingredients for the dipping sauce in a small bowl and set aside.

4 If you don't have a sushi roll mat, use a sheet of baking parchment slightly larger than the nori sheets (which will enable you to store the rolls for a few hours before serving) or you might find it just as easy to roll without either. To assemble a roll, place a sheet of nori, shiny side down, on a clean, flat surface. Spread a thin layer of rice, about 5cm (2in) thick, on top of the sheet. Sprinkle the toasted sesame seeds and a few drops of toasted sesame oil over the rice. Carefully arrange one or two of each of the sliced vegetables at one end of the nori sheet so that they all lie horizontally across the rice. Fold the nori sheet over the vegetables and continue to roll it up. Seal the end of the nori sheet by running a little water along the seam side with your finger. Repeat this process until you have the desired amount of rolls.

5 To serve, dip a serrated knife into water and slice the nori rolls into bite-sized pieces. Stand the rolls upright on a serving plate with the bowl of dipping sauce on the side.

CABBAGE MOMOS

 **AIDS HEALTHY DIGESTION**

 **HELPS STRENGTHEN THE IMMUNE SYSTEM**

 **SUPPORTS HEALTHY LIVER FUNCTION**

These dumplings, known as momos, are traditionally served at Bhutanese social gatherings. They can be filled with either meat or vegetables, but they are always served with a hot chilli relish locally known as ezze (p195). Both cabbage and warming chilli stimulate the digestion, help strengthen the immune system, combat seasonal infections, and cleanse the liver.

MAKES 24 MOMOS

For the filling

¼ medium cabbage, finely chopped

3 large onions, finely chopped

3 carrots, finely chopped

1 tbsp chopped lovage or celery leaves

1 tbsp chopped parsley or coriander leaves

olive oil, for frying

200g (7oz) cream cheese (preferably home-made kefir cheese, p332)

2 garlic cloves, very finely crushed or powdered

1 tbsp soy sauce

¼ tsp salt

For the dough

500g (1lb 2oz) wholewheat flour

2 eggs, beaten

2 tsp baking powder

1 tsp salt

1 For the filling, fry the chopped vegetables, lovage or celery, and parsley or coriander, in a very little olive oil over a medium heat in a heated wok for 5–6 minutes. Stir in the cream or kefir cheese, garlic, soy sauce, and salt and set aside.

2 Make the dough for the momos by sifting the flour into a large bowl, adding the beaten eggs, and mixing lightly. Stir in 150ml (5fl oz) of water and the baking powder and salt. Combine the ingredients well, then transfer the dough onto a floured surface. Knead the dough lightly until it is smooth. Cover with a damp cloth and set aside for 5–10 minutes. This will allow the baking powder time to activate so that the momos swell when steaming.

3 Roll the dough into a large sausage and cut into 24 even-sized pieces. Roll each piece into a thin circle 9 10cm (4in) wide. Place a tablespoonful of the filling in the centre of the dough circle, gather the edges of the circle together, pinch the edges together with your fingers, and twist to seal. Repeat with the rest of the dough circles and filling.

4 Stand the momos in an oiled steaming basket. Place over a large saucepan of simmering water, cover, and steam for 12–14 minutes. If you don't own a steaming basket, place the momos in a heatproof colander or sieve over a saucepan filled with a 5cm (2in) layer of water; the base should not touch the water. Cover with the lid and bring the water to the boil; steam for 12–14 minutes. Serve the momos with Ezze relish (p195).

MUSHROOM FRITTATA WITH CHERRY TOMATOES AND BASIL

 HELPS STRENGTHEN THE IMMUNE SYSTEM  **AIDS HEALTHY DIGESTION**  **HELPS EASE RHEUMATIC PAIN**  **PROTECTS THE HEART AND BLOOD VESSELS**

This is an ideal meal if you are convalescing. Like other mushrooms, morels (*Morchella esculenta*) are rich in the essential amino acids that the body needs to build protein, while shiitake and crimini mushrooms help improve digestion and have anti-inflammatory properties. Wash the morels thoroughly under running water, as their sponge-like caps often contain soil and grit.

SERVES 4

For the braised tomatoes

½ tbsp ghee, or clarified butter, for greasing

200g (7oz) ripe cherry tomatoes

salt and freshly ground black pepper

1 tbsp freshly chopped basil leaves, to garnish

For the frittata

25g (scant 1oz) dried morels, soaked in boiling water for 5 minutes to rehydrate, or 75g (2½oz) fresh morels, cleaned and finely chopped

100g (3½oz) shiitake mushrooms, sliced

100g (3½oz) crimini mushrooms, sliced

2 tbsp ghee

salt and freshly ground black pepper

2 tbsp finely chopped chives

8 eggs, beaten

3 tbsp crème fraîche

1 Preheat the oven to 180°C (350°F/Gas 4). To braise the tomatoes, grease a baking tray with the ghee, add the cherry tomatoes, season with salt and black pepper, and cook in the oven for 8–10 minutes or until the tomatoes are cooked.

2 Meanwhile, place a large, non-stick frying pan over a medium heat and dry-fry all the mushrooms for 1–2 minutes to enhance their flavour, and allow them to release some of their moisture. Add 1 tablespoon of the ghee, allow to melt, and sauté the mushrooms for 3–5 minutes, adding salt and black pepper to taste. Add half the chopped chives to the mushrooms, reserving the rest to use as a garnish. Remove the mushrooms from the pan and set aside.

3 Beat together the eggs and crème fraîche in a medium bowl with a little more salt and black pepper to taste. Melt the remaining tablespoon of ghee in the pan and pour in the egg mixture. Cook for 2–3 minutes over a low heat until the base is firm, then add the mushrooms and cover with a lid to cook for 3–5 minutes, until both the base and top of the frittata are set.

4 To serve, sprinkle the frittata with the rest of the chives, divide between 4 serving plates, and add the braised cherry tomatoes. Garnish the tomatoes with the basil and serve immediately.

BUCKWHEAT PANCAKES WITH NETTLES AND FETA CHEESE

HELPS BUILD RED BLOOD CELLS

HELPS ALLEVIATE DRY COUGHS

HELPS REMOVE TOXINS FROM THE BODY

PROMOTES A HEALTHY COMPLEXION

When combined, nettles and buckwheat enrich the blood, helping to increase red blood cells and restore metabolic balance. This dish is ideal for anyone with anaemia, a dry cough, or a weak constitution. It can also aid those in need of a detox, or recovering from a long illness. Young nettles in spring are best, as they are small yet potent; wear gloves to gather them.

SERVES 4

For the pancakes

125–150g (4½–5½oz) buckwheat flour

a pinch of salt

1 egg

60ml (2fl oz) milk

1 tbsp olive oil

1 tsp butter, plus extra for greasing

For the filling

100g (3½oz) young nettle leaves, finely chopped

100g (3½oz) feta cheese

3 eggs

100g (3½oz) ricotta cheese

2 tbsp crème fraîche

a pinch of salt

1 Place the flour in a mixing bowl with the salt, and make a well in the centre. Crack the egg into the well and add the milk. Using a wooden spoon, stir the egg and milk, letting the flour gradually tumble in. Gradually add 100–125ml (3½–4fl oz) of water, little by little, stirring continuously until all the flour has been incorporated and the mixture is lump-free. If necessary, adjust the liquids or add a little more flour. If you have time, place the batter in the refrigerator to rest for 30 minutes to allow the milled grain to swell, which helps make the batter light rather than stodgy.

2 Preheat the oven to 180°C (350°F/Gas 4). Place the nettle leaves in a bowl and crumble in the feta cheese. Add the eggs, ricotta cheese, crème fraîche, and salt, combine all the ingredients together, and set aside.

3 To make the pancakes, heat the olive oil and butter in a medium frying pan. When hot enough, add a ladle of the batter and swirl it around the base of the pan to make a thin pancake. Cook for 2–3 minutes or until golden, then toss or turn the pancake and cook on the other side. Repeat until you have 8 pancakes.

4 Spread some of the filling over a pancake and roll it up. Repeat with the rest of the pancakes and the filling, then arrange all the pancake rolls in a greased baking dish. Pour the remaining filling over the pancakes, and bake in the preheated oven for 20–25 minutes until cooked through and golden in appearance. The filling may ooze out of the pancakes during cooking, but this won't detract from the final look and flavour of the dish. Serve hot with a salad.

Buckwheat flour (p113) is rich in natural antioxidants that help protect the heart.

ARTICHOKES IN A SWEET SPICY SAUCE

HAS A MILD DIURETIC ACTION　　**HELPS LOWER CHOLESTEROL**　　**SUPPORTS HEALTHY LIVER FUNCTION**　　**PROMOTES A HEALTHY COMPLEXION**

Globe artichokes are not only good to eat, they are a therapeutic herb – a bitter digestive remedy that helps stimulate and strengthen the urinary system and support the liver. Artichokes also help with fat metabolism and can reduce "unhealthy" (LDL) cholesterol levels in the blood. The hot sauce supports detoxification, which in turn can help improve the condition of the skin.

SERVES 4

4–8 artichokes
2 tbsp lemon juice
½ tsp salt
1 garlic clove, finely chopped
2 tbsp dry white wine
2 tbsp olive oil
350g (12oz) quinoa, rinsed and soaked until sprouted (p204)
salt and freshly ground black pepper
3 tbsp pine nuts, toasted (optional)
3 tbsp fresh pomegranate seeds (optional)

For the dressing

4 tbsp roasted sesame oil
150ml (5fl oz) Marsala wine
2 tbsp teriyaki sauce
3 tbsp fresh orange juice
2 garlic cloves, minced
1 medium-hot chilli, deseeded, finely chopped
2 tbsp finely chopped flat leaf parsley leaves
2 tbsp chopped lemon thyme leaves

1 Trim the artichoke heads by removing the tough outer scales to expose the paler, softer leaves, and cutting away the spiky leaves on the top. If the artichokes have their stems intact, peel off the stringy outer layer with a sharp knife. Slice each artichoke in half lengthways and scrape away the furry choke with a spoon. Place the artichokes in a large bowl of water with the lemon juice to prevent them discolouring.

2 Bring a large saucepan of water to the boil. Turn the heat down, add the salt, garlic, wine, olive oil, and artichoke halves and poach gently for 20 minutes. Remove the artichokes from the water and drain.

3 Heat the sesame oil with 2 tablespoons of water in another large saucepan, and add the artichoke halves. Let them brown gently for 2–3 minutes, then remove and set aside.

4 Add the Marsala wine, teriyaki sauce, orange juice, garlic, and chilli to the pan. Mix the ingredients briefly, then add the parsley and thyme, and remove the pan from the heat.

5 To assemble the dish, divide the sprouted quinoa between 4 serving plates and season with salt and black pepper. Swirl a spoonful of the sauce over the sprouted quinoa and arrange 1–2 artichoke halves on top of each portion. Spoon more sauce over the artichokes, sprinkle with toasted pine nuts and pomegranate seeds, if using, and serve.

TIP: Start 1–3 days ahead to sprout the quinoa, depending on how big you like the sprouts. Rinse and drain the quinoa every 8–12 hours.

Artichokes (p62) support immune function by detoxifying the liver and gall bladder.

WILD RICE SALAD

 PROTECTS AGAINST FREE-RADICAL DAMAGE    **AIDS HEALTHY DIGESTION**    **PROTECTS THE HEART AND BLOOD VESSELS**

Black wild rice, which was once cultivated solely for China's emperors to consume, is a nutritious protein and antioxidant-rich grain with a nutty taste and chewy texture. Rice is classified as a sweet, neutral food in Chinese medicine, and is eaten to ease many stomach and digestive problems including diarrhoea, indigestion, and constipation. Its fibre helps protect the heart.

SERVES 4

115g (4oz) black wild rice

240ml (8fl oz) vegetable or chicken stock

a pinch of salt

2 kaffir lime leaves

1 tsp orange zest

1 tsp lemon zest

30g (1oz) sun-dried tomatoes, chopped

1 large red pepper, deseeded and diced

2 tbsp chopped coriander leaves

For the dressing

2 tbsp basil oil

1 tbsp blackberry vinegar

a pinch of salt

1 Rinse the rice in cold water, drain, and transfer to a medium saucepan. Add the stock, salt, kaffir lime leaves, and citrus zest. Bring to the boil, then cover, reduce the heat, and simmer for 25–30 minutes or until the rice is cooked and water has been absorbed.

2 Meanwhile, make the dressing. Place all the ingredients in a bowl or screw-top jar, add 1 tablespoon of water, and mix well. When the rice is cooked pour the dressing over the rice while it is still hot, mix in the sun-dried tomatoes, and set aside until the rice has cooled.

3 When the rice is cold, mix in the chopped pepper. Garnish with the coriander leaves, and serve.

Fresh Coriander Leaf Pesto With Pasta

 **HELPS ELIMINATE TRACES OF METALS**

 **PROTECTS AGAINST NEURO-DEGENERATION**

 **AIDS HEALTHY DIGESTION**

PROTECTS THE HEART AND BLOOD VESSELS

This dish offers the detoxifying properties of fresh coriander, which is a good chelating agent, helping to remove traces of heavy metals from the body. High levels of heavy metals are implicated in certain arthritic conditions, depression, memory loss, muscle pain, and weakness. Coriander seeds aid digestion, and pine nuts, cashew nuts, and almonds help support heart health.

SERVES 4

a large bunch of organic coriander leaves

6 tbsp olive oil

1 garlic clove

¼ tsp ground coriander

2 tbsp blanched almonds

2 tbsp cashews

2 tbsp pine nuts

2 tbsp lemon juice

225g (8oz) fresh pasta, such as spelt spaghetti

100g (3½oz) sun-dried tomatoes in olive oil, drained and chopped

freshly ground black pepper

grated Parmesan cheese, to garnish

a small handful of chopped coriander leaves, to garnish

1 Place the coriander leaves and olive oil in a food processor or blender and blitz until finely blended. Add the garlic, ground coriander, almonds, cashews, pine nuts, and lemon juice, and blitz the ingredients to a paste. Alter the consistency and flavour of the pesto slightly, if you like, by adding a little more olive oil and/or lemon juice keeping to a 3:1 ratio of oil to juice.

2 Cook the pasta according to the packet instructions and drain. Immediately stir the pesto through the hot pasta so it melts, then add the sun-dried tomatoes, and toss the ingredients together. Season with black pepper, sprinkle generously with grated Parmesan and coriander leaves, and serve.

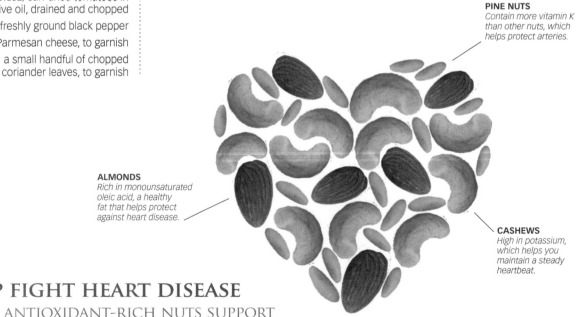

PINE NUTS
Contain more vitamin K than other nuts, which helps protect arteries.

ALMONDS
Rich in monounsaturated oleic acid, a healthy fat that helps protect against heart disease.

CASHEWS
High in potassium, which helps you maintain a steady heartbeat.

HELP FIGHT HEART DISEASE
THREE ANTIOXIDANT-RICH NUTS SUPPORT ARTERIES, STRENGTHEN BLOOD VESSELS, AND LOWER BLOOD PRESSURE.

Braised Red Chicory And Celery Heart Salad

 AIDS DETOXIFICATION SYSTEM

 **PROMOTES A HEALTHY DIGESTIVE TRACT**

 **HELPS MAINTAIN WATER BALANCE**

 HAS NATURAL SEDATIVE PROPERTIES

A detoxifying meal with significant benefits for the body. Chicory, which has a bitter taste, stimulates digestion, improves both gall bladder and liver function, and cleanses the urinary tract. Celery helps regulate the body's water balance. Both vegetables are a good source of fibre and have important sedative and stress-relieving properties. This recipe makes a perfect side dish for a meal.

SERVES 4

1 tbsp olive oil

2 long (or banana) shallots, finely chopped

2 garlic cloves, minced

1 small chilli, deseeded and finely chopped

1 large bunch of celery, split into inner and outer sticks, with inner sticks finely chopped

8 heads of red chicory, halved

1 tsp chopped lemon thyme leaves

salt and white pepper

1 Preheat the oven to 180°C (350°F/Gas 4). Heat the oil with a tablespoon of water in a medium saucepan over a medium heat. Add the shallots, allow to soften, then add the garlic, chilli, and chopped inner sticks of celery, or celery hearts, and cook for 2–3 minutes.

2 Meanwhile, juice the outer sticks and leaves of the celery in a juicer. Add the celery juice to the pan.

3 Arrange the chicory bulbs in an ovenproof ceramic dish with a lid. Pour the shallot and celery mixture over the chicory, cover with the lid, and bake in the oven for 20 minutes.

4 Transfer the chicory bulbs to a serving plate. Pour the celery mixture into a small saucepan, bring to the boil, add the lemon thyme, and boil for 3 minutes to reduce the liquid. Add salt and white pepper to taste, pour the mixture over the chicory bulbs, and serve.

Red chicory (p73) is a variant of blanched white chicory. It contains high amounts of volatile oils that aid digestion.

Main Meals

MAKE SURE YOUR MAIN MEAL FORMS A **HEALTHY** CENTREPIECE TO YOUR DAY – WHATEVER TIME OF DAY YOU EAT IT. **FRESH** INGREDIENTS BALANCED FOR FLAVOUR, COLOUR, AND TEXTURE – AND MOST IMPORTANTLY **HEALING POWER** – ARE KEY.

SPROUTED QUINOA WITH VEGETABLES

 EASY TO DIGEST AND GLUTEN-FREE

 HELPS BALANCE BLOOD SUGAR LEVELS

 MAINTAINS HEALTHY BLOOD VESSELS

 HELPS PROTECT EYE HEALTH

Sprouted seeds and grains are not just a pretty garnish. This gluten-free, fibre-rich dish is easy to digest and helps keep blood sugar levels stable. It's packed with vitamins, minerals, amino acids, and beneficial digestive enzymes that helps us extract maximum nutrition from food. Peppers, courgettes, and green mango supply antioxidants to support cardiovascular and eye health.

SERVES 4

2 tbsp broccoli seeds

400g (14oz) quinoa

1 large red pepper, deseeded and finely diced

1 large orange pepper, deseeded and finely diced

1 fennel bulb, finely diced

1 yellow courgette, finely diced

1 small unripe mango, peeled, stone removed, and finely diced

1 garlic clove, minced

juice of 1 lime

3 tbsp extra virgin olive oil

salt and freshly ground black pepper

1 To sprout the broccoli seeds, place them in a large glass jar, pour in enough tepid water to liberally cover the seeds, fasten muslin cloth over the mouth of the jar with an elastic band, and set aside overnight. The next morning, pour the water out through the muslin cloth, pour in more water to rinse the seeds, and drain. Leave the jar upside down at an angle of 45 degrees, away from direct sunlight, so the excess water can drain away. Repeat the rinsing process every morning and evening for 3–5 days depending on the room temperature and how quickly the seeds sprout. Once sprouted, store the seeds in a glass jar with a sealed lid in the refrigerator and consume within 1–2 days.

2 To sprout the quinoa, place the seeds in a large glass jar, pour in enough tepid water to liberally cover the seeds, fasten muslin cloth over the mouth of the jar, and set aside for 2 hours. Pour the water out through the muslin cloth, pour in more water to rinse the seeds, and drain. Leave the jar upside down at an angle of 45 degrees, away from direct sunlight, so the excess water can drain away. Repeat the rinsing process the following day and you may find that little shoots are already breaking through. The quinoa is ready when most of the seeds have sprouted.

3 To assemble the dish, combine all the sprouts and diced peppers, fennel, courgette, and mango in a large bowl.

4 In a small bowl, mix together the minced garlic, lime juice, and olive oil and add a pinch of salt. Pour this dressing over the ingredients in the bowl, mix well, and add black pepper. Taste and adjust the seasoning if necessary before serving.

Yellow courgette (p60) skin is rich in antioxidant carotenes, such as lutein, which promote healthy eyes.

Spicy Raw Vegetable Spaghetti

 HAS A DIURETIC ACTION   **PROMOTES CLEAR SKIN**   **HELPS EASE CONSTIPATION**    **PROMOTES DETOX AT CELL LEVEL**

Raw vegetables provide more enzymes, vitamins, and other essential nutrients than if cooked, and the combination of ingredients used here has a cleansing effect on the body. A spiralizer is a gadget that turns the vegetables into lovely spaghetti-like strands, which changes their texture – the root vegetables in particular taste surprisingly light and vibrant.

SERVES 4

a handful of pine nuts

2 tbsp furikake, or 1 tbsp each of black and white sesame seeds

2 carrots, peeled

2 medium beetroots, peeled

1 green and 1 yellow courgette, stalks removed

3 small radishes

a large bunch of fresh coriander leaves, large stalks removed, and finely chopped

For the dressing

juice of 3 celery sticks (about 4 tbsp)

1 tbsp hemp oil

2 tbsp pumpkin seed oil

1 tbsp fresh lemon juice

2 tsp tahini

salt and freshly ground black pepper

1 To make the dressing, combine all the ingredients in a food processor or blender, then set aside.

2 To toast the pine nuts and sesame seeds, heat a small frying pan over a medium heat, add the pine nuts and seeds, and dry-fry, stirring until lightly golden.

3 Put the carrots, beetroots, courgettes, and radishes through a vegetable spiralizer to turn them into long thick ribbons. Alternatively, use a vegetable peeler.

4 Place all the vegetable strips except the beetroot in a serving bowl and toss with the chopped coriander leaves (adding the beetroot separately prevents the whole salad turning pink). Distribute between 4 serving plates, add the beetroot, pour over the dressing, scatter a few of the pine nuts and furikake or sesame seeds over each portion, and serve.

Furikake is a Japanese seasoning of sesame seeds, seaweed, and other flavourings. Sprinkling a little over a salad, rice, or noodles is a great way of increasing the nutrient density of a dish.

SEA BASS WITH SPINACH AND MANGO

HELPS COMBAT ANAEMIA

HELPS PROTECT EYE HEALTH

AIDS HEALTHY DIGESTION

HAS A DIURETIC ACTION

This dish of firm-textured oily fish and iron-rich spinach helps to lower blood pressure and to prevent recurring headaches and dizziness. Antioxidants in the mango support healthy vision. The cooling effect of the spinach is balanced by the heat of chilli, garlic, and ginger – all of which promote healthy circulation and digestion, and also help to remove excess water from the body.

SERVES 4

4 sea bass, about 250g (9oz) each

a pinch of salt

15g (½oz) fresh root ginger, finely chopped

2 small chillies, deseeded and finely chopped

4 garlic cloves, finely chopped

1 lemon, cut in half, with one half thinly sliced and the other half juiced

2 heaped tsp wholegrain mustard

6 tbsp olive oil

8 tbsp white wine

200g (7oz) spinach leaves

For the sauce

1 medium mango, peeled, stoned, and roughly chopped

2 tsp lime juice

1 tbsp olive oil

1 If you have time, soak the fish in a large bowl of salted water (1 tablespoon of salt to 1 litre/1¾ pints of water) half an hour before cooking to clean them thoroughly. Preheat the oven to 180°C (350°F/Gas 4). Pat the fish dry with kitchen paper and place in a large ceramic baking dish. Sprinkle with the salt and pack the insides of the fish with the ginger, chilli, and garlic. Arrange a few lemon slices on top of each fish. Blend the mustard, lemon juice, olive oil, and the wine (or 8 tablespoons of water) in a jug and pour over the fish. Cover with foil and bake for 25–35 minutes, or until the fish flakes easily when you test it with a fork.

2 Meanwhile, prepare the sauce. Put the mango flesh, lime juice, and olive oil in a food processor or blender, blitz briefly, and set aside.

3 Boil a large saucepan of water, add the spinach, and cook for 30 seconds or until it wilts. Drain off the hot water, quickly rinse the spinach in cold water to halt the cooking process, then drain again. Place the sea bass on 4 serving plates. Divide the spinach into 4 portions, arranging it around the edge of each fish if you like. Drizzle a little of the mango sauce over the sea bass and serve the rest of the sauce in a small bowl on the side.

Kale With Buckwheat Noodles

 **HELPS LOWER CHOLESTEROL**

 **CONTAINS ANTI-CANCER SUBSTANCES**

HELPS FIGHT INFLAMMATION

This dish of buckwheat noodles and kale benefits the heart. Kale is the ultimate leafy vegetable, full of antioxidants, omega-3 fatty acids, and natural substances that give it anti-inflammatory properties and can help reduce the risk of oestrogen-related cancers. Any type of kale will do for this quick, easy dish, and it is best cooked lightly for a minimal amount of time.

SERVES 4

400g (14oz) soba buckwheat noodles

2 tbsp walnut oil, plus extra for sprinkling

1 red chilli, deseeded and finely diced

2 garlic cloves, crushed

2 tbsp tamari soy sauce

600g (1lb 5oz) fresh kale, cut into strips with the spines removed

2 tbsp fresh orange juice

4 tbsp walnut pieces, toasted, to garnish

1 Cook the soba noodles according to the packet instructions. Add a dash of walnut oil and a pinch of salt to the water before you add the noodles, if you like.

2 Meanwhile, place a large heavy-based saucepan with a lid over a moderate heat and add the walnut oil with 2 tablespoons of water. When the oil has warmed, add the chilli and crushed garlic, and stir. Add the tamari soy sauce, followed by the kale, and stir to coat the leaves in the other ingredients.

3 Add the orange juice, put the lid on, and let the kale steam for 2–3 minutes or until it is just cooked. Stir occasionally as it cooks, to stop it sticking to the base of the pan, and add a dash of water if necessary. Remove from the heat. Arrange the soba noodles on a warmed serving dish, pile the kale on top, and scatter over the toasted walnuts. Sprinkle a few drops of walnut oil over the dish and serve.

Vegetable Hot Pot

 PROMOTES A SENSE OF WELL-BEING

 **HELPS REMOVE TOXINS FROM THE BODY**

 **HELPS FIGHT INFLAMMATION**

 **AIDS OPTIMAL DIGESTIVE HEALTH**

Dishes such as this medley of vegetables and spices, cooked slowly over a low heat, are warming, sustaining, and uplifting for the mind and body. Sweet potato helps remove toxins and calm inflammation, while cabbage and garlic are anti-parasitic and help improve digestion. The art of this dish lies in carefully layering the ingredients, so each diner receives a little of all the vegetables.

SERVES 4–6

150g (5½oz) shallots, quartered

1 tbsp ghee or clarified butter

200ml (7fl oz) vegetable stock

100ml (3½fl oz) dry white wine

600–800g (1lb 5oz–1¾lb) white cabbage, outside leaves removed, and cut into 8 segments

1 medium (200g/7oz) sweet potato, peeled and cut into 6 segments

2 small carrots, peeled and sliced

6 garlic cloves, minced

2 small chillies, deseeded and chopped

4 inner celery sticks and leaves, chopped (discard stringy outer sticks)

250g (9oz) baby plum tomatoes

6 bay leaves

1 tsp ground coriander

1 tsp freshly ground black pepper

2 tsp smoked paprika

1 tbsp olive oil

salt

a small handful of chopped coriander leaves, to garnish (optional)

1 Place half the shallots in a heavy-based casserole pot with a lid, add half the ghee and a splash of vegetable stock and wine, and mix. Add some of the cabbage segments, sweet potato, and carrots, half the garlic, 1 chilli, half the chopped celery and tomatoes, 3 bay leaves, and a dash of the spices to create a layer of ingredients. Repeat with the rest of the ghee, vegetables, and spices to create another layer.

2 Sprinkle the olive oil over the top. Mix the stock and wine, season with a little salt, and pour two-thirds of the liquid into the pot. Bring it to a simmer on the hob, cover with a lid, and simmer on a gentle heat for 1 hour, occasionally adding more wine and stock blend. Remove the lid for the last 15 minutes of cooking time for any excess stock to evaporate. Remove from the heat, lift out the bay leaves if possible and discard, and serve. Garnish each portion with coriander leaves, if using.

Marinated Tofu With Shiitake And Noodles

 **HELPS FIGHT INFLAMMATION**   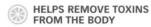 **HELPS REMOVE TOXINS FROM THE BODY**    **HELPS LOWER BLOOD PRESSURE**

Soya is a traditional remedy for inflammatory conditions of the lungs and gut. Its phytoestrogens (plant hormones) can also help protect the heart and lower blood pressure. In small amounts, unfermented soya can help neutralize toxins in the body – helpful if you have a hangover – although high, regular consumption can lower the absorption of some minerals in food.

SERVES 6

300g (10oz) organic marinated tofu, cut into bite-sized cubes

4 tbsp sunflower oil

a pinch of salt

approximately 300g (10oz) medium noodles (egg or rice) for 6 people

300g (10oz) fresh shiitake mushrooms, halved or quartered

1 carrot, julienned

250g (9oz) mung bean sprouts, rinsed and drained

250g (9oz) mangetout, cut in half

100g (3½oz) baby corn, halved

1–2 tbsp tamari soy sauce

1 tbsp black sesame seeds

a small handful of coriander leaves, chopped, to garnish

For the marinade

3 garlic cloves, crushed

3cm (1½in) fresh ginger root, grated

1 small chilli, deseeded and finely chopped

3 tbsp mirin sauce

2 tbsp toasted sesame oil

3 tbsp teriyaki sauce

3 small shallots, finely sliced

1 Arrange the tofu in a flat dish. Mix together the marinade ingredients and pour over the tofu cubes, making sure they are thoroughly covered. Cover the dish and leave to marinate overnight in the refrigerator. Turn the cubes over at some point to allow the flavours to infuse completely.

2 Remove the tofu cubes from the marinade and drain for a moment to let the juices drip away. Reserve the marinade.

3 Heat 2 tablespoons of the sunflower oil with 2 tablespoons of water in a wok over a medium heat. Add the tofu cubes and fry until lightly browned on all sides, turning them gently so they don't break. Remove from the wok and transfer to a warm dish.

4 Meanwhile, bring a large saucepan of water to the boil, add a pinch of salt, and cook the noodles according to the packet instructions. Drain the noodles and rinse in cold water to prevent them cooking any more.

5 Scrape off any burned remnants of tofu in the bottom of the wok and add another tablespoon each of sunflower oil and water. Add the shiitake mushrooms and stir-fry for 2–3 minutes, then transfer to a warm dish. Add the carrot, mung bean sprouts, mangetout, baby corn, and tamari soy sauce, and stir-fry briefly. Then transfer to the warm dish of mushrooms.

6 Wipe the wok down again, and heat the last tablespoon of oil. Add the reserved marinade, let it heat through, then add the cooked noodles and stir-fry them briefly too. Return all the vegetables to the wok and mix them into the noodles. Add the tofu and mix it in gently. Sprinkle the black sesame seeds on top, then transfer to 6 warmed noodle bowls. Sprinkle the chopped coriander leaves over each portion and serve.

Mung beans (p115) produce the thick, juicy sprouts that are popular in Asian cuisine. They are renowned for their detoxifying properties.

STIR-FRIED SPRING VEGETABLES

FEEDS GOOD BACTERIA IN THE GUT   **HELPS FIGHT INFLAMMATION**   **HELPS LOWER BLOOD PRESSURE**   **HELPS BALANCE BLOOD SUGAR LEVELS**

Eating plenty of fresh, young, green vegetables in spring is a good way to cleanse the body after the dark days of winter. Asparagus stimulates the digestion by acting as a prebiotic. It also contains compounds that have an anti-inflammatory effect, so it is beneficial if you have high blood pressure and blood sugar imbalance. Young mint and chives gently invigorate the body.

SERVES 4

2 tbsp olive oil

350g (12oz) asparagus, cut into 5cm (2in) pieces

250g (9oz) mangetout, trimmed

150g (5½oz) wild garlic leaves, chopped

200g (7oz) small spinach leaves

1 tbsp raspberry vinegar

2 tbsp chopped mint leaves

2 tbsp finely chopped chives

1 Heat the olive oil and a dash of water in a wok over a high heat. Add the asparagus and mangetout and stir-fry for 3 minutes, then add the wild garlic leaves and spinach and stir until they wilt.

2 Remove the wok from the heat and add the raspberry vinegar, mint, and chives. Combine and serve while hot with steamed rice or quinoa.

Asparagus (p77) contains antioxidants that help fight free-radical damage and has a mild laxative effect – perfect for a spring detox.

WOOD PIGEON BREASTS WITH GOJI BERRIES

⚡ **HELPS MAINTAIN ENERGY LEVELS**　　🔄 **ENHANCES VIGOUR AND A SENSE OF WELL-BEING**　　♀ **REPLACES IRON LOST IN MENSTRUATION**　　**HELPS TONE THE KIDNEYS**

Wood pigeon meat is lean, tender, and nutritious. In China, it is regarded as an excellent kidney tonic, but it is most commonly eaten to help combat male and female infertility by boosting blood circulation and improving energy levels. It also helps build iron levels after substantial blood loss, such as at childbirth or heavy menstruation. Goji berries are added to give a metabolic boost.

SERVES 4

4 whole pigeons

25g (scant 1oz) dried shiitake mushrooms

2 medium carrots, halved lengthways

1 medium onion, peeled and quartered

1 medium red chilli, whole

4 garlic cloves in their skins

½ tsp black peppercorns

a pinch of salt

4 tsp cornflour

20g (¾oz) goji berries

a dash of olive oil

coriander leaves, chopped, to garnish

1 Remove the breast meat in whole pieces from each bird and reserve. Place the filleted birds in a large casserole pot and add the mushrooms, carrots, onion, chilli, garlic, black peppercorns, and salt. Pour in enough water to just cover, bring it to the boil, and simmer over a low heat for 1½ hours, skimming off any impurities from the top of the stock as necessary. Watch the liquid level and add more water if needed. Towards the end of the cooking time, you should have approximately 500ml (16fl oz) or more of stock remaining.

2 Strain the stock, reserving the cooking liquid, shiitake mushrooms, garlic cloves, and some of the peppercorns. Discard the rest of the ingredients including the pigeon meat, bones, and skin. Shred the mushrooms and squeeze the softened garlic cloves from their skins. Set the garlic paste aside.

3 Return the stock to the casserole pot, reserving 4 tablespoons in a mug, and set over a medium-high heat. Thicken the liquid by mixing the cornflour with the reserved stock in the mug and adding it to the pot. Add the goji berries, shredded mushrooms, and the garlic paste and simmer the stock for 10–20 minutes until it thickens to the consistency of double cream. Adjust the seasoning if required.

4 Add a dash of olive oil to a frying pan and warm over a medium heat. Add the reserved pigeon breasts and pan-fry for 2 minutes on each side until just cooked through. Transfer to the casserole pot and cook for 2–3 minutes.

5 Arrange the breasts on a warm serving plate, spoon over a little of the sauce, and garnish with the coriander leaves. Serve with the remaining sauce in a jug and some boiled rice.

Goji berries *(p36) are rich in pyridoxine (vitamin B6), which supports efficient metabolism.*

GINGER CHICKEN

 PROTECTS AGAINST COLDS AND FLU

 **AIDS HEALTHY DIGESTION**

 **SUPPLIES OXYGEN TO CELLS**

 **BOOSTS RECOVERY AFTER CHILDBIRTH**

The marinade in this chicken dish contains fresh ginger, which is one of the most important foods for helping prevent and treat common colds. Its warming nature is enhanced here with lime, garlic, and honey – all known to help boost the immune system. This dish is ideal if you need to increase your resistance to seasonal bugs or build your strength after an illness.

SERVES 4

1 organic free-range chicken, approximately 1.5kg (3lb 3oz), cut into 8 pieces

1 tbsp ghee or clarified butter

1kg (2¼lb) potatoes, peeled and thinly sliced

½–1 tsp salt

1 tbsp paprika

½ tsp freshly ground black pepper

For the marinade

4 tbsp tamari soy sauce

1 heaped tbsp finely chopped fresh root ginger

3–5 garlic cloves, crushed

zest and juice of 1–2 limes

3 tbsp honey

1 Prepare the marinade by mixing the tamari soy sauce, ginger, garlic, lime juice, and honey in a clean plastic container with a lid. Add the chicken pieces and marinate for 8–12 hours or overnight in the refrigerator.

2 Preheat the oven to 220°C (425°F/Gas 7). Grease a large ovenproof dish with the ghee. Arrange the sliced potatoes in thin layers in the dish and sprinkle the salt, paprika, and black pepper on top. Place the chicken pieces on top of the potatoes. Pour any remaining marinade on top and season with salt and black pepper. Bake in the oven for 45–50 minutes or until the chicken juices run clear when the meat is pierced with a sharp knife, and the potatoes are cooked. Serve with salad.

Ghee (p120) is a good source of lauric acid, a healthy fat with antibacterial and antifungal properties.

Quinoa And Vegetable Stack

 **HELPS MAINTAIN ENERGY LEVELS**

 **SUPPORTS TISSUE GROWTH AND REPAIR**

 **EASY TO DIGEST AND GLUTEN-FREE**

 **HELPS STRENGTHEN THE IMMUNE SYSTEM**

High in protein and fibre, quinoa contains all the essential amino acids the body needs to sustain energy levels and support healthy tissue growth and repair. It is also gluten-free which makes it a good choice for anyone with gluten sensitivity. The sauerkraut brings multiple benefits for immunity and gut health and a selection of colourful fresh vegetables add valuable nutrients.

SERVES 4

5 small shallots or small red onions, finely sliced

1 medium-hot chilli, finely chopped

2 large red Romano peppers, or other red pepper, cut in half lengthways, deseeded, and sliced into 1cm (½in) strips

3 medium yellow courgettes, cut into 5mm (¼in) slices

100g (3½oz) shiitake mushrooms, stalks removed, sliced

2 garlic cloves, crushed

sea salt and freshly ground black pepper

2 tbsp olive oil

300g (10oz) quinoa

a sprig of parsley, chopped, to garnish

a drizzle of extra virgin olive oil

6 tbsp sauerkraut, to serve (optional)

1 Pour in enough water to cover the base of a medium saucepan and heat gently. Add the shallots and cook gently with the lid on until tender, adding more water if necessary. Add the chilli and sauté gently. Add the peppers and allow to soften, then add the courgettes. Lastly, add the shiitake mushrooms and garlic, season to taste with a pinch of sea salt, stir for a minute, and drizzle in the olive oil. Stir the mixture, place the lid back on, then switch off the heat and leave the pan on the hob to keep warm.

2 Cook the quinoa according to the packet instructions, then drain and set aside.

3 When you are ready to serve the food, take a serving dish, place a large cook's ring on it, and fill with a 2.5cm (1in) layer of the quinoa. Spoon a layer of vegetables on top of the quinoa and sprinkle with some chopped parsley. Remove the ring and repeat with 3 more stacks of quinoa, vegetables, and parsley. Sprinkle the stacks with black pepper and a drizzle of extra virgin olive oil, and serve with some sauerkraut arranged around the base of the stacks.

4 If you don't have a cook's ring, use a dome-shaped small bowl brushed with olive oil. Fill the bottom half of the bowl with the vegetables, top with quinoa, place the serving dish face down on the bowl, turn both upside down, and gently remove the bowl. Sprinkle the parsley over the top, season, drizzle with the extra virgin olive oil, and serve with the sauerkraut.

SAUERKRAUT PARCELS

 PROMOTES A HEALTHY DIGESTIVE TRACT    **CALMING AND COMFORTING**

Fermented cabbage, or sauerkraut, is rich in vitamin C and contains a type of lactic acid that aids digestion by clearing harmful bacteria and combating toxins, food stagnation, and wind. Some nutritionists also maintain that it is an effective preventative for cancer and degenerative diseases. Whole sauerkraut leaves can sometimes be found in Polish or Italian delicatessens.

SERVES 4

salt and freshly ground black pepper

2 tbsp wine vinegar

6 black peppercorns

16 whole sauerkraut leaves, or large cabbage leaves, stalks and leaf veins removed

1 tbsp olive oil

2 medium onions, finely diced

3 garlic cloves, crushed

500g (1lb 2oz) minced meat (pork, beef, or a mixture of the two)

125g (4½oz) white or brown rice, rinsed

2 tsp paprika

2 tbsp chopped flat-leaf parsley leaves

300g (10oz) sauerkraut

200g (7oz) smoked rib of pork or smoked bacon, chopped

For the sauce

1 tbsp olive oil

3 tsp plain flour

a pinch of salt

a few black peppercorns

20g (¾oz) tomato purée

1 small chilli, deseeded and finely chopped

115g (4oz) crème fraîche

1 If using fresh cabbage leaves instead of the whole fermented sauerkraut leaves, bring a large saucepan of water to the boil and add a pinch of salt, the wine vinegar, and black peppercorns. Place the leaves into the water, 2 at a time, and blanch for 2–3 minutes: watch them carefully and remove as soon as they begin to wilt. Set aside to dry on kitchen paper.

2 Heat the olive oil in a frying pan and sauté the onions and garlic until soft and translucent. Add the minced meat and cook for 10–15 minutes until it is lightly browned. Add the rice, paprika, and parsley, stirring well for 2–3 minutes. Remove from the heat and set aside to cool to a manageable temperature.

3 Place a ball of the stuffing in the centre of a sauerkraut or cabbage leaf. Fold in the sides of the leaf and roll it up to form a closed parcel. Repeat with the rest of the stuffing and cabbage leaves.

4 Arrange a layer of sauerkraut in the bottom of a large saucepan with a lid, followed by the cabbage parcels, loose ends facing down, and topped with the smoked pork or bacon. Carefully add hot water to the pan until it half-covers the contents of the pan. If necessary, weigh the parcels down with a small heatproof plate. Put the lid on and simmer over a low heat for 2 hours or until cooked, making sure the water doesn't evaporate. The water should remain at the same level, half-covering the contents of the pan, throughout the cooking time.

5 Meanwhile, make the sauce. Heat the olive oil in a small saucepan, add the flour and allow to brown slightly, then add the salt, black peppercorns, tomato purée, chilli, crème fraîche, and enough water to make a sauce with the consistency of pouring cream. When the sauerkraut parcels are cooked, divide between 4 serving plates and pour some of the hot sauce over each portion.

TIP: Try making your own sauerkraut leaves by using the recipe on p330.

Savoy Cabbage Parcels

 **HELPS MAINTAIN ENERGY LEVELS**

 HELPS BUILD MUSCLE

 **ENHANCES VIGOUR**

 **CALMING AND COMFORTING**

This dish is great comfort food, but it is also packed with healthy ingredients that boost energy levels. It is a good choice for men of all ages, as quinoa provides protein and essential amino acids that help the body build muscle, while walnuts can help improve men's fertility and are heart-healthy. This also makes an ideal complete meal for vegetarians and vegans.

SERVES 4

300g (10oz) quinoa

60g (2oz) walnuts, roughly chopped

50g (1¾oz) sun-dried tomatoes, chopped

2 garlic cloves, finely chopped

1 medium red onion, finely chopped

4 small shallots, finely chopped

6 tbsp chopped parsley

100g (3½oz) fresh or dried unsweetened cranberries

2 tsp ground pimento

½ tsp ground coriander

2 level tsp Italian herbs seasoning

Himalayan salt and freshly ground black pepper

1 large Savoy cabbage, leaves removed

4 bay leaves

2 tsp plain flour, arrowroot, or kudzu (a popular Asian thickener)

thick natural yogurt, to serve

1 To make the stuffing, wash the quinoa grains, allow to drip-dry, and put in a mixing bowl with the walnuts, tomatoes, garlic, onion, shallots, parsley, and cranberries. Season with the pimento, ground coriander, Italian seasoning, and salt and black pepper, and combine all the ingredients thoroughly.

2 Choose 10–12 tender medium-sized cabbage leaves and blanch in boiling water for 1–2 minutes, removing them as soon as they wilt. Reserve the cabbage water. Allow the leaves to cool for a moment, then cut away the thick vein at the back of each leaf.

3 Place a spoonful of stuffing in the centre of a cabbage leaf. Fold in the sides of the leaf and roll it up to form a closed parcel. Repeat with the rest of the stuffing and cabbage leaves.

4 Tightly arrange the parcels, loose ends facing down, in the bottom of a medium saucepan with a lid. Layer the parcels if necessary, adding the bay leaves as you work.

5 Add the reserved cabbage water to the pan, making sure that the base of the pan is covered but the parcels are only partially covered with liquid. Bring to the boil, reduce the heat, put on the lid, and simmer gently for 30 minutes.

6 Dissolve the flour in a mug of water and add it to the pan. Simmer for another 15 minutes or until the sauce has thickened and the parcels are cooked. Serve accompanied with a spoonful of thick yogurt.

Savoy cabbage (p52) is a source of sulphur, essential for healthy bones, cartilage, tendons, and skin.

CHANTERELLES AND CHILLIES WITH PASTA

 **HELPS STRENGTHEN
THE IMMUNE SYSTEM**   **PROMOTES HEALTHY
SKIN**   **HELPS PROTECT
EYE HEALTH**

Like many mushrooms, chanterelles are rich in the amino acids that are essential for building protein in the body. They also contain vitamin A and so benefit eye health. Kamut is an ancient grain closely related to modern wheat. Even though it contains gluten, it has been found to be more easily digestible for people with allergies or intolerances to wheat.

SERVES 4

400g (14oz) fresh chanterelle mushrooms, sliced

4 tsp olive oil

2–3 garlic cloves, crushed

1–2 small chillies, deseeded and finely chopped

5 tbsp soured cream

salt and freshly ground black pepper

500g (1lb 2oz) pasta, such as tagliatelle or spaghetti, made from kamut wheat

1 tbsp finely chopped flat-leaf parsley leaves, to garnish

1 Place the mushrooms in a medium saucepan and dry-fry them over a low heat, shaking the pan gently, until their juices run. Then, turn the heat up so the liquid evaporates and the mushrooms are soft, but reasonably dry. Add 3 teaspoons of the olive oil to coat the mushrooms, then add the garlic, chillies, and soured cream, and let the mixture simmer over a low heat for 2–6 minutes. Season with salt and black pepper to taste.

2 Meanwhile, cook the pasta according to the packet instructions until it is al dente, adding the last teaspoon of olive oil to the cooking water to prevent it boiling over and to enhance the flavour of the pasta. Drain and transfer to a warmed serving dish. Spoon the sauce over the pasta, garnish with the parsley, combine the ingredients well, and serve with a green salad.

Chanterelle mushrooms (p91)
contain vitamins D and K, which work
together to protect the heart and bones.

SALMON WITH DILL AND TAMARI SAUCE

 HELPS MAINTAIN ENERGY LEVELS

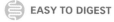 **EASY TO DIGEST**

 **HELPS IMPROVE CIRCULATION**

This simply baked salmon dish is paired with fresh dill for a classic combination of flavours. Salmon is considered a good food to eat if you are feeling debilitated or are convalescing after an illness, as it helps to improve energy levels and is easily digested. It is also rich in omega-3 fatty acids and selenium, which promote heart health and support healthy ageing.

SERVES 4

4 salmon fillets, approximately 300g (10oz) each
4 tbsp tamari soy sauce
a generous dash of lemon juice
4 tbsp olive oil
4 garlic cloves, finely chopped
4 thin slices of lemon
2 tbsp chopped dill leaves

1 Preheat the oven to 180°C (350°F/Gas 4). Place the salmon fillets in a ceramic baking dish. Blend the tamari soy sauce, lemon juice, olive oil, and a dash of water in a small bowl, add the garlic, combine the ingredients together well, and pour over the fish.

2 Arrange the lemon slices on top of the fish and sprinkle the dill on top. Cover with foil and bake for 20–25 minutes. Carefully insert a sharp knife into the centre of one fillet to check if the fish is cooked; the flesh should be opaque. Serve either hot or cold.

57% DAILY INTAKE OF VITAMIN B5

MORE THAN 100% DAILY INTAKE OF VITAMIN B6

MORE THAN 100% DAILY INTAKE OF VITAMIN B12

MORE THAN 100% DAILY INTAKE OF VITAMIN D

BOOST YOUR VITAMIN INTAKE

EACH LARGE SALMON FILLET PROVIDES EXCELLENT QUANTITIES OF VITAMIN D AND AN ARRAY OF KEY B VITAMINS.

Marinated Duck With Mango Salsa

 **HELPS MAINTAIN ENERGY LEVELS**

 HAS A DIURETIC ACTION

 SOOTHES AND TONES THE DIGESTIVE TRACT

 **ENHANCES SPERM QUALITY**

Duck meat is considered an empowering food in traditional Chinese medicine: it provides the body with energy and helps to increase stamina levels. Its diuretic properties help to reduce water retention and, coupled with a sweet and sour mango salsa, it benefits the digestive system and can help to alleviate nausea. It is also thought to boost men's sperm count.

SERVES 4

3 kaffir lime leaves

1 tsp clear honey

zest of 1 orange and juice of 2 oranges

1 tbsp tamari soy sauce

¼ tsp five-spice powder

4 duck breasts, without skin

125g (4½oz) jasmine rice

4 fresh figs (optional) to garnish

For the mango salsa

2 medium mangoes, peeled and diced, with stones removed

3 spring onions, finely chopped

1 small green chilli pepper, deseeded and finely chopped

1 small red chilli pepper, deseeded and finely chopped

4 tbsp chopped coriander leaves

3 tbsp chopped basil leaves

1 small cucumber, deseeded and finely diced

1 large tomato, deseeded and finely diced

1 tbsp balsamic vinegar

2 tbsp extra virgin olive oil

salt and freshly ground black pepper

1 Place the kaffir lime leaves in a large mixing bowl, cover with 4 tablespoons of boiling water, and leave to infuse for 15 minutes. Add the honey and stir until it dissolves. Add the orange zest and juice, tamari soy sauce, and five-spice powder and blend well. Immerse the duck breasts in the marinade, ensure they are well coated, and set aside to marinate for 30 minutes.

2 Meanwhile, bring a medium saucepan of water to the boil and cook the jasmine rice according to the packet instructions.

3 Heat a heavy-based frying pan over a high heat. Remove the duck breasts from the marinade and transfer them to the pan to brown on both sides. Lower the heat, strain the marinade juices, and add them to the pan. Cook the duck breasts for a further 5–6 minutes, turning them frequently so they don't stick or burn on the base of the pan. Test to see how well-cooked the meat is by carefully cutting into the centre of the breast with a sharp knife. The centre of the meat should still be pink after this time, so let it cook for a little longer if you prefer it well done. Remove the pan from the heat and set aside briefly. Make 2 deep cuts at right angles in the top of each fig, if using, and open out the 4 tips to create a flower petal effect.

4 Transfer the duck breasts from the pan to a chopping board and slice diagonally into thin slices. Add all the mango salsa ingredients to the pan with the marinade juices and stir to mix and warm through. To assemble the dish, place a cook's ring in the centre of each serving plate, half-fill with cooked jasmine rice, top up with some of the warm mango salsa, and carefully remove the ring. Arrange a sliced duck breast on each portion, position a fig "flower" on top of the duck, and serve.

VENISON CASSEROLE WITH CRANBERRIES

 HELPS RELEASE CELLULAR ENERGY   **HELPS INCREASE LIBIDO**   **STRENGTHENS THE REPRODUCTIVE SYSTEM**   **FIGHTS URINARY TRACT INFECTIONS**

Colder months are the time for this warming venison stew, best eaten at lunchtime to benefit from its energizing properties; iron-rich venison is traditionally eaten to help combat fatigue, as well as impotence and infertility. Cranberries are both astringent and antibacterial, and are commonly used to help prevent infections in the urinary tract, kidneys, and bladder.

SERVES 6

1 tbsp vegetable oil

1kg (2¼lb) lean venison shoulder, chopped into 2.5cm (1in) cubes

2 tbsp plain flour, seasoned

1 tsp whole coriander seeds, coarsely crushed

200g (7oz) small shallots, quartered

100g (3½oz) crimini or brown button mushrooms, sliced

70g (2¼oz) dried apricots (without sulphur), roughly chopped

150g (5½oz) fresh or frozen cranberries

3 kaffir lime leaves

1 tbsp cacao nibs or dark chocolate (optional)

375ml (13fl oz) red wine

salt and freshly ground black pepper

1 Preheat the oven to 180°C (350°F/Gas 4). Heat the vegetable oil in a large, heavy casserole pan with a lid. Toss the venison in the flour and add it to the pan in small batches to brown on a medium-high heat. Set aside the browned meat, turn the heat down, and add the coriander seeds, followed by the shallots and mushrooms, to brown. Add a little water if necessary.

2 Add the apricots to the pan and gently stir them in. Return the meat back into the pan together with all the juices, and add the cranberries and kaffir lime leaves. Stir in the cacao nibs and red wine, and stir everything thoroughly, put the lid on, and place in the oven.

3 Let the stew cook for 1–1½ hours or until the meat is tender and the juices have thickened. Remove the kaffir lime leaves, add salt and black pepper to taste, and serve with boiled rice.

TIP: If you can't find fresh or frozen cranberries, substitute with 100g (3½oz) of fresh blueberries and 50g (1¾oz) of dried cranberries instead.

MEDITERRANEAN VEGETABLE MEDLEY

 HELPS STRENGTHEN THE IMMUNE SYSTEM    **HELPS IMPROVE CIRCULATION**   ✺ **HELPS REMOVE TOXINS FROM THE BODY**

This summer dish is full of vegetables with antioxidant and anti-inflammatory phytonutrients that help protect the body at a cellular level. Try to cut the peppers, aubergine, and tomatoes the same size to improve the look and cooking time of this simple dish. The courgettes are best left in larger cubes, as they cook quickly and their nutrients can be lost if they are overcooked.

SERVES 4

1 tbsp olive oil

4 shallots, finely chopped

salt and freshly ground black pepper

a pinch of oregano or marjoram

2 red peppers, deseeded and chopped

2 yellow peppers, deseeded and chopped

1 medium aubergine, chopped

1 medium courgette, chopped

4 tomatoes, skinned (optional), and chopped

2 garlic cloves, crushed

2 tbsp olive oil

4 tbsp finely chopped parsley leaves, plus leaves to garnish

1 Heat the olive oil in a large, heavy-based saucepan over a medium to low heat. Add the shallots and a pinch of salt, and stir until the shallots begin to turn translucent. Add a dash of water to bring the temperature down and to add moisture to the pan. After 2–3 minutes add the oregano or marjoram and the peppers. Cook until the peppers have softened.

2 Add the aubergine and the courgette, and when the liquid in the pan has reduced, add the tomatoes. Let the mixture simmer for 15 minutes over a low heat, taking care not to let the vegetables stick to the base of the pan and burn.

3 Add the garlic and a little more olive oil for added flavour and cook for a further 5 minutes. Mix in the chopped parsley and add salt and black pepper to taste. Serve on a bed of brown basmati rice with some parsley scattered on top.

Aubergines (p64) *have the ability to help remove harmful toxins from the body.*

FRENCH BEAN STEW

AIDS HEALTHY DIGESTION

HELPS BALANCE BLOOD SUGAR LEVELS

HAS A DIURETIC ACTION

This blend of vegetables enhances digestion, balances blood sugar levels, and helps remove excess fluid from the body. Fresh beans also have a diuretic effect. Tender, golden-yellow, French beans are best for this recipe, although any fresh beans will taste good. Look for young, succulent beans that aren't stringy and which snap easily if you bend them in half.

SERVES 4

2 large tomatoes, skinned and chopped

2 large potatoes, peeled and diced

2 tbsp olive oil

1 onion, finely chopped

2 carrots, sliced into thin rounds

1 chilli pepper, deseeded and finely chopped (optional)

800g (1¾lb) tender, yellow French beans, topped and tailed, and sliced into 3cm (1¼in) pieces

3 garlic cloves, chopped

salt and freshly ground black pepper

1 tbsp chopped dill leaves, plus a few extra leaves to garnish

1 Cut a cross on the top of each tomato, dip in boiling water for 20 seconds, remove, and when cold enough to handle, remove the skin and finely chop the flesh.

2 Place the potatoes in a saucepan, cover with cold water, bring to the boil, turn down the heat, and simmer until the potatoes are cooked.

3 Meanwhile, heat the olive oil in a large saucepan with a lid over a medium heat. Add the onion and sauté until soft and translucent. Add the carrots and chilli pepper (if using), stir, and sauté for 2–3 minutes. Add the beans, stir briefly, then lower the heat, cover with the lid, and allow the beans to sweat for 1–2 minutes. Add the garlic and tomatoes and allow them to cook in the vegetable juices for 2–3 minutes. Add 1–2 tablespoons of water if the vegetables are beginning to catch on the base of the pan.

4 When the beans are al dente (cooked, but still slightly crunchy), add the cooked potatoes and a small amount of their cooking water. Add some seasoning and the dill, combine with the other ingredients, and cook for a further 2–3 minutes. Remove from the heat, transfer to 4 serving bowls, and garnish with dill leaves.

Red tomatoes (p65) enhance the cleansing effect of this recipe and are a good source of heart-friendly lycopene.

GRILLED MACKEREL WITH CHARD

 **PROTECTS THE HEART AND BLOOD VESSELS**

 **HELPS FIGHT INFLAMMATION**

 **HELPS BALANCE BLOOD SUGAR LEVELS**

HELPS BUILD STRONG BONES

Mackerel is beneficial for cardiovascular health, and here it is combined with Swiss chard, which is known for its anti-inflammatory, antioxidant, and detoxifying properties. In addition, Swiss chard helps balance blood sugar levels, protect the body from chronic oxidative stress, and support bone health. Choose young leaves with narrow stems for an even cooking time.

SERVES 4

4 whole mackerel, filleted

2 celery sticks, chopped

2 garlic cloves, chopped, plus 2 garlic cloves, crushed

1 chilli, deseeded and chopped

a bunch of parsley leaves, roughly chopped

juice of 1 lemon

2 tbsp olive oil

500g (1lb 2oz) Swiss chard, chopped, with stems removed and finely chopped

1 tbsp blackberry vinegar (p334) or the juice of ½ lemon

salt and freshly ground black pepper

For the dressing

juice of 1 lemon

2 tbsp teriyaki sauce

1 tsp finely grated fresh ginger root

2 tbsp olive oil

1 tsp honey

salt and freshly ground black pepper

1 With a sharp knife, make several diagonal scores through the skin along the length of each mackerel fillet to prevent them curling up while being grilled. Place the fillets in a shallow dish.

2 Place the celery, chopped garlic, chilli, parsley, and lemon juice in a blender or food processor, add 100ml (3½fl oz) of water, and blitz. Pour this marinade over the mackerel fillets, ensuring they are thoroughly coated, and set aside to marinate for 1 hour. Meanwhile, prepare the dressing by blending all the ingredients together.

3 Heat the grill to high. Remove the mackerel from the marinade and place the fillets, skin-side up, on the grill pan. Cook for 4–5 minutes or until the skin is crisp and the flesh is cooked through and flakes when tested with a fork.

4 Meanwhile, heat the olive oil and 4 tablespoons of water in a large heavy-based saucepan over a medium heat. Add the 2 crushed garlic cloves and chard leaves and stems, and stir thoroughly. Cook until the leaves wilt, then sprinkle with blackberry vinegar and remove from the heat. Add seasoning to taste and a dash more of the vinegar, if you like.

5 Transfer the mackerel fillets to 4 warm serving plates, pour the dressing over each portion, and place a serving of chard beside it.

Mackerel (p128) is abundant in healthy fats and nutrients that help support the cardiovascular and nervous systems.

GRILLED SARDINES WITH TOMATO SALSA

 **HELPS IMPROVE CIRCULATION**    **SUPPLIES OXYGEN TO CELLS**    **HELPS STRENGTHEN TENDONS AND BONES**   **HELPS CALM THE NERVES**

Salty-sweet sardines boost circulation and help build red blood cells, which in turn increase the flow of oxygen around the body, and strengthen tendons and bones. Here, they are cooked with flavoursome ingredients including basil, which has a soothing and supporting action on the mind and cognitive processes, and rosemary, which has anti-inflammatory properties.

SERVES 4

6–8 large sprigs of rosemary
8 fresh sardines
1–2 tbsp olive oil
sea salt and freshly ground black pepper
1–2 lemons, cut into quarters, to serve

For the salsa

8 tomatoes, skinned, deseeded and finely diced
1 red chilli, deseeded and finely diced
3 spring onions, finely chopped
2 tbsp chopped basil leaves
1 garlic clove, finely chopped (optional)
2 tbsp raspberry vinegar, or red wine vinegar
4 tbsp olive oil
sea salt and freshly ground black pepper

1 To make the tomato salsa, mix all the ingredients well and season to taste.

2 Preheat the grill to a moderate heat. Arrange the large rosemary sprigs on a grill pan and lay the sardines on top. Drizzle with the olive oil and season with sea salt and black pepper.

3 Grill the sardines for 3–5 minutes on each side or until cooked (they should be opaque, but still firm).

4 Divide the sardines and salsa between 4 serving plates, place 1–2 lemon quarters on each plate, and serve with a green salad and boiled new potatoes.

Rosemary (p101) is rich in the compound borneol, which acts as an energizing tonic for the nervous system.

BARLOTTO WITH CHESTNUT PURÉE

 **HELPS MAINTAIN ENERGY LEVELS**  **HELPS IMPROVE CIRCULATION**  **PROMOTES BOWEL REGULARITY**  **HELPS STRENGTHEN LOWER LIMBS**

Barlotto is a version of risotto made with barley instead of short-grain rice. Barley is a good source of soluble fibre and together with sweet chestnuts assists the digestive and urinary systems. Black barley, an ancient grain that hasn't been hulled, is even more of a healing, energizing food, if you can find it. Toasting the barley first gives it a fragrant, nutty flavour.

SERVES 4

250g (9oz) pearl barley
20g (¾oz) dried shiitake mushrooms
1 tsp sea salt or other unrefined salt
1 tbsp ghee, or clarified butter
8 small shallots, finely diced
1 medium carrot, diced
1 fennel bulb, cored and thinly sliced
2 garlic cloves, minced
¼ tsp freshly ground white pepper
150g (5½oz) chestnut purée
1 large glass of dry white wine

For the vegetable stock

10g (¼oz) astragalus root (optional)
1 large carrot
2 celery sticks
6 thin slices of fresh ginger root
3 thick slices of celeriac
3 shallots, quartered
4 small garlic cloves, with the skin left on
1 tbsp coriander seeds
a small handful of parsley leaves

1 To toast the barley, preheat the oven to 180°C (350°F/Gas 4), arrange the grains in a thin layer on a baking sheet, and place in the oven for 10–12 minutes. Toast the barley until it turns light golden, agitating it occasionally so it toasts evenly.

2 Put all the stock ingredients in a large saucepan and cover with 3 litres (5¼ pints) of water. Simmer on a low heat until it reduces to roughly 2 litres (3½ pints) of stock. Strain through a colander into another pan. Discard the other vegetables. Squeeze the cooked garlic from its skin and add the paste to the strained stock.

3 Add the dried shiitake mushrooms and salt to the stock in the pan, and bring it back to the boil. Lower the temperature and simmer for 15 minutes to ensure the mushrooms have reconstituted fully.

4 Strain, reserving the stock, and mince the mushrooms. Place a heavy frying pan over a medium heat and add the ghee. Once the ghee has melted, add the shallots, cook for 2–3 minutes, then add the carrots, minced shiitake mushrooms, fennel, garlic, and white pepper, and cook for 10 minutes or until the vegetables have softened.

5 Stir in the toasted barley, making sure all the grains are well coated in the vegetable juices. Add a ladle of the hot stock and stir constantly until it is absorbed, then repeat with more stock. After 10 minutes of cooking, stir in the chestnut purée, and after 25 minutes, add the white wine. Cook for a further 5–15 minutes until the barley is cooked through, but still al dente (slightly firm to the bite). Remove from the heat and serve with a green salad.

GRIDDLED VEGETABLE ROLL WITH CASHEW AND BRAISED GARLIC CREAM

 **HELPS LOWER CHOLESTEROL**    **HELPS FIGHT COLDS AND FLU**    **AIDS HEALTHY DIGESTION**

These lightly cooked summer vegetables are bursting with nutrients that support the heart and blood vessels, and also enhance immunity and digestion. A sauce laced with a powerful combination of garlic and cashew nuts enhances these tasty rolls' ability to help lower blood cholesterol, and protect against viruses, colds, and flu.

SERVES 4

2 tbsp olives in brine, drained and chopped

2 tbsp sun-dried tomatoes in oil, drained and chopped

1 red pepper, sliced in half and deseeded

1 yellow pepper, sliced in half and deseeded

a dash of olive oil

2 aubergines, sliced thinly lengthways

2 courgettes, thinly sliced

2 small fennel bulbs, trimmed and quartered

2 marinated artichoke hearts in oil, drained and quartered

For the cashew and braised garlic cream

2 large garlic bulbs

4 tbsp olive oil

1 small sprig of rosemary

60g (2oz) cashew nuts

a pinch of salt

1 tbsp finely chopped parsley leaves

1 garlic clove, finely chopped

1 To make the braised garlic cream, preheat the oven to 180°C (350°F/Gas 4). Place the garlic bulbs, olive oil, and rosemary sprig in a small baking dish, cover with foil or a lid, and bake for 30–40 minutes or until the cloves are soft and just beginning to brown. Remove from the oven and, when cool enough to handle, squeeze the softened garlic from its skins into a small bowl.

2 Place the cashews and 60g (2oz) of the braised garlic purée in a food processor or blender, add 120ml (4fl oz) of water, and blitz until smooth and sticky. Slowly add another 120ml (4fl oz) of water or more until the consistency is like heavy cream and pourable. Add the salt to taste and blitz again. Stir in the parsley leaves and garlic and set aside.

3 Increase the oven temperature to 190°C (375°F/Gas 5). Mix the olives and sun-dried tomatoes in a small bowl and set aside. Place the halved peppers on a baking sheet and bake in the oven for 15–20 minutes or until their skins start blistering and turning slightly brown. Remove from the oven, transfer to a bowl, cover with cling film, and leave to sweat and cool. Once cool enough to handle, remove the skins and cut the flesh into quarters.

4 Brush a griddle pan (or barbecue) with the olive oil and heat over a high heat. Add the aubergine slices in batches and griddle for 2–3 minutes on each side. Repeat with the courgettes and fennel.

5 To assemble the vegetable rolls, place an aubergine slice on a chopping board, cover with 1 or 2 slices of griddled courgette, and place a slice each of red and yellow pepper on top. Place an artichoke quarter on top of the layered vegetables at one side and a fennel quarter next to it. Carefully roll up the layered aubergine slice and fasten with a cocktail stick. Repeat with the rest of the ingredients. Arrange the vegetable rolls on a serving plate, scatter the olives and sun-dried tomatoes around them, drizzle the cashew and braised garlic cream on top, and serve with a kamut and pine nut salad, if you like.

FRAGRANT RICE AND MILLET

 **AIDS HEALTHY DIGESTION**

 **PROMOTES A SENSE OF WELL-BEING**

HAS ANTIFUNGAL PROPERTIES

This fragrant blend of brown rice, millet, vegetables, nuts, and herbs is a great dinner party dish. Cinnamon, cardamom, and coriander are all warming, digestive stimulants, and cardamom is also thought to help stimulate the mind and spirit. Millet is a diuretic, but it is also known to have antifungal properties and is often used in the treatment of candida.

SERVES 4

115g (4oz) mixed walnuts and hazelnuts, halved

150g (5½oz) long grain brown rice

115g (4oz) millet

1 tbsp olive oil

60g (2oz) red onion, finely chopped

1 medium leek, sliced

20 coriander seeds, crushed

6 cardamom pods, crushed

a pinch of ground cinnamon

1 litre (1¾ pints) vegetable or chicken stock

225g (8oz) mixed peppers, sliced in half and deseeded

2 tbsp chopped coriander leaves

salt and freshly ground black pepper

For the dressing

1 tsp tamari soy sauce

juice of 1 lime

2 tbsp chicken stock

1 Soak the mixed nuts in water for 30 minutes. Preheat the oven to 180°C (350°F/Gas 4).

2 Rinse the nuts in fresh water and leave to drain for 2–3 minutes. Then scatter onto a baking tray and toast in the oven for 30 minutes, shaking or stirring them every 6–10 minutes until dry and light brown in colour. Remove the nuts from the oven as soon as they are toasted and increase the temperature to 190°C (375°F/Gas 5).

3 Meanwhile, rinse the rice and millet in fresh water and drain. Heat the olive oil in a medium saucepan over a low heat and cook the onion, leek, and spices in the pan for 2 minutes. Add the rice, millet, and stock and simmer for 30 minutes or until all the liquid has been absorbed and the grains are soft. Avoid stirring the rice mixture while it cooks, as this will release starch and alter the texture.

4 Transfer the mixture to a serving bowl, remove the cardamom pods if possible, and set aside to cool.

5 Put the mixed peppers on a baking sheet and bake for 15–20 minutes or until their skins start blistering and turning slightly brown. Remove from the oven, transfer to a bowl, cover with cling film, and leave to sweat and cool. Once cool enough to handle, remove the skins and dice the flesh.

6 Mix together all the ingredients for the dressing. Combine the peppers, nuts, and coriander leaves with the cooled grains, pour over the dressing, adjust the seasoning to taste, and serve.

Cardamom (p116) is an excellent spice to aid digestion, and even boasts of antibacterial properties.

SWEET TREATS

WE ALL NEED A **LITTLE SWEETNESS** IN OUR LIVES.
WHETHER HOT OR COLD, DESSERTS WITH FRESH
FRUITS, NUTS, AND SEEDS AT THEIR CORE SUPPLY
THE **ANTIOXIDANTS**, PHYTONUTRIENTS, HEALTHY
OILS, AND **FLAVOURS** THAT CAN UPLIFT AND HEAL.

Fresh Fig Delight With Pear And Red Wine Sauce

 **SUPPORTS HEALTHY LUNG FUNCTION**

 **PROMOTES BOWEL REGULARITY**

 **PROMOTES A SENSE OF WELL-BEING**

 **HELPS FIGHT INFLAMMATION**

This impressive dessert combines a fig-filled sponge cake with a crisp almond base. It benefits the lungs and large intestine, 2 organs whose functions are closely related. Pears and almonds are cooling and uplifting and help lubricate the lungs, alleviating dry coughs, and also benefit the skin. Figs help to relieve constipation, alleviate inflammation, and build muscle.

SERVES 8

For the base

200g (7oz) ground almonds

3 tbsp caster sugar

50g (1¾oz) tbsp butter, melted

pinch of salt

For the cake

175g (6oz) butter, softened, plus extra for greasing

175g (6oz) granulated sugar

4 eggs, beaten

grated zest of 1 organic lemon

1 tsp vanilla extract

150g (5½oz) plain flour

2 tsp baking powder

4 tbsp whole blanched almonds

8–10 figs, quartered

For the sauce

3 soft pears, peeled, cored, and fincly chopped

50ml (2fl oz) red wine

¼ tsp allspice powder

1 tbsp maple syrup

freshly ground black pepper

1 Preheat the oven to 180°C (350°F/Gas 4). First, make the almond base. Mix together the ingredients for the base in a mixing bowl, combining well. Press the almond mixture evenly onto the base of a 23cm (9in) springform cake tin. Bake for 10 minutes, or until crisp, then remove from the oven and set aside on a wire rack to cool. Reduce the oven temperature to 150°C (300°F/Gas 2).

2 Next, make the cake mixture. Beat the softened butter and granulated sugar together in a clean bowl until pale and creamy. Then beat in the eggs, lemon zest, and vanilla extract until thoroughly combined. Sift in the flour and baking powder and fold into the wet ingredients until the cake mixture is smooth. Finally, fold in the whole almonds. Smear a little butter around the inside of the springform tin.

3 Arrange the quartered figs over the almond base and cover with the cake mixture. Bake in the oven for about 60 minutes, or until the top is golden and the sides of the cake have pulled away slightly from the edge of the tin. Remove from the oven and unclip the side of the springform tin, leaving the cake on its base. Set aside on a wire rack to cool.

4 For the sauce, place the pears, red wine, and allspice powder in a medium saucepan, bring to a simmer, cover, and cook over a low heat for 20 minutes, or until the pears are soft. Transfer to a blender or food processor and blitz until smooth. Add the maple syrup and a pinch of black pepper and blitz again. Add more maple syrup to taste, if needed.

5 Place a slice of the cake on a serving plate and serve with a little of the sauce drizzled around it.

ALMOND AND RASPBERRY CAKE

 HELPS CLEAR CONGESTION

 SUPPORTS HEALTHY LIVER AND KIDNEYS

 HELPS CALM NERVES

 HELPS PROTECT EYE HEALTH

This dense, gluten-free cake is made with ground almonds instead of flour. Almonds soothe and support the respiratory system, helping to remove phlegm. Raspberries have a tonic effect on the liver, and a calming effect on the mind. Rich in antioxidants, they also support healthy vision. In traditional Chinese medicine, raspberries are used to treat impotence and infertility in men.

SERVES 6

250g (9oz) butter, plus extra for greasing

250g (9oz) caster sugar

5 eggs, separated

250g (9oz) ground almonds

1 tsp vanilla extract

200g (7oz) raspberries

1 Preheat the oven to 140°C (275°F/Gas 1). Grease a 25cm (10in) springform cake tin with the butter and line the base with baking parchment, making sure the paper is exactly the same size as the base.

2 Cream the butter and sugar in a large bowl. Add an egg yolk, mix well, then add a little of the ground almonds and combine well. Repeat until all the yolks and almonds have been added to the mix. Add the vanilla extract and combine well.

3 In a clean separate large bowl, beat the egg whites to stiff peaks with an electric hand whisk. Gently fold the egg whites into the cake mix with a metal spoon to keep the mix as fluffy and light as possible. Keep 6–12 raspberries aside to use as decoration later. Transfer half the mix to the prepared cake tin, arrange half the raspberries on top, then add the rest of the cake mix and finish with the rest of the raspberries. Don't combine the raspberries with the cake mix, as they will break up and discolour the cake.

4 Bake in the oven for 45 minutes–1 hour until cooked through. To test if the cake is cooked, insert a clean skewer into the centre of the cake. If the skewer is clean when you take it out, remove the cake from the oven. If not, cook for a little longer and test again.

5 Place the cake on a wire rack and allow to cool. Once cool, carefully remove the springform tin and baking parchment. Decorate the top of the cake with the reserved raspberries and serve.

ELDERBERRY AND BLACKBERRY NUTTY CRUMBLE

 HELPS FIGHT COLDS AND FLU

HAS A MILD DIURETIC ACTION

PROTECTS THE HEART AND BLOOD VESSELS

The best time to make this crumble is when elderberries are fully ripened and blackberries are just beginning to ripen in the hedgerows. They are both worth foraging for, as they enhance immunity, especially against colds and flu. They also have a mild diuretic action, and help maintain healthy blood vessels. If elderberries are no longer in season, use blueberries instead.

SERVES 4–6

550g (1¼lb) cooking apples, cored, peeled, and sliced

200g (7oz) fresh elderberries

250g (9oz) fresh blackberries

For the topping

150g (5½oz) plain flour

100g (3½oz) organic butter

200g (7oz) ground almonds

2 tbsp molasses sugar, or other dark brown soft sugar

50g (1¾oz) walnuts, finely chopped

crème fraîche, to serve

1 Preheat the oven to 180°C (350°F/Gas 4). To make the crumble topping, place the flour in a mixing bowl, add the butter, and rub it into the flour with your fingertips. Add the ground almonds and molasses sugar and mix together well until the mixture resembles breadcrumbs. Add the chopped walnuts and mix them in well.

2 Place the apples in a large saucepan with a little water and simmer for 10 minutes over a low heat. Transfer the softened apples to a large, deep baking dish and add the berries. Completely cover the fruits with the crumble topping, press it down lightly, bake in the oven for 35–40 minutes or until golden on top, then serve either hot or warm with the crème fraîche.

Elderberries (p35) are a good source of antioxidant anthocyanins, which help fight free-radical damage.

NUTTY SUGAR LOAF

 PROMOTES A SENSE OF WELL-BEING

 **PROMOTES BOWEL REGULARITY**

 **HELPS KEEP JOINTS SUPPLE**

Containing walnuts, chestnuts, hazelnuts, and sprouted spelt, this is a deeply satisfying dish that helps to improve digestion and bowel regularity, and also to strengthen and improve movement in muscles and joints. This recipe, great for a party, requires some advanced preparation, as the spelt grains need 3–4 days to sprout.

SERVES 6–8

250g (9oz) spelt grains

150g (5½oz) hazelnuts

100g (3½oz) walnuts

150g (5½oz) fresh sweet chestnuts, cooked, with skins removed

70g (2½oz) unrefined caster sugar

1 tbsp vanilla extract

mascarpone cheese, to serve

1 To sprout the spelt grains, start soaking them 3–4 days before you need them. Soak 100g (3½oz) of the grains for 8–12 hours in clean water in a large, clean, wide-mouthed glass jar covered with cheesecloth or muslin, and with the cloth secured in place with a rubber band. Strain the water from the grains, rinse the grains in fresh water, drain, then set the jar aside, out of direct sunlight. Rinse and drain the grains again 8–12 hours later. It usually takes 2–3 rinsing cycles for the spelt to sprout; the grains are sprouted when most of them have a tiny rootlet just pushing through. They are ready to use 8 hours later.

2 Preheat the oven to 180°C (350°F/Gas 4). To toast the hazelnuts, put them on a baking sheet and place in the oven for 15 minutes, keeping an eye on them and shaking the tray occasionally so they don't burn, or they will taste bitter. Transfer to a bowl and cover with cling film to let the nuts sweat for 2–3 minutes. Transfer a small batch of nuts to a piece of kitchen paper and rub them roughly to remove the majority of the skins. Repeat with the rest of the hazelnuts. Transfer to a blender or food processor and blitz briefly until coarsely chopped.

3 To toast the walnuts, soak in 450ml (15fl oz) of water for 30 minutes, then drain. Transfer to a baking sheet and place in the oven for 25–30 minutes, turning them regularly until they become dry and light brown in colour. Set aside to cool.

4 Cook the remaining spelt in plenty of water for 1 hour 20 minutes or until soft, and set aside to cool.

5 Use a coffee grinder, hand grinder, or a powerful blender to grind the cooked spelt, walnuts, and chestnuts, and transfer the ground ingredients to a mixing bowl. Add the whole sprouted spelt grains, caster sugar, and vanilla extract, and combine all the ingredients well.

6 Using your hands, mould the dry mixture into a sugar loaf shape on a serving plate (if you find the mixture too dry, blend a small quantity in a blender or food processor to bind it together, and use as a base on which to build the other ingredients). Alternatively, press into individual serving bowls and turn out before serving. Cover with the toasted, coarsely ground hazelnuts. To serve, cut a slice from the sugar loaf and serve with a spoonful of mascarpone cheese.

WARM FRUIT SALAD IN SWEET WINE SAUCE

 HELPS REMOVE TOXINS FROM THE BODY

 **HAS AN UPLIFTING EFFECT**

 **HELPS EASE CONSTIPATION**

 **HELPS LOWER BLOOD PRESSURE**

The subtle flavours and textures of warmed fresh fruits, tossed in a sweet wine syrup, result in a deliciously different twist on a classic fruit salad. This combination of soft and crunchy fresh fruits and pistachio nuts is detoxifying, uplifting, and has a tonic effect on the whole body. The abundant fibre in the fruit supports healthy digestion and potassium helps lower blood pressure.

SERVES 4

3 tbsp butter

3 tbsp caster sugar

300ml (10fl oz) sweet Marsala wine

1 ripe pear, cored and quartered

4 figs, halved

2 peaches, quartered, with stones removed

2 nectarines, quartered, with stones removed

1 apple, cored and quartered

100g (3½oz) pistachio nuts, shelled and roughly chopped

1 Preheat the oven to 200°C (400°F/Gas 6). Melt the butter in a small saucepan, add the sugar and Marsala wine, and cook over a low heat for 5–10 minutes until it is a syrupy consistency. Remove from the heat and set aside to cool.

2 Place all the fruits in a bowl, add the pistachio nuts, and pour in two-thirds of the cooled Marsala syrup. Gently toss everything together to coat the fruit. Turn the fruit mixture out onto a baking tray and bake in the oven for 25–35 minutes until the fruit is warmed through, but not completely cooked.

3 Remove from the oven and spoon the warm fruit salad onto individual plates. Mix the remaining Marsala syrup with the juices from the baking dish, drizzle it over the fruit portions, and serve.

Nectarines (p22) of all types, including the white-fleshed variety, can help remove excess water from the body.

CHERRY STRUDEL

 PROTECTS AGAINST FREE-RADICAL DAMAGE   **PROTECTS THE HEART AND BLOOD VESSELS**   **HELPS EASE JOINT INFLAMMATION**   **HELPS RELIEVE INSOMNIA**

The tart morello cherries in this recipe are particularly rich in antioxidants which help protect the heart and fight free-radical damage and inflammation, especially in the joints. They also contain melatonin, which aids restful sleep. if you can't find morello cherries, choose a sweet variety and marinate in the zest of an orange and the juice of half a lemon for a sharper flavour.

SERVES 4

35g (1¼oz) fresh breadcrumbs

50g (1¾oz) caster sugar

25g (scant 1oz) ground almonds

25g (scant 1oz) ground walnuts

5 sheets ready-made filo pastry

35g (1¼oz) unsalted butter, melted, plus a little extra for brushing

½ tsp ground cinnamon

325g (11oz) fresh morello cherries, pitted

3 tbsp flaked almonds (optional)

icing sugar, for dusting

1 To make the filling, mix the breadcrumbs, caster sugar, and ground almonds together in a bowl and set aside.

2 Preheat the oven to 190°C (375°F/Gas 5). If you can't find ground walnuts, blitz some walnut pieces in a food processor or blender. Arrange a sheet of baking parchment on a flat surface. Lay a sheet of filo pastry on the parchment, with one of the longer edges of the pastry rectangle facing you. Brush the surface of the pastry with some of the melted butter and sprinkle over a little of the cinnamon. Repeat with the rest of the pastry sheets, butter, and cinnamon. Scatter the breadcrumb filling over the pastry stack, leaving a 5cm (2in) border around the edge (this will help when you fold the pastry edges over to prevent the filling escaping). If you want to make 2 strudels, cut the pastry in half, leaving a 10cm (4in) space in the middle. Scatter the ground walnuts over the filling and heap the cherries in a thick strip along the centre of the pastry, leaving a 5cm (2in) gap at either end.

3 Fold in the short edges of the pastry rectangle. Then, using the baking parchment, fold over the long edge of the pastry rectangle nearest you, and roll up the pastry to enclose the filling and create a long roll. Brush the surface of the rolled pastry with more melted butter and scatter over the flaked almonds, if using.

4 Lift the baking parchment with the strudel, seam-side down, onto a large baking sheet and bake in the oven for 30 minutes or until the pastry is golden. Allow to cool for about 10 minutes, then dust with icing sugar and serve.

Morello cherries (p20) are coloured brightly with red pigments that produce a greater pain-relieving effect than aspirin.

Baked Quince

 **SUPPORTS HEALTHY LIVER FUNCTION**　　 **HELPS IMPROVE CIRCULATION**　　 **HELPS RELIEVE JOINT AND MUSCLE PAIN**　　 **SOOTHES STOMACH UPSETS**

Quince is a well-regarded medicinal fruit and a liver remedy in traditional Chinese, Tibetan, and Bhutanese medicine. It helps increase blood circulation to the muscles and tendons, and is used in the treatment of rheumatic pain and cramp in calf muscles. It is also used to treat deficiency in the spleen and the associated symptoms of vomiting, diarrhoea, and dyspepsia.

SERVES 4

4 small or 2 large quince, peeled, cored, and quartered

½ tsp cardamom pods

1 tbsp soft brown sugar

4 tbsp sweet dessert wine, plus a little for drizzling (Marsala or Muscat are good choices)

4 tbsp mascarpone cheese

1 Preheat the oven to 180°C (350°F/Gas 4). Put the quince in a baking dish, scatter over the cardamom pods and sugar, and drizzle over half the dessert wine and 2 tablespoons of water. Bake in the oven until cooked through and golden in colour, about 1 hour. Check the quince occasionally to make sure it doesn't dry out and add more wine or water if needed.

2 Mix the rest of the sweet wine and the mascarpone in a bowl. Transfer the quince to 4 small serving bowls and drizzle with the cooking juices. Place 1 tablespoon of the flavoured mascarpone on top of each portion and serve.

ROSE PETAL AND WHITE WINE SORBET

 **HELPS RELAX AND UNWIND THE MIND**

 **HELPS IMPROVE CIRCULATION**

HELPS EASE MENSTRUAL CRAMPS

Roses have a deeply calming effect on the nervous system. Here they are combined with a small amount of sweet wine, which helps relax blood vessels and boosts their beneficial effect on circulation. Roses are also a good remedy for menstrual cramps and premenstrual symptoms. Highly perfumed roses (*Rosa damascena* or *Rosa gallica*) are best for this recipe.

SERVES 4

10 fresh red rose heads or a large handful of red rose petals, plus extra petals for decoration

300ml (10fl oz) sweet dessert wine (Marsala or Muscat are good choices)

250g (9oz) caster sugar

2 tsp agar flakes

juice of 1 lemon, strained

juice of 1 orange, strained

1 Combine half the roses and the sweet dessert wine in a jug and refrigerate. Infuse the rest of the roses in 450ml (14fl oz) of boiling water and set aside to cool.

2 Strain the infused liquid and discard the petals. Transfer the liquid to a saucepan and add the sugar. Set the pan over a gentle heat and stir frequently until the sugar has dissolved. Bring to the boil and boil (at 110°C/ 230°F, if you have a sugar thermometer) for 5–8 minutes or until you have a light syrup. Remove from the heat and set aside to cool.

3 Melt the agar flakes in 50ml (2fl oz) of hot water and add it to the syrup. Stir, transfer to a bowl, and then refrigerate until completely cold.

4 Combine the chilled dessert wine and fresh rose petal mixture with the rose syrup. Stir in the strained lemon and orange juices and pour the mixture into an ice cream maker. Process the sorbet for 20–30 minutes or until it is cold and the right consistency. Spoon the ingredients into a freezerproof container and freeze if not serving immediately. If you don't have an ice cream maker, pour the wine and syrup mixture into a freezerproof container and place in the freezer. Take it out every hour to give it a stir until the mixture is completely frozen.

CALM YOUR MOOD

A SMALL AMOUNT OF WHITE WINE RELAXES YOUR BLOOD VESSELS. INFUSED WITH ROSE PETALS – TRADITIONALLY USED TO TREAT NERVOUS TENSION – IT WILL ALSO HELP TO INCREASE YOUR SENSE OF WELL-BEING.

BANANA AND CRANBERRY ICE CREAM

 **HELPS EASE CONSTIPATION**

 **HELPS LOWER BLOOD PRESSURE**

 **FIGHTS URINARY TRACT INFECTIONS**

Ice cream without any cream – ideal for those who are allergic to cow's milk. Ripe bananas promote bowel regularity and can help lower blood pressure, while cranberries have antibacterial properties that treat urinary tract infections (UTIs). In traditional Chinese medicine, cold food is thought to disrupt healthy digestion, so keep frozen foods for occasional treats.

SERVES 4

4 ripe bananas, sliced
200g (7oz) cranberries
1 tbsp caster sugar
1 tsp vanilla extract
50g (1¾oz) pistachio nuts, shelled and chopped

1 Put the bananas and cranberries in the freezer and remove when semi-frozen. If they are completely frozen, allow to thaw slightly for about an hour. Place them in a blender or food processor and blitz until the fruits are coarsely combined and still have some texture. Divide between 4 freezerproof serving bowls (enamel bowls are freezer-safe) and place in the freezer for 3 hours. Alternatively, freeze the ice cream in a clean plastic container.

2 Meanwhile, place the sugar in a small saucepan over a low heat and add just enough water to wet the sugar. When the sugar has dissolved completely, add the vanilla extract and mix in the pistachios, then remove from the heat and allow to cool.

3 Remove the bowls, or container, from the freezer, allow to sit at room temperature for a short while, then use an ice-cream scoop to divide the ice cream between 4 serving bowls. Drizzle the sugar solution and nuts over the top of each portion and serve.

TIP: If you have a weak digestive system, you may like to add a few drops of freshly squeezed ginger juice, instead of water, to the sugar to dissolve it (grate fresh ginger root, wrap in a piece of muslin, squeeze the muslin, and collect the juice). Children may also benefit from ginger juice, as their digestive systems are still developing, but make sure they are familiar with, and enjoy the taste of, ginger before you include it. If you can't find fresh or frozen cranberries, use blueberries, which freeze well and taste just as good.

ALMOND AND PISTACHIO MACAROONS

 SUPPORTS LUNG FUNCTION

 **PROMOTES A HEALTHY DIGESTIVE TRACT**

 **HELPS IMPROVE CIRCULATION**

 **ENHANCES VIGOUR AND CONFIDENCE**

Almonds and pistachios are both good sources of protein and, together with cardamom, are beneficial for your respiratory system, circulation, and digestive health. They are also traditionally regarded as an aphrodisiac for both men and women. This recipe makes quite a number of macaroons, so halve the quantities if you like.

MAKES 45

3 egg whites
250g (9oz) caster sugar
1 tsp crushed cardamom seeds
400g (14oz) ground almonds
2 tbsp rose water
20g (¾oz) whole pistachios, shelled

1 Preheat the oven to 150°C (300°F/Gas 2). Put the egg whites in a mixing bowl and whisk into soft or stiff peaks with an electric hand whisk, gradually adding the sugar as you whisk. When all the sugar has been incorporated, add the cardamom, ground almonds, and rose water and combine all the ingredients together.

2 Line a baking tray with baking parchment. Wet your hands with water so the mixture won't stick to your fingers. Divide the mixture into small walnut-sized balls and arrange on the baking parchment, allowing sufficient space around each ball. Place a pistachio in the centre of each.

3 Bake for 10–12 minutes, then transfer to a wire rack to cool. Store the macaroons in an airtight container. They will keep for up to 2 weeks.

Almonds (p92) are rich in cholesterol-lowering monounsaturated fatty acids.

DRINKS

SOOTHING, **UPLIFTING**, AND NUTRITIOUS DRINKS AND BEAUTIFUL BLENDS **DELIVER NUTRIENTS** QUICKLY AND IN AN EASILY **ABSORBABLE** FORM – WHETHER YOU OPT FOR REFRESHING COOL DRINKS OR **NURTURING** HOT BROTHS AND TEAS.

HOT LEMONADE WITH GINGER AND HONEY

 HELPS FIGHT COLDS AND FLU    **AIDS HEALTHY DIGESTION**    **HELPS IMPROVE CIRCULATION**    **CONTAINS SLOW-RELEASE SUGARS**

Lemon juice, mint, and ginger are the perfect trio to help combat the symptoms of a cold. The thin skin and fibrous root of fresh ginger have anti-inflammatory properties that can lessen the aches and pains, while honey is a natural antibiotic and lemon and mint have antibacterial benefits. Drink this healing tea as soon as you feel the first signs of a cold.

SERVES 2

3cm (1in) piece fresh ginger root, grated

zest and juice of 1 lemon

1 tbsp clear honey

1 tbsp chopped mint leaves

1 Place the grated fresh ginger root in a small saucepan, cover with 400ml (14fl oz) of water and bring to the boil. Turn the heat down to low and simmer for 15 minutes.

2 Strain the mixture through a strainer, add the lemon juice and zest, spoon in the honey and mix well. Add the mint leaf and serve in heatproof glasses. Drink the tea and eat the chopped mint leaves.

ALOE AND HONEY HOT TODDY

 **HELPS STRENGTHEN THE IMMUNE SYSTEM**    **HELPS REMOVE TOXINS FROM THE BODY**

Honey and aloe are known to help the body detoxify and to strengthen the immune system, which in turn enables all the major organs to function more efficiently. Traditionally, the variety of aloe known as *Aloe arborescens* (which produces red flowers when in bloom) is used for this recipe; it has a high concentration of complex sugars and other phytonutrients that work synergistically.

SERVES 2

150g (5½oz) aloe leaves

100g (3½oz) clear honey

3 tbsp grappa or Cognac

1 Clean the fresh aloe leaves with a damp cloth, cut off and discard the spines, chop the leaves, and put them in a blender or food processor. Add the honey and grappa or Cognac and blitz. Add a dash of water if you want to dilute the flavour slightly.

2 Boil half a kettle of water and pour into a glass jug, allow to cool for 3 minutes. Pour the aloe mixture into 2 heatproof glasses, and pour over the slightly cooled boiling water. Drink while warm. If taking as a therapeutic drink, allow to cool, transfer to a dark glass bottle and store in the refrigerator for up to 1 week. Take 1–2 tablespoons a day.

BLACKBERRY LEMONADE

 **HELPS SOOTHE A SORE THROAT** **SUPPORTS HEALTHY KIDNEY FUNCTION** **HELPS REMOVE TOXINS FROM THE BODY** **HELPS ALLEVIATE HEAVY PERIODS**

Blackberries are a great medicine if you have a painful or swollen throat, mouth, or gums. Their antioxidant, kidney-toning, and detoxifying properties make them a must-have ingredient when in season. Collect the leaves too, as a blackberry leaf infusion enhances the anti-inflammatory effects further. Serve with ice, or as a warm drink if you have a throat condition.

SERVES 2

4 tsp dried blackberry leaves, or 12 fresh leaves

300g (10oz) blackberries, rinsed

2 lemons, juiced, plus a few thin slices for decoration (optional)

3 tbsp maple syrup

1 To make an infusion with the leaves, boil 300ml (10fl oz) of water, pour over the leaves, and leave to infuse for 10 minutes. Strain the mixture, reserving the liquid to use in the lemonade. Discard the leaves.

2 Place the blackberries in a food processor or blender and blitz to a pulp. If you don't like the gritty texture of the seeds in your drink, strain the pulp through a colander and collect the smooth juice.

3 Pour the lemon juice, blackberry juice, and 250ml (9fl oz) of the blackberry leaf infusion into a jug, add the maple syrup, and stir well. Pour into large glasses, decorate each with a slice of lemon, and serve.

BARLEY GRASS AND BARLEY LEMONADE

 **REMOVES TOXINS AND ALKALIZES THE BODY** 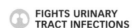 **FIGHTS URINARY TRACT INFECTIONS**  **HELPS KEEP JOINTS SUPPLE**

This juice combines the benefits of the dry barley grain with those of the fresh barley juice to provide a powerful, alkalizing, anti-inflammatory, and purifying drink. It helps support healthy joints and benefits the intestines, urinary system, and skin, all of which eliminate waste materials from the body. It also helps revitalize and energize the body and slows signs of ageing.

SERVES 4

100g (3½oz) whole, non-hulled barley (optional)

100g (3½oz) pearl barley

2.5cm (1in) lemon peel, cut into 4 strips

6 tbsp lemon juice

2 tbsp honey, or more as desired

6 tbsp barley grass juice

4 lemon slices, to garnish

1 If you want to grow your own barley grass, soak the non-hulled barley in a large bowl of water overnight. Drain and arrange the soaked barley on a garden tray filled with organic compost. Gently press the grains down into the compost and leave to germinate. Mist twice daily until it grows to 12–15cm (5-6in) high, when it is ready to harvest (about 10 days).

2 Place the pearl barley into a fine mesh strainer, pour boiling water over it, and allow to drain. Transfer to a medium saucepan, add the lemon peel and 1.2 litres (2 pints) of water, and bring to the boil. Reduce the heat to low and simmer for 25 minutes. Remove from the heat and strain into a clean container. Add the lemon juice and honey to taste, mix well, and refrigerate until chilled. Juice the barley grass (if you have grown it yourself) just before serving and stir into the lemonade or simply add the shop-bought barley grass juice. To serve, pour into tall glasses, add a slice of lemon to each glass, and stir.

Blackberry Lemonade ▶

SOUR CHERRY DRINK

 **AIDS RECOVERY AND
MUSCLE STRENGTH**

**HELPS PROMOTE
PEACEFUL SLEEP**

**HELPS WITH FAT AND
SUGAR METABOLISM**

A popular drink in eastern Europe and western Asia where sour cherries commonly grow, this is a must-have remedy for building strength after a hard day's work, aiding recovery from a tough workout, and relaxing your mind to get a good night's sleep. Cherries also help balance blood sugar, and assist the liver in metabolising fat after a meal.

SERVES 4

100g (3½oz) dried sour cherries, stoned

200g (7oz) sugar

1 tbsp vanilla extract

675g (1½lb) sour cherries, stoned

maple syrup to taste (optional)

1 lime, thinly sliced, to garnish (optional)

1 Rinse the dried cherries, transfer to a bowl, cover with water, and stir to remove some of the oil they are coated in. Drain and repeat. Transfer to a large bowl, cover with water, and soak for 6 hours or overnight to reconstitute. Drain, set aside the cherries, and reserve the soaking water.

2 Measure the soaking water and top up with fresh water if necessary to make 200ml (7fl oz). Transfer to a small saucepan, add the sugar, set over a low heat, and let the sugar dissolve. Bring to the boil, turn the heat down, simmer for 10 minutes, and add the soaked cherries. Simmer for 20–30 minutes or until the cherries are soft and the syrup has thickened. Strain the mixture, return the syrup to the pan, and discard the fruit. Bring the syrup back to the boil, remove from the heat, and stir in the vanilla extract. Set aside to cool while you juice the fresh sour cherries.

3 Mix 200ml (7fl oz) each of cherry juice and syrup in a jug and dilute with water. Add maple syrup to taste, and lime slices, if using. Store any unused syrup in a sterilized glass bottle in the refrigerator for 1–2 weeks.

ELDERBERRY SYRUP

 **PROTECTS AGAINST
COLDS AND FLU**

 **HELPS CLEAR
CONGESTION**

 **HELPS MAINTAIN
WATER BALANCE**

 **HELPS EASE
CONSTIPATION**

Pungent, bitter-sweet, ripe elderberries are rich in antioxidants that help prevent and treat colds, coughs, and flu by promoting sweating, strengthening the lungs, maintaining water balance and bowel regularity, and shifting mucous. Use this syrup as a quick flu remedy or in cooking.

SERVES 2

300g (10oz) elderberries

4cm (1¾in) fresh ginger root, grated

300g (10oz) caster sugar

juice of 2 lemons

1 Put the berries and ginger into a medium saucepan and add 300ml (10fl oz) of water. Bring to the boil, cover with a lid, turn the heat down, and simmer over a low heat for 20–30 minutes or until the fruit is soft.

2 Strain the fruit through a muslin cloth or a very fine sieve, collect the liquid, and decant it into a clean saucepan. Discard the fruit and ginger.

3 Add the sugar to the pan and allow it to dissolve over a low heat, stirring constantly. When it has dissolved, add the lemon juice and increase the heat. Bring to the boil and boil for 10–15 minutes until the liquid becomes syrupy. Transfer to a heat-sterilized bottle, seal, label, and date. Store in the refrigerator and use within 6 weeks.

WINTER PICK-ME-UP JUICE

 **PROTECTS AGAINST COLDS AND FLU**

 **HELPS MAINTAIN ENERGY LEVELS**

 **HELPS BUILD RED BLOOD CELLS**

There is usually a brief window in autumn when wild rosehips, blackberries, and blueberries can be harvested at the same time. The high antioxidant levels of these wild berries help to boost your immunity and energy levels, and traditionally they are considered to be a blood tonic. Cinnamon is rich in antioxidants too, and is also an effective aid in the treatment of colds and flu.

SERVES 2

115g (4oz) rosehips, halved and deseeded
115g (4oz) blackberries
115g (4oz) raspberries
115g (4oz) blueberries
¼ tsp cinnamon
2 tbsp elderberry syrup (left)
coconut water, to dilute

1 Put all ingredients, except the coconut water, in a food processor or blender and blitz until smooth. Top up with the coconut water to achieve the desired consistency.

BLUEBERRIES

ROSEHIPS

BLACKBERRIES

RASPBERRIES

FIGHT THE COLD

THIS JUICE IS THE PERFECT WINTER GUARD. ANTIOXIDANT RICH BERRIES ENHANCE YOUR IMMUNITY AND FIGHT COLDS AND FLU. THIS QUANTITY OF ROSEHIP ALONE ACCOUNTS FOR MORE THAN 1½ TIMES YOUR RECOMMENDED DAILY INTAKE OF VITAMIN C.

HEALTH BOOST JUICE

 PROTECTS AGAINST COLDS AND FLU **HELPS REMOVE TOXINS FROM THE BODY** **AIDS HEALTHY DIGESTION**

This juice is a beneficial tonic, especially in the winter. Onion squash, which has a mild sweet flavour, supplies anti-inflammatory and antioxidant properties, while fragrant ginger can improve digestion. Tart grapefruit helps ward off common colds, improves liver function, and treats gallstones, and salty-tasting celery has a diuretic action that helps detoxify the body.

SERVES 2

100g (3½oz) onion squash
1 small piece fresh ginger root, skin on
1 large grapefruit, peeled and pith removed
2 celery sticks and leaves, roughly chopped

1 Cut the squash in half, scoop out all the seeds, and discard or reserve them to roast later and use as an ingredient in other recipes (such as Pre-soaked Barley Breakfast, p190), or as a topping for salads and soups. Leave the skin on the squash to benefit from its nutrients and chop the flesh if necessary, so it fits through the hopper of your juicer.

2 Juice all the ingredients and combine in a jug. Strain through a sieve to remove the grapefruit pips and serve immediately in long glasses.

COOLING, SOOTHING JUICE

 PROMOTES A HEALTHY DIGESTIVE TRACT   **HELPS REMOVE PARASITES IN THE GUT**   **HELPS IMPROVE CIRCULATION**

Aloe vera has a cooling, anti-inflammatory effect on the gut; it helps relieve constipation and can help clear intestinal parasites. Turmeric has a similarly soothing effect on the gut, relieving pain and tension, and also helps improve circulation. Fresh ginger tones and stimulates the digestive tract, but it can raise blood pressure; if you suffer from high blood pressure, omit the ginger.

SERVES 2

2cm (¾in) piece fresh turmeric root
2cm (¾in) piece fresh ginger root
1 green dessert apple
2 celery sticks
2 small leaves of aloe vera
coconut water, to dilute

1 Using a juicer, juice the turmeric root, ginger root, apple, and celery and combine the juices in a jug.

2 Using a sharp knife, remove the spine from each aloe vera leaf, slice the leaves open lengthways, and scrape out the gel. Add the gel to the juices in the jug and mix thoroughly. Pour into 2 long glasses, dilute with coconut water until the juice is your preferred consistency, and serve.

STAY SUPPLE JUICE

 **HELPS FIGHT INFLAMMATION**   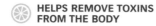 **HELPS REMOVE TOXINS FROM THE BODY**    **HELPS COMBAT FATIGUE**

This pungent vegetable juice addresses the cause of joint problems. Cucumber, spinach, and turmeric combine to relieve joint inflammation and stimulate the circulation, and, together with chilli and ginger, they help expel accumulated toxins from the body by encouraging bowel movements, promoting sweating, and acting as a mild diuretic.

SERVES 2

1 small cucumber, skin on

60g (2oz) spinach leaves

4cm (1½in) piece fresh ginger root, skin on

4cm (1½in) piece fresh turmeric root, skin on

4 celery sticks

2 green apples, skin on

½ fresh red chilli, deseeded

1 Using a juicer, juice each ingredient, transfer to a glass jug, stir to mix well, and serve. Consume immediately to avoid any loss of valuable nutrients.

FIVE-FLAVOUR JUICE

 **AIDS DETOXIFICATION SYSTEM**    **SUPPORTS AND PROTECTS THE LIVER**    **PROMOTES HEALTHY SKIN**

Traditional Chinese medicine categorizes foods into 5 flavours – bitter, sweet, salty, sour, and hot. This recipe includes all 5 flavours to help keep the body in balance. In addition, hot black radish is a traditional Chinese remedy for liver conditions, while beetroot and carrot are both packed with antioxidants that increase oxygen and nutrient levels in the blood and benefit the skin.

SERVES 2

1 medium black radish or turnip

1 large beetroot

2 large carrots

8 celery sticks

4 small Seville oranges, with half the peel removed

1 Using a juicer, juice each ingredient, transfer to a glass jug, stir to mix well, and serve. Consume immediately to avoid any loss of valuable nutrients.

BUILD-ME-UP JUICE

 AIDS DETOXIFICATION SYSTEM  **HELPS RELEASE CELLULAR ENERGY**  **HELPS IMPROVE CIRCULATION**  **AIDS HEALTHY DIGESTION**

This particular blend of root vegetables is high in antioxidants and phytonutrients that help revitalize the blood by improving circulation and increasing oxygen levels. It also supports the health of major organs, such as the heart, liver, and kidneys, builds body tissues and fluids, and enhances the digestive process by promoting bowel regularity and general intestinal health.

SERVES 2

2 large carrots
1 large beetroot
4 celery sticks
½ celeriac root, peeled
2 fennel bulbs
2cm (¾in) piece fresh ginger root, skin on
1 small lemon, peel on
coconut water, to dilute

1 Using a juicer, juice each ingredient, transfer to a glass jug, stir to mix well, and add enough coconut water to taste. Serve in tall glasses and consume immediately to avoid any loss of valuable nutrients.

ALERT AND JOYFUL JUICE

 SUPPORTS HEALTHY LIVER FUNCTION   **HELP PREVENT URINARY TRACT INFECTIONS**   **HELPS ENHANCE FOCUS**

According to traditional Chinese medicine, sour flavours are said to tonify and enhance liver function, promote the elimination of waste products through the intestines and urinary system, calm emotions, improve your sense of well-being, and focus the mind. Adjust the flavour of this sour-based juice to your liking by adding some coconut water to modify its acidity.

SERVES 2

8 heaped tbsp fresh or frozen cranberries
1 small Seville orange, peel on, and quartered
1 red pepper, deseeded
3 celery sticks
1 small cucumber
¼ chilli, deseeded
1cm (½in) piece fresh ginger root, skin on
coconut water, to dilute

1 Using a juicer, juice each ingredient, transfer to a glass jug, stir to mix well, and add enough coconut water to taste. Serve in tall glasses and consume immediately to avoid any loss of valuable nutrients.

Rose Syrup

 HELPS TO RELAX AND UNWIND THE MIND    **HELPS STRENGTHEN THE IMMUNE SYSTEM**

Mildly sedative and immune-enhancing rose syrup can be used to sweeten herbal infusions, poured over pancakes and ice cream, drizzled over fruit salads, used in a sorbet, or drunk as a cordial diluted with water. Highly perfumed damask rose (*Rosa damascena*) or French rose (*Rosa gallica*) are best for this recipe. Keeping the temperature low is key to preserving their benefits.

MAKES 500ML (16FL OZ)

225g (8oz) unrefined granulated sugar
juice of 1 lemon
juice of 1 orange
100g (3½oz) dried red rose petals, or the petals of 10 fresh red rose heads

1 Dissolve the sugar in 300ml (10fl oz) of water in a small saucepan over a low heat without letting it boil (which will make the mixture cloudy).

2 Add the citrus juices, then turn the heat right down and simmer for 5 minutes. Over the next 15 minutes, gradually add the rose petals and stir thoroughly before adding more. Remove from the heat, allow to cool, and strain.

3 Meanwhile, sterilize a heatproof glass bottle and lid: wash them in hot soapy water, drain upside down, then place in a cool oven (140°C/275°F/Gas 1) for 15 minutes. Pour the hot syrup into the sterilized glass bottle, seal, and label. Keep refrigerated and use within 6 weeks.

Valentine's Special

 PROMOTES A SENSE OF WELL-BEING   **HELPS COMBAT FATIGUE**   **HELPS IMPROVE CIRCULATION**

This is a feel-good drink: nutritious, healthy, and life-enhancing. It contains antioxidant-rich soft fruits and coconut water, which help rehydrate the body and reduce feelings of fatigue, while the pistachios, cardamom, and concentrated rose in the rose syrup are said to keep love on your mind! If you prefer, add yogurt instead of the coconut water to make a smoothie.

SERVES 2

½ punnet raspberries, washed
½ punnet blueberries, washed
a dash of rose syrup
¼ tsp cardamom seeds, crushed (no more than 10 pods)
2 tbsp pistachio nuts, shelled
250ml (9oz) coconut water, to top up

1 Put all the ingredients in a powerful food processor or blender and blitz to a smooth consistency. If serving immediately, pour into long glasses and serve. Otherwise the drink will last for up to 2 days if stored in a tightly sealed bottle and refrigerated.

Valentine's Special

Winter Wake Up

 SUPPORTS HEALTHY LIVER FUNCTION    **HELPS CLEAR CONGESTION**    **HELPS IMPROVE CIRCULATION**

Bitter Seville oranges add a fantastic cleansing element to this juice, benefitting liver function and enhancing bowel regularity. This effect is enhanced by fennel, which helps clear mucous in the lungs, and coriander, which helps eliminate any traces of heavy metals in the body. Ginger boosts the circulation and carrots act as an anti-inflammatory and anti-allergic agent.

SERVES 2

4 Seville oranges, 3 peeled
1 large fennel bulb
1 large carrot
1 small bunch of coriander leaves and stalks
1cm (½in) piece fresh ginger root

1 Using a juicer, juice all the ingredients and combine in a jug. Mix well and serve in long glasses.

Party Aftermath

 AIDS DETOXIFICATION SYSTEM   **HELPS MAINTAIN WATER BALANCE**   **AIDS DIGESTION, EASES CONSTIPATION**

This is a juice to get you going the morning after. All these ingredients have strong detoxifying properties, that stimulate the digestive and urinary systems to eliminate accumulated waste. Sauerkraut, which is traditionally used to maintain a healthy digestive system, is also included to help combat a hangover, especially if accompanied by stomach upset.

SERVES 2

1 cucumber
4 celery sticks
1 small bunch of flat-leaf parsley
1 small bunch of coriander leaves
¼ lemon with peel on
4 tbsp sauerkraut (p330)
1 tbsp milk thistle tincture
freshly ground black pepper, to garnish

1 Using a juicer, juice the cucumber, celery, parsley, coriander, lemon, and sauerkraut and combine in a jug. Add the milk thistle tincture and mix well. Pour into long glasses, sprinkle a dash of black pepper on top, and serve.

DEEPLY PURIFYING JUICE

 HELPS REMOVE TOXINS FROM THE BODY　 **AIDS HEALTHY/OPTIMAL DIGESTION**　 **PROTECTS AGAINST FREE-RADICAL DAMAGE**

This deeply nurturing juice strengthens the body's normal detoxifying processes as it is rich in chlorophyll, which enhances intestinal health and helps eliminate stored toxins. Barley grass and wheat grass supply valuable enzymes that support healthy digestion, help to regulate metabolism, and help protect vital tissues and organs from oxidative stress, and therefore premature ageing.

SERVES 2

a bunch of wheat grass
a bunch of barley grass
1 bunch of flat-leaf parsley
8 large dandelion leaves
½ small cucumber
2 celery sticks
1cm (½in) piece fresh ginger root

1 Using a juicer, juice all the ingredients and combine thoroughly in a jug. Pour into 2 glasses, top up with filtered water or spring water to adjust the taste if necessary, and serve.

A CUP OF HAPPINESS

 HAS AN UPLIFTING EFFECT　 **HELPS COMBAT FATIGUE**

Plants can have as powerful an effect on our mind and emotions as they can on our bodies. The herbs in this blend have long been used to promote an improved sense of well-being and to alleviate feelings of melancholy, depression, and exhaustion. Take this tea for a quick lift, especially if you are recovering from a long convalescence or long-term debilitation.

SERVES 2

1 tsp dried St John's wort (*Hypericum perforatum*), chopped
1 tsp dried skullcap (*Scutellaria lateriflora*), chopped
1 tsp dried silk tree flowers (*Albizia julibrissin*), chopped

1 Place the dried herbs in a teapot and cover with 500ml (16fl oz) of boiling water. Leave to infuse for 15 minutes, then strain and drink.

TIP: Silk tree flower can be sourced from Chinese herbalists.

MINT AND FRIENDS TEA

 AIDS HEALTHY DIGESTION

HELPS TO RELAX AND UNWIND THE MIND

The aromatic plants in this refreshing tea are useful digestive aids, helping to relieve stomach cramps and bloating. They may also relieve nervous tension headaches, as they generally help to relax the mind and ease tension. It's up to you how long you choose to infuse the herbs, according to your palate.

MAKE 2 CUPS

1 tbsp mint leaves, plus a few small leaves to garnish
½ tbsp fennel leaves
½ tbsp dill leaves
½ tbsp marjoram leaves

1 Remove the leaves from their stalks (although including a few odd stalks is not a problem, as they contain a lot of flavour). Chop each herb separately and transfer to a teapot.

2 Cover with hot, but not boiling, water (water at a temperature of 75–80°C/165–175°F is best for infusing the fine fragrant compounds in these plants).

3 Allow the herbs to infuse for 5 minutes or more, strain, and serve in heatproof glasses decorated with a few small mint leaves on top.

Sweet marjoram contains a natural analgesic that can ease abdominal cramps.

MARSHMALLOW AND LIQUORICE TEA

HELPS TO RELAX AND UNWIND THE MIND

HELPS TO REHYDRATE SKIN AND LUNGS

PROTECTS AGAINST COLDS AND FLU

This is a refreshing, fragrant tea that is especially beneficial if you work in a crowded, centrally heated, stressful office environment. Together these herbs help calm, relax, and focus the mind. They also help protect against airborne microorganisms and provide relief from the effects of central heating by moistening and soothing the respiratory system and rehydrating the skin.

SERVES 2

30g (1oz) dried marshmallow root (*Althea officinalis*), chopped

20g (¾oz) dried marshmallow leaf (*Althea officinalis*), chopped

20g (¾oz) dried linden flower (*Tilia cordata*), chopped

20g (¾oz) dried vervain (*Verbena officinalis*), chopped

10g (¼oz) dried liquorice (*Glycyrrhiza glabra*), chopped

1 Combine all the dried herbs thoroughly in a bowl, transfer to a dark container, metal tea caddy, or a biscuit tin, and label and date.

2 To make the tea, place 20g (¾oz) of the dried herbs in a small saucepan with a lid, cover with 600ml (1 pint) of water and bring to the boil. Reduce the heat, cover with the lid, and let it simmer for 10 minutes. Remove from the heat, leave to infuse for 10 more minutes, strain, and serve. Alternatively, pour the strained tea into a flask and sip throughout the day.

3 To make an occasional drink, place 1 heaped teaspoon of the dried herbs, or an infuser ball filled with the herbal blend, in a mug. Cover with 250ml (9fl oz) of boiling water, leave to stand for 10 minutes, strain, and drink.

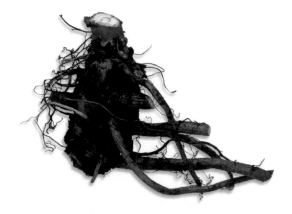

Marshmallow root *(p99) soothes irritation and inflammation, and is particularly useful for treating gastric ulcers and irritable bowel syndrome.*

DEEP SLEEP TEA

 HELPS PROMOTE PEACEFUL SLEEP    **RELAXES THE HEART**

Restful, refreshing sleep comes when we are able to switch off our minds fully and consciously let go of any physical tension in our bodies. This calming tea helps take the edge off ragged emotions, lowers stress levels, and releases any tension in your muscles. It also helps to naturally slow your heartbeat so you can and drift off to sleep easily.

SERVES 2

15g (½oz) dried valerian root (*Valeriana officinalis*), chopped

25g (scant 1oz) dried hawthorn flowers (*Crataegus sp.*), chopped

30g (1oz) dried passion flower leaf (*Passiflora incarnata*), chopped

20g (¾oz) dried schisandra berries (*Schisandra chinensis*), chopped

10g (¼oz) dried chamomile flowers (*Matricaria recutita*), chopped

1 Blitz the valerian root briefly in a coffee grinder or blender if it is too thick to chop easily by hand.

2 Combine all the ingredients thoroughly in a bowl, transfer to a dark container, metal tea caddy, or a biscuit tin, and label and date.

3 Place 20g (¾oz) of the dried herbs in a small saucepan with a lid, cover with 600ml (1 pint) of water, and bring to the boil. Reduce the heat, cover with the lid, and let it simmer for 10 minutes. Remove from the heat, leave to infuse for 10 more minutes, strain, and serve. Alternatively, pour the strained tea into a flask and sip throughout the day.

4 To make an occasional drink, place 1 heaped teaspoon of the dried herbs, or an infuser ball filled with the herbal blend, in a mug. Cover with 250ml (9fl oz) of boiling water, leave to stand for 10 minutes, and strain. Add 1 tablespoon of Cherry Syrup (p308), if you prefer, as it is also an effective sleep aid; stir well and drink.

DEEPLY WARMING TEA

 PROTECTS FROM COLDS AND FLU   **FIGHTS RESPIRATORY INFECTIONS**

Drinking 1 or 2 cups of this immune-boosting tea a day provides extra health insurance in cooler weather: it helps strengthen the body's innate immunity against colds, flu, and upper respiratory infections. It is particularly beneficial if you have chronic immune deficiency.

SERVES 2

25g (scant 1oz) astragalus root (*Astragalus membranaceus*), finely chopped

20g (¾oz) dried elderberries (*Sambucus nigra*)

20g (¾oz) dried echinacea root (*Echinacea purpurea*), chopped

15g (½oz) fresh ginger root, finely chopped

20g (¾oz) dried elderflowers (*Sambucus nigra*), rubbed

1 Combine all the dried herbs thoroughly in a bowl, transfer to a dark container, metal tea caddy, or a biscuit tin, and label and date.

2 Place 20g (¾oz) of the dried herbs and the ginger in a small saucepan with a lid, cover with 600ml (1 pint) of water and bring to the boil. Reduce the heat, cover with the lid, and let it simmer for 10 minutes. Remove from the heat, leave to infuse for 10 more minutes, strain, and serve. Alternatively, pour the strained tea into a flask and sip throughout the day.

3 To make an occasional drink, place 1 heaped teaspoon of the dried herbs, or an infuser ball filled with the herbal blend, in a mug. Cover with 250ml (9fl oz) of boiling water, leave to stand for 10 minutes, strain, and drink.

Deep Cleansing Tea

 HELPS REMOVE TOXINS FROM THE BODY　　 **PROMOTES CLEAR SKIN**　　 **HELPS KEEP JOINTS SUPPLE**

This tea comprises herbs that have deep-cleansing properties and help remove toxic accumulations from the body while its antioxidant content improves skin tone. It can also benefit those who suffer from recurrent inflammatory arthritic conditions such as gout. If you grow your own blackcurrants, harvest and dry the leaves to use throughout the year.

MAKES 5 DAYS' SUPPLY

20g (¾oz) dried blackcurrant leaves, chopped

20g (¾oz) dried red clover flowers, chopped

20g (¾oz) dried celery seeds, chopped

20g (¾oz) dried nettle leaves, chopped

20g (¾oz) dried dandelion leaves, chopped

1 Combine all the ingredients in a bowl, transfer to a sealed container, label, date, and store in a cupboard away from direct light.

2 To make the tea, put 20g (¾oz) of the dried leaves and 650ml (1¼ pints) of water in a saucepan, cover with a lid, and bring to the boil. Lower the heat and simmer for 10 minutes. Remove from the heat, leave to infuse for 10 minutes, and strain the liquid into a flask. Sip throughout the day. To make a single drink, take 1 heaped teaspoon of dried herbs, or fill an infuser ball with the herb blend, cover with 250ml (9fl oz) of boiling water, leave to stand for 10 minutes, strain, and drink.

Deep Nurture Tea

 **HELPS PROTECT AGAINST POLLUTION**　　 **PROTECTS AGAINST FREE-RADICAL DAMAGE**　　 **REMOVES ENERGY-DRAINING TOXINS**　　 **PROMOTES HEALTHY SKIN**

The antioxidant, anti-ageing nutrients in this tea help to protect the body against environmental pollutants; wild fruits supply unique antioxidants that aren't typically found in commercially grown fruits and vegetables. Adding wild fruits to your diet can help enrich your blood, which in turn supports your energy production, skin health, and benefits your overall well-being.

MAKES 5 DAYS' SUPPLY

20g (¾oz) dried rosehips, chopped

10g (¼oz) dried bilberries, chopped

20g (¾oz) goji berries, chopped

20g (¾oz) dried orange peel (p220, step 1), chopped

10g (¼oz) dried hibiscus flowers, chopped

15g (½oz) dried schisandra berries, chopped

5g (⅛oz) dried liquorice root, chopped

1 Combine all the ingredients in a bowl, transfer to a sealed container, label, date, and store in a cupboard away from direct light.

2 To make the tea, put 20g (¾oz) of the dried leaves and 650ml (1¼ pints) of water in a saucepan, cover with a lid, and bring to the boil. Lower the heat and simmer for 10 minutes. Remove from the heat, leave to infuse for 10 minutes, and strain the liquid into a flask. Sip throughout the day. To make a single drink, take 1 heaped teaspoon of dried herbs, or fill an infuser ball with the herb blend, cover with 250ml (9fl oz) of boiling water, leave to stand for 10 minutes, strain, and drink.

RAINBOW VEGETABLE BROTH

 HELPS COMBAT FATIGUE   **HAS A MILD DIURETIC ACTION**   **HELPS STRENGTHEN THE IMMUNE SYSTEM**

This is an alkalizing broth that lifts energy levels by balancing the body's pH and fluid levels. Using vegetables in season assures a broad range of essential nutrients. Drink on its own at any time of day, or use as a base for stock for soup. Broths like this are excellent if you are convalescing, and will fortify you against illness if you include them in your daily diet.

SERVES 2

½ leek, chopped
1 spring onion, quartered
1 celery stick with leaves, chopped
1 carrot, chopped
1 potato with skin on, chopped
1 small beetroot with skin on, chopped
1 small radish with skin on, chopped
2 slices of fresh root ginger
1 sprig of parsley
1 tsp coriander seeds
1 litre (1¾ pints) mineral water
1 wakame seaweed, chopped (optional)

1 Place all the ingredients in a large saucepan, add the mineral water, and bring to the boil. Cover with a lid and simmer for 1½–2 hours over a low heat.

2 Remove the pan from the heat and strain the liquid. Discard the vegetables. Pour the hot broth into a flask, add the chopped wakame seaweed, and seal. Drink glassfuls of the broth throughout the day.

1 CELERY STICK
1 SPRING ONION
½ LEEK
1 BEETROOT
1 POTATO
1 CARROT
1 RADISH

EAT A RAINBOW
INCLUDING A VARIETY OF VIBRANTLY COLOURED FRUIT AND VEGETABLES IN YOUR DIET GIVES YOUR IMMUNE SYSTEM THE BENEFIT OF A RANGE OF ANTIOXIDANTS.

Astragalus And Schisandra Broth

PROMOTES A SENSE OF WELL-BEING

HELPS FIGHT COLDS AND FLU

HELPS DETOX AND ALKALIZE THE BODY

We are so used to thinking of herbal teas and other plant essences as occasional or emergency "therapy" that we have almost forgotten the nutritional and health benefits they bring as part of a daily diet. This blend of medicinal herbs, spices, and vegetables – which doubles as a soup and a herbal drink – provides valuable electrolytes and helps balance the natural pH of the body.

SERVES 2

6g (⅛oz) astragalus root

6g (⅛oz) schisandra berries

6g (⅛oz) wood ear fungus

6 thin slices of fresh ginger root, peeled

4 garlic cloves, skins on

4 shallots, skins on

1 tbsp coriander seeds

½ tsp aniseeds

60g (2oz) celeriac root, peeled and chopped

1 large carrot, sliced

1 strand of kelp or wakame

10 black peppercorns

1 Place all the ingredients in a medium saucepan, cover with 600ml (1 pint) of water, and bring to the boil. Reduce the heat and simmer for 1½ hours, then strain.

2 If serving as a soup, transfer to 2 serving bowls. If using as a drink pour into 2 heatproof glasses and serve. You can also use all this broth as part of an individual detox treatment – store it in a flask and sip it throughout the day.

Kelp *(p131) has a high iodine content, which supports a healthy thyroid function.*

SEAWEED AND MISO BROTH

 **HELPS LOWER
CHOLESTEROL**

 **HAS A POWERFUL
DIURETIC ACTION**

**HELPS CALM
THE NERVES**

Traditionally, seaweeds are used to alkalize the blood, help lower blood cholesterol, for their diuretic properties, and to help protect the body against the effects of radiation. This Asian-inspired broth combines various seaweeds with flavours such as lemongrass and makrut lime leaves, which relax the mind and alleviate stress. It can be served as a drink or a soup.

**SERVES 1
(MAKES 600ML/1 PINT)**

5g (⅛oz) wakame

5g (⅛oz) dulse

1 small blade of kelp

2 stalks of lemongrass

3 makrut lime leaves

½ tbsp coriander seeds

60g (2oz) celery root, chopped

1.5cm (½in) piece fresh ginger root, chopped

1 carrot, chopped

1 tbsp barley miso

1 tbsp chopped coriander leaves

1 Rinse the seaweeds in a bowl of cold water to help remove some of their salty taste.

2 Place all the ingredients except the barley miso and coriander leaves in a medium saucepan, cover with 650ml (1 pint) of water and bring to the boil. Reduce the heat to a simmer and cook with the lid on for 1½ hours on a low heat.

3 Strain the liquid and pour it into a flask. Discard the ingredients in the sieve. Add the barley miso and allow it to dissolve, then add the coriander leaves. If using as a drink pour into 2 heatproof glasses and serve. You can also use all this broth as part of an individual detox treatment – store it in a flask and sip it throughout the day.

Dulse (p131) is a good source
of chlorophyll, which helps
remove toxins from the body.

OILS, DRESSINGS, AND EXTRAS

IT'S THE LITTLE EXTRAS THAT MAKE A MEAL. BEAUTIFUL BREADS AND "LIVING" FERMENTED FOOD CONDIMENTS, DEEPLY **FLAVOURED** OILS, AND **FRUITY** VINEGARS ALL ADD VARIETY AND BRING YOU THE BEST OF HEALTH.

FLATBREAD WITH SWEET POTATO AND CORIANDER

 HELPS KEEP JOINTS SUPPLE   **SUPPORTS AND PROTECTS THE LIVER**   **HELPS IMPROVE CIRCULATION**

This is a take on traditional Indian paratha, and is a versatile bread that tastes equally good freshly baked and spread with soft kefir cheese (p332) or eaten as an accompaniment to all sorts of hot dishes and salads. Its main ingredients are sweet potato, turmeric powder, and coriander, which together have anti-inflammatory benefits, support the liver, and help improve circulation.

MAKES 8–10

1 sweet potato

100g (3½oz) plain flour, plus more for dusting

70g (2½oz) chickpea flour

½ tsp salt

2 tbsp ghee, or clarified butter

1 small red onion, finely chopped

1 garlic clove, finely chopped

1 tsp coriander seeds, crushed

1 tsp turmeric powder

25g (scant 1oz) coriander leaves, chopped

juice of ½ lime

1 Preheat the oven to 180°C (350°F/Gas 4). Wrap the sweet potato in foil and bake for 25 minutes or until soft. When the potato is cool enough to handle, peel off the skin and discard, and chop the flesh finely.

2 Combine the 2 flours in a small bowl, add the salt, and mix well. Set aside while you heat 1 tablespoon of the ghee in a small saucepan. Add the chopped onion and cook over a medium heat until it has softened. Add the garlic, coriander seeds, and turmeric powder, stir for 1 minute, then remove from the heat and add the coriander leaves, sweet potato, and lime juice, and mix well.

3 Transfer the sautéed ingredients to a large bowl and mix thoroughly. When all the ingredients are combined, knead into a dough and leave to stand for 15 minutes.

4 Remove the dough from the bowl, place it on a lightly floured work surface, and shape into a long roll. Divide into 8 or 10 equal amounts and shape into small balls. Roll each ball out into a 3–5mm (⅛–¼in) thick round that will fit in a heavy-based frying pan. Repeat with the rest of the dough balls. The thinner the flatbreads, the quicker they will cook.

5 Heat the frying pan over a moderate heat and place a flatbread in it. Cook for about 3 minutes. Brush the surface of the flatbread with some of the remaining ghee before turning it over to cook on the other side for 3 more minutes. Keep in a warm place while you cook the rest of the flatbreads, then serve.

Sweet potato (p88), especially this dark-skinned variety, contains high levels of beta-carotene and can therefore help strengthen the immune system.

SOURDOUGH RYE BREAD

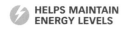 **HELPS MAINTAIN ENERGY LEVELS**  **HELPS STRENGTHEN BONES**  **PROMOTES HEALTHY SKIN AND HAIR**  **HELPS LOWER BLOOD PRESSURE**

Good-quality bread is the ultimate slow food: taking time to make it means you get a flavourful loaf. Rye grain, commonly used to make sourdough bread, boosts energy levels, strengthens bones and fingernails, enhances the condition of hair, and is also thought to benefit the heart and circulatory system. Buy freshly milled wholemeal rye flour that supplies the most nutrients.

MAKES 1 LOAF

For the sourdough starter

200g (7oz) wholemeal rye flour
400ml (14fl oz) spring water

For the bread

450g (1lb) sourdough starter
1 tbsp blackstrap molasses
450–500g (1lb–1lb 2oz) wholemeal rye flour
1 tbsp sunflower seeds
2 tbsp pumpkin seeds
1 tbsp caraway seeds
a pinch of salt
1 tsp coriander seeds
a knob of butter, plus extra for greasing

1 To make the sourdough starter, mix 50g (1¾oz) of the rye flour with 100ml (3½fl oz) of spring water in a large clean jar, cover with a clean kitchen cloth, and leave in a warm place for 24 hours. The ideal room temperature for the starter to ferment is 18–20°C (64–68°F). When the dough starter develops a bubbly texture and a fragrant sour smell, "feed" it with 50g (1¾oz) more rye flour and 100ml (3½fl oz) of spring water. Stir, add a little more water or flour if necessary to keep it smooth, and leave for another 24 hours. It should now be bubbling, with a fruity sour taste. Add a further 100g (3½oz) of flour and 200ml (7fl oz) more spring water and leave overnight to rise and become a fragrant, light dough.

2 Place 450g (1lb) of the starter dough in a large bowl, add 100ml (3½fl oz) of water and the blackstrap molasses, and stir. Add about 400g (14oz) of the rye flour to begin with and work it in with your hands; it will be quite a sticky mixture. Add more flour if necessary until the dough is of a manageable consistency – neither too thin nor too thick – allowing for the fact that it is likely to thicken with standing, and that seeds will be added to it. Cover with a clean kitchen cloth and set aside to stand in the bowl in a warm place for a few hours; if the starter is vigorous enough, the dough should double in size within 8–12 hours.

3 Add the pumpkin, sunflower, and caraway seeds, and salt to the risen dough and mix in thoroughly using your hands. Heat a small frying pan, add the coriander seeds, dry-fry until they release their aroma, then transfer to a pestle and mortar and crush to a powder. Grease the inside of a 900g (2lb) loaf tin with a little butter and sprinkle in the coriander powder, making sure it covers the insides of the tin evenly. Place the dough in the tin, smooth the top, dust with a little flour, cover with a clean kitchen cloth, and leave in a warm place to rest for a few hours or until it has visibly risen.

4 Preheat the oven to 210°C (410°F/Gas 6½) and bake the loaf for 10 minutes. Lower the oven to 180°C (350°F/Gas 4) and bake for a further 45 minutes. Remove the loaf from the oven, mix 2 tablespoons of boiling water with a knob of butter, and pour the liquid over the hot bread. Turn the oven off, return the loaf to the oven, and leave for 30 minutes, or until completely cold. Remove from the oven, cover with a linen cloth, and set aside on a wire rack to cool completely. Rye bread flavour improves during storage. Kept wrapped in a linen cloth in a wooden bread bin, or in a fabric bread bag, it will last for 5–6 days.

SAUERKRAUT

 FEEDS GOOD BACTERIA IN THE GUT   **HAS AN UPLIFTING EFFECT**   **HELPS STRENGTHEN THE IMMUNE SYSTEM**   **CONTAINS ANTI-CANCER SUBSTANCES**

Preserving vegetables in a brine solution, known as lacto-fermentation, encourages the growth of gut-friendly bacteria. Home-made sauerkraut not only tastes better, it is richer in enzymes that support a healthy gut which, in turn, can improve both physical and emotional health. It also preserves the immune-boosting and cancer-fighting properties of cabbage.

MAKES 1.35KG (3LB)

2.5–3kg (5½–6½lb) hard white or red cabbage, or half red and half white cabbage

about 60g (2oz) coarse sea or rock salt (see method)

1 tbsp caraway seeds

1 Remove the outer leaves of the cabbage, slice in half, remove the cores, quarter, and shred finely in a food processor or using a sharp knife. Weigh the shredded cabbage and calculate the amount of salt you need: approximately 60g (2oz) of salt per 2.5kg (5½lb) of cabbage.

2 Place the cabbage in a large, clean bowl and sprinkle the salt evenly over it. Using your hands, work the salt thoroughly into the cabbage – imagine you are making pastry – until it begins to feel wet. Leave for a few minutes for the salt to soften the cabbage and draw out its juices.

3 Pack into a very large sterilized crock or jar. Add 5cm (2in) of shredded cabbage at a time and scatter with the caraway seeds. Pack each layer down with a clean tamper such as the end of a rolling pin, a large pestle, or a jam jar. Leave 7.5cm (3in) of space at the top of the jar. Add any juices from the bowl and top up with cold brine (1½ tbsp of salt to 1 litre/1¾ pints of boiled cooled water) to cover the cabbage.

4 Place the jar on a tray, place clean muslin over the cabbage, and place a snug-fitting plate or saucer on top. Place a large jar or sandwich bag filled with water on top of the plate.

5 Leave in a well-ventilated place at room temperature (the ideal temperature is 20–22°C/68–72°C). Check every day that the cabbage is submerged. Remove any scum regularly and replace with clean muslin.

6 Fermentation is complete when all the bubbling has ceased; if the room temperature is ideal, the sauerkraut will be ready in 3–4 weeks. Pot up into sterilized jars, seal, and store in the refrigerator.

TIP: If the room temperature is below 13°C (55°F), fermentation will stop, and if it is higher than 24°C (76°F) it will spoil. If your sauerkraut develops a pinkish hue on its surface, goes dark, or is very soft and mushy, it has not fermented properly and shouldn't be eaten.

KIMCHI

 HELPS FIGHT INFECTION  **HELPS IMPROVE CIRCULATION**  **ENCOURAGES HEALTHY DIGESTION**  **CONTAINS ANTI-CANCER SUBSTANCES**

A traditional Korean cabbage dish, kimchi has numerous variations and this is one of the simplest. The mixture of spices in kimchi can help the body fend off bacterial and viral infections. The spices also have a strengthening effect on the circulation and digestion. Since kimchi uses cabbage as its base, it also contains a range of cancer-fighting nutrients.

MAKES 450–600G (1–1LB 5OZ)

1 small head Chinese leaves
2 tbsp sea salt
4 spring onions, chopped
2.5cm (1in) piece fresh ginger root, peeled and grated
1 garlic clove, crushed
4 tbsp rice vinegar
1 tbsp Thai fish sauce (nam pla)
juice of 1 lime
2 tbsp sesame oil
2 tbsp toasted sesame seeds
2 tbsp sambal oelek

1 Cut the head of the Chinese leaves lengthways into quarters, then into 5cm (2in) chunks. Place in a colander over a bowl. Add the sea salt, toss well, and leave to stand overnight at room temperature.

2 Wash the Chinese leaves thoroughly to remove the salt, tossing them with your hands to rinse thoroughly. Drain and dry on kitchen paper.

3 Transfer to a freezerproof container (large enough to hold up to 600g/1lb 5oz of Chinese leaves) with a lid. Add the remaining ingredients and toss together thoroughly.

4 Place the lid on the container, leave at room temperature overnight to marinate, then allow the flavours to develop in the refrigerator for a few more days. Store in the refrigerator and use within 2 weeks.

Chinese leaves are a good source of antioxidants and vitamin C, which can help to protect from certain kinds of cancer.

KEFIR MILK

 FEEDS GOOD BACTERIA IN THE GUT   **HELPS STRENGTHEN THE IMMUNE SYSTEM**   **PROMOTES A SENSE OF WELL-BEING**

Milk cultured with kefir grains benefits the digestive system, which is closely linked to the immune, endocrine, circulatory, and central nervous systems. The smooth functioning of these internal systems in turn helps boost a feeling of well-being. For best results, use unpasteurized milk, otherwise use whole pasteurized non-homogenized cow's, sheep's, or goat's milk.

MAKES 1 LITRE (1¾ PINTS)

1 tbsp kefir grains

1 litre (1¾ pints) unpasteurized or whole pasteurized, non-homogenized milk at room temperature

1 Put the kefir grains in a clean glass jar and add the milk. Cover with a clean kitchen towel and store in a dark place, such as a kitchen cupboard, for 18 hours–1 day.

2 Strain the milk using a clean plastic sieve. Reserve the kefir grains and add to a new batch of milk.

3 Store the kefir milk in a jug or a bottle in the refrigerator and use within 1 week, although it is best drunk fresh. It will continue to ferment at a lower rate during this time and have a consistency of thick milk.

KEFIR MILK CHEESE

 FEEDS GOOD BACTERIA IN THE GUT   **HELPS STRENGTHEN THE IMMUNE SYSTEM**   **PROMOTES A SENSE OF WELL-BEING**

Using kefir grains gives you a degree of control over the quality of dairy products you include in your diet. This soft, creamy cheese boosts immunity and digestion by enhancing intestinal health. Most of the lactose in kefir cheese is pre-digested by bacteria and yeasts before you ingest it, and some proteins are also broken down, so some lactose-intolerant people can tolerate it.

MAKES APPROXIMATELY 300G (10OZ)

1 tbsp kefir grains

1 litre (1¾ pints) unpasteurized or whole pasteurized, non-homogenized milk at room temperature

1 Put the kefir grains in a clean glass jar and add the milk. Cover with a clean kitchen towel and store in a dark place such as a kitchen cupboard for 2–4 days or until the liquid separates into liquid whey and solid curds. The live kefir grains usually remain on the top layer of the curd; use a plastic spoon to remove as many of them as you can and reserve in the refrigerator to add to a new batch of milk, if you like.

2 Strain the curd and whey using a clean plastic sieve positioned over a large glass bowl. Retain the curd and use the whey for soups or as a drink, if you like. Store the cheese in a covered ceramic bowl in the refrigerator and use within 1 week on crackers or toasted rye bread.

3 If you want a smoother, denser soft cheese, wrap the curds in a piece of cheesecloth and hang it overnight or until the cheese is as firm as you like (the firmer you want the cheese, the longer you leave it to drain). If you want to add extra flavours, mix with cracked linseeds or other seeds and nuts, or fresh herbs, such as marjoram, basil, lemon thyme, and dill.

CORIANDER AND JUNIPER OIL

 PROMOTES A SENSE OF WELL-BEING  **HELPS IMPROVE CIRCULATION**  **PROMOTES PROSTATE HEALTH**

An aromatic oil blend to liven up your life. The therapeutic action of this combination of seed oils and spices has a warming, strengthening, and energizing quality that can help enhance your sense of well-being and sexual drive. Use it as part of a dressing for salads or on its own to flavour cooked rice, spaghetti, or noodles.

MAKES 200ML (7FL OZ)

15g (½oz) peppercorns
30g (1oz) coriander seeds
15g (½oz) juniper berries
¼–½ tsp chilli flakes
150ml (5fl oz) sunflower oil

For the base oil

2 tbsp walnut oil
2 tbsp pumpkin oil
1½ tbsp hemp seed oil
1½ tbsp black seed oil

1 Put the dried ingredients in a pestle and mortar and crush roughly. Transfer to a clean heatproof glass jar and cover with the sunflower oil.

2 Preheat the oven to 50°C (120°F/Gas ¼), then turn it off. Wrap the base of the jar in a cloth (to prevent the glass cracking while standing on the hot metal shelves) and place it, unsealed, in the oven. The dried ingredients need to infuse at a temperature of around 40°C (104°F) for 6–8 hours, so you may need to turn the oven on and then off again briefly every so often, to keep the mixture warm.

3 Strain the oil and discard the dried ingredients; you should have at least 100ml (3½fl oz) of flavoured oil. Pour into a sterilized dark glass bottle and add the walnut, pumpkin, and hemp and black seed oils. Seal, shake well, label, and date. Store in the refrigerator and use within 3 weeks.

ROSE AND FENNEL SEED OIL

 RELIEVES MENOPAUSAL AND PMS SYMPTOMS   **HELPS FIGHT INFLAMMATION**  **PROMOTES HEALTHY SKIN**

This is a rejuvenating oil blend to help us age beautifully. The body loses its ability to convert dietary fats into gamma-linolenic-acid (GLA) with age and as this dietary oil blend contains significant levels of GLA, it may be helpful in age-related conditions resulting from GLA deficiency. It can also be useful for relieving menopausal symptoms and premenstrual syndrome.

MAKES 200ML (7FL OZ)

10g (¼oz) dried thyme
5g (⅛oz) fennel seeds
5g (⅛oz) dried rose petals
5g (⅛oz) dried marigold flowers
150ml (5fl oz) sunflower oil

For the base oil

3 tbsp evening primrose oil
2 tbsp borage oil
2 tbsp hemp seed oil
1 tbsp black seed oil

1 Put the dried ingredients in a pestle and mortar and crush roughly. Transfer to a clean heatproof glass jar and cover with the sunflower oil.

2 Preheat the oven to 50°C (120°F/Gas ¼), then turn it off. Wrap the base of the jar in a cloth (to prevent the glass cracking while standing on the hot metal shelves) and place it, unsealed, in the oven. The dried ingredients need to infuse at a temperature of around 40°C (104°F) for 6–8 hours, so you may need to turn the oven on and then off again briefly every so often, to keep the mixture warm.

3 Strain the oil and discard the dried ingredients; you should have at least 100ml (3½fl oz) of oil. Pour into a sterilized dark glass bottle and add the evening primrose, borage, and hemp and black seed oils. Seal, shake well, label, and date. Store in the refrigerator and use within 3 weeks.

ROSE AND RASPBERRY VINEGAR

 HAS A MILD DIURETIC ACTION

 ENHANCES DIGESTION OF FATS

 PROMOTES HEALTHY SKIN AND HAIR

 HELPS EASE MENSTRUAL CRAMPS

Infused vinegars are useful and versatile. This vinegar can be used as a flavouring for food, or drink 1 teaspoonful in a cup of warm water every morning to improve detoxification. For the best result, use the fragrant, old-fashioned roses *Rosa damascena* or *Rosa gallica* to benefit from their healing qualities, and choose a good-quality organic apple cider vinegar.

MAKES 300ML (10FL OZ)

100g (3½oz) fresh raspberries
2 tbsp fresh rose petals
300ml (10fl oz) organic apple cider vinegar

1 Put the raspberries and rose petals in a clean glass jar, cover with the vinegar so the berries are completely submerged, and seal tightly with the lid. Leave in a dark cupboard to infuse for 2–3 weeks, then strain, pour the vinegar into a clean bottle, and seal, label, and date. Reserve the raspberries, if you like, and use in a smoothie. Use within 3 months.

BLACKBERRY VINEGAR

 HELPS FIGHT COLDS AND FLU

 PROMOTES A HEALTHY COMPLEXION

 HELPS IMPROVE CIRCULATION

If picked when fully ripe, blackberries are a perfect foraging food, with many health benefits: they contain anthocyanins, salicylic acid, ellagic acid, and fibre, which are good for skin and hair. Traditionally, blackberry vinegar is used as a gargle for sore throats, and as a drink to avert the onset of cold or flu. Choose a good-quality organic apple cider vinegar.

MAKES 300ML (10FL OZ)

100g (3½oz) fresh blackberries
300ml (10fl oz) organic apple cider vinegar

1 Put the blackberries into a clean glass jar, cover with the vinegar so the blackberries are completely submerged, and seal tightly with the lid. Leave in a dark cupboard to infuse for 2–3 weeks, then strain, pour the vinegar into a clean bottle, and seal, label, and date. Reserve the blackberries, if you like, and use in a smoothie. Use within 3 months.

Rose and Raspberry Vinegar ▶

TURMERIC AND GINGER OIL

 **HELPS FIGHT INFLAMMATION** **PROTECTS THE HEART AND BLOOD VESSELS** **AIDS HEALTHY DIGESTION**

This is a blend of fine seed oils and anti-inflammatory medicinal plants. Together they make an oil that is particularly beneficial for arthritic and rheumatic conditions, and protects the heart and digestive tract. This warming, immune-enhancing oil is delicious as a salad dressing, or drizzle a spoonful or two onto steamed vegetables or yogurt, or add to smoothies.

MAKES 400ML (14FL OZ)

20g (¾oz) dried oregano
5g (⅛oz) dried sage leaves
10g (¼oz) juniper berries
10g (¼oz) dried rosemary leaves
1 tsp ground turmeric
1 tsp ground ginger
250ml (9fl oz) sunflower oil
3 tbsp flaxseed oil
3 tbsp hemp oil
3 tbsp borage oil
3 tbsp rosehip oil

1 Place the oregano, sage leaves, juniper berries, and rosemary leaves in a blender or food processor, and blitz to reduce their volume. Place the herbs and ground spices into a glass jar and cover with the sunflower oil.

2 Preheat the oven to 50°C (120°F/Gas ¼), then turn it off. Wrap the base of the jar in a cloth (to prevent the glass cracking while standing on the hot metal shelves) and put it, unsealed, in the oven. The dried ingredients need to infuse at a temperature of around 40°C (104°F) for 6–8 hours, so you may need to turn the oven briefly on and then off again every so often to keep the mixture warm.

3 Strain the oil and discard the dried ingredients; you should have at least 100ml (3½fl oz) of flavoured oil. Pour into a sterilized glass bottle and add the flax oil, hemp oil, borage oil, and rosehip oil. Seal and shake to blend. Label and date, store in the refrigerator, and use within 3–4 weeks.

BASIL OIL

 **HELPS EASE BRONCHIAL COMPLAINTS** **HELPS ALLEVIATE PMS** **PROMOTES A SENSE OF WELL-BEING**

Basil is beneficial for the respiratory, reproductive, and nervous systems. It is a good remedy for conditions that require relief from congestion, such as sinusitis, a loss of smell, and some bronchial conditions. Basil is traditionally known as a herb that awakens joy and courage as it helps restore vitality, enhance memory, and lift your mood.

MAKES 240ML (8FL OZ)

a small bunch of basil
110ml (3¼fl oz) extra virgin olive oil
110ml (3¼fl oz) grapeseed oil

1 Bring 500ml (16fl oz) of water to the boil in a saucepan. Fill another small pan with cold water and add some ice cubes to it to make an iced water bath. Holding the bunch of basil by its stems, immerse the leaves into the boiling water for 8 seconds. Plunge the wilted basil leaves into the iced water bath to prevent them from discolouring and cooking further. Dry with kitchen paper, cut off the stems, and put the leaves into a blender or food processor. Add the two oils, and blitz until smooth.

2 Use immediately, or if you want to store it for a few days in a refrigerator, leave to infuse for 1–2 hours, then strain the oils through a muslin cloth and discard the minced basil leaves. Transfer to a sterilized bottle, seal, label, and date. Store in the refrigerator and use within 3–4 weeks.

 Turmeric and Ginger Oil

VITAMIN SUPPLEMENTS CHART

The better quality your food is, the more abundant it will be in the vitamins that are essential to your continued health and well-being. Processing, cooking, and storage, as well as soil-damaging pesticides and fertilisers can leave food nutrient poor. Supplementing at optimal levels can help fill the gap between what you need and what you often get – see p17 for details about ADI and Supplemental Range.

Nutrient	Functions	Rich Food Sources	Notes	Average Dietary Intake /Supplemental Range
Vitamin A and Carotenoids	**Vitamin A:** Antioxidant; vision and night vision; growth and reproduction; collagen production; moistness of mucosa. **Carotenoids:** Precursors to vitamin A; antioxidant; healthy heart and circulation; healthy mucosa.	**Vitamin A:** Fish-liver oils; animal liver; oily fish; egg yolks; whole milk; and butter. **Carotenoids:** Green and yellow fruits and vegetables; dark green leafy vegetables; sweet peppers; sweet potato; broccoli; carrots; dried apricots; prunes; kale; parsley; spinach; squash; and watercress.	Animal sources of Vitamin A may be much better absorbed than vegetable sources.	**Vitamin A –** ADI: 5,000–9,000IU SR: 10,000+ **Beta-carotene –** ADI: 5–8mg SR: 10–40mg
Vitamin B1 – Thiamin	Release of energy from carbohydrates; growth; appetite regulation; healthy digestion and nervous system.	Yeast extract; wheat germ; wholemeal flour; sunflower seeds; brown rice; brazil nuts; pecans; pork; beans; buckwheat; oatmeal; hazelnuts; rye; liver; cashews.	Unstable to light and heat e.g. milling flour causes 60–80% loss.	ADI: 1–5mg SR: 5–150mg
Vitamin B2 – Riboflavin	Combines with protein to regulate respiration; growth; healthy skin and eyes.	Yeast; animal liver; kidneys; almonds; wheat germ; wild rice; mushrooms; egg yolks; millet; wheat bran; oily fish; kale; cashews; sunflower.	Unstable to light.	ADI: 1.5–2mg SR: 10–200mg
Vitamin B3 – Niacin	Required for energy release and synthesis of steroids and fatty acids; healthy digestion, skin, and nervous system.	Yeast; wild rice; brown rice; wholemeal flour; peanuts; animal liver; turkey; trout; mackerel; chicken; sesame seeds; sunflower seeds; lean red meat; buckwheat; barley; almonds.	Relatively stable.	ADI: 15–20mg SR: 100–3,000mg
Vitamin B5 – Pantothenic Acid	Regulates carbohydrate and fat metabolism; resistance to stress; healthy immune system; digestion.	Yeast; animal liver; kidneys; peanuts; mushrooms; split peas; brown rice; soybeans; eggs; oatmeal; buckwheat; sunflower seeds; lentils; rye flour; cashews; oily fish; turkey; broccoli; avocados.	Unstable to heat (cooking), freezing and canning. Considerable loss when milling grains.	ADI: 5–10mg SR: 20–500mg
Vitamin B6 – Pyridoxine, Pyridoxal-5-phosphate	Metabolism of carbohydrate and protein; synthesis of hormones and fatty acids; healthy nervous system, hormone-balance growth, and skin.	Yeast; sunflower seeds; wheat germ; tuna; liver; soybeans; walnuts; oily fish; lentils; buckwheat flour; beans; brown rice; hazelnuts; bananas; pork; avocados; whole wheat flour; sweet chestnuts; egg yolk; kale; rye flour.	Unstable to light and cooking. Milling flour causes 75% losses.	ADI: 1.6–2.6mg SR: 10–150mg

Nutrient	Functions	Rich Food Sources	Notes	Average Dietary Intake /Supplemental Range
Vitamin B12 – Cobalamin	DNA synthesis; new red blood cells; lipid production; myelin sheath; healthy nervous system, blood cells, gut mucosa, skin.	Liver; shellfish; kidneys; oily fish; egg yolk; lamb; beef; cheese.	Plants do not contain bioactive forms of B12 so vegans must supplement.	ADI: 2–50ug SR: 300–5000ug
Folic Acid	DNA and RNA synthesis; new blood cells; protein synthesis; growth; healthy digestion; nervous system; red blood cells.	Yeast; Black-eyed peas; soya beans; wheat germ; liver; kidney beans; mung beans; asparagus; lentils; walnuts; spinach; kale; beet greens; peanuts; broccoli; barley; whole wheat cereal; Brussels sprouts; almonds; oatmeal; cabbage; figs; avocado.	Unstable to heat and light. Storage and cooking causes losses. Supplementation may be advisable before and during pregnancy.	ADI: 400ug SR: 500ug–5mg
Vitamin C – Ascorbic Acid	Antioxidant; healthy immune system, bones, teeth, gums, cartilage, capillaries, connective tissue, healing; synthesis of steroid hormones, absorption of iron, regulating cholesterol.	Acerola cherry; sweet peppers; kale; parsley; leafy vegetables; broccoli; watercress; strawberries; papaya; oranges; grapefruit; cabbage; lemon juice; elderberries; liver; mangoes; asparagus; oysters; radishes; raspberries.	Unstable to heat and light. Cooking may cause 10-90% losses.	ADI: 75–125mg SR: 250–2,000mg
Vitamin D – Calciferol	Controls calcium absorption for healthy bones and teeth; healthy immune system and nervous system; cancer-protective; hormone-balance.	Fish liver oils; sardines (tinned and fresh); salmon; tuna; shrimps; butter; sunflower seeds; liver; eggs; milk; mushrooms; cheese.	Synthesized by the action of sunlight on the skin. Supplementation may be advisable if not exposed to sunlight regularly.	ADI: 1–5mg SR: 5–150mg
Vitamin E – Tocopherol, etc.	Antioxidant; healthy immune system; heart and circulation; lipid balance; sex hormone regulator; fertility; gestation; growth.	Sunflower seeds; sunflower oil; safflower oil; almonds; sesame oil; peanut oil; corn oil; wheat germ; peanuts; olive oil; butter; spinach; oatmeal; salmon; brown rice; rye flour; pecans; wholewheat bread; carrots.	Losses caused by heat and light. Milling of flour causes up to 80% loss.	ADI: 30mg SR: 100–800mg
Vitamin K – Phylloquinone, Menaquinone	Blood clotting; calcium metabolism; blood sugar-balance; healthy lung tissue; heart and circulation; metabolism; bones; skin; bacterial synthesis in the gut.	Broccoli; lettuce; cabbage; liver; spinach; watercress; asparagus; cheese; butter; oats; peas; whole wheat; green beans; pork; eggs; kelp.	Unstable to light. If bowel microflora are healthy up to 50% of Vitamin K needs are manufactured in the gut.	ADI: 70–150ug SR: 1–20mg
Bioflavonoids – Citrin, Hesperidin, Rutin, Quercetin, etc.	Antioxidant; anti-inflammatory; healthy immune system; cancer-protective (Quercetin); healthy blood vessels (Rutin).	Apples; black and red berries; blackcurrants; buckwheat; citrus fruit; apricots; garlic; green-growing shoots of plants; onions; rosehips; cherries.	Some loss during cooking and processing.	ADI: N/A SR: 500–3,000mg
Essential Fatty Acids – Omega oils	Regulate inflammation; healthy blood coagulation; lipid balance; reproduction and growth; brain function; nervous system; eyes; skin; joints; metabolism; hormones; heart and circulation.	Fish liver oils; oily fish; milk; cheese; Linseed oil; hempseed oil; canola; soya oil; walnut oil; blackcurrant seed oil.	Hydrogenation, light, heat.	3–8% of calories

MINERAL SUPPLEMENTS CHART

Just like vitamins, minerals are essential for our overall health and have specific roles to play in building bones, making hormones and regulating heartbeat. Modern food production and farming methods remove important minerals from our food. Since the body cannot make its own, so it's essential to obtain minerals in adequate amounts from either food or good quality supplements (find more on p17).

Nutrient	Functions	Rich Food Sources	Notes	Average Dietary Intake/ Supplemental Range
Boron	Activates Vitamin D; bone and joint health.	Drinking water; almonds; apples; dates; nuts; beans; peanuts; prunes; soya.	Available from most plants grown where boron is present in the soil.	ADI: 2–3mg SR: 2–10mg
Calcium	Bone and teeth formation; regulates nerve and muscle function; hormones and blood pressure.	Kelp; seaweed; cheese; carob; molasses; almonds; yeast; parsley; corn; watercress; goats milk; tofu; figs; sunflower seeds; yogurt; beet greens; green leafy vegetables; wheat bran; cows milk; buckwheat; sesame seeds; olives; broccoli.	Water softeners remove calcium. Excess phytates (rhubarb, spinach, grains and cereals) can decrease absorption.	ADI: 800–1400mg SR: 1000–2500mg
Chromium	Glucose metabolism; growth; insulin and cholesterol regulation.	Brewer's yeast; beef; liver; whole wheat bread; rye flour; chilli; oysters; potatoes.	Refining flour causes up to 50% losses.	ADI: 50–200ug SR: 100–300ug
Copper	Synthesis of enzymes required for iron absorption; red blood cell formation; maintenance of skin, bone and nerve formation; collagen synthesis.	Oysters; shellfish; nuts; brazil nuts; almonds; hazelnuts; walnuts; pecans; legumes; split peas; liver; buckwheat; peanuts; lamb; sunflower oil; crab; copper water pipes.	Zinc and calcium are antagonists (high levels prevent absorption of copper).	ADI: 1–3mg SR: 2–10mg Metabolism of copper is highly individual.
Iodine	Synthesis of thyroid hormones.	Seaweed; kelp; clams; prawns; haddock; shellfish; salmon; sardines; liver; pineapple; eggs; peanuts; wholemeal bread; cheese; pork; lettuce; spinach.	Often added to table salt but not sea salt.	ADI: 150ug SR: 100–1000ug
Iron	Red blood cell function; energy release; growth; bone regulation; healthy respiration, skin, and nails.	Kelp; yeast; molasses; wheat bran; pumpkin seeds; liver; sunflower seeds; millet; parsley; clams; almonds; prunes; cashews; red meat; raisins; nuts; chard; dandelion leaves; dates; cooked dry beans; eggs; lentils; brown rice; dried apricots; raw chocolate.	Vitamin C enhances iron absorption.	ADI: 10–20mg SR: 15–50mg

Nutrient	Functions	Rich Food Sources	Notes	Average Dietary Intake /Supplemental Range
Magnesium	Synthesis of proteins, carbohydrates and lipids; DNA repair; energy production; modulation of muscle activity; homeostasis of calcium; heart and circulation health.	Kelp; seaweed; wheat bran and wheat germ; almonds; cashews; molasses; brewer's yeast; buckwheat; brazil nuts; nuts; millet; rye; tofu; beet greens; coconut meat; soya; spinach; brown rice; figs; apricots; dates; prawns; sweet corn; avocado.	Milling/refining of grains and cereals causes up to 90% losses.	ADI: 350mg SR: 300–800mg
Manganese	Antioxidant; enzyme activator; bone and ligament formation.	Nuts: pecans, brazil, almonds; barley; rye; buckwheat; split peas; wholemeal bread; spinach; oats; raisins; rhubarb; Brussels sprouts; avocado; beans.	Milling/refining of cereals causes 80–90% losses.	ADI: 2.5–7mg SR: 2–20mg
Molybdenum	Regulates iron, copper, and fat metabolism; teeth health; anti-carcinogenic.	Lentils; liver, dried beans; cauliflower; wheat germ; spinach; kidney; brown rice; garlic; oats; eggs; rye; corn; barley; fish; chicken; beef; potatoes; onions; coconut.	Refining flour causes up to 80% losses.	ADI: 75–250ug SR: 100–1000ug
Phosphorus	Healthy bones; calcium homeostasis; RNA and DNA synthesis; energy metabolism and production; Vitamin B activator.	Brewer's yeast; wheat bran and wheat germ; pumpkin seeds; brazil nuts; sesame seeds; dried beans; almonds; cheese; rye; peanuts; cashews; liver; scallops; millet; barley; seaweed; chicken; brown rice; eggs; garlic; crab; mushrooms; milk.	Because phosphorus is so widespread in food, dietary phosphorus deficiency is extremely rare.	ADI: 800mg SR: 400–3000mg
Potassium	Blood pressure regulation; water balance regulation; hormone balance; muscle and nerve health.	Seaweed; sunflower seeds; wheat germ; almonds; raisins; nuts; dates; figs; yams; garlic; spinach; millet; dried beans; mushrooms; broccoli; banana; red meat; squash; chicken; carrots; potato.	Diuretics and certain medicines cause your body to lose potassium.	ADI: 4,500-5,100mg SR: 3–8g
Selenium	Antioxidant; detoxification of chemicals; anti-carcinogenic; sperm health; reproductive system health; fertility; thyroid health; DNA repair.	Butter; herring; wheat germ; brazil nuts; cider vinegar; scallops; barley; lobster; prawns; oats; chard; shellfish; crab; milk; fish; red meat; molasses; garlic; barley; eggs; mushrooms; alfalfa.	Milling/refining of cereals causes 40–50% losses.	ADI: 50–200ug SR: 200–800ug
Zinc	Antioxidant; anti-carcinogenic; immune system regulator; anti-viral; DNA and RNA synthesis; enzyme activator; wound healing; skin; hair; muscle and respiratory health; fertility; reproductive health; growth; insulin synthesis.	Oysters; ginger; red meat; nuts; dried beans; liver; milk; egg yolk; whole wheat; rye; oats; brazil nuts; peanuts; chicken; sardines; buckwheat; oily fish; prawns; white fish.	Milling/refining of cereals causes 80% losses, freezing of vegetables causes 25–50% losses.	ADI: 15mg SR: 10–70mg

References for vitamins and minerals supplements charts: Osiecki, H., "*The Nutrient Bible 8th Edition*" (2010, Bioconcepts, Australia) Liska et al, "*Clinical Nutrition: A Functional Approach*" (2004, The Institute for Functional Medicine, Washington, USA)

INDEX BY HEALTH AREA

Beneficial foods are grouped under each specific health area.

INDEX

Index entries in italic are full recipes from the recipe section (pp176–337). In addition, the main source of information for each food gives suggestions about other culinary uses.

ACKNOWLEDGMENTS

The authors would like to thank Peter Kindersley whose tireless support for organic food and a natural lifestyle helped to create this book. Thanks also to Daphne Lambert for recipe inspiration and feedback, and for allowing us to reproduce her Almond and Raspberry Cake recipe on page 268; to Alex Savage for assisting with research; and to all at Dorling Kindersley for helping to steer this volume from concept to completion.

Dorling Kindersley would like to thank the great team at Neal's Yard Remedies.

Recipe photography Stuart West
Art direction Kat Mead
Food styling Jane Lawrie
Prop styling Liz Hippisley
Additional ingredients photography Ian O'Leary
Proofreading Sue Morony, Kokila Manchanda, and Neha Ruth Samuel
Indexing Marie Lorimer
Recipe testing Hülya Balci, Amy Carter, Francesa Dennis, Katy Greenwood, Clare Nielsen-Marsh, and Ann Reynolds
Editorial assistance Martha Burley
Design assistance Collette Sadler and Pooja Verma

Jacket images: Front: Dorling Kindersley: Stuart West bl, b, bc, br; Back: Dorling Kindersley: Stuart West tl, t, tc, tr

All other images © Dorling Kindersley
For further information see: **www.dkimages.com**